Taste of Home

Slow Cooker
THROUGHOUT THE YEAR

Taste of Home
Slow Cooker
THROUGHOUT THE YEAR

EDITORIAL
EDITOR-IN-CHIEF **Catherine Cassidy**
CREATIVE DIRECTOR **Howard Greenberg**
EDITORIAL OPERATIONS DIRECTOR **Kerri Balliet**

MANAGING EDITOR, PRINT AND DIGITAL BOOKS **Mark Hagen**
ASSOCIATE CREATIVE DIRECTOR **Edwin Robles Jr.**

EDITOR **Michelle Rozumalski**
CONTRIBUTING ART DIRECTOR **Jennifer Ruetz**
LAYOUT DESIGNER **Nancy Novak**
EDITORIAL PRODUCTION MANAGER **Dena Ahlers**
COPY CHIEF **Deb Warlaumont Mulvey**
COPY EDITOR **Mary C. Hanson**
CONTENT OPERATIONS MANAGER **Colleen King**
CONTENT OPERATIONS ASSISTANT **Shannon Stroud**
EXECUTIVE ASSISTANT **Marie Brannon**

CHIEF FOOD EDITOR **Karen Berner**
FOOD EDITORS **James Schend; Peggy Woodward, RD**
ASSOCIATE FOOD EDITOR **Krista Lanphier**
ASSOCIATE EDITOR/FOOD CONTENT **Annie Rundle**
RECIPE EDITORS **Mary King; Jenni Sharp, RD; Irene Yeh**

TEST KITCHEN AND FOOD STYLING MANAGER **Sarah Thompson**
TEST COOKS **Nicholas Iverson (lead), Matthew Hass, Lauren Knoelke**
FOOD STYLISTS **Kathryn Conrad (senior), Leah Rekau, Shannon Roum**
PREP COOKS **Megumi Garcia, Melissa Hansen, Nicole Spohrleder, Bethany VanOpdorp**

PHOTOGRAPHY DIRECTOR **Stephanie Marchese**
PHOTOGRAPHERS **Dan Roberts, Jim Wieland**
PHOTOGRAPHER/SET STYLIST **Grace Natoli Sheldon**
SET STYLISTS **Stacey Genaw, Melissa Haberman, Dee Dee Jacq**

BUSINESS ANALYST **Kristy Martin**
BILLING SPECIALIST **Mary Ann Koebernik**

BUSINESS
GENERAL MANAGER, TASTE OF HOME COOKING SCHOOLS **Erin Puariea**

VICE PRESIDENT, BRAND MARKETING **Jennifer Smith**
VICE PRESIDENT, CIRCULATION AND CONTINUITY MARKETING **Dave Fiegel**

READER'S DIGEST NORTH AMERICA
VICE PRESIDENT, BUSINESS DEVELOPMENT AMD MARKETING **Alain Begun**
PRESIDENT, BOOKS AND HOME ENTERTAINMENT **Harold Clarke**
GENERAL MANAGER, CANADA **Philippe Cloutier**
VICE PRESIDENT, OPERATIONS **Mitch Cooper**
CHIEF OPERATING OFFICER **Howard Halligan**
VICE PRESIDENT, CHIEF SALES OFFICER **Mark Josephson**
VICE PRESIDENT, GENERAL MANAGER, MILWAUKEE **Frank Quigley**
VICE PRESIDENT, DIGITAL SALES **Steve Sottile**
VICE PRESIDENT, CHIEF CONTENT OFFICER **Liz Vaccariello**
VICE PRESIDENT, GLOBAL FINANCIAL PLANNING AND ANALYSIS **Devin White**

THE READER'S DIGEST ASSOCIATION, INC.
PRESIDENT AND CHIEF EXECUTIVE OFFICER **Robert E. Guth**

A TASTE OF HOME READER'S DIGEST BOOK

FOR OTHER TASTE OF HOME BOOKS AND PRODUCTS, VISIT US AT TASTEOFHOME.COM.

FOR MORE READER'S DIGEST PRODUCTS AND INFORMATION, VISIT RD.COM (IN THE UNITED STATES) OR SEE RD.CA (IN CANADA).

INTERNATIONAL STANDARD BOOK NUMBER **978-1-61765-383-4**
LIBRARY OF CONGRESS CONTROL NUMBER **2013944816**

PICTURED ON FRONT COVER **Blueberry Grunt, page 177; Mango & Coconut Chicken Soup, page 161; Mexican Pot Roast Filling, page 295; and Beef Stew Provencal, page 328.**

PRINTED IN CHINA
1 3 5 7 9 10 8 6 4 2

Table of Contents

GREEN BEANS AND NEW POTATOES

MOROCCAN CHICKEN

Slow Cooking 101

The original slow cooker, called a Crock-Pot®, was introduced in 1971 by Rival®. Today, the term "slow cooker" and the name Crock-Pot® are often used interchangeably; however, Crock-Pot® is a brand, and a slow cooker is the appliance.

Most slow cookers have two or more settings. Food cooks faster on the high setting, but the low setting is ideal for all-day cooking or for less tender cuts of meat. Use the "warm" setting to keep food hot until it's ready to serve. The slow cooker recipes in this book refer to cooking on either "high" or "low" settings.

Some newer slow cookers seem to heat up faster than older ones. If you have an older model and a recipe directs to cook on low, you may want to set the slow cooker on the highest setting for the first hour of cooking to be sure the food is thoroughly cooked.

When using your slow cooker...

- Slow cookers come in a range of sizes, from 1½ to 7 quarts. It's important to use the right size for the amount of food you're making. To serve a dip from a buffet, the smallest slow cookers are ideal. For entertaining or potluck dinners, the larger sizes work best. Check the chart below to find a useful size for your household.

- To cook properly and safely, manufacturers and the USDA recommend slow cookers be filled at least half full but no more than two-thirds full.

- With many slow cooker recipes, the ingredients are added at once and are cooked all day. For make-ahead convenience, place the food items in the crock the night before, cover and refrigerate overnight (the removable stoneware insert makes this an easy task). In the morning, place the crock in the slow cooker and select the proper temperature.

- Do not preheat your slow cooker. An insert that has been in the refrigerator overnight should always be put into a cold base unit. Stoneware is sensitive to dramatic temperature changes, and cracking or breakage could occur if the base is preheated.

- After the recipe is finished cooking, if there are any leftovers, allow them to cool, then refrigerate. Slow cookers should not be used to reheat leftovers. Instead, use a microwave, stovetop burner or oven to reheat foods to 165°. This ensures that the food has been thoroughly heated and it is safe to eat.

- Following a power outage of less than two hours, you can finish cooking food from your slow cooker on the stovetop or microwave. If it's been more than two hours or you are unsure how long the power has been out, discard the food for your safety.

Slow Cooker Size

HOUSEHOLD SIZE	SLOW COOKER CAPACITY
1 person	1½ quarts
2 people	2 to 3½ quarts
3 or 4 people	3½ to 4½ quarts
4 or 5 people	4½ to 5 quarts
6 or more people	5 to 7 quarts

Useful Handles for Lifting Food

Layered dishes or meat loaves are easier to get out of the slow cooker using foil handles. Here's how to make and use them:

1
For a 3-qt. slow cooker, cut three 20x3-inch strips of heavy-duty foil (or 25x3-inch strips for large slow cookers). Or cut 6-inch wide strips from regular foil and fold in half lengthwise. Criss-cross the strips to resemble spokes of a wheel.

2
Place the foil strips on the bottom and up the sides of the ceramic insert. Let the strips hang over the edge. To prevent food from sticking to the foil, coat the foil strips with cooking spray.

3
Place the foods in the order suggested by the recipe in center of the foil strips and lower until the food rests on the bottom of the slow cooker.

4
After the food is cooked, grasp the foil strips together and carefully lift the food from the crock. Remove the strips from the food before serving.

CONVERTING RECIPES FOR THE

Slow Cooker

Almost any recipe that bakes in the oven or simmers on the stovetop can be easily converted for the slow cooker. Here are some guidelines.

- Before converting recipes, check the manufacturer's guidelines for your particular slow cooker. Find a recipe that is similar to the one you want to convert and use it as a guide. Note the amount and size of meat and vegetables, heat setting, cooking time and liquid.

- Since there is no evaporation, adjusting the amount of liquid in your recipe may be necessary. If a recipe calls for 6 to 8 cups of water, try starting with 5 cups. Conversely, recipes should include at least a little liquid. If a recipe does not include liquid, add ½ cup of water or broth.

- In general, 1 hour of simmering on the range or baking at 350° in the oven is equal to 8-10 hours on low or 4-6 hours on high in a slow cooker. Check the chart at right.

- Flour and cornstarch are often used to thicken soups, stews and sauces that are cooked in a slow cooker.

Tips for Tasty Outcomes

- No peeking! Refrain from lifting the lid while food cooks in the slow cooker, unless you're instructed in a recipe to stir or add ingredients. The loss of steam can mean an extra 20-30 minutes of cooking time each time you lift the lid.

- Be sure the lid is well-placed over the ceramic insert, not tilted or askew. The steam during cooking creates a seal.

- When food is finished cooking, remove it from the slow cooker within 1 hour and promptly refrigerate any leftovers.

- Slow cooking may take longer at higher altitudes.

- Don't forget your slow cooker when you go camping, if electricity is available. When space is limited and you want "set-it-and-forget-it" meals, it's a handy appliance.

- Reheating food in a slow cooker isn't recommended. Cooked food can be heated on the stovetop or in the microwave and then put into a slow cooker to keep hot for serving.

- Use a slow cooker on a buffet table to keep soup, stew, savory dips or mashed potatoes hot.

Cook Times

15 to 30 minutes in Conventional Oven
Slow Cooker
Low: 4 to 6 hours
High: 1½ to 2 hours
35 to 45 minutes in Conventional Oven
Slow Cooker
Low: 6 to 8 hours
High: 3 to 4 hours
50 minutes or more in Conventional Oven
Slow Cooker
Low: 8 to 10 hours
High: 4 to 6 hours

When a range in cooking time is provided, this accounts for variables such as thickness of meat, how full the slow cooker is and the temperature of the food going into the cooker. As you become used to how your slow cooker works, you'll be better able to judge which end of the range to use.

A Melting Pot of Ingredients

Beans

Minerals in water and variations in voltage affect different types of dried beans in different ways; therefore, dried beans can be tricky to work with in the slow cooker. As a result, dried beans should always be soaked before adding to a slow cooker recipe. To soak beans, place them in a Dutch oven or stockpot and add water to cover by 2 inches. Bring to a boil, and boil for 2 minutes. Remove from the heat, cover and let stand for 1 hour. Drain and rinse the beans, discarding the liquid. Sugar, salt and acidic ingredients, such as vinegar, have a hardening effect on beans and prevent them from becoming soft and tender. It's best not to cook beans with these flavorings, but to add them only after the beans are fully cooked. Lentils and split peas do not need to be soaked.

Couscous

For the best results when preparing couscous, cook on a stovetop instead of in a slow cooker.

Dairy

Milk-based products tend to break down during slow cooking. Add items like milk, sour cream, cream cheese or cream during the last hour of cooking unless the recipe instructs otherwise. Cheeses don't generally hold up over extended periods of cooking, so they should be added near the end of cooking. Condensed cream soups can be cooked in slow cookers for extended periods of time with minimal curdling concerns.

Fish & Seafood

Since fish and seafood cook quickly in a slow cooker and can break down if cooked too long, they are often added toward the end of the cooking time.

Meats

For enhanced flavor and appearance, meat may be browned before going into the slow cooker. Browning, although not vital, may improve the color and flavor of meat. When cooking a roast over 3 pounds, be sure to cut it in half before placing it in the slow cooker to ensure that it thoroughly cooks. Frozen meats should be completely thawed before being placed in a slow cooker. Trim excess fat from meat or poultry before placing in a slow cooker. A slow cooker retains heat, and large amounts of fat could raise the temperature of the cooking liquid, causing the meat to overcook and become tough.

Oats

Quick-cooking and old-fashioned oats are often interchangeable in recipes. However, old-fashioned oats hold up better in a slow cooker.

Pasta

If added to a slow cooker when dry, pasta tends to become very sticky. It's best to cook it according to the package directions and stir it into the slow cooker just before serving. Small types of pasta, such as orzo, may be cooked in the slow cooker. To keep them from becoming mushy, add during the last hour of cooking.

Rice

Converted rice is ideal for all-day cooking. If using instant rice, add it during the last 30 minutes of cooking.

Vegetables

Vegetables, especially potatoes and root vegetables (such as carrots), tend to cook slower than meat. Place these vegetables on the bottom and around the sides of the slow cooker, and put meat on top of the vegetables. Add tender vegetables, like peas and zucchini, or those you'd prefer to be crisp-tender, during the last 50-60 minutes.

RACHEL KUNKEL'S
BBQ CHICKEN SLIDERS
page 82

Spring

Spring has sprung! Celebrate the season with these slow-cooked dishes. Whether planning a St. Patrick's Day party, hosting Easter dinner, organizing a quaint luncheon or simply thinking about supper, you can't go wrong with these all-time favorites.

Spring

APPETIZERS & BEVERAGES

It's time to shake the winter blues and get together with a group of friends and family! Whip up these easy bites for a surefire celebration that welcomes longer days, warmer weather and Mother Nature's freshest ingredients!

KELLY BYLER'S
SOUTHWESTERN NACHOS

Southwestern Nachos

Guests will go crazy when you serve two heaping pans of this cheesy nacho casserole featuring tender chunks of pork. You don't need to worry about filling the chip bowl...the tortilla chips are conveniently baked right in the dish!

—**KELLY BYLER** GOSHEN, IN

PREP: 40 MIN. • **COOK:** 7¼ HOURS • **MAKES:** 30 SERVINGS

- 2 boneless whole pork loin roasts (3½ pounds each)
- 1 cup unsweetened apple juice
- 6 garlic cloves, minced
- 1 teaspoon salt
- 1 teaspoon liquid smoke, optional
- 2½ cups barbecue sauce, divided
- ⅓ cup packed brown sugar
- 2 tablespoons honey
- 1 package (10 ounces) tortilla chip scoops
- 1½ cups frozen corn
- 1 can (15 ounces) black beans, rinsed and drained
- 1 medium tomato, seeded and chopped
- 1 medium red onion, chopped
- ⅓ cup minced fresh cilantro
- 1 jalapeno pepper, seeded and chopped
- 2 teaspoons lime juice
- 1 package (16 ounces) process cheese (Velveeta), cubed
- 2 tablespoons 2% milk

1. Cut each roast in half; place in two 5-qt. slow cookers. Combine the apple juice, garlic, salt and liquid smoke if desired; pour over meat. Cover and cook on low for 7-8 hours or until tender.

2. Shred pork with two forks; place in a very large bowl. Stir in 2 cups barbecue sauce, brown sugar and honey. Divide tortilla chips between two greased 13-in. x 9-in. baking dishes; top with pork mixture. Combine the corn, beans, tomato, onion, cilantro, jalapeno and lime juice; spoon over pork mixture.

3. Bake, uncovered, at 375° for 15-20 minutes or until heated through. Meanwhile, in a small saucepan, melt cheese with milk. Drizzle cheese sauce and remaining barbecue sauce over nachos.

NOTE *Wear disposable gloves when cutting hot peppers; the oils can burn skin. Avoid touching your face.*

top tip Smart Supper

Make the most of your slow cooker and your leftovers! Place any leftover cooked beef, pork or chicken in a resealable freezer storage bag. Keep adding leftover cooked meats to the bag, regardless of how they're seasoned or prepared. When the bag is full, set the frozen contents into a slow cooker and top with bottled barbecue sauce. Cook on low for 8 hours, then shred the meat for no-fuss sandwiches.

JALAPENO SPINACH DIP

Jalapeno Spinach Dip

Everyone loves spinach dip, and this version is as easy as it is delicious. Just mix the ingredients together in the slow cooker for a savory and creamy appetizer.

—**MICHAELA DEBELIUS** WADDELL, AZ

PREP: 10 MIN. • **COOK:** 2 HOURS
MAKES: 16 SERVINGS (¼ CUP EACH)

- 2 packages (10 ounces each) frozen chopped spinach, thawed and squeezed dry
- 2 packages (8 ounces each) cream cheese, softened
- 1 cup grated Parmesan cheese
- 1 cup half-and-half cream
- ½ cup finely chopped onion
- ¼ cup chopped seeded jalapeno peppers
- 2 teaspoons Worcestershire sauce
- 2 teaspoons hot pepper sauce
- 1 teaspoon garlic powder
- 1 teaspoon dill weed
  Tortilla chips

In a 1½-qt. slow cooker, combine the first 10 ingredients. Cover and cook on low for 2-3 hours or until heated through. Serve with chips.
NOTE *Wear disposable gloves when cutting hot peppers; the oils can burn skin. Avoid touching your face.*

⑤ INGREDIENTS Warm Strawberry Fondue

You need only a handful of ingredients to fix this spring fondue. Use grapes, bananas, strawberries and angel food cake cubes as dippers.

—**SHARON MENSING** GREENFIELD, IA

START TO FINISH: 15 MIN. • **MAKES:** 1½ CUPS

- 1 package (10 ounces) frozen sweetened sliced strawberries, thawed
- ¼ cup half-and-half cream
- 1 teaspoon cornstarch
- ½ teaspoon lemon juice
  Angel food cake cubes and fresh fruit

1. In a food processor, combine the strawberries, cream, cornstarch and lemon juice; cover and process until smooth.
2. Pour into saucepan. Bring to a boil; cook and stir for 2 minutes or until slightly thickened. Transfer to a fondue pot or 1½-qt. slow cooker; keep warm. Serve with cake cubes and fruit.

WARM STRAWBERRY FONDUE

JAN HABERSTICH'S
SPINACH ARTICHOKE DIP

Spinach Artichoke Dip

Here's a creamy, delicious appetizer that's perfect for special occasions. It's especially good served with Asiago cheese bread for dipping.

—**JAN HABERSTICH** WATERLOO, IA

PREP: 15 MIN. • **COOK:** 2 HOURS • **MAKES:** 3 CUPS

- 1 can (14 ounces) water-packed artichoke hearts, rinsed, drained and chopped
- 1 cup fresh baby spinach, chopped
- ½ cup sour cream
- ½ cup mayonnaise
- ½ cup shredded part-skim mozzarella cheese
- ½ cup shredded Parmesan cheese
- ⅓ cup chopped red onion
- ¼ teaspoon garlic powder
  Assorted crackers or breads

In a 1½-qt. slow cooker, combine the first eight ingredients. Cover and cook on low for 2-3 hours or until heated through. Serve with crackers or breads.

Buffalo Wing Dip

If you love spicy wings, you'll love this dip. It's super cheesy, full of rich flavor and really tastes like buffalo wings!

—**TASTE OF HOME TEST KITCHEN**

PREP: 20 MIN. • **COOK:** 2 HOURS • **MAKES:** 6 CUPS

- 2 packages (8 ounces each) cream cheese, softened
- ½ cup ranch salad dressing
- ½ cup sour cream
- 5 tablespoons crumbled blue cheese
- 2 cups shredded cooked chicken

BUFFALO WING DIP

MEXICAN FONDUE

- ½ cup buffalo wing sauce
- 2 cups (8 ounces) shredded cheddar cheese, divided
- 1 green onion, sliced
  Tortilla chips

1. In a small bowl, combine the cream cheese, dressing, sour cream and blue cheese. Transfer to a 3-qt. slow cooker. Layer with chicken, wing sauce and 1 cup cheese. Cover and cook on low for 2-3 hours or until heated through.

2. Sprinkle with remaining cheese and onion. Serve with tortilla chips.

Mexican Fondue

A handful of items and a few moments of prep work are all you'll need for my festive fondue. Not only does it take advantage of canned goods and other convenience items, but the slow cooker does all the work!

—**NELLA PARKER** HERSEY, MI

PREP: 15 MIN. • **COOK:** 1½ HOURS • **MAKES:** 4½ CUPS

- 1 can (14¾ ounces) cream-style corn
- 1 can (14½ ounces) diced tomatoes, drained
- 3 tablespoons chopped green chilies
- 1 teaspoon chili powder
- 1 package (16 ounces) process cheese (Velveeta), cubed
  French bread cubes

1. In a small bowl, combine the corn, tomatoes, green chilies and chili powder. Stir in cheese. Pour mixture into a 1½-qt. slow cooker coated with cooking spray.

2. Cover and cook on high for 1½ hours, stirring every 30 minutes or until cheese is melted. Serve warm with bread cubes.

"I have a large family, work full-time and coach soccer and football. So I appreciate recipes like this one that are easy to assemble. The rich creamy dip is a fun appetizer for any spring gathering. "

—**TERI LEE RASEY** CADILLAC, MI

Hot Crab Dip

PREP: 5 MIN. • **COOK:** 3 HOURS • **MAKES:** ABOUT 5 CUPS

- ½ cup milk
- ⅓ cup salsa
- 3 packages (8 ounces each) cream cheese, cubed
- 2 packages (8 ounces each) imitation crabmeat, flaked
- 1 cup thinly sliced green onions
- 1 can (4 ounces) chopped green chilies
   Assorted crackers

In a small bowl, combine milk and salsa. Transfer to a greased 3-qt. slow cooker. Stir in cream cheese, crab, onions and chilies. Cover and cook on low for 3-4 hours, stirring every 30 minutes. Serve with crackers.

HOT CRAB DIP

MARMALADE MEATBALLS

[5]INGREDIENTS Marmalade Meatballs

I brought this snappy dish to work for a potluck. I started cooking the meatballs in the morning, and by lunch time they were ready. They disappeared fast!

—**JEANNE KISS** GREENSBURG, PA

PREP: 10 MIN. • **COOK:** 4 HOURS • **MAKES:** ABOUT 5 DOZEN

- 1 bottle (16 ounces) Catalina salad dressing
- 1 cup orange marmalade
- 3 tablespoons Worcestershire sauce
- ½ teaspoon crushed red pepper flakes
- 1 package (32 ounces) frozen fully cooked homestyle meatballs, thawed

In a 3-qt. slow cooker, combine the salad dressing, marmalade, Worcestershire sauce and pepper flakes. Stir in meatballs. Cover and cook on low for 4-5 hours or until heated through.

Barbecue Sausage Bites

This sweet-and-tangy appetizer pairs pineapple chunks with barbecue sauce and three kinds of sausage. It'll tide over even the biggest appetites until dinner.

—**REBEKAH RANDOLPH** GREER, SC

PREP: 10 MIN. • **COOK:** 2½ HOURS • **MAKES:** 12-14 SERVINGS

- 1 package (16 ounces) miniature smoked sausages
- ¾ pound fully cooked bratwurst links, cut into ½-inch slices
- ¾ pound smoked kielbasa or Polish sausage, cut into ½-inch slices
- 1 bottle (18 ounces) barbecue sauce
- ⅔ cup orange marmalade
- ½ teaspoon ground mustard
- ⅛ teaspoon ground allspice
- 1 can (20 ounces) pineapple chunks, drained

1. In a 3-qt. slow cooker, combine the sausages. In a small bowl, whisk the barbecue sauce, marmalade, mustard and allspice. Pour over sausage mixture; stir to coat.

2. Cover and cook on high for 2½-3 hours or until heated through. Stir in pineapple. Serve with toothpicks.

SEAFOOD CHEESE DIP

(5) INGREDIENTS Seafood Cheese Dip

This cheesy recipe has a savory combination of seafood flavors and clings nicely to slices of toasted bread.

—**MICHELLE DOMM** ATLANTA, NY

PREP: 15 MIN. • **COOK:** 1½ HOURS • **MAKES:** 5 CUPS

- 1 package (32 ounces) process cheese (Velveeta), cubed
- 2 cans (6 ounces each) lump crabmeat, drained
- 1 can (10 ounces) diced tomatoes and green chilies, undrained
- 1 cup frozen cooked salad shrimp, thawed
  French bread baguettes, sliced and toasted

In a greased 3-qt. slow cooker, combine the cheese, crab, tomatoes and shrimp. Cover and cook on low for 1½-2 hours or until cheese is melted, stirring occasionally. Serve with baguettes.

BARBECUE SAUSAGE BITES

IDA TUEY'S
SWEET 'N' TANGY CHICKEN WINGS

Sweet 'n' Tangy Chicken Wings

Here's a festive recipe that's perfect for a crowd. Put the wings in before you prepare for the party, and in a few hours, you'll have wonderful appetizers!

—**IDA TUEY** SOUTH LYON, MI

PREP: 20 MIN. • **COOK:** 3¾ HOURS
MAKES: ABOUT 2½ DOZEN

- 3 pounds chicken wingettes (about 30)
- ½ teaspoon salt, divided
  Dash pepper
- 1½ cups ketchup
- ¼ cup packed brown sugar
- ¼ cup red wine vinegar
- 2 tablespoons Worcestershire sauce
- 1 tablespoon Dijon mustard
- 1 teaspoon minced garlic
- 1 teaspoon liquid smoke, optional
  Sesame seeds, optional

1. Sprinkle chicken wings with a dash of salt and pepper. Broil 4-6 in. from the heat for 5-10 minutes on each side or until golden brown. Transfer to a greased 5-qt. slow cooker.
2. Combine the ketchup, brown sugar, vinegar, Worcestershire sauce, mustard, garlic, liquid smoke if desired and remaining salt; pour over wings. Toss to coat.
3. Cover and cook on low for 3¼-3¾ hours or until chicken juices run clear. Sprinkle with sesame seeds if desired.

Spicy Apple Tea

Ideal for a chilly spring morning, this comforting beverage is one of my slow-cooker staples.

—**KAREN LARA** KAMLOOPS, BC

PREP: 15 MIN. • **COOK:** 2 HOURS
MAKES: 21 SERVINGS (¾ CUP EACH)

- 2 quarts water
- 2 quarts unsweetened apple juice
- 1 cup packed brown sugar
- 4 individual black tea bags
- 4 cinnamon sticks (3 inches)
- 1 tablespoon minced fresh gingerroot
- 1 tablespoon whole allspice
- 1 tablespoon whole cloves

1. In a 6-qt. slow cooker, combine the water, apple juice, brown sugar and tea bags. Place the cinnamon sticks, ginger, allspice and cloves on a double thickness of cheesecloth; bring up corners of cloth and tie with string to form a bag. Place in slow cooker.
2. Cover and cook on high for 2-3 hours or until heated through. Discard tea bags and spice bag. Serve warm in mugs.

⑤INGREDIENTS
Pretty Orange Cider

As the season warms up, this pretty beverage is sure to be a hit. You just might want to double this recipe, then fill the punchbowl for guests!

—**MARK MORGAN** WATERFORD, WI

START TO FINISH: 20 MIN.
MAKES: 1½ QUARTS

- 4 cups apple cider or juice
- 2 cups orange juice
- 3 tablespoons red-hot candies
- 1½ teaspoons whole allspice
- 4½ teaspoons honey

1. In a large saucepan, combine the cider, juice and candies. Place the allspice on a double thickness of cheesecloth; bring up corners of cloth and tie with string to form a bag. Add to pan. Bring to a boil. Reduce heat; cover and simmer for 5 minutes or until flavors are blended.
2. Discard spice bag; stir in honey. Transfer to a 3-qt. slow cooker; keep warm over low heat.

PRETTY ORANGE CIDER

1. In a 5-qt. slow cooker, combine the noodles, cereal, cashews and coconut. In a small bowl, whisk the butter, soy sauce, curry powder and ginger; drizzle over cereal mixture and mix well.

2. Cover and cook on low for 2½ hours, stirring every 30 minutes. Serve warm or at room temperature.

Reuben Spread

I love anything with Reuben flavor, and this appetizer is a favorite. It's a warm and yummy crowd-pleaser, perfect for rallying your game-day crowd!

—**JUNE HERKE** WATERTOWN, SD

PREP: 10 MIN. • **COOK:** 4 HOURS • **MAKES:** 3¾ CUPS

- 2 packages (8 ounces each) cream cheese, cubed
- 4 cups (16 ounces) shredded Swiss cheese
- 1 can (14 ounces) sauerkraut, rinsed and well drained
- 4 packages (2 ounces each) thinly sliced deli corned beef, chopped
- ½ cup Thousand Island salad dressing
  Snack rye bread

In a 1½-qt. slow cooker, combine the first five ingredients. Cover and cook on low for 4 hours; stir to blend. Serve with snack rye bread.

CRISPY SNACK MIX

Crispy Snack Mix

This recipe proves that you can make just about anything in the slow cooker...even a delightfully crisp snack mix!

—**JANE PAIR SIMS** DE LEON, TX

PREP: 10 MIN. • **COOK:** 2½ HOURS • **MAKES:** ABOUT 2½ QUARTS

- 4½ cups crispy chow mein noodles
- 4 cups Rice Chex
- 1 can (9¾ ounces) salted cashews
- 1 cup flaked coconut, toasted
- ½ cup butter, melted
- 2 tablespoons reduced-sodium soy sauce
- 2¼ teaspoons curry powder
- ¾ teaspoon ground ginger

top tip — Quick Fix

Toasting nuts and coconut truly enhances the flavors. In addition, toasted coconut helps maintain the perfect texture in snack mixes, garnishes and more. To toast nuts or coconut, spread in a 15-in. x 10-in. x 1-in. baking pan. Bake at 350° for 5-10 minutes or until lightly browned, stirring occasionally. Or, spread in a dry nonstick skillet and heat over low heat until lightly browned, stirring occasionally.

REUBEN SPREAD

MARINATED CHICKEN WINGS

Marinated Chicken Wings

I've made these nicely flavored chicken wings many times for get-togethers. They're so moist and tender—I always get lots of compliments and many requests for the recipe.

—**JANIE BOTTING** SULTAN, WA

PREP: 5 MIN. + MARINATING • **COOK:** 3 HOURS
MAKES: 20 SERVINGS

- 20 whole chicken wings (about 4 pounds)
- 1 cup soy sauce
- ¼ cup white wine or reduced-sodium chicken broth
- ¼ cup canola oil
- 1 tablespoon sugar
- 2 garlic cloves, minced
- 1 teaspoon ground ginger

1. Cut chicken wings into three sections; discard wing tips. Place wings in a large resealable plastic bag. In a small bowl, whisk remaining ingredients until blended. Add to chicken; seal bag and turn to coat. Refrigerate overnight.
2. Transfer chicken and marinade to a 5-qt. slow cooker. Cook, covered, on low 3-4 hours or until chicken is tender. Using tongs, remove wings to a serving plate.
NOTE *Uncooked chicken wing sections (wingettes) may be substituted for whole chicken wings.*

Fruit Salsa

Serve this fruity salsa anywhere you'd use ordinary salsa. My son and I experimented with different ingredients to find the combination we liked best. Preparing it in a slow cooker not only minimizes prep time but also maximizes flavor.

—**FLORENCE BUCHKOWSKY** PRINCE ALBERT, SK

PREP: 10 MIN. • **COOK:** 2 HOURS • **MAKES:** 4 CUPS

- 3 tablespoons cornstarch
- 4 teaspoons white vinegar
- 1 can (11 ounces) mandarin oranges, undrained
- 1 can (8½ ounces) sliced peaches, undrained
- ¾ cup pineapple tidbits
- 1 medium onion, chopped
- ½ each medium green, sweet red and yellow peppers, chopped
- 3 garlic cloves, minced
    Tortilla chips

1. In a 3-qt. slow cooker, combine cornstarch and vinegar until smooth. Stir in the fruits, onion, peppers and garlic.
2. Cover and cook on high for 2-3 hours or until thickened and heated through, stirring occasionally. Serve with tortilla chips.

SARA NOWACKI'S
PIZZA DIP

Pizza Dip

Everybody loves this simple pizza-flavored dip. If you have any left over, spoon it on a toasted English muffin for a delightful open-faced sandwich.

—**SARA NOWACKI** FRANKLIN, WI

PREP: 10 MIN. • **COOK:** 1½ HOURS
MAKES: 5½ CUPS

- 2 **packages (8 ounces each) cream cheese, cubed**
- 1 **can (15 ounces) pizza sauce**
- 1 **package (8 ounces) sliced pepperoni, chopped**
- 1 **can (3.8 ounces) chopped ripe olives, drained**
- 2 **cups (8 ounces) shredded part-skim mozzarella cheese**
  Bagel chips or garlic toast

1. Place cream cheese in a 3-qt. slow cooker. Combine the pizza sauce, pepperoni and olives; pour over cream cheese. Top with mozzarella cheese.
2. Cover and cook on low for 1-2 hours or until cheese is melted. Stir; serve warm with bagel chips or garlic toast.

Hearty Broccoli Dip

You'll need just five ingredients to stir up my no-fuss spring appetizer. People often ask me to bring the creamy dip to potlucks and parties. I never leave with leftovers.

—**SUE CALL** BEECH GROVE, IN

PREP: 15 MIN. • **COOK:** 2 HOURS
MAKES: 5½ CUPS

- 1 **pound ground beef**
- 1 **pound process cheese (Velveeta), cubed**
- 1 **can (10¾ ounces) condensed cream of mushroom soup, undiluted**
- 3 **cups frozen chopped broccoli, thawed**
- 2 **tablespoons salsa**
  Tortilla chips

1. In a large skillet, cook beef over medium heat until no longer pink; drain. Transfer to a 3-qt. slow cooker. Add cheese, soup, broccoli and salsa; mix well.
2. Cover and cook on low for 2-3 hours or until heated through, stirring after 1 hour. Serve with chips.

Creamy Chipped Beef Fondue

My mother often served fondue at parties, and I've since followed in that tradition. It's nice to offer a hearty appetizer that requires very little work.

—**BETH FOX** LAWRENCE, KS

START TO FINISH: 15 MIN.
MAKES: ABOUT 4 CUPS

- 1⅓ to 1½ **cups milk**
- 2 **packages (8 ounces each) cream cheese, softened**
- 1 **package (2½ ounces) thinly sliced dried beef, chopped**
- ¼ **cup chopped green onions**
- 2 **teaspoons ground mustard**
- 1 **loaf (1 pound) French bread, cubed**

In a large saucepan, heat milk and cream cheese over medium heat; stir until smooth. Stir in beef, onions and mustard; heat through. Transfer to a fondue pot or 1½-qt. slow cooker; keep warm. Serve with bread cubes.

Spring

Spring is a great time to round out meals with root vegetables such as carrots and potatoes. Best of all, these savory slow-cooked options free up oven space for entrees. So go ahead and add these sides to your lineup for a fuss-free dinner!

GLORIA SCHUTZ'S
SHOEPEG CORN SIDE DISH

Shoepeg Corn Side Dish

I took this dish to a potluck and everyone asked for the recipe. If shoepeg corn isn't available in your region, then regular canned corn works well, too.
—GLORIA SCHUTZ TRENTON, IL

PREP: 20 MIN. • **COOK:** 3 HOURS • **MAKES:** 8 SERVINGS

- 1 can (14½ ounces) French-style green beans, drained
- 2 cans (7 ounces each) white or shoepeg corn
- 1 can (10¾ ounces) condensed cream of mushroom soup, undiluted
- 1 jar (4½ ounces) sliced mushrooms, drained
- ½ cup slivered almonds
- ½ cup shredded cheddar cheese
- ½ cup sour cream
- ¾ cup French-fried onions

In a 3-qt. slow cooker, combine the first seven ingredients. Cover and cook on low for 3-4 hours or until vegetables are tender, stirring occasionally. Sprinkle with onions during the last 15 minutes of cooking.

Slow Cooker Goetta

Being German, my husband's grandfather introduced goetta to me. I found a slow cooker recipe and changed some of the ingredients to make this the best goetta in town! It makes a lot, but it freezes well for busy nights ahead.
—SHARON GEERS WILMINGTON, OH

PREP: 45 MIN. • **COOK:** 4 HOURS
MAKES: 2 LOAVES (16 SLICES EACH)

- 6 cups water
- 2½ cups steel-cut oats
- 6 bay leaves
- 3 tablespoons beef bouillon granules
- ¾ teaspoon salt
- 1 teaspoon each garlic powder, rubbed sage and pepper
- ½ teaspoon ground allspice
- ½ teaspoon crushed red pepper flakes
- 2 pounds bulk pork sausage
- 2 medium onions, chopped

1. In a 5-qt. slow cooker, combine water, oats and seasonings. Cook, covered, on high 2 hours. Remove bay leaves.
2. In a large skillet, cook sausage and onions over medium heat 8-10 minutes or until no longer pink, breaking up sausage into crumbles. Drain, reserving 2 tablespoons drippings. Stir sausage mixture and reserved drippings into oats. Cook, covered, on low 2 hours.
3. Transfer mixture to two plastic wrap-lined 9x5-in. loaf pans. Refrigerate, covered, overnight.
4. To serve, slice each loaf into 16 slices. In a large skillet, cook goetta, in batches, over medium heat 3-4 minutes on each side or until lightly browned and heated through.

Loaded Mashed Potatoes

Every year Mom made cream cheese mashed potatoes for Thanksgiving. I've tailored the recipe to my family and have carried on the tradition. I also prepare them in a slow cooker, which is convenient because it frees up oven space. For extra convenience, make the side dish a day early.

—ANN NOLTE RIVERVIEW, FL

PREP: 25 MIN. + CHILLING • **COOK:** 3 HOURS
MAKES: 10 SERVINGS

- 3 **pounds potatoes (about 9 medium), peeled and cubed**
- 1 **package (8 ounces) cream cheese, softened**
- 1 **cup (8 ounces) sour cream**
- ½ **cup butter, cubed**
- ¼ **cup 2% milk**
- 1½ **cups (6 ounces) shredded cheddar cheese**
- 1½ **cups (6 ounces) shredded pepper jack cheese**
- ½ **pound bacon strips, cooked and crumbled**
- 4 **green onions, chopped**
- ½ **teaspoon onion powder**
- ½ **teaspoon garlic powder**

1. Place potatoes in a Dutch oven and cover with water. Bring to a boil. Reduce heat; cover and cook for 10-15 minutes or until tender. Drain. Mash potatoes with cream cheese, sour cream, butter and milk. Stir in the cheeses, bacon, onions and seasonings. Transfer to a large bowl; cover and refrigerate overnight.

2. Transfer to a greased 3- or 4-qt. slow cooker. Cover and cook on low for 3 to 3½ hours.

AU GRATIN GARLIC POTATOES

LOADED MASHED POTATOES

Au Gratin Garlic Potatoes

Cream cheese and a can of cheese soup turn ordinary sliced potatoes into a rich side dish that's a perfect accompaniment to almost any meal.

—TONYA VOWELS VINE GROVE, KY

PREP: 10 MIN. • **COOK:** 6 HOURS • **MAKES:** 6-8 SERVINGS

- ½ **cup milk**
- 1 **can (10¾ ounces) condensed cheddar cheese soup, undiluted**
- 1 **package (8 ounces) cream cheese, cubed**
- 1 **garlic clove, minced**
- ¼ **teaspoon ground nutmeg**
- ⅛ **teaspoon pepper**
- 2 **pounds potatoes, peeled and sliced**
- 1 **small onion, chopped**
  Paprika, optional

1. In a large saucepan, heat milk over medium heat until bubbles form around side of saucepan. Remove from the heat. Add the soup, cream cheese, garlic, nutmeg and pepper; stir until smooth.

2. Place the potatoes and onion in a 3-qt. slow cooker. Pour the milk mixture over the potato mixture; mix well. Cover and cook on low for 6-7 hours or until potatoes are tender. Sprinkle with paprika if desired.

Lemon Red Potatoes

Butter, lemon juice, parsley and chives enhance my easy side dish. I usually prepare these potatoes when I'm having company. Since they cook in the slow cooker, there's plenty of room on the stove for other dishes.

—**TARA BRANHAM** AUSTIN, TX

PREP: 5 MIN. • **COOK:** 2½ HOURS
MAKES: 6 SERVINGS

- 1½ **pounds medium red potatoes**
- ¼ **cup water**
- ¼ **cup butter, melted**
- 3 **tablespoons minced fresh parsley**
- 1 **tablespoon lemon juice**
- 1 **tablespoon minced chives**
  Salt and pepper to taste

1. Cut a strip of peel from around the middle of each potato. Place potatoes and water in a 3-qt. slow cooker. Cover and cook on high for 2½ to 3 hours or until tender (do not overcook); drain.
2. In a small bowl, combine the butter, parsley, lemon juice and chives. Pour over the potatoes and toss to coat. Season with salt and pepper.

Garlic & Herb Mashed Potatoes

Can you keep a secret? Cream cheese is the "secret ingredient" in these comforting spuds. Simply mix, mash and let them simmer in the slow cooker.

—**FRIEDA BLIESNER** MCALLEN, TX

PREP: 30 MIN. • **COOK:** 2 HOURS
MAKES: 10 SERVINGS

- 4 **pounds Yukon Gold potatoes (about 12 medium), peeled and cubed**
- 1 **package (8 ounces) cream cheese, softened and cubed**
- 1 **cup (8 ounces) sour cream**
- ½ **cup butter, cubed**
- ⅓ **cup heavy whipping cream**
- 3 **tablespoons minced chives**
- 3 **garlic cloves, minced**
- 1 **tablespoon minced fresh parsley**
- 1 **teaspoon minced fresh thyme**
- ½ **teaspoon salt**
- ¼ **teaspoon pepper**

1. Place potatoes in a Dutch oven and cover with water. Bring to a boil. Reduce heat; cover and cook for 10-15 minutes or until tender. Drain. Mash potatoes with cream cheese, sour cream, butter and cream. Stir in the remaining ingredients.
2. Transfer to a greased 3- or 4-qt. slow cooker. Cover and cook on low for 2-3 hours or until heated through.

Harvard Beets

Fresh beets are delicious when combined with an aromatic spice and hint of orange. These have the perfect balance of sweet and sour flavors.

—**TASTE OF HOME TEST KITCHEN**

PREP: 15 MIN. • **COOK:** 7 HOURS
MAKES: 6 SERVINGS

- 2 **pounds small fresh beets, peeled and halved**
- ½ **cup sugar**
- ¼ **cup packed brown sugar**
- 2 **tablespoons cornstarch**
- ½ **teaspoon salt**
- ¼ **cup orange juice**
- ¼ **cup cider vinegar**
- 2 **tablespoons butter**
- 1½ **teaspoons whole cloves**

1. Place beets in a 3-qt. slow cooker. In a small bowl, combine the sugar, brown sugar, cornstarch and salt. Stir in orange juice and vinegar. Pour over beets; dot with butter. Place cloves on a double thickness of cheesecloth; bring up corners of cloth and tie with string to form a bag. Place bag in slow cooker.
2. Cover and cook on low for 7-8 hours or until tender. Discard spice bag.

Name Game

Harvard Beets are simmered in a sugar-vinegar sauce, often flavored with orange juice. The history of this dish isn't clear. Many believe the beets are called this because they resemble the color of a Harvard Crimson football jersey. Others think the beets originated in a tavern in England named "Harwood," which eventually came to be pronounced "Harvard."

LEMON RED POTATOES

HARVARD BEETS

CHEDDAR SPIRALS

⑤ INGREDIENTS Cheddar Spirals

Our kids just love this cheesy pasta and will sample spoonfuls right from the slow cooker when they walk by. It's ideal any time of the year, really. Try it alongside ham for a delightful dinner.
—**HEIDI FERKOVICH** PARK FALLS, WI

PREP: 20 MIN. • **COOK:** 2½ HOURS
MAKES: 15 SERVINGS (¾ CUP EACH)

- 1 **package (16 ounces) spiral pasta**
- 2 **cups half-and-half cream**
- 1 **can (10¾ ounces) condensed cheddar cheese soup, undiluted**
- ½ **cup butter, melted**
- 4 **cups (16 ounces) shredded cheddar cheese**

Cook pasta according to package directions; drain. In a 5-qt. slow cooker, combine the cream, soup and butter until smooth; stir in the cheese and pasta. Cover and cook on low for 2½ hours or until cheese is melted.

top tip Must-Try Main Dish

When I need a slow-cooked entree, I turn to Cheddar Spirals. Make it a main course by stirring cooked cocktail sausages, sliced Polish sausage or cubed ham into the slow cooker during the last half hour of cooking.
—**HEIDI F.** PARK FALLS, WI

Black-Eyed Peas & Ham

We have these slow-cooked black-eyed peas regularly at our house. They're supposed to bring good luck!

—**DAWN FRIHAUF** FORT MORGAN, CO

PREP: 20 MIN. • **COOK:** 6 HOURS • **MAKES:** 12 SERVINGS

- 1 package (16 ounces) dried black-eyed peas, rinsed and sorted
- ½ pound fully cooked boneless ham, finely chopped
- 1 medium onion, finely chopped
- 1 medium sweet red pepper, finely chopped
- 5 bacon strips, cooked and crumbled
- 1 large jalapeno pepper, seeded and finely chopped
- 2 garlic cloves, minced
- 1½ teaspoons ground cumin
- 1 teaspoon reduced-sodium chicken bouillon granules
- ½ teaspoon salt
- ½ teaspoon cayenne pepper
- ¼ teaspoon pepper
- 6 cups water
  Minced fresh cilantro, optional
  Hot cooked rice

In a 6-qt. slow cooker, combine the first 13 ingredients. Cover and cook on low for 6-8 hours or until peas are tender. Sprinkle with cilantro if desired. Serve with rice.

NOTE *Wear disposable gloves when cutting hot peppers; the oils can burn skin. Avoid touching your face.*

BLACK-EYED PEAS & HAM

CREAMY HASH BROWN POTATOES

Creamy Hash Brown Potatoes

I like to fix a batch of these cheesy slow cooker potatoes for potlucks and other big gatherings. Frozen hash browns, canned soup and flavored cream cheese make it so quick to put together.

—**JULIANNE HENSON** STREAMWOOD, IL

PREP: 5 MIN. • **COOK:** 3½ HOURS • **MAKES:** 12-14 SERVINGS

- 1 package (32 ounces) frozen cubed hash brown potatoes
- 1 can (10¾ ounces) condensed cream of potato soup, undiluted
- 2 cups (8 ounces) shredded Colby-Monterey Jack cheese
- 1 cup (8 ounces) sour cream
- ¼ teaspoon pepper
- ⅛ teaspoon salt
- 1 carton (8 ounces) spreadable chive and onion cream cheese

1. Place potatoes in a lightly greased 3-qt. slow cooker. In a large bowl, combine the soup, cheese, sour cream, pepper and salt. Pour over potatoes and mix well.

2. Cover and cook on low for 3½ to 4 hours or until potatoes are tender. Stir in cream cheese.

PECAN-COCONUT SWEET POTATOES

"This recipe has truly evolved over the many years we have made it. This version is a favorite at our Christmas dinners."
—JUDY BATSON TAMPA, FL

Banana Applesauce

PREP: 20 MIN. • **COOK:** 3 HOURS
MAKES: 5½ CUPS

- 8 medium apples, peeled and cubed
- 1 medium ripe banana, thinly sliced
- 1 cup raisins
- ¾ cup orange juice
- ½ cup packed brown sugar
- ¼ cup honey
- ¼ cup butter, melted
- 2 teaspoons pumpkin pie spice
- 1 small lemon
- 1 envelope instant apples and cinnamon oatmeal
- ½ cup boiling water

1. Place the apples, banana and raisins in a 3-qt. slow cooker coated with cooking spray. In a small bowl, combine the orange juice, brown sugar, honey, butter and pie spice; pour over apple mixture. Cut ends off lemon. Cut into six wedges and remove seeds. Transfer to slow cooker. Cover and cook on high for 3-4 hours or until apples are soft.

2. Discard lemon. Mash apple mixture. In a small bowl, combine oatmeal and water. Let stand for 1 minute. Stir into applesauce.

Pecan-Coconut Sweet Potatoes

It's great to be able to make a tempting sweet potato dish well ahead by putting it in the slow cooker. My tasty recipe includes sweet coconut and crunchy pecans. It's yummy!
—REBECCA CLARK WARRIOR, AL

PREP: 20 MIN. • **COOK:** 5 HOURS
MAKES: 6 SERVINGS

- 2 pounds sweet potatoes, peeled and cut into ¾-inch cubes
- ¼ cup packed brown sugar
- 2 tablespoons flaked coconut
- 2 tablespoons chopped pecans, toasted
- 1 teaspoon vanilla extract
- ½ teaspoon salt
- ¼ teaspoon ground cinnamon
- 1 tablespoon butter, melted
- ½ cup miniature marshmallows

1. Place sweet potatoes in a 3-qt. slow cooker coated with cooking spray. In a small bowl combine the brown sugar, coconut, pecans, vanilla, salt and cinnamon; sprinkle over sweet potatoes. Drizzle with butter.

2. Cover and cook on low for 5-6 hours or until potatoes are tender, sprinkling with marshmallows during the last 5 minutes of cooking.

Homemade Spices

For pumpkin pie spice, combine 4 teaspoons ground cinnamon, 2 teaspoons ground ginger, 1 teaspoon ground cloves and 1/2 teaspoon ground nutmeg.

COWBOY CALICO BEANS

Spanish Hominy

I received this recipe from a good friend who is a fabulous cook. The colorful side dish gets its zesty flavor from spicy canned tomatoes with green chilies.

—**DONNA BROCKETT** KINGFISHER, OK

PREP: 15 MIN. • **COOK:** 6 HOURS
MAKES: 12 SERVINGS

- 4 cans (15½ ounces each) hominy, rinsed and drained
- 1 can (14½ ounces) diced tomatoes, undrained
- 1 can (10 ounces) diced tomatoes and green chilies, undrained
- 1 can (8 ounces) tomato sauce
- ¾ pound sliced bacon, diced
- 1 large onion, chopped
- 1 medium green pepper, chopped

1. In a 5-qt. slow cooker, combine the hominy, tomatoes and tomato sauce.
2. In a large skillet, cook bacon until crisp; remove with a slotted spoon to paper towels. Drain, reserving 1 tablespoon of drippings.
3. In the same skillet, saute onion and green pepper in drippings until tender. Stir onion mixture and bacon into hominy mixture. Cover and cook on low for 6-8 hours or until heated through.

Cowboy Calico Beans

This filling dish is a tradition at the table when my girlfriends and I go up North for a girls' weekend. The husbands and kids are left at home, but the slow cooker comes with us!

—**JULIE BUTSCH** HARTLAND, WI

PREP: 30 MIN. • **COOK:** 4 HOURS
MAKES: 8 SERVINGS

- 1 pound lean ground beef (90% lean)
- 1 large sweet onion, chopped
- ½ cup packed brown sugar
- ¼ cup ketchup
- 3 tablespoons cider vinegar
- 2 tablespoons yellow mustard
- 1 can (16 ounces) butter beans, drained
- 1 can (16 ounces) kidney beans, rinsed and drained
- 1 can (15 ounces) pork and beans
- 1 can (15¼ ounces) lima beans, rinsed and drained

1. In a large skillet, cook beef and onion over medium heat until meat is no longer pink; drain.
2. Transfer to a 3-qt. slow cooker. Combine the brown sugar, ketchup, vinegar and mustard; add to meat mixture. Stir in the beans. Cover and cook on low for 4-5 hours or until heated through.

SPANISH HOMINY

CATHY BELL'S
GREEN BEANS WITH BACON AND TOMATOES

BLACK BEAN POTATO AU GRATIN

Green Beans with Bacon and Tomatoes

If needed, this recipe can easily be doubled or tripled to serve larger crowds. Garlic salt can be substituted for the seasoned salt if you like.

—**CATHY BELL** JOPLIN, MO

PREP: 15 MIN. • **COOK:** 4½ HOURS • **MAKES:** 12 SERVINGS (¾ CUP)

1 package (14 ounces) thick-sliced bacon strips, chopped
1 large red onion, chopped
2 packages (16 ounces each) frozen cut green beans
1 can (28 ounces) petite diced tomatoes, undrained
¼ cup packed brown sugar
1 tablespoon seasoned pepper
½ teaspoon seasoned salt
1 can (16 ounces) red beans, rinsed and drained

1. In a large skillet, cook bacon over medium heat until partially cooked but not crisp, stirring occasionally. Remove with a slotted spoon; drain on paper towels. Discard drippings, reserving 2 tablespoons. Add onion to drippings; cook and stir over medium-high heat until tender.

2. In a 4- or 5-qt. slow cooker, combine green beans, tomatoes, brown sugar, pepper, salt, bacon and onion. Cook, covered, on low 4 hours. Stir in red beans. Cook 30 minutes longer or until heated through.

Black Bean Potato au Gratin

The addition of black beans and vegetables adds both protein and fiber to this side dish. For a Southwestern twist, try adding a handful or two of cooked chorizo sausage, and replace the peas with one cup of frozen corn kernels.

—**ERIN CHILCOAT** CENTRAL ISLIP, NY

PREP: 25 MIN. • **COOK:** 8 HOURS • **MAKES:** 6 SERVINGS

2 cans (15 ounces each) black beans, rinsed and drained
1 can (10¾ ounces) condensed cream of mushroom soup, undiluted
1 medium sweet red pepper, chopped
1 cup frozen peas
1 cup chopped sweet onion
1 celery rib, thinly sliced
2 garlic cloves, minced
1 teaspoon dried thyme
¼ teaspoon coarsely ground pepper
1½ pounds medium red potatoes, cut into ¼-inch slices
1 teaspoon salt
1 cup (4 ounces) shredded cheddar cheese

In a large bowl, combine the beans, soup, red pepper, peas, onion, celery, garlic, thyme and pepper. Spoon half of mixture into a greased 3- or 4-qt. slow cooker. Layer with half of the potatoes, salt and cheese. Repeat layers. Cover and cook on low for 8-10 hours or until potatoes are tender.

EASY BEANS & POTATOES WITH BACON

Easy Beans & Potatoes with Bacon

I love the combination of green beans with bacon, so I created this recipe. It's great for times when you have company because you can start the side dish in the slow cooker and continue preparing the rest of your dinner.

—BARBARA BRITTAIN SANTEE, CA

PREP: 15 MIN. • **COOK:** 6 HOURS • **MAKES:** 10 SERVINGS

- 8 **bacon strips, chopped**
- 1½ **pounds fresh green beans, trimmed and cut into 2-inch pieces (about 4 cups)**
- 4 **medium potatoes, peeled and cubed (½-inch)**
- 1 **small onion, halved and sliced**
- ¼ **cup reduced-sodium chicken broth**
- ½ **teaspoon salt**
- ¼ **teaspoon pepper**

1. In a large skillet, cook bacon over medium heat until crisp, stirring occasionally. Remove to paper towels with a slotted spoon; drain, reserving 1 tablespoon drippings. Cover and refrigerate bacon until serving.

2. In a 5-qt. slow cooker, combine the remaining ingredients; stir in reserved drippings. Cover and cook on low for 6-8 hours or until potatoes are tender. Stir in bacon; heat through.

Scalloped Potatoes & Ham

I adapted an oven favorite to cook on its own while I'm away. It's ready to serve when I get home, making it a real winner!

—**JONI HILTON** ROCKLIN, CA

PREP: 25 MIN. • **COOK:** 8 HOURS
MAKES: 16 SERVINGS (¾ CUP EACH)

- 1 can (10¾ ounces) condensed cheddar cheese soup, undiluted
- 1 can (10¾ ounces) condensed cream of mushroom soup, undiluted
- 1 cup 2% milk
- 10 medium potatoes, peeled and thinly sliced
- 3 cups cubed fully cooked ham
- 2 medium onions, chopped
- 1 teaspoon paprika
- 1 teaspoon pepper

1. In a small bowl, combine the soups and milk. In a greased 5-qt. slow cooker, layer half of the potatoes, ham, onions and soup mixture. Repeat layers. Sprinkle with paprika and pepper.

2. Cover and cook on low for 8-10 hours or until potatoes are tender.

SLOW-COOKED VEGETABLES

SCALLOPED POTATOES & HAM

Slow-Cooked Vegetables

I like to simmer an assortment of garden-fresh vegetables for this satisfying side dish. My sister-in-law shared the recipe with me. It's a favorite at potlucks.

—**KATHY WESTENDORF** WESTGATE, IA

PREP: 10 MIN. • **COOK:** 7 HOURS • **MAKES:** 8 SERVINGS

- 4 celery ribs, cut into 1-inch pieces
- 4 small carrots, cut into 1-inch pieces
- 2 medium tomatoes, cut into chunks
- 2 medium onions, thinly sliced
- 2 cups cut fresh green beans (1-inch pieces)
- 1 medium green pepper, cut into 1-inch pieces
- ¼ cup butter, melted
- 3 tablespoons quick-cooking tapioca
- 1 tablespoon sugar
- 2 teaspoons salt, optional
- ⅛ teaspoon pepper

1. Place the vegetables in a 3-qt. slow cooker. In a small bowl, combine the butter, tapioca, sugar, salt if desired and pepper; pour over vegetables and stir well.

2. Cover and cook on low for 7-8 hours or until vegetables are tender. Serve with a slotted spoon.

SWEET & SPICY BEANS

Sweet & Spicy Beans

My husband and I love this sweet and savory bean dish. It can be used as a side, but we normally eat it as a dip with crunchy corn "scoop" chips. I've shared the colorful slow cooker recipe many times with friends and family.

—**SONDRA POPE** MOORESVILLE, NC

PREP: 10 MIN. • **COOK:** 5 HOURS
MAKES: 12 SERVINGS (⅔ CUP EACH)

- 1 can (16 ounces) **kidney beans, rinsed and drained**
- 1 can (15¼ ounces) **whole kernel corn, drained**
- 1 can (15 ounces) **garbanzo beans or chickpeas, rinsed and drained**
- 1 can (15 ounces) **black beans, rinsed and drained**
- 1 can (15 ounces) **chili with beans**
- 1 cup **barbecue sauce**
- 1 cup **salsa**
- ⅓ cup **packed brown sugar**
- ¼ teaspoon **hot pepper sauce**
  Chopped green onions, optional

In a 4- or 5-qt. slow cooker, combine the first nine ingredients. Cover and cook on low for 5-6 hours. Top with green onions if desired.

SLOW-COOKED MAC 'N' CHEESE

Onion-Garlic Hash Browns

Quick to assemble, this is a simple recipe that I've served many times. Stir in hot sauce if you like a bit of heat. I love to top my finished dish with a sprinkling of shredded cheddar cheese.

—**CINDI HAYWARD** ARDMORE, AL

PREP: 20 MIN. • **COOK:** 3 HOURS • **MAKES:** 12 SERVINGS

- 1 **large red onion, chopped**
- 1 **small sweet red pepper, chopped**
- 1 **small green pepper, chopped**
- ¼ **cup butter, cubed**
- 1 **tablespoon olive oil**
- 4 **garlic cloves, minced**
- 1 **package (30 ounces) frozen shredded hash brown potatoes**
- ½ **teaspoon salt**
- ½ **teaspoon pepper**
- 3 **drops hot pepper sauce, optional**
- 2 **teaspoons minced fresh parsley**

1. In a large skillet, saute onion and peppers in butter and oil until crisp-tender. Add garlic; cook 1 minute longer. Stir in the hash browns, salt, pepper and pepper sauce if desired.
2. Transfer to a 5-qt. slow cooker coated with cooking spray. Cover and cook on low for 3-4 hours or until heated through. Sprinkle with parsley before serving.

Slow-Cooked Mac 'n' Cheese

The name of this recipe alone is enough to make mouths water. It's comfort food at its finest: rich, hearty and extra-cheesy. It serves nine as a side dish, though you might want to make it your main course!

—**SHELBY MOLINA** WHITEWATER, WI

PREP: 25 MIN. • **COOK:** 2 HOURS • **MAKES:** 9 SERVINGS

- 2 **cups uncooked elbow macaroni**
- 1 **can (12 ounces) reduced-fat evaporated milk**
- 1½ **cups fat-free milk**
- ⅓ **cup egg substitute**
- 1 **tablespoon butter, melted**
- 8 **ounces reduced-fat process cheese (Velveeta), cubed**
- 2 **cups (8 ounces) shredded sharp cheddar cheese, divided**

1. Cook macaroni according to package directions; drain and rinse in cold water. In a large bowl, combine the evaporated milk, milk, egg substitute and butter. Stir in the process cheese, 1½ cups sharp cheddar cheese and macaroni.
2. Transfer to a 3-qt. slow cooker coated with cooking spray. Cover and cook on low for 2-3 hours or until center is set, stirring once. Sprinkle with remaining sharp cheddar cheese.

ONION-GARLIC HASH BROWNS

GLAZED SPICED CARROTS

Glazed Spiced Carrots

Glazed carrots are a classic side dish for special occasions. This recipe is easy to put together, leaving your oven and stovetop free for other dishes.

—TASTE OF HOME TEST KITCHEN

PREP: 10 MIN. • **COOK:** 6 HOURS • **MAKES:** 6 SERVINGS

- 2 **pounds fresh baby carrots**
- ½ **cup peach preserves**
- ¼ **cup packed brown sugar**
- ½ **cup butter, melted**
- 1 **teaspoon vanilla extract**
- ½ **teaspoon ground cinnamon**
- ¼ **teaspoon salt**
- ⅛ **teaspoon ground nutmeg**
- 2 **tablespoons cornstarch**
- 2 **tablespoons water**
  Toasted chopped pecans, optional

1. Place carrots in a 3-qt. slow cooker. Combine the preserves, brown sugar, butter, vanilla, cinnamon, salt and nutmeg. Combine cornstarch and water until smooth; stir into preserve mixture. Pour over carrots.

2. Cover and cook on low for 6-8 hours or until tender. Stir carrots; sprinkle with pecans if desired.

Potluck Macaroni and Cheese

Here's an easy way to satisfy a crowd with America's most popular comfort food. The dish turns out cheesy, rich and extra-creamy.

—JENNIFER BABCOCK CHICOPEE, MA

PREP: 25 MIN. • **COOK:** 2 HOURS
MAKES: 16 SERVINGS (¾ CUP EACH)

- 3 **cups uncooked elbow macaroni**
- 1 **pound process cheese (Velveeta), cubed**
- 2 **cups (8 ounces) shredded Mexican cheese blend**
- 2 **cups (8 ounces) shredded white cheddar cheese**
- 1¾ **cups milk**
- 1 **can (12 ounces) evaporated milk**
- 3 **eggs, lightly beaten**
- ¾ **cup butter, melted**

1. Cook macaroni according to package directions; drain. Place in a greased 5-qt. slow cooker. Stir in the remaining ingredients.

2. Cover and cook on low for 2-3 hours or until a thermometer reads 160°, stirring once.

JENNIFER BABCOCK'S
POTLUCK MACARONI AND CHEESE

⑤ INGREDIENTS Italian Mushrooms

It's hard to believe that only four ingredients can create such a rich and flavorful dish! It's great with beef.

—KIM REICHERT ST. PAUL, MN

PREP: 10 MIN. • **COOK:** 4 HOURS • **MAKES:** 6 SERVINGS

- 1 **pound medium fresh mushrooms**
- 1 **large onion, sliced**
- ½ **cup butter, melted**
- 1 **envelope Italian salad dressing mix**

In a 3-qt. slow cooker, layer mushrooms and onion. Combine butter and salad dressing mix; pour over vegetables. Cover and cook on low for 4-5 hours or until vegetables are tender. Serve with a slotted spoon.

NACHO HASH BROWN CASSEROLE

Nacho Hash Brown Casserole

This tasty slow cooker recipe produces the best hash browns ever. Soft and super cheesy, they make a sensational side dish for meat or poultry.

—PAT HABIGER SPEARVILLE, KS

PREP: 15 MIN. • **COOK:** 3¼ HOURS • **MAKES:** 8 SERVINGS

- 1 **package (32 ounces) frozen cubed hash brown potatoes, thawed**
- 1 **can (10¾ ounces) condensed cream of celery soup, undiluted**
- 1 **can (10¾ ounces) condensed nacho cheese soup, undiluted**
- 1 **large onion, finely chopped**
- ⅓ **cup butter, melted**
- 1 **cup (8 ounces) reduced-fat sour cream**

In a greased 3-qt. slow cooker, combine the first five ingredients. Cover and cook on low for 3-4 hours or until potatoes are tender. Stir in sour cream. Cover and cook 15-30 minutes longer or until heated through

top tip Simple Shortcut

For finely chopped onions, try slicing an onion and laying the slices on a cutting board. Next, simply run a pizza cutter back and forth over the slices.

—HAZEL G. SPRING HILL, FL

ITALIAN MUSHROOMS

Stuffed Sweet Onions

This unique dish is perfect to serve alongside steak or pork chops. Even if you're not an onion fan, the low heat and long cooking time mellows and sweetens the naturally sharp onion flavor that some people dislike.

—ERIN CHILCOAT CENTRAL ISLIP, NY

PREP: 45 MIN. • **COOK:** 4 HOURS • **MAKES:** 4 SERVINGS

- 4 medium sweet onions
- 2 small zucchini, shredded
- 1 large garlic clove, minced
- 1 tablespoon olive oil
- 1 teaspoon dried basil
- 1 teaspoon dried thyme
- ¼ teaspoon salt
- ¼ teaspoon pepper
- ½ cup dry bread crumbs
- 4 thick-sliced bacon strips, cooked and crumbled
- ¼ cup grated Parmesan cheese
- ¼ cup reduced-sodium chicken broth

1. Peel onions and cut a ¼-in. slice from the top and bottom. Carefully cut and remove the center of each onion, leaving a ½-in. shell; chop removed onion.

2. In a large skillet, saute the zucchini, garlic and chopped onions in oil until tender and juices are reduced. Stir in the basil, thyme, salt and pepper. Remove from the heat. Stir in the bread crumbs, bacon and Parmesan cheese. Fill onion shells with zucchini mixture.

3. Place in a greased 3- or 4-qt. slow cooker. Add broth to the slow cooker. Cover and cook on low for 4-5 hours or until onions are tender.

STUFFED SWEET ONIONS

Spring

ENTREES

Spring chicken...glazed ham... St. Patty's Day favorites...these are just a few of the light and lively main courses you'll find here. Ideal for warmer weather, these slow-cooked dinners make mealtime a breeze.

DARLENE MORRIS'
CHICKEN MOLE

Chicken Mole

Even if you're not familiar with mole, don't be afraid of this versatile Mexican sauce. I love sharing the recipe because it's a great one to experiment with.
—**DARLENE MORRIS** ANGIE, LA

PREP: 25 MIN. • **COOK:** 6 HOURS • **MAKES:** 12 SERVINGS

- 12 bone-in chicken thighs (about 4½ pounds), skin removed
- 1 teaspoon salt

MOLE SAUCE
- 1 can (28 ounces) whole tomatoes, drained
- 1 medium onion, chopped
- 2 dried ancho chilies, stems and seeds removed
- ½ cup sliced almonds, toasted
- ¼ cup raisins
- 3 ounces bittersweet chocolate, chopped
- 3 tablespoons olive oil
- 1 chipotle pepper in adobo sauce
- 3 garlic cloves, peeled and halved
- ¾ teaspoon ground cumin
- ½ teaspoon ground cinnamon
- Fresh cilantro leaves, optional

1. Sprinkle chicken with salt; place in a 5- or 6-qt. slow cooker. Place the tomatoes, onion, chilies, almonds, raisins, chocolate, oil, chipotle pepper, garlic, cumin and cinnamon in a food processor; cover and process until blended. Pour over chicken.
2. Cover and cook on low for 6-8 hours or until chicken is tender; skim fat. Serve chicken with sauce and sprinkle with cilantro if desired.

Light Ham Tetrazzini

This creamy pasta is an easy way to serve a hungry crowd. If you're bringing this tetrazzini to a potluck, cook and add the spaghetti to the slow cooker just before heading to the event.
—**SUSAN BLAIR** STERLING, MI

PREP: 15 MIN. • **COOK:** 4 HOURS • **MAKES:** 10 SERVINGS

- 2 cans (10¾ ounces each) reduced-fat reduced-sodium condensed cream of mushroom soup, undiluted
- 2 cups sliced fresh mushrooms
- 2 cups cubed fully cooked ham
- 1 cup fat-free evaporated milk
- ¼ cup white wine or water
- 2 teaspoons prepared horseradish
- 1 package (14½ ounces) uncooked multigrain spaghetti
- 1 cup shredded Parmesan cheese

1. In a 5-qt. slow cooker, combine the soup, mushrooms, ham, milk, wine and horseradish. Cover and cook on low for 4 hours.
2. Cook spaghetti according to package directions; drain. Add spaghetti and cheese to slow cooker; toss to coat.

Best Short Ribs Vindaloo

My sister shared this dish with me, and I made a few modifications to fit my tastes. I love the aroma as it simmers all day!

—**LORRAINE CARLSTROM** NELSON, BC

PREP: 30 MIN. + MARINATING • **COOK:** 8¼ HOURS
MAKES: 4 SERVINGS

- 1 tablespoon cumin seeds
- 2 teaspoons coriander seeds
- 1 tablespoon butter
- 1 medium onion, finely chopped
- 8 garlic cloves, minced
- 1 tablespoon minced fresh gingerroot
- 2 teaspoons mustard seed
- ½ teaspoon ground cloves
- ¼ teaspoon kosher salt
- ¼ teaspoon ground cinnamon
- ¼ teaspoon cayenne pepper
- ½ cup red wine vinegar
- 4 bay leaves
- 2 pounds bone-in beef short ribs
- 1 cup fresh sugar snap peas, halved
  Hot cooked rice and plain yogurt

1. In a dry small skillet over medium heat, toast cumin and coriander seeds until aromatic, stirring frequently. Cool. Coarsely crush seeds in a spice grinder or with a mortar and pestle.
2. In a large saucepan, heat butter over medium heat. Add the onion, garlic and ginger; cook and stir for 1 minute. Add the mustard seed, cloves, salt, cinnamon, cayenne pepper and crushed seeds; cook and stir 1 minute longer. Cool completely.
3. In a large resealable plastic bag, combine the vinegar, bay leaves and onion mixture. Add ribs; seal bag and turn to coat. Refrigerate overnight.

BEST SHORT RIBS VINDALOO

CANTONESE SWEET AND SOUR PORK

4. Transfer rib mixture to a 4-qt. slow cooker. Cover and cook on low for 8-10 hours or until meat is tender. Stir in peas; cook 8-10 minutes longer or until peas are crisp-tender. Skim fat; discard bay leaves. Serve rib mixture with rice and yogurt.

Cantonese Sweet and Sour Pork

Step away from the takeout menu. There'll be no reason to dial up delivery once you get a bite of my take on traditional sweet and sour pork. The tender vegetables, juicy pork and flavorful sauce are delicious over rice.

—**NANCY TEWS** ANTIGO, WI

PREP: 20 MIN. • **COOK:** 7½ HOURS • **MAKES:** 6 SERVINGS

- 1 can (15 ounces) tomato sauce
- 1 medium onion, halved and sliced
- 1 medium green pepper, cut into strips
- 1 can (4½ ounces) sliced mushrooms, drained
- 3 tablespoons brown sugar
- 4½ teaspoons white vinegar
- 2 teaspoons steak sauce
- 1 teaspoon salt
- 1½ pounds pork tenderloin, cut into 1-inch cubes
- 1 tablespoon olive oil
- 1 can (8 ounces) unsweetened pineapple chunks, drained
  Hot cooked rice

1. In a large bowl, combine the first eight ingredients; set aside.
2. In a large skillet, brown pork in oil in batches. Transfer to a 3- or 4-qt. slow cooker. Pour tomato sauce mixture over pork. Cover and cook on low for 7-8 hours or until the meat is tender.
3. Add pineapple; cover and cook 30 minutes longer or until heated through. Serve with rice.

THAI PORK

Thai Pork

My husband and I both work long hours. This slow cooker recipe is large enough that the two of us can eat as much yummy pork as we like and still have leftovers!
—**DAWN SCHMIDT** DURHAM, NC

PREP: 20 MIN. • **COOK:** 8 HOURS
MAKES: 8 SERVINGS

- 2 **medium sweet red peppers, julienned**
- 1 **boneless pork shoulder butt roast (3 pounds)**
- ⅓ **cup reduced-sodium teriyaki sauce**
- 3 **tablespoons rice vinegar**
- 2 **garlic cloves, minced**
- ½ **teaspoon crushed red pepper flakes**
- ¼ **cup creamy peanut butter**
- 4 **cups hot cooked rice**
- ½ **cup chopped unsalted peanuts**
- 4 **green onions, sliced**

1. Place peppers in a 3-qt. slow cooker. Cut roast in half; place on top of peppers. Combine the teriyaki sauce, vinegar and garlic; pour over roast. Sprinkle with pepper flakes. Cover and cook on low for 8-9 hours or until meat is tender.

2. Remove meat from slow cooker. When cool enough to handle, shred meat with two forks. Reserve 2 cups cooking juices; skim fat. Stir peanut butter into reserved juices.

3. Return pork and cooking juices to slow cooker; heat through. Serve with rice; sprinkle with peanuts and the green onions.

Tangy Chicken Thighs

I love this dish because it turns affordable chicken thighs into a rich and delicious meal. The creamy sauce is what makes it! Serve with a crisp side salad or fresh spring vegetables.

—**DUTCHMOM4MI**
TASTE OF HOME ONLINE COMMUNITY

PREP: 25 MIN. • **COOK:** 4¾ HOURS
MAKES: 6 SERVINGS

- 1 **envelope Italian salad dressing mix**
- ½ **teaspoon pepper**
- 6 **boneless skinless chicken thighs (about 1½ pounds)**
- 2 **tablespoons butter, melted**
- 1 **large onion, chopped**
- 2 **garlic cloves, minced**
- 1 **can (10¾ ounces) condensed cream of chicken soup, undiluted**
- 1 **package (8 ounces) cream cheese, softened and cubed**
- ¼ **cup chicken broth**
  Hot cooked noodles or rice, optional

1. Combine salad dressing mix and pepper. In a 3-qt. slow cooker, layer half of the chicken, butter, salad dressing mixture, onion and garlic. Repeat layers. Cover and cook on low for 4-5 hours or until chicken is tender. Skim the fat.

2. In a small bowl, combine the soup, cream cheese and broth until blended; add to slow cooker. Cover and cook for 45 minutes or until heated through.

3. Remove chicken to a serving platter; stir sauce until smooth. Serve chicken with the sauce and noodles or rice if desired.

DUTCHMOM4MI'S TANGY
CHICKEN THIGHS

Tangy Lamb Tagine

I love lamb stew but wanted to try something a bit different, so I created this recipe that relies on Moroccan spices. It's a wonderful way to use lamb, and it's easy to make in the slow cooker. The stew tastes even better served a day or two later, when the flavors have really had a chance to meld.

—**BRIDGET KLUSMAN** OTSEGO, MI

PREP: 40 MIN. • **COOK:** 8 HOURS • **MAKES:** 8 SERVINGS

- 3 **pounds lamb stew meat, cut into 1½-inch cubes**
- 1 **teaspoon salt**
- 1 **teaspoon pepper**
- 4 **tablespoons olive oil, divided**
- 6 **medium carrots, sliced**
- 2 **medium onions, chopped**
- 6 **garlic cloves, minced**
- 2 **teaspoons grated lemon peel**
- ¼ **cup lemon juice**
- 1 **tablespoon minced fresh gingerroot**
- 1½ **teaspoons ground cinnamon**
- 1½ **teaspoons ground cumin**
- 1½ **teaspoons paprika**
- 2½ **cups reduced-sodium chicken broth**
- ¼ **cup sweet vermouth**
- ¼ **cup honey**
- ½ **cup pitted dates, chopped**
- ½ **cup sliced almonds, toasted**

LUCKY CORNED BEEF

1. Sprinkle lamb with salt and pepper. In a Dutch oven, brown meat in 2 tablespoons oil in batches. Using a slotted spoon, transfer to a 4- or 5-qt. slow cooker.

2. In the same skillet, saute the carrots, onions, garlic and lemon peel in remaining oil until crisp-tender. Add the lemon juice, ginger, cinnamon, cumin and paprika; cook and stir 2 minutes longer. Add to slow cooker.

3. Stir in the broth, vermouth, honey and dates. Cover and cook on low for 8-10 hours or until lamb is tender. Sprinkle with almonds.

Lucky Corned Beef

It's not really luck—just an amazing Irish recipe! With this in your slow cooker by sunrise, you can bet to fill seats at the dinner table by sundown.

—**HEATHER PARRAZ** ROCHESTER, WA

PREP 20 MIN. • **COOK:** 9 HOURS • **MAKES:** 10 SERVINGS

- 6 **medium red potatoes, quartered**
- 2 **medium carrots, cut into chunks**
- 1 **large onion, sliced**
- 2 **corned beef briskets with spice packets (3 pounds each)**
- ¼ **cup packed brown sugar**
- 2 **tablespoons sugar**
- 2 **tablespoons coriander seeds**
- 2 **tablespoons whole peppercorns**
- 4 **cups water**

1. In a 6-qt. slow cooker, combine the potatoes, carrots and onion. Add briskets (discard spice packets from corned beef or save for another use). Sprinkle the brown sugar, sugar, coriander and peppercorns over meat. Pour water over top.

2. Cover and cook on low for 9-11 hours or until meat and vegetables are tender.

3. Remove meat and vegetables to a serving platter. Thinly slice one brisket across the grain and serve with vegetables. Save the remaining brisket for another day or another use.

TANGY LAMB TAGINE

Slow Cooker Two-Meat Manicotti

I wanted to create my ideal version of a stuffed manicotti, which requires a fantastic filling and a meat sauce to die for. This recipe is the final result, and I don't mind saying that it's a huge success!

—**SHALIMAR WIECH** GLASSPORT, PA

PREP: 45 MIN. • **COOK:** 4 HOURS • **MAKES:** 7 SERVINGS

- ½ pound medium fresh mushrooms, chopped
- 2 small green peppers, chopped
- 1 medium onion, chopped
- 1½ teaspoons canola oil
- 4 garlic cloves, minced
- ¾ pound ground sirloin
- ¾ pound bulk Italian sausage
- 2 jars (23½ ounces each) Italian sausage and garlic spaghetti sauce
- 1 carton (15 ounces) ricotta cheese
- 1 cup minced fresh parsley
- ½ cup shredded part-skim mozzarella cheese, divided
- ½ cup grated Parmesan cheese, divided
- 2 eggs, lightly beaten
- ½ teaspoon salt
- ¼ teaspoon pepper
- ⅛ teaspoon ground nutmeg
- 1 package (8 ounces) manicotti shells

1. In a large skillet, saute the mushrooms, peppers and onion in oil until tender. Add garlic; cook 1 minute longer. Remove from pan.

2. In the same skillet, cook beef and sausage over medium heat until no longer pink; drain. Stir in mushroom mixture and spaghetti sauce; set aside.

3. In a small bowl, combine the ricotta cheese, parsley, ¼ cup mozzarella cheese, ¼ cup Parmesan cheese, eggs and seasonings. Stuff into uncooked manicotti shells.

LEMON CHICKEN BREASTS WITH VEGGIES

4. Spread 2¼ cups sauce onto the bottom of a 6-qt. slow cooker. Arrange five stuffed manicotti shells over sauce; repeat two times, using four shells on the top layer. Top with remaining sauce. Sprinkle with remaining cheeses. Cover and cook on low for 4-5 hours or until pasta is tender.

Lemon Chicken Breasts with Veggies

My recipe's everything you need for a satisfying spring meal. After all, why bake chicken when this slow-cooked version is so fuss-free? Flecked with herbs, these chicken breasts are nestled with crisp-tender veggies in a subtle lemon sauce.

—**AMBER OTIS** MORRIS, OK

PREP: 25 MIN. • **COOK:** 8 HOURS • **MAKES:** 6 SERVINGS

- 1 pound fresh baby carrots
- 3 cups cubed red potatoes
- 1 package (14 ounces) frozen pearl onions, thawed
- 2 celery ribs, thinly sliced
- 6 bone-in chicken breast halves (10 ounces each), skin removed
- 1 can (10¾ ounces) condensed cream of chicken soup, undiluted
- ½ cup water
- ½ cup lemon juice
- 1 teaspoon dried parsley flakes
- 1 teaspoon dried thyme
- ½ teaspoon pepper
- ¼ teaspoon salt

1. In a 5- or 6-qt. slow cooker, combine the carrots, potatoes, onions and celery. Top with chicken.

2. Combine the soup, water, lemon juice, parsley, thyme, pepper and salt; pour over chicken and vegetables. Cover and cook on low for 8-9 hours or until chicken and vegetables are tender.

SLOW COOKER TWO-MEAT MANICOTTI

LAURA EHLERS'
SPECIAL SAUERBRATEN

"After simmering in the slow cooker for hours, this rump roast has taken on the flavors of the sauce and is fork-tender. My family always looks forward to having it for dinner. I serve it with corn."
—**LAURA EHLERS** LAFAYETTE, IN

Special Sauerbraten

PREP: 25 MIN. • **COOK:** 6 HOURS • **MAKES:** 6 SERVINGS

- 1 beef rump roast or bottom round roast (3 to 4 pounds), cut in half
- 1 tablespoon olive oil
- 1½ cups cider vinegar
- 1 medium onion, chopped
- ⅔ cup packed brown sugar
- 1 envelope onion soup mix
- ⅓ cup shredded carrot
- 2 tablespoons beef bouillon granules
- 1 tablespoon Worcestershire sauce
- 1 bay leaf
- 1 garlic clove, minced
- 1 teaspoon salt
- 1 teaspoon celery seed
- 1 teaspoon ground ginger
- ½ teaspoon mixed pickling spices
- ¼ teaspoon ground allspice
- ¼ teaspoon pepper
- ¼ cup cornstarch
- ½ cup water

1. In a large skillet, brown meat in oil on all sides. Transfer meat and drippings to a 5-qt. slow cooker. In a large bowl, combine the vinegar, onion, sugar, soup mix, carrot, bouillon, Worcestershire sauce and seasonings; pour over roast. Cover and cook on low for 6-8 hours or until tender.
2. Remove meat to a serving platter; keep warm. Strain cooking juices, discarding vegetables and seasonings.
3. Skim fat from cooking juices; transfer juices to a large saucepan. Bring to a boil. Combine cornstarch and water until smooth; gradually stir into the pan. Bring to a boil; cook and stir for 2 minutes or until thickened. Serve with beef.

top tip Pickling Spices

Not sure what to do with extra pickling spices? Fill a tea ball with some of the spices, then hang it in your slow cooker when making soups or stews.

HEARTY CHEESE TORTELLINI

Hearty Cheese Tortellini

Simple enough for an everyday meal but impressive enough for company, my recipe is sure to become a staple in your home, too. I like to serve it with steamed broccoli covered in a cheese sauce and fresh bread.
—**CHRISTINE EILERTS** TULSA, OK

PREP: 30 MIN. • **COOK:** 6¼ HOURS •**MAKES:** 6 SERVINGS

- ½ pound bulk Italian sausage
- ½ pound lean ground beef (90% lean)
- 1 jar (24 ounces) marinara sauce
- 1 can (14½ ounces) Italian diced tomatoes
- 1 cup sliced fresh mushrooms
- 1 package (9 ounces) refrigerated cheese tortellini
- 1 cup (4 ounces) shredded part-skim mozzarella cheese

1. In a small skillet, cook sausage and beef over medium heat until no longer pink; drain. Transfer to a 3-qt. slow cooker. Stir in the marinara sauce, tomatoes and mushrooms. Cover and cook on low for 6-7 hours or until heated through.
2. Prepare tortellini according to package directions; stir into meat mixture. Sprinkle with cheese. Cover and cook for 15 minutes or until cheese is melted.

"Flag this dish for holidays where you crave the mouthwatering combo of smoky ham, pineapple and stone-ground mustard. Perfect for a large group, it comes together quickly." —**CAROLE RESNICK** CLEVELAND, OH

HAM WITH CRANBERRY-PINEAPPLE SAUCE

Ham with Cranberry-Pineapple Sauce

PREP: 15 MIN. • **COOK:** 5 HOURS
MAKES: 20 SERVINGS (4½ CUPS SAUCE)

- 1 fully cooked boneless ham (5 to 6 pounds)
- 12 whole cloves
- 1 can (20 ounces) crushed pineapple, undrained
- 1 can (14 ounces) whole-berry cranberry sauce
- 2 garlic cloves, minced
- 2 tablespoons stone-ground mustard
- ½ teaspoon coarsely ground pepper
- 2 tablespoons cornstarch
- 2 tablespoons cold water

1. Score the ham, making ½-in.-deep diamond shapes; insert a clove in each diamond. Place ham in a 5-qt. slow cooker. In a large bowl, combine the pineapple, cranberry sauce, garlic, mustard and pepper; pour over ham.
2. Cover and cook on low for 5-6 hours or until a thermometer reads 140°. Remove meat to a cutting board and keep warm; remove and discard cloves.
3. Transfer sauce to a small saucepan. Bring to a boil. Combine cornstarch and water until smooth; gradually stir into pan. Bring to a boil; cook and stir for 2 minutes or until thickened. Slice ham and serve with sauce.

Savory Mustard Pork Roast

Here, a unique mixture of honey and molasses with diced tomatoes and red wine yields the most delightful sauce for a pork roast.

—**EZRA ELKON** CHARLES TOWN, WV

PREP: 20 MIN.
COOK: 6 HOURS + STANDING
MAKES: 8 SERVINGS

- 1 boneless pork shoulder butt roast (3 to 4 pounds)
- ¾ teaspoon salt
- ¼ teaspoon pepper
- 1 tablespoon canola oil
- 1 can (14½ ounces) diced tomatoes, drained
- 1 medium onion, chopped
- 1 can (14½ ounces) beef broth
- ½ cup dry red wine
- ¾ cup stone-ground mustard
- 6 garlic cloves, minced
- 2 tablespoons honey
- 2 tablespoons molasses
- 1 teaspoon dried thyme
- 2 tablespoons cornstarch
- 2 tablespoons cold water

1. Sprinkle roast with salt and pepper; brown in oil in a large skillet on all sides. Transfer to a 5-qt. slow cooker. Add tomatoes and onion; pour broth and wine around meat. Combine the mustard, garlic, honey, molasses and thyme; pour over pork. Cover and cook on low for 6-7 hours or until the meat is tender.
2. Remove roast; cover and let stand for 15 minutes before slicing. Meanwhile, skim fat from cooking juices; transfer juices to a small saucepan. Bring to a boil. Combine cornstarch and water until smooth; gradually stir into the pan. Bring to a boil; cook and stir for 2 minutes or until thickened. Slice pork and serve with the sauce.

SAVORY MUSTARD PORK ROAST

SOY-GINGER CHICKEN

Soy-Ginger Chicken

Bone-in chicken becomes moist and tender when cooked with sliced carrots and green onions in a rich ginger-soy sauce that's brightened with brown sugar, balsamic vinegar and coriander.

—**KAEL HARVEY** BROOKLYN, NY

PREP: 25 MIN. • **COOK:** 5 HOURS
MAKES: 4 SERVINGS

- 4 **bone-in chicken thighs (about 1½ pounds), skin removed**
- 4 **chicken drumsticks (about 1 pound), skin removed**
- 2 **medium carrots, sliced**
- 4 **green onions, thinly sliced**
- ⅓ **cup soy sauce**
- 2 **tablespoons brown sugar**
- 1 **piece fresh gingerroot (about 2 inches), peeled and thinly sliced**
- 5 **garlic cloves, minced**
- 1 **tablespoon balsamic vinegar**
- 1 **teaspoon ground coriander**
- ½ **teaspoon pepper**
- 1 **tablespoon cornstarch**
- 1 **tablespoon cold water**
  Hot cooked rice and minced fresh cilantro

1. Place chicken, carrots and green onions in a 3-qt. slow cooker. Combine the soy sauce, brown sugar, ginger, garlic, vinegar, coriander and pepper in a small bowl. Pour over top. Cover and cook on low for 5-6 hours or until chicken is tender.
2. Remove chicken to a serving platter; keep warm. Pour juices into a small saucepan. Bring to a boil. Combine cornstarch and water until smooth; gradually stir into pan. Bring to a boil; cook and stir for 1-2 minutes or until thickened. Serve with the chicken and rice; sprinkle servings with cilantro.

Spinach and Sausage Lasagna

Dig into the rich layers of this hearty lasagna that features plenty of Italian sausage and gooey cheese. No-cook noodles, frozen spinach and jarred spaghetti sauce simplify the prep, but it tastes far from ordinary!

—**KATHLEEN MORROW** HUBBARD, OH

PREP: 25 MIN. • **COOK:** 3 HOURS
MAKES: 8 SERVINGS

- 1 **pound bulk Italian sausage**
- 1 **jar (24 ounces) garden-style spaghetti sauce**
- ½ **cup water**
- 1 **teaspoon Italian seasoning**
- ½ **teaspoon salt**
- 1 **carton (15 ounces) ricotta cheese**
- 1 **package (10 ounces) frozen chopped spinach, thawed and squeezed dry**
- 2 **cups (8 ounces) shredded part-skim mozzarella cheese, divided**
- 9 **no-cook lasagna noodles
  Grated Parmesan cheese**

1. Cook sausage in a large skillet over medium heat until no longer pink; drain. Stir in the spaghetti sauce, water, Italian seasoning and salt. Combine ricotta, spinach and 1 cup mozzarella cheese in a small bowl.
2. Spread 1 cup sauce mixture in a greased oval 5-qt. slow cooker. Layer with three noodles (breaking noodles if necessary to fit), 1¼ cups sauce mixture and half of the cheese mixture. Repeat layers. Layer with remaining noodles and sauce mixture; sprinkle with the remaining mozzarella cheese.
3. Cover and cook on low for 3-4 hours or until noodles are tender. Sprinkle servings with Parmesan cheese.

SPINACH AND SAUSAGE LASAGNA

GARDEN CHICKEN CACCIATORE

Garden Chicken Cacciatore

When I have company, I take advantage of the slow cooker so I can spend more time with my guests. Served with hot cooked pasta, green salad and a dry red wine, this is the perfect meal for a spring dinner party.
—**MARTHA SCHIRMACHER** STERLING HEIGHTS, MI

PREP: 15 MIN. • **COOK:** 8½ HOURS • **MAKES:** 12 SERVINGS

- 12 **boneless skinless chicken thighs (about 3 pounds)**
- 2 **medium green peppers, chopped**
- 1 **can (14½ ounces) diced tomatoes with basil, oregano and garlic, undrained**
- 1 **can (6 ounces) tomato paste**
- 1 **medium onion, sliced**
- ½ **cup reduced-sodium chicken broth**
- ¼ **cup dry red wine or additional reduced-sodium chicken broth**
- 3 **garlic cloves, minced**
- ¾ **teaspoon salt**
- ⅛ **teaspoon pepper**
- 2 **tablespoons cornstarch**
- 2 **tablespoons cold water**

1. Place chicken in a 4-qt. slow cooker. In a small bowl, combine the green peppers, tomatoes, tomato paste, onion, broth, wine, garlic, salt and pepper. Cover and cook on low for 8-10 hours or until chicken is tender.

2. Combine cornstarch and water until smooth; gradually stir into slow cooker. Cover and cook on high 30 minutes longer or until sauce is thickened.

Louisiana Round Steak

This beefy main dish is always a big hit with the men in our family. After simmering in a slow cooker, the steak takes on a robust flavor, and the filling portions are just what we love.
—**MEGAN ROHLCK** VERMILLION, SD

PREP: 20 MIN. • **COOK:** 7 HOURS • **MAKES:** 6 SERVINGS

- 2 **pounds sweet potatoes, peeled and cut into 1-inch pieces**
- 1 **large onion, chopped**
- 1 **medium green pepper, sliced**
- 2 **beef top round steaks (¾ inch thick and 1 pound each)**
- 1 **teaspoon salt, divided**
- 2 **tablespoons olive oil**
- 1 **garlic clove, minced**
- 3 **tablespoons all-purpose flour**
- 1 **can (28 ounces) diced tomatoes, undrained**
- ½ **cup beef broth**
- 1 **teaspoon sugar**
- ½ **teaspoon dried thyme**
- ½ **teaspoon pepper**
- ¼ **teaspoon hot pepper sauce**

1. Place the sweet potatoes, onion and green pepper in a 6-qt. slow cooker. Cut each steak into three serving-size pieces; sprinkle with ½ teaspoon salt. In a large skillet over medium heat, brown steaks in oil in batches on both sides. Place steaks over vegetables, reserving drippings in pan.

2. Add garlic to drippings; cook and stir for 1 minute. Stir in flour until blended. Stir in the remaining ingredients and remaining salt. Bring to a boil, stirring constantly. Cook and stir for 4-5 minutes or until thickened. Pour over meat. Cover and cook on low for 7-9 hours or until beef is tender.

MEGAN ROHLCK'S
LOUISIANA ROUND STEAK

Creamy Chicken & Broccoli Stew

Shh! Don't tell anyone! This recipe is so simple, but you'd never know it. My husband, who normally doesn't even like chicken, asks for it regularly.

—MARY WATKINS LITTLE ELM, TX

PREP: 15 MIN. • **COOK:** 6 HOURS • **MAKES:** 8 SERVINGS

- 8 **bone-in chicken thighs, skin removed (about 3 pounds)**
- 1 **cup Italian salad dressing**
- ½ **cup white wine or chicken broth**
- 6 **tablespoons butter, melted, divided**
- 1 **tablespoon dried minced onion**
- 1 **tablespoon garlic powder**
- 1 **tablespoon Italian seasoning**
- ¾ **teaspoon salt, divided**
- ¾ **teaspoon pepper, divided**
- 1 **can (10¾ ounces) condensed cream of mushroom soup, undiluted**
- 1 **package (8 ounces) cream cheese, softened**
- 2 **cups frozen broccoli florets, thawed**
- 2 **pounds red potatoes, quartered**

1. Place chicken in a 4-qt. slow cooker. Combine the salad dressing, wine, 4 tablespoons butter, onion, garlic powder, Italian seasoning, ½ teaspoon salt and ½ teaspoon pepper in a small bowl; pour over chicken.

2. Cover and cook on low for 5 hours. Skim fat. Combine the soup, cream cheese and 2 cups of liquid from slow cooker in a small bowl until blended; add to slow cooker.

3. Cover and cook 45 minutes longer or until chicken is tender, adding the broccoli during the last 30 minutes of cooking.

ASIAN RIBS

4. Meanwhile, place potatoes in a large saucepan and cover with water. Bring to a boil. Reduce heat; cover and simmer for 15-20 minutes or until tender. Drain and return to pan. Mash potatoes with the remaining butter, salt and pepper. Serve with chicken and broccoli mixture.

Asian Ribs

My husband adores this dish, and I love how good it makes the house smell! The tangy, salty-sweet sauce with fresh ginger and garlic is delicious with rice or noodles.

—JULIE KO ROGERS, AR

PREP: 15 MIN. • **COOK:** 6 HOURS
MAKES: 6 SERVINGS (ABOUT 4 CUPS SAUCE)

- 6 **pounds pork baby back ribs, cut into serving-size pieces**
- 1⅓ **cups packed brown sugar**
- 1 **cup reduced-sodium soy sauce**
- ¼ **cup rice vinegar**
- ¼ **cup sesame oil**
- ¼ **cup minced fresh gingerroot**
- 6 **garlic cloves, minced**
- 1 **teaspoon crushed red pepper flakes**
- ¼ **cup cornstarch**
- ¼ **cup cold water**
  Thinly sliced green onions and sesame seeds, optional

1. Place ribs in a 6-qt. slow cooker. In a small bowl, combine the brown sugar, soy sauce, vinegar, oil, ginger, garlic and pepper flakes; pour over ribs. Cover and cook on low for 6-7 hours or until meat is tender.

2. Remove meat to a serving platter; keep warm. Skim fat from cooking juices; transfer to a small saucepan. Bring to a boil.

3. Combine cornstarch and water until smooth. Gradually stir into the pan. Bring to a boil; cook and stir for 2 minutes or until thickened. Serve with ribs. Garnish with onions and sesame seeds if desired.

CREAMY CHICKEN & BROCCOLI STEW

Chicken & Mushroom Alfredo

PREP: 20 MIN. • **COOK:** 4 HOURS • **MAKES:** 4 SERVINGS

- 4 **bone-in chicken breast halves (12 to 14 ounces each), skin removed**
- 2 **tablespoons canola oil**
- 1 **can (10¾ ounces) condensed cream of chicken soup, undiluted**
- 1 **can (10¾ ounces) condensed cream of mushroom soup, undiluted**
- 1 **cup chicken broth**
- 1 **small onion, chopped**
- 1 **jar (6 ounces) sliced mushrooms, drained**
- ¼ **teaspoon garlic salt**
- ¼ **teaspoon pepper**
- 8 **ounces fettuccine**
- 1 **package (8 ounces) cream cheese, softened and cubed**
  Shredded Parmesan cheese, optional

CHICKEN & MUSHROOM ALFREDO

VEGETARIAN STUFFED PEPPERS

1. In a large skillet, brown chicken in oil in batches. Transfer to a 4- or 5-qt. slow cooker. In a large bowl, combine the soups, broth, onion, mushrooms, garlic salt and pepper; pour over meat. Cover and cook on low for 4-5 hours or until chicken is tender.

2. Cook fettuccine according to package directions; drain. Remove chicken from slow cooker and keep warm. Turn slow cooker off and stir in cream cheese until melted. Serve with fettucine. Top with Parmesan cheese if desired.

Vegetarian Stuffed Peppers

My favorite appliance is my slow cooker, and I use it more than anyone I know. I love the convenience of walking in the door and having a meal ready to go. For recipes like my stuffed peppers, you don't have to worry about boiling the peppers first and preparing the filling separately.

—**MICHELLE GURNSEY** LINCOLN, NE

PREP: 15 MIN. • **COOK:** 3 HOURS • **MAKES:** 4 SERVINGS

- 4 **medium sweet red peppers**
- 1 **can (15 ounces) black beans, rinsed and drained**
- 1 **cup (4 ounces) shredded pepper jack cheese**
- ¾ **cup salsa**
- 1 **small onion, chopped**
- ½ **cup frozen corn**
- ⅓ **cup uncooked converted long grain rice**
- 1¼ **teaspoons chili powder**
- ½ **teaspoon ground cumin**
  Reduced-fat sour cream, optional

1. Cut and discard tops from peppers; remove seeds. In a large bowl, mix beans, cheese, salsa, onion, corn, rice, chili powder and cumin; spoon into peppers. Place in a 5-qt. slow cooker coated with cooking spray.

2. Cook, covered, on low 3-4 hours or until peppers are tender and filling is heated through. If desired, serve with sour cream.

KELLY GRAHAM'S
MOM'S SCALLOPED POTATOES AND HAM

Mom's Scalloped Potatoes and Ham

Mom's friend gave her this recipe years ago, and she shared it with me. When we have leftover ham to use up, this is the most-requested dish at my house.
—**KELLY GRAHAM** ST. THOMAS, ON

PREP: 20 MIN. • **COOK:** 8 HOURS
MAKES: 9 SERVINGS

- 10 medium potatoes, peeled and thinly sliced
- 3 cups cubed fully cooked ham
- 2 large onions, thinly sliced
- 2 cups (8 ounces) shredded cheddar cheese
- 1 can (10¾ ounces) condensed cream of mushroom soup, undiluted
- ½ teaspoon paprika
- ¼ teaspoon pepper

1. In a greased 6-qt. slow cooker, layer half of the potatoes, ham, onions and cheese. Repeat layers. Pour soup over top. Sprinkle with paprika and pepper.
2. Cover and cook on low for 8-10 hours or until potatoes are tender.

Butter & Herb Turkey

My kids love turkey for dinner, and this easy recipe lets me make it whenever I want. No special occasion required! The meat is so tender that it falls right off the bone.
—**ROCHELLE POPOVIC** SOUTH BEND, IN

PREP: 10 MIN. • **COOK:** 5 HOURS
MAKES: 12 SERVINGS (3 CUPS GRAVY)

- 1 bone-in turkey breast (6 to 7 pounds)
- 2 tablespoons butter, softened
- ½ teaspoon dried rosemary, crushed
- ½ teaspoon dried thyme
- ¼ teaspoon garlic powder
- ¼ teaspoon pepper
- 1 can (14½ ounces) chicken broth
- 3 tablespoons cornstarch
- 2 tablespoons cold water

1. Rub turkey with butter. Combine the rosemary, thyme, garlic powder and pepper; sprinkle over turkey. Place in a 6-qt. slow cooker. Pour broth over top. Cover and cook on low for 5-6 hours or until tender.
2. Remove turkey to a serving platter; keep warm. Skim fat from cooking juices; transfer to a small saucepan. Bring to a boil. Combine cornstarch and water until smooth. Gradually stir into the pan. Bring to a boil; cook and stir for 2 minutes or until thickened. Serve with turkey.

Steak San Marino

As a busy pastor's wife and mother of three, I find that this delicious, inexpensive dish helps my day run smoother. The steak is so tender and flavorful, my kids gobble it up, and my husband asks for seconds.
—**LAEL GRIESS** HULL, IA

PREP: 15 MIN. • **COOK:** 7 HOURS
MAKES: 6 SERVINGS

- ¼ cup all-purpose flour
- ½ teaspoon salt
- ½ teaspoon pepper
- 1 beef top round steak (1½ pounds), cut into six pieces
- 2 large carrots, sliced
- 1 celery rib, sliced
- 1 can (8 ounces) tomato sauce
- 2 garlic cloves, minced
- 1 bay leaf
- 1 teaspoon Italian seasoning
- ½ teaspoon Worcestershire sauce
- 3 cups hot cooked brown rice

1. In a large resealable plastic bag, combine the flour, salt and pepper. Add beef, a few pieces at a time, and shake to coat. Transfer to a 4-qt. slow cooker.
2. In a small bowl, combine the carrots, celery, tomato sauce, garlic, bay leaf, Italian seasoning and Worcestershire sauce. Pour over beef. Cover and cook on low for 7-9 hours or until beef is tender. Discard bay leaf. Serve with rice.

top tip **Enticing Extras**

To beef up the sauce in Steak San Marino, simply stir in a can of diced Italian-style tomatoes toward the end of the cooking cycle and heat through.

STEAK SAN MARINO

AMAZING SLOW COOKER ORANGE CHICKEN

"Orange chicken is my favorite Chinese takeout food, but I know that it's very high in sodium and fat. So I got to work at home and created a healthier version. Now I have peace of mind knowing what ingredients are in it and that it's better for my family."
—**BARB MILLER** OAKDALE, MN

Amazing Slow Cooker Orange Chicken

PREP: 25 MIN. • **COOK:** 4 HOURS
MAKES: 8 SERVINGS

- 1 **cup chicken stock**
- 1 **cup orange juice**
- 1 **cup orange marmalade**
- ½ **cup ketchup**
- ¼ **cup Dijon mustard**
- 2 **tablespoons brown sugar**
- 2 **tablespoons rice vinegar**
- 2 **tablespoons reduced-sodium soy sauce**
- 1 **tablespoon minced fresh gingerroot**
- 1 **teaspoon garlic powder**
- ¾ **teaspoon crushed red pepper flakes**
- 2 **tablespoons molasses, optional**
- 2 **pounds boneless skinless chicken breasts, cut into ¾-inch pieces**
- ½ **cup cornstarch**
- ¾ **teaspoon salt**
- ½ **teaspoon pepper**
- 1 **large sweet red pepper, cut into 1-inch pieces**
- 2 **cups fresh broccoli florets**
  Hot cooked rice
  Optional toppings: chopped green onions, peanuts and fresh cilantro

1. In a small bowl, combine the first 11 ingredients; stir in molasses if desired. In a 4-qt. slow cooker, combine chicken, cornstarch, salt and pepper; toss to coat. Top with red pepper. Pour stock mixture over top. Cover and cook on low for 4 hours or until chicken is tender.
2. Stir in broccoli. Cover and cook on high 30-40 minutes longer or until broccoli is crisp-tender. Serve with rice. Sprinkle with toppings of your choice.

Fiesta Beef Bowls

This easy entree will knock your socks off! Zesty ingredients turn round steak into a phenomenal meal-in-one delight.
—**DEBORAH LINN** VALDEZ, AK

PREP: 25 MIN. • **COOK:** 8½ HOURS
MAKES: 6 SERVINGS

- 1½ **pounds boneless beef top round steak**
- 1 **can (10 ounces) diced tomatoes and green chilies**
- 1 **medium onion, chopped**
- 2 **garlic cloves, minced**
- 1 **teaspoon dried oregano**
- 1 **teaspoon chili powder**
- 1 **teaspoon ground cumin**
- ¼ **teaspoon salt**
- ¼ **teaspoon pepper**
- 2 **cans (15 ounces each) pinto beans, rinsed and drained**
- 3 **cups hot cooked rice**
- ½ **cup shredded cheddar cheese**
- 6 **tablespoons sliced ripe olives**
- 6 **tablespoons thinly sliced green onions**
- 6 **tablespoons guacamole**

1. Place round steak in a 3-qt. slow cooker. In a small bowl, combine the tomatoes, onion, garlic and seasonings; pour over steak. Cover and cook on low for 8-9 hours or until meat is tender.
2. Remove meat from slow cooker. Add beans to tomato mixture. Cover and cook on high for 30 minutes or until beans are heated through. When cool enough to handle, slice meat. In individual bowls, layer the rice, meat and bean mixture. Top with cheese, olives, onions and guacamole.

FIESTA BEEF BOWLS

Easy Citrus Ham

I created this entree many years ago with items I already had on hand. Since then, it has become a family staple. The ham is succulent with a mild citrus flavor. I was asked to share the recipe with a church social and there were so many raves, I knew the recipe was a winner!

—**SHEILA CHRISTENSEN** SAN MARCOS, CA

PREP: 15 MIN.
COOK: 4 HOURS + STANDING
MAKES: 10-12 SERVINGS

- 1 **boneless fully cooked ham (3 to 4 pounds)**
- ½ **cup packed dark brown sugar**
- 1 **can (12 ounces) lemon-lime soda, divided**
- 1 **medium navel orange, thinly sliced**
- 1 **medium lemon, thinly sliced**
- 1 **medium lime, thinly sliced**
- 1 **tablespoon chopped crystallized ginger**

1. Cut ham in half; place in a 5-qt. slow cooker. In a small bowl, combine brown sugar and ¼ cup soda; rub over ham. Top with orange, lemon and lime slices. Add candied ginger and remaining soda to the slow cooker.

2. Cover and cook on low for 4-5 hours or until a thermometer reads 140°, basting occasionally with cooking juices. Let stand for 10 minutes before slicing.

EASY CITRUS HAM

CARAMELIZED ONION CHUCK ROAST

Caramelized Onion Chuck Roast

Wonderfully fork-tender, this tasty roast with sweet onions makes the perfect comfort food at the end of a long day.

—**JEANNIE KLUGH** LANCASTER, PA

PREP: 25 MIN. • **COOK:** 8 HOURS
MAKES: 8 SERVINGS

- 1 cup water
- 1 cup beer or beef broth
- ½ cup beef broth
- ¼ cup packed brown sugar
- 3 tablespoons Dijon mustard
- 2 tablespoons cider vinegar
- 1 boneless beef chuck roast (4 pounds), trimmed
- 1 teaspoon onion salt
- 1 teaspoon coarsely ground pepper
- 1 tablespoon olive oil
- 3 large sweet onions, halved and sliced
- 2 tablespoons cornstarch
- 2 tablespoons cold water

1. In a large bowl, combine the first six ingredients; set aside. Sprinkle roast with onion salt and pepper. In a large skillet, brown meat in oil on all sides.

Place onions and roast in a 5-qt. slow cooker; pour beer mixture over top. Cover and cook on low for 8-10 hours or until meat is tender.

2. Remove roast and onions and keep warm. Skim fat from cooking juices; transfer 2 cups to a small saucepan. Bring liquid to a boil. Combine cornstarch and water until smooth; gradually stir into the pan. Bring to a boil; cook and stir for 2 minutes or until thickened. Serve gravy with roast and onions.

Island Pork Roast

This delicious dinner is a nice mixture of tangy and sweet. It is especially good when served over rice. The leftovers make wonderful sandwiches.

—**HEATHER CAMPBELL** LAWRENCE, KS

PREP: 25 MIN. • **COOK:** 5 HOURS
MAKES: 10 SERVINGS

- 1 boneless pork loin roast (about 4 pounds)
- 1 large onion, sliced
- 2 cans (8 ounces each) unsweetened pineapple chunks, undrained
- ½ cup sugar
- ½ cup lime juice
- ½ cup soy sauce
- ¼ cup packed brown sugar
- 2 tablespoons teriyaki sauce
- 2 garlic cloves, minced
- 1 teaspoon ground ginger
- 1 teaspoon curry powder
- ¼ teaspoon salt
- ¼ teaspoon pepper
- 1 bay leaf
- ¼ cup cornstarch
- ½ cup cold water

1. Cut roast in half. Place onion in a 4- or 5-qt. slow cooker. Add pork. Drain pineapple, reserving juice; set pineapple aside. In a small bowl, combine the sugar, lime juice, soy sauce, brown sugar, teriyaki sauce, garlic, ginger, curry, salt, pepper, bay leaf and reserved juice. Pour over the roast.

2. Cover and cook on low for 5-6 hours or until a thermometer reads 160°. Add the pineapple during the last hour of cooking.

3. Remove the meat, onion and pineapple to a serving platter; keep warm.

4. Discard bay leaf from slow cooker. Skim fat from cooking juices; transfer to a small saucepan. Bring liquid to a boil. Combine cornstarch and water until smooth; gradually stir into the pan. Bring to a boil; cook and stir for 2 minutes or until thickened. Serve with the pork.

top tip

Beverage Basics

Enjoy Island Pork Roast with glasses of ice water, seasoned with cucumber slices and fresh mint. Let the cucumber and mint sit in a pitcher of water for at least 1 hour before serving. You could also serve the roast with a light-bodied white wine such as Sauvignon Blanc or Pinot Grigio.

HEATHER CAMPBELL'S
ISLAND PORK ROAST

BBQ Chicken Baked Potatoes

PREP: 15 MIN. • **COOK:** 6 HOURS • **MAKES:** 10 SERVINGS

- 4½ pounds bone-in chicken breast halves, skin removed
- 2 tablespoons garlic powder
- 1 large red onion, sliced into thick rings
- 1 bottle (18 ounces) honey barbecue sauce
- 1 cup Italian salad dressing
- ½ cup packed brown sugar
- ½ cup cider vinegar
- ¼ cup Worcestershire sauce
- 2 tablespoons liquid smoke, optional
- 10 medium potatoes, baked
  Crumbled blue cheese and chopped green onions, optional

1. Place chicken in a greased 5- or 6-qt. slow cooker; sprinkle with garlic powder and top with onion. Combine the barbecue sauce, salad dressing, brown sugar, vinegar, Worcestershire sauce and liquid smoke if desired; pour over chicken.

2. Cover and cook on low for 6-8 hours or until chicken is tender. When cool enough to handle, remove chicken from bones; discard bones and onion. Skim fat from the cooking juices.

3. Shred meat with two forks and return to slow cooker; heat through. Serve with potatoes, blue cheese and green onions if desired.

HEALTHY SLOW-COOKED MEAT LOAF

Healthy Slow-Cooked Meat Loaf

What could be easier than an Italian-inspired meat loaf made in the slow cooker? No fuss, easy cleanup and great taste; it's all right here!

—**SHARON DELANEY-CHRONIS** SOUTH MILWAUKEE, WI

PREP: 15 MIN. • **COOK:** 3 HOURS • **MAKES:** 8 SERVINGS

- 1 cup soft bread crumbs
- 1½ cups spaghetti sauce, divided
- 1 egg, lightly beaten
- 2 tablespoons dried minced onion
- 1 teaspoon salt
- ½ teaspoon garlic powder
- ½ teaspoon Italian seasoning
- ¼ teaspoon pepper
- 2 pounds lean ground beef (90% lean)

1. Cut four 20-in. x 3-in. strips of heavy-duty foil; crisscross so they resemble the spokes of a wheel. Place strips on the bottom and up the sides of a 3-qt. slow cooker. Coat strips with cooking spray.

2. In a large bowl, combine the bread crumbs, 1 cup of spaghetti sauce, egg, onion, and seasonings. Crumble beef over mixture and mix well. Shape into a loaf; place in the center of the strips.

3. Spoon remaining spaghetti sauce over meat loaf. Cover and cook on low for 3-4 hours or until a thermometer reads 160°. Using foil strips as handles, remove meat loaf to a platter.

"These baked potatoes are meals in themselves, with a smoky barbecue flavor that will make your mouth water. You can top them with your favorite cheese and garnish." —**AMBER MASSEY** ARGYLE, TX

BBQ CHICKEN BAKED POTATOES

Beef Braciole

My great aunt used to make the most amazing braciole, but it was a laborious and time-consuming effort. I took her basic recipe and transformed it into a slow cooker version, making it easier for today's hurried world. My great aunt always served the flank steak sliced over orzo that had been tossed with olive oil and Romano cheese. Delicioso!

—LISA RENSHAW KANSAS CITY, MO

PREP: 30 MIN. • **COOK:** 6 HOURS • **MAKES:** 6 SERVINGS

- 2 jars (24 ounces each) tomato basil pasta sauce
- 1 teaspoon crushed red pepper flakes
- 1 beef flank steak (1½ pounds)
- ½ teaspoon salt
- ½ teaspoon pepper
- 2 eggs, beaten
- ½ cup seasoned bread crumbs
- 8 thin slices prosciutto or deli ham
- 1 cup (4 ounces) shredded Italian cheese blend
- 2 tablespoons olive oil

1. In a 5- or 6-qt. oval slow cooker, combine pasta sauce and pepper flakes. Pound steak with a meat mallet to ½-in. thickness; sprinkle with salt and pepper.
2. In a small bowl, combine eggs and bread crumbs. Spoon over beef to within 1 in. of edges; press onto meat. Layer with prosciutto and cheese. Roll up jelly-roll style, starting with a long side; tie at 2-in. intervals with kitchen string.
3. In a Dutch oven, brown meat in oil on all sides. Transfer to slow cooker; spoon sauce over meat. Cover and cook on low for 6-8 hours or until beef is tender.
4. Remove meat from sauce and discard string. Cut into slices; serve with sauce.

BEEF BRACIOLE

ZIPPY SPAGHETTI SAUCE

Zippy Spaghetti Sauce

Here's a spaghetti sauce that's perfect when you need a set-it-and-forget-it meal. Serve with any type of pasta you like, then toss up a green salad, and dinner is ready!

—ELAINE PRIEST DOVER, PA

PREP: 20 MIN. • **COOK:** 6 HOURS • **MAKES:** ABOUT 3 QUARTS

- 2 pounds lean ground beef (90% lean)
- 1 cup chopped onion
- ½ cup chopped green pepper
- 2 cans (15 ounces each) tomato sauce
- 1 can (28 ounces) diced tomatoes, undrained
- 1 can (12 ounces) tomato paste
- ½ pound sliced fresh mushrooms
- 1 cup grated Parmesan cheese
- ½ to ¾ cup dry red wine or beef broth
- ½ cup sliced pimiento-stuffed olives
- ¼ cup dried parsley flakes
- 1 to 2 tablespoons dried oregano
- 2 teaspoons Italian seasoning
- 2 teaspoons minced garlic
- ½ teaspoon salt
- 1 teaspoon pepper
  Hot cooked pasta

1. In a large skillet, cook the beef, onion and green pepper over medium heat until meat is no longer pink; drain. Transfer to a 5-qt. slow cooker.
2. Stir in the tomato sauce, tomatoes, tomato paste, mushrooms, cheese, wine, olives, parsley, oregano, Italian seasoning, garlic, salt and pepper.
3. Cover and cook on low for 6-8 hours. Serve with pasta.

ROXANNE CHAN'S
CASABLANCA CHUTNEY CHICKEN

> "If you enjoy Indian food, you'll love this idea. An array of spices and dried fruit simmer with chicken thighs for an aromatic and satisfying meal. To make it complete, serve over jasmine or basmati rice."
> —ROXANNE CHAN ALBANY, CA

Casablanca Chutney Chicken

PREP: 25 MIN. • **COOK:** 7 HOURS • **MAKES:** 4 SERVINGS

- 1 pound boneless skinless chicken thighs, cut into ¾-inch pieces
- 1 can (14½ ounces) chicken broth
- ⅓ cup finely chopped onion
- ⅓ cup chopped sweet red pepper
- ⅓ cup chopped carrot
- ⅓ cup chopped dried apricots
- ⅓ cup chopped dried figs
- ⅓ cup golden raisins
- 2 tablespoons orange marmalade
- 1 tablespoon mustard seed
- 2 garlic cloves, minced
- ½ teaspoon curry powder
- ¼ teaspoon crushed red pepper flakes
- ¼ teaspoon ground cumin
- ¼ teaspoon ground cinnamon
- ¼ teaspoon ground cloves
- 2 tablespoons minced fresh parsley
- 2 tablespoons minced fresh mint
- 1 tablespoon lemon juice
- 4 tablespoons chopped pistachios

1. In a 3-qt. slow cooker, combine the first 16 ingredients. Cover and cook on low for 7-8 hours or until the chicken is tender.

2. Stir in the parsley, mint and lemon juice; heat through. Sprinkle each serving with pistachios.

Glazed Kielbasa

You only need three ingredients to prepare this pleasantly sweet sausage. Reduced-fat or turkey kielbasa can also be used.
—JODY SANDS TAYLOR RICHMOND, VA

PREP: 5 MIN. • **COOK:** 4 HOURS • **MAKES:** 12 SERVINGS

- 3 pounds smoked kielbasa or Polish sausage, cut into 1-inch chunks
- ½ cup packed brown sugar
- 1½ cups ginger ale

Place sausage in a 3-qt. slow cooker; sprinkle with brown sugar. Pour ginger ale over the top. Cover and cook on low for 4-5 hours or until heated through.

German Potato Salad with Sausage

Hearty and saucy, this dish is an old family recipe that was updated using canned cream of potato soup to ease preparation. The sausage and sauerkraut make it a satisfying main course.
—TERESA MCGILL TROTWOOD, OH

PREP: 30 MIN. • **COOK:** 6 HOURS • **MAKES:** 5 SERVINGS

- 8 bacon strips, finely chopped
- 1 large onion, chopped
- 1 pound smoked kielbasa or Polish sausage, halved and cut into ½-inch slices
- 2 pounds medium red potatoes, cut into chunks
- 1 can (10¾ ounces) condensed cream of potato soup, undiluted
- 1 cup sauerkraut, rinsed and well drained
- ½ cup water
- ¼ cup cider vinegar
- 1 tablespoon sugar
- ½ teaspoon salt
- ½ teaspoon coarsely ground pepper

1. In a large skillet, cook bacon over medium heat until crisp. Remove to paper towels with a slotted spoon to drain. Saute onion in drippings for 1 minute. Add sausage; cook until lightly browned. Add potatoes; cook 2 minutes longer. Drain.

2. Transfer sausage mixture to a 3-qt. slow cooker. In a small bowl, combine the soup, sauerkraut, water, vinegar, sugar, salt and pepper. Pour over sausage mixture. Sprinkle with bacon. Cover and cook on low for 6-7 hours or until potatoes are tender.

GERMAN POTATO SALAD WITH SAUSAGE

CHICKEN THIGHS WITH GINGER-PEACH SAUCE

Potato Pizza Casserole

Here's a fun, full-flavored meal the whole family will go for. It's great on weeknights when everyone arrives home hungry at the same time!

—TYLER SHERMAN WILLIAMSBURG, VA

PREP: 25 MIN. • **COOK:** 4 HOURS
MAKES: 8 SERVINGS

- 1 pound ground beef
- ½ pound sliced fresh mushrooms
- 1 medium green pepper, chopped
- 1 small onion, chopped
- 2 jars (14 ounces each) pizza sauce
- 1 can (10¾ ounces) condensed cheddar cheese soup, undiluted
- ½ cup 2% milk
- 1 teaspoon Italian seasoning
- ½ teaspoon garlic salt
- ¼ teaspoon crushed red pepper flakes
- 1 package (32 ounces) frozen cubed hash brown potatoes, thawed
- 15 slices pepperoni, chopped
- 2 cups (8 ounces) shredded Italian cheese blend

1. In a large skillet, cook the beef, mushrooms, green pepper and onion until meat is no longer pink; drain.
2. Meanwhile, in a large bowl, combine the pizza sauce, soup, milk, Italian seasoning, garlic salt and pepper flakes. Stir in the potatoes, pepperoni and beef mixture.
3. Transfer half of the meat mixture to a 5-qt slow cooker. Sprinkle with half of the cheese; repeat layers. Cover and cook on low for 4-5 hours or until potatoes are tender.

"This sweet and sour chicken dinner has become a meal-in-one favorite on Sundays. It's easy to prepare and requires very little cleanup, plus the slow cooker leaves me plenty of time to do other things."

—LISA RENSHAW KANSAS CITY, MO

Chicken Thighs with Ginger-Peach Sauce

PREP: 15 MIN. • **COOK:** 4 HOURS
MAKES: 10 SERVINGS

- 10 boneless skinless chicken thighs (about 2½ pounds)
- 1 cup sliced peeled fresh or frozen peaches
- 1 cup golden raisins
- 1 cup peach preserves
- ⅓ cup chili sauce
- 2 tablespoons minced crystallized ginger
- 1 tablespoon reduced-sodium soy sauce
- 1 tablespoon minced garlic Hot cooked rice, optional

1. Place chicken in a 4-qt. slow cooker coated with cooking spray. Top with peaches and raisins. In a small bowl, combine the preserves, chili sauce, ginger, soy sauce and garlic. Spoon over the top.
2. Cover and cook on low for 4-5 hours or until chicken is tender. Serve with rice if desired.

POTATO PIZZA CASSEROLE

Greek Shrimp Orzo

One of our favorite dishes, Greek Shrimp Orzo, is delicious, satisfying and reheats well. My husband would rather have 'the orzo dish' than go out to eat. Serve it with crusty bread and a simple salad.
—**MOLLY SEIDEL** EDGEWOOD, NM

PREP: 45 MIN. • **COOK:** 2 HOURS
MAKES: 6 SERVINGS

- 2 cups uncooked orzo pasta
- 2 tablespoons minced fresh basil or 2 teaspoons dried basil
- 3 tablespoons olive oil, divided
- 1½ tablespoons chopped shallot
- 2 tablespoons butter
- 1 can (14½ ounces) diced tomatoes, drained
- 2 tablespoons minced fresh oregano or 2 teaspoons dried oregano
- 3 garlic cloves, minced
- 1 pound uncooked large shrimp, peeled and deveined
- 1 cup oil-packed sun-dried tomatoes, chopped
- 2½ cups (10 ounces) crumbled feta cheese
- 1½ cups pitted Greek olives

1. Cook orzo according to package directions; rinse in cold water and drain. Transfer to a large bowl. Add basil and 1 tablespoon oil; toss to coat and set aside.

2. In a large skillet, saute shallot in butter and remaining oil until tender. Add the diced tomatoes, oregano and garlic; cook and stir for 1-2 minutes. Add shrimp and sun-dried tomatoes; cook and stir for 2-3 minutes or until shrimp turn pink.

3. Transfer to a greased 5-qt. slow cooker. Stir in the orzo mixture, cheese and olives. Cover and cook on low for 2-3 hours or until heated through.

GUINNESS CORNED BEEF AND CABBAGE

Guinness Corned Beef and Cabbage

Passed down through multiple generations, this robust corned beef and cabbage is requested often in our house. The Irish stout beer adds excellent richness to the meat. Just throw the ingredients in the slow cooker, and let them simmer until they're delicious!
—**KARIN BRODBECK** RED HOOK, NY

PREP: 20 MIN. • **COOK:** 8 HOURS
MAKES: 9 SERVINGS

- 2 pounds red potatoes, quartered
- 1 pound carrots, cut into 3-inch pieces
- 2 celery ribs, cut into 3-inch pieces
- 1 small onion, quartered
- 1 corned beef brisket with spice packet (3 to 3½ pounds)
- 8 whole cloves
- 6 whole peppercorns
- 1 bay leaf
- 1 bottle (12 ounces) Guinness (dark beer) or beef broth
- ½ small head cabbage, thinly sliced
  Prepared horseradish

1. In a 6-qt. slow cooker, combine the potatoes, carrots, celery and onion. Add brisket (discard spice packet from corned beef or save for another use). Place the cloves, peppercorns and bay leaf on a double thickness of cheesecloth; bring up corners of cloth and tie with string to form a bag. Place in slow cooker. Pour beer over top.

2. Cover and cook on low for 8-10 hours or until meat and vegetables are tender, adding cabbage during the last hour of cooking. Discard spice bag.

3. Thinly slice corned beef across the grain. Serve with vegetables and horseradish.

Spring-Thyme Chicken Stew

During a long spring, my husband and I were in need of something warm, comforting, and bright. This chicken was the perfect thing. It filled the house with the aroma of Mom's cooking back home, and it brought us much comfort and delight!

—**AMY CHASE** VANDERHOOF, BC

PREP: 15 MIN. • **COOK:** 7 HOURS • **MAKES:** 4 SERVINGS

- 1 pound small red potatoes, halved
- 1 large onion, finely chopped
- ¾ cup shredded carrots
- 3 tablespoons all-purpose flour
- 6 garlic cloves, minced
- 2 teaspoons grated lemon peel
- 2 teaspoons dried thyme
- ½ teaspoon salt
- ¼ teaspoon pepper
- 1½ pounds boneless skinless chicken thighs, halved
- 2 cups reduced-sodium chicken broth
- 2 bay leaves
- 2 tablespoons minced fresh parsley

1. Place potatoes, onion and carrots in a 3-qt. slow cooker. Sprinkle with flour, garlic, lemon peel, thyme, salt and pepper; toss to coat. Place chicken over top. Add broth and bay leaves.

2. Cook, covered, on low 7-9 hours or until the chicken and vegetables are tender. Remove bay leaves. Sprinkle with parsley.

SPRING-THYME CHICKEN STEW

"Here, spice-coated chicken thighs simmer in a rich sauce. This savory entree is perfect for an everyday meal or potluck. With a little planning, it's an easy dish to prepare in the morning so dinner is ready when you are."

—**JUDY ARMSTRONG** PRAIRIEVILLE, LA

Mediterranean Chicken in Eggplant Sauce

PREP: 45 MIN. • **COOK:** 5 HOURS • **MAKES:** 8 SERVINGS

- ⅓ cup all-purpose flour
- 2 teaspoons paprika
- 2 teaspoons ground cumin
- 1 teaspoon salt
- 1 teaspoon freshly ground pepper
- 3 pounds boneless skinless chicken thighs, cut into 2-inch pieces
- 2 tablespoons olive oil
- 1¼ cups white wine or chicken broth
- 1 small eggplant (1 pound), peeled and cubed
- 1 jar (12 ounces) roasted sweet red peppers, drained
- 1 medium onion, chopped
- 1 jalapeno pepper, seeded and chopped
- 2 tablespoons tomato paste
- 1 tablespoon brown sugar
- 3 garlic cloves, minced
- 1 cup pitted ripe olives, halved
- ¼ cup minced fresh Italian parsley
- 1 cup (4 ounces) crumbled feta cheese
- 8 naan flatbreads, quartered

1. In a large bowl, combine the first five ingredients. Add chicken; toss to coat. In a large skillet, brown chicken in oil in batches. Transfer to a 4-qt. slow cooker.

2. Add wine to the skillet, stirring to loosen browned bits from pan. Stir in the eggplant, red peppers, onion, jalapeno, tomato paste, brown sugar and garlic. Bring to a boil. Reduce heat; simmer, uncovered, for 5 minutes. Cool slightly. Transfer to a blender; cover and process until pureed. Pour over chicken.

3. Cover and cook on low for 5-6 hours or until chicken is tender, adding olives and parsley during the last 30 minutes. Just before serving, sprinkle with feta cheese. Serve with naan flatbreads.

NOTE *Wear disposable gloves when cutting hot peppers; the oils can burn skin. Avoid touching your face.*

JUDY ARMSTRONG'S
MEDITERRANEAN CHICKEN IN EGGPLANT SAUCE

SWEET 'N' TENDER CABBAGE ROLLS

Sweet 'n' Tender Cabbage Rolls

I've used this recipe for more than 30 years, and the extra time it takes to assemble the rolls is well worth the effort. You can also roll them up them the night before and cook the next day. I always make two batches because they go so fast.

—SONJA BENZ CARMEL, IN

PREP: 40 MIN. • **COOK:** 7 HOURS • **MAKES:** 7 SERVINGS

- 1 **large head cabbage**
- 2 **eggs, lightly beaten**
- ½ **cup 2% milk**
- 2 **cups cooked long grain rice**
- 2 **jars (4½ ounces each) sliced mushrooms, well drained**
- 1 **small onion, chopped**
- 2 **teaspoons salt**
- 1 **teaspoon dried parsley flakes**
- 1 **teaspoon dried oregano**
- 1 **teaspoon dried basil**
- ½ **teaspoon pepper**
- 2 **pounds lean ground beef (90% lean)**

SAUCE
- 2 **cans (8 ounces each) tomato sauce**
- ½ **cup packed brown sugar**
- 2 **tablespoons lemon juice**
- 2 **teaspoons Worcestershire sauce**

1. Cook cabbage in boiling water just until leaves fall off head. Set aside 14 large leaves for rolls. (Refrigerate remaining cabbage for another use.) Cut out the thick vein from the bottom of each reserved leaf, making a V-shaped cut.

2. In a large bowl, combine the eggs, milk, rice, mushrooms, onion and seasonings. Crumble beef over mixture and mix well. Place about ½ cup on each cabbage leaf; overlap cut ends and fold in sides, beginning from the cut end. Roll up completely to enclose filling.

3. Place seven rolls, seam side down, in a 5-qt. slow cooker. Combine sauce ingredients; pour half over cabbage rolls. Top with remaining rolls and sauce. Cover and cook on low for 7-8 hours or until a thermometer reads 160°.

STOVETOP SWEET 'N' TENDER CABBAGE ROLLS *Prepare as directed in steps 1-3. Place rolls in a Dutch oven. Combine tomato sauce, brown sugar, lemon juice and Worcestershire sauce; pour over cabbage rolls. Bring to a boil. Reduce heat; cover and simmer for 60-70 minutes, spooning sauce over rolls occasionally during cooking.*

"Here's a great recipe to make ahead! I cut up fresh chicken, put it in a bag with the remaining ingredients and freeze. To cook, just remove the bag a day early to thaw in the fridge, then pour all the contents into the slow cooker." —SARAH NEWMAN MAHTOMEDI, MN

Indonesian Peanut Chicken

PREP: 15 MIN. • **COOK:** 4 HOURS • **MAKES:** 6 SERVINGS

- 1½ pounds boneless skinless chicken breasts, cut into 1-inch cubes
- ⅓ cup chopped onion
- ⅓ cup water
- ¼ cup reduced-fat creamy peanut butter
- 3 tablespoons chili sauce
- ¼ teaspoon salt
- ¼ teaspoon cayenne pepper
- ¼ teaspoon pepper
- 3 cups hot cooked brown rice
- 6 tablespoons chopped salted peanuts
- 6 tablespoons chopped sweet red pepper

1. Place chicken in a 4-qt. slow cooker. In a small bowl, combine the onion, water, peanut butter, chili sauce, salt, cayenne and pepper; pour over chicken. Cover and cook on low for 4-6 hours or until chicken is no longer pink.

2. Shred meat with two forks and return to slow cooker; heat through. Serve with rice. Sprinkle with peanuts and red pepper.

INDONESIAN PEANUT CHICKEN

SPICED LAMB STEW WITH APRICOTS

Spiced Lamb Stew with Apricots

My family loves lamb, especially my son. During his first year of college, he said he became a vegetarian. When he came home, I had a pot of this slow-cooked lamb stew simmering on the counter. When my husband and I wanted to eat dinner, there were only a few shreds of meat left floating in the gravy—and my son confessed that he was the culprit!

—**ARLENE ERLBACH** MORTON GROVE, IL

PREP: 30 MIN. • **COOK:** 5 HOURS • **MAKES:** 5 SERVINGS

- 2 pounds lamb stew meat, cut into ¾-inch cubes
- 3 tablespoons butter
- 1½ cups chopped sweet onion
- ¾ cup dried apricots
- ½ cup orange juice
- ½ cup chicken broth
- 2 teaspoons paprika
- 2 teaspoons ground allspice
- 2 teaspoons ground cinnamon
- 1½ teaspoons salt
- 1 teaspoon ground cardamom
  Hot cooked couscous
  Chopped dried apricots, optional

1. In a large skillet, brown lamb in butter in batches. With a slotted spoon, transfer to a 3-qt. slow cooker. In the same skillet, saute onion in drippings until tender. Stir in the apricots, orange juice, broth and seasonings; pour over the lamb.

2. Cover and cook on high for 5-6 hours or until meat is tender. Serve with couscous. Sprinkle with chopped apricots if desired.

ROBIN HAAS'
PINEAPPLE CURRY CHICKEN

Pineapple Curry Chicken

Curry has a moderate to strong delivery, so add it early in the cooking process for good balance with the pineapple, coconut and ginger.

—ROBIN HAAS CRANSTON, RI

PREP: 25 MIN. • **COOK:** 6 HOURS
MAKES: 6 SERVINGS

- 2 cans (8 ounces each) unsweetened pineapple chunks, undrained
- 6 bone-in chicken breast halves, skin removed (12 ounces each)
- 1 can (15 ounces) garbanzo beans or chickpeas, rinsed and drained
- 1 large onion, cut into 1-inch pieces
- 1 cup julienned carrots
- 1 medium sweet red pepper, cut into strips
- ½ cup light coconut milk
- 2 tablespoons cornstarch
- 2 tablespoons sugar
- 3 teaspoons curry powder
- 2 garlic cloves, minced
- 2 teaspoons minced fresh gingerroot
- 1 teaspoon salt
- 1 teaspoon pepper
- 1 teaspoon lime juice
- ½ teaspoon crushed red pepper flakes
  Hot cooked rice
- ⅓ cup minced fresh basil
  Toasted flaked coconut, optional

1. Drain pineapple, reserving ¾ cup juice. Place the chicken, beans, vegetables and pineapple in a 6-qt. slow cooker.

2. In a small bowl, combine coconut milk and cornstarch until smooth. Stir in the sugar, curry powder, garlic, ginger, salt, pepper, lime juice, pepper flakes and reserved juice; pour over the chicken.

3. Cover and cook on low for 6-8 hours or until chicken is tender. Serve with rice; sprinkle with basil and, if desired, coconut.

"A simple mango coleslaw accompanies tender shredded pork in my popular recipe. We like it with corn bread."
—JANICE ELDER CHARLOTTE, NC

CONGA LIME PORK

Conga Lime Pork

PREP: 20 MIN. • **COOK:** 4 HOURS
MAKES: 6 SERVINGS

- 1 teaspoon salt, divided
- ½ teaspoon pepper, divided
- 1 boneless pork shoulder butt roast (2 to 3 pounds)
- 1 tablespoon canola oil
- 1 large onion, chopped
- 3 garlic cloves, peeled and thinly sliced
- ½ cup water
- 2 chipotle peppers in adobo sauce, seeded and chopped
- 2 tablespoons molasses
- 2 cups broccoli coleslaw mix
- 1 medium mango, peeled and chopped
- 2 tablespoons lime juice
- 1½ teaspoons grated lime peel
- 6 prepared corn muffins, halved

1. Sprinkle ¾ teaspoon salt and ¼ teaspoon pepper over roast. In a large skillet, brown the pork in oil on all sides. Transfer meat to a 3- or 4-qt. slow cooker.

2. In the same skillet, saute onion until tender. Add garlic; cook 1 minute longer. Add water, chipotle peppers and molasses, stirring to loosen browned bits from pan. Pour over pork. Cover and cook on high for 4-5 hours or until meat is tender.

3. Remove roast; cool slightly. Skim fat from cooking juices. Shred pork with two forks and return to slow cooker; heat through. In a large bowl, combine the coleslaw mix, mango, lime juice, lime peel and remaining salt and pepper.

4. Place muffin halves cut-side down on an ungreased baking sheet. Broil 4 in. from the heat for 2-3 minutes or until lightly toasted. Serve pork with muffins; top with slaw.

"I put this dish together regularly because it's so simple to prepare. The combination of seasonings truly makes it a standout main course."

—**JENN TIDWELL** FAIR OAKS, CA

SLOW-COOKED CARIBBEAN POT ROAST

Slow-Cooked Caribbean Pot Roast

PREP: 30 MIN. • **COOK:** 6 HOURS
MAKES: 10 SERVINGS

- 2 **medium sweet potatoes, cubed**
- 2 **large carrots, sliced**
- ¼ **cup chopped celery**
- 1 **boneless beef chuck roast (2½ pounds)**
- 1 **tablespoon canola oil**
- 1 **large onion, chopped**
- 2 **garlic cloves, minced**
- 1 **tablespoon all-purpose flour**
- 1 **tablespoon sugar**
- 1 **tablespoon brown sugar**
- 1 **teaspoon ground cumin**
- ¾ **teaspoon salt**
- ¾ **teaspoon ground coriander**
- ¾ **teaspoon chili powder**
- ½ **teaspoon dried oregano**
- ⅛ **teaspoon ground cinnamon**
- ¾ **teaspoon grated orange peel**
- ¾ **teaspoon baking cocoa**
- 1 **can (15 ounces) tomato sauce**

1. Place potatoes, carrots and celery in a 5-qt. slow cooker. In a large skillet, brown meat in oil on all sides. Transfer meat to slow cooker.

2. In the same skillet, saute onion in drippings until tender. Add garlic; cook 1 minute longer. Combine the flour, sugar, brown sugar, seasonings, orange peel and cocoa. Stir in tomato sauce; add to skillet and heat through. Pour over beef.

3. Cover and cook on low for 6-8 hours or until beef and vegetables are tender.

Ratatouille with a Twist

Before this variation came along, my family always ate ratatouille as a veggie side. My husband's suggestion to incorporate sausage turned out to be a big hit, and now it's an entree! Use sweet Italian sausages if you'd like less heat.

—**SUSAN TREMBLAY** BERLIN, NH

PREP: 25 MIN. • **COOK:** 6 HOURS
MAKES: 6 SERVINGS

- 4 **hot Italian sausage links (4 ounces each)**
- 4 **cups chopped zucchini**
- 1 **can (14½ ounces) stewed tomatoes, cut-up**
- 1 **can (10¾ ounces) condensed tomato soup, undiluted**
- 1 **medium onion, chopped**
- 1 **garlic clove, minced**
- ½ **teaspoon dried basil**
- ½ **teaspoon dried oregano**
  Hot cooked pasta

In a large skillet, cook sausages until no longer pink. Cut into ½-in. slices; transfer to a 3-qt. slow cooker. Add the zucchini, tomatoes, soup, onion, garlic, basil and oregano. Cover and cook on low for 6-8 hours or until flavors are blended. Serve with pasta.

top tip Summer Squash

Summer squash have edible thin skins and soft seeds. Zucchini, patty pan and yellow are the most common varieties. Choose firm summer squash with brightly colored skin that's free from spots and bruises. Generally, the smaller the squash, the more tender it will be. Refrigerate summer squash in a plastic bag for up to 5 days. Before using, wash squash and trim both ends. One pound of summer squash equals about 3 medium squash or 2 ½ cups chopped squash.

Slow-Cooked Shepherd's Pie

Shepherd's pie is to the British what meat loaf is to Americans, so as a young child living in the UK, shepherd's pie was a weekly staple. This is my go-to recipe when I'm longing for the sights and smells of my mother's kitchen.

—**MARI SITKIEWICZ** DOWNERS GROVE, IL

PREP: 35 MIN. • **COOK:** 5¼ HOURS
MAKES: 5 SERVINGS

- 2 pounds medium Yukon Gold potatoes, peeled and quartered
- 2 tablespoons butter
- ¼ to ⅓ cup 2% milk
- ¾ teaspoon salt, divided
- ½ teaspoon pepper, divided
- 1 pound ground beef
- 1 large onion, chopped
- 2 garlic cloves, minced
- 3 tablespoons tomato paste
- 1¾ cups sliced fresh mushrooms
- 2 medium carrots, chopped
- 1 cup beef broth
- ¼ cup dry white wine
- 2 teaspoons Worcestershire sauce
- ½ teaspoon dried thyme
- ⅓ cup frozen peas
- ½ cup shredded Monterey Jack cheese
- 1 tablespoon minced fresh parsley

1. Place potatoes in a large saucepan and cover with water. Bring to a boil. Reduce heat; cover and cook for 10-15 minutes or until tender. Drain, then shake potatoes over low heat for 1 minute to dry. Mash potatoes, gradually adding butter and enough milk to reach desired consistency. Stir in ½ teaspoon salt and ¼ teaspoon pepper.

2. Meanwhile, in a large skillet, cook the beef, onion, and garlic over medium heat until the meat is no longer pink; drain.

3. Add the tomato paste; cook for 2 minutes. Add the mushrooms, carrots, broth, wine, Worcestershire sauce and thyme. Bring to a boil. Reduce heat; simmer, uncovered, until most of the liquid is evaporated. Stir in peas. Season with remaining salt and pepper.

4. Transfer beef mixture to a greased 4-qt. slow cooker. Spread mashed potatoes over top. Cover and cook on low for 5-6 hours or until bubbly. Sprinkle with cheese. Cover and cook 10 minutes longer or until cheese is melted. Just before serving, sprinkle with parsley.

MANGO-PINEAPPLE CHICKEN TACOS

Mango-Pineapple Chicken Tacos

I lived in the Caribbean as a child, and the fresh tropical fruits in this slow cooker change-of-pace recipe always bring me back to my childhood.

—**LISSA NELSON** PROVO, UT

PREP: 25 MIN. • **COOK:** 5 HOURS
MAKES: 16 SERVINGS

- 2 medium mangoes, peeled and chopped
- 1½ cups cubed fresh pineapple or canned pineapple chunks, drained
- 2 medium tomatoes, chopped
- 1 medium red onion, finely chopped
- 2 small Anaheim peppers, seeded and chopped
- 2 green onions, finely chopped
- 1 tablespoon lime juice
- 1 teaspoon sugar
- 4 pounds bone-in chicken breast halves, skin removed
- 3 teaspoons salt
- ¼ cup packed brown sugar
- 32 taco shells, warmed
- ¼ cup minced fresh cilantro

1. In a large bowl, combine the first eight ingredients. Place chicken in a 6-qt. slow cooker; sprinkle with salt and brown sugar. Top with mango mixture. Cover and cook on low for 5-6 hours or until chicken is tender.

2. Remove chicken; cool slightly. Strain cooking juices, reserving mango mixture and ½ cup juices. Discard remaining juices. When cool enough to handle, remove the chicken from bones; discard bones.

3. Shred chicken with two forks. Return chicken and reserved mango mixture and cooking juices to slow cooker; heat through. Serve in taco shells; sprinkle with cilantro.

SLOW-COOKED SHEPHERD'S PIE

Spring

SOUPS & SANDWICHES

Nothing tops the popular combination of soup and sandwich, so why not use your slow cooker to create the tasty duo? Loaded with convenience, the recipes found here deliver spring's freshest flavors.

NICHOLE JONES' TURKEY SLOPPY JOES

Turkey Sloppy Joes

The chili sauce and ground turkey that are used to make these sloppy joes create a deliciously unique flavor. The creamy avocado adds a special spring-summer touch people love.

—**NICHOLE JONES** PLEASANT GROVE, UT

PREP: 35 MIN. • **COOK:** 4 HOURS • **MAKES:** 8 SERVINGS

- 1½ pounds lean ground turkey
- 2 medium onions, finely chopped
- 4 garlic cloves, minced
- 1 jar (12 ounces) chili sauce
- 1 jalapeno pepper, seeded and chopped
- 1 tablespoon Worcestershire sauce
- 2 teaspoons dried oregano
- 1 teaspoon ground cumin
- 1 teaspoon paprika
- ½ teaspoon salt
- ½ teaspoon pepper
- 2 cups (8 ounces) shredded Monterey Jack cheese
- 8 onion rolls, split
- 2 medium ripe avocados, peeled and thinly sliced

1. In a large skillet coated with cooking spray, cook the turkey, onions and garlic over medium heat until meat is no longer pink; drain.

2. Transfer to a 1½-qt. slow cooker. Stir in the chili sauce, jalapeno, Worcestershire sauce, oregano, cumin, paprika, salt and pepper. Cover and cook on low for 4-5 hours or until heated through. Just before serving, stir in cheese. Serve on rolls topped with avocado.

NOTE *Wear disposable gloves when cutting hot peppers; the oils can burn skin. Avoid touching your face.*

Zesty Garbanzo Sausage Soup

Even the busiest home cooks will have time to prepare this Cajun-inspired soup. If your family prefers spicier flavors, use medium salsa instead of mild.

—**PRISCILLA DOYLE** LUTZ, FL

PREP: 20 MIN. • **COOK:** 6½ HOURS • **MAKES:** 7 SERVINGS

- 2 cans (15 ounces each) garbanzo beans or chickpeas, rinsed and drained
- 3 cups water
- 1 jar (16 ounces) mild salsa
- 1 can (14½ ounces) diced tomatoes, undrained
- 2 celery ribs, chopped
- 1 cup sliced fresh or frozen okra
- 1 medium onion, chopped
- 2 teaspoons Cajun seasoning
- 1 pound smoked kielbasa or Polish sausage, cut into 1-inch pieces

In a 5-qt. slow cooker, combine the first eight ingredients. Cover and cook on low for 6-8 hours or until vegetables are tender. Stir in kielbasa. Cover and cook 30 minutes longer or until heated through.

Mojito Pulled Pork

This fork-tender pulled pork tastes fabulous on a bun, in a wrap or tortilla. My kids like to eat it spooned over rice, which goes well with its citrus-flavored juices.

—**MINDY OSWALT** WINNETKA, CA

PREP: 20 MIN. • **COOK:** 7 HOURS • **MAKES:** 16 SERVINGS

- 1 boneless pork shoulder roast (4 to 5 pounds)
- 2 teaspoons salt
- 2 teaspoons dried oregano
- 2 teaspoons each ground cumin, paprika and pepper
- 1 bunch fresh cilantro, divided
- 2 medium onions, halved and sliced
- ¼ cup canned chopped green chilies
- 4 garlic cloves, minced
- 2 cans (14½ ounces each) reduced-sodium chicken broth
- ⅔ cup orange juice
- ½ cup lime juice
- 16 sandwich buns, split
  Barbecue sauce

1. Cut roast in half. Combine the salt, oregano, cumin, paprika and pepper; rub over pork. Place in a 4- or 5-qt. slow cooker.

2. Mince cilantro to measure ¼ cup; set aside. Trim remaining cilantro, discarding stems. Add the whole cilantro leaves, onions, chilies and garlic to the slow cooker. Combine the broth, orange juice and lime juice; pour over roast. Cover and cook on low for 7-9 hours or until the meat is tender.

3. Remove roast; cool slightly. Skim fat from cooking juices; set aside 3 cups juices. Discard remaining juices. Shred pork with two forks and return to slow cooker. Stir in minced cilantro and reserved cooking juices; heat through. Spoon ½ cup meat onto each bun. Serve with barbecue sauce.

MOJITO PULLED PORK

ITALIAN PULLED PORK SANDWICHES

Italian Pulled Pork Sandwiches

Enjoy all the flavors of classic Italian sausage sandwiches with a healthier alternative that uses spicy and tender pulled pork instead.

—**DELLARIO LIA** MIDDLEPORT, NY

PREP: 20 MIN. • **COOK:** 8 HOURS • **MAKES:** 12 SERVINGS

- 1 tablespoon fennel seed, crushed
- 1 tablespoon steak seasoning
- 1 teaspoon cayenne pepper, optional
- 1 boneless pork shoulder butt roast (3 pounds)
- 1 tablespoon olive oil
- 2 medium green or sweet red peppers, thinly sliced
- 2 medium onions, thinly sliced
- 1 can (14½ ounces) diced tomatoes, undrained
- 12 whole wheat hamburger buns, split

1. In a small bowl, combine fennel seed, steak seasoning and cayenne if desired. Cut roast in half. Rub seasoning mixture over pork. In a large skillet, brown roast in oil on all sides. Place in a 4- or 5-qt. slow cooker. Add peppers, onions and tomatoes; cover and cook on low for 7-9 hours or until meat is tender.

2. Remove roast; cool slightly. Skim fat from cooking juices. Shred pork with two forks and return to slow cooker; heat through. Using a slotted spoon, place ½ cup meat mixture on each bun.

NOTE *This recipe was tested with Montreal Steak Seasoning. Look for it in the spice aisle.*

MACHACA BEEF DIP SANDWICHES

Machaca Beef Dip Sandwiches

The winning combination of beef, cumin, chili powder and the spicy heat of chipotle peppers makes these sandwiches game-day food at its finest!

—KAROL CHANDLER-EZELL NACOGDOCHES, TX

PREP: 20 MIN. • **COOK:** 8 HOURS • **MAKES:** 6 SERVINGS

- 1 **boneless beef chuck roast (2 to 3 pounds)**
- 1 **large sweet onion, thinly sliced**
- 1 **can (14½ ounces) reduced-sodium beef broth**
- ½ **cup water**
- 3 **chipotle peppers in adobo sauce, chopped**
- 1 **tablespoon adobo sauce**
- 1 **envelope au jus gravy mix**
- 1 **tablespoon Creole seasoning**
- 1 **tablespoon chili powder**
- 2 **teaspoons ground cumin**
- 6 **French rolls, split**
  Guacamole and salsa, optional

1. Place roast in a 3- to 4-qt. slow cooker; top with onion. Combine the broth, water, chipotle peppers, adobo sauce, gravy mix, Creole seasoning, chili powder and cumin; pour over meat. Cover and cook on low for 8-10 hours or until meat is tender.

2. Remove roast; cool slightly. Skim fat from cooking juices. Shred beef with two forks and return to slow cooker; heat through. Using a slotted spoon, place meat on rolls. Serve with cooking juices and guacamole or salsa if desired.

NOTES *Wear disposable gloves when cutting hot peppers; the oils can burn skin. Avoid touching your face. The following spices may be substituted for 1 tablespoon Creole seasoning: ¾ teaspoon each salt, garlic powder and paprika; and a pinch each of dried thyme, ground cumin and cayenne pepper.*

Vegetable Pork Soup

Packed with tender pork, veggies and savory flavor, this nutritious soup fills the house with a wonderful aroma as it simmers.

—DEB HALL HUNTINGTON, IN

PREP: 20 MIN. • **COOK:** 7 HOURS• **MAKES:** 6 SERVINGS (2 QUARTS)

- 1 pork tenderloin (1 pound), cut into 1-inch pieces
- 1 teaspoon garlic powder
- 2 teaspoons canola oil
- 1 can (28 ounces) diced tomatoes
- 4 medium carrots, cut into ½-inch pieces
- 2 medium potatoes, cubed
- 1 can (12 ounces) light or nonalcoholic beer
- ¼ cup quick-cooking tapioca
- 2 bay leaves
- 1 tablespoon Worcestershire sauce
- 1 tablespoon honey
- 1 teaspoon dried thyme
- ¼ teaspoon salt
- ¼ teaspoon pepper
- ⅛ teaspoon ground nutmeg

1. Sprinkle pork with garlic powder. In a large skillet, brown pork in oil; drain.

2. Transfer to a 4-qt. slow cooker. Add the remaining ingredients. Cover and cook on low for 7-8 hours or until meat is tender. Discard bay leaves.

VEGETABLE PORK SOUP

TEX-MEX SHREDDED BEEF SANDWICHES

⑤ INGREDIENTS

Tex-Mex Shredded Beef Sandwiches

Slow cooker meals, like this shredded beef sandwich, are my favorite kind because after I combine a few ingredients and let them cook, there is time for me to do my own thing. Plus, I have a hearty, satisfying and enticing meal all ready when I come home!

—KATHERINE WHITE CLEMMONS, NC

PREP: 5 MIN. • **COOK:** 8 HOURS • **MAKES:** 8 SERVINGS

- 1 boneless beef chuck roast (3 pounds)
- 1 envelope chili seasoning
- ½ cup barbecue sauce
- 8 onion rolls, split
- 8 slices cheddar cheese

1. Cut roast in half; place in a 3-qt. slow cooker. Sprinkle with chili seasoning. Pour barbecue sauce over top. Cover and cook on low for 8-10 hours or until meat is tender.

2. Remove roast; cool slightly. Shred meat with two forks. Skim fat from cooking juices. Return meat to slow cooker; heat through. Using a slotted spoon, place ½ cup meat mixture on each roll bottom; top with cheese. Replace tops.

Coffee-Braised Pulled Pork Sandwiches

I love coffee with meat...it adds such depth of flavor. My recipe not only combines those two items, it's also made in a slow cooker so it's ready for us to dig in as we walk in the door. It may take longer then 9 hours, depending on the fat content of the pork. It makes a great sandwich with the pepper jack cheese.

—JACQUELYNN SANDERS BURNSVILLE, MN

PREP: 30 MIN. • **COOK:** 8 HOURS • **MAKES:** 10 SERVINGS

- 1 **boneless pork shoulder butt roast (3 to 3½ pounds)**
- ⅓ **cup ground coffee beans**
- ½ **teaspoon salt**
- ½ **teaspoon pepper**
- 2 **tablespoons canola oil**
- 2 **celery ribs, chopped**
- 1 **large carrot, chopped**
- 1 **medium onion, chopped**
- 2 **cups chicken stock**
- 1½ **cups strong brewed coffee**
- 2 **tablespoons minced fresh parsley**
- 1 **teaspoon coriander seeds**
- 1 **teaspoon ground cumin**
- 1 **teaspoon whole peppercorns, crushed**
- 1 **cinnamon stick (3 inches)**
- 1 **bay leaf**
- 10 **hoagie or kaiser buns, split**
- 10 **slices pepper jack cheese**

1. Cut roast into thirds. Combine the ground coffee, salt and pepper; rub over roast. In a large skillet, brown meat in oil on all sides; drain.

2. Transfer meat to a 5-qt. slow cooker. Add the celery, carrot, onion, chicken stock, brewed coffee, parsley, coriander seeds, cumin, peppercorns, cinnamon stick and bay leaf; pour over roast.

COFFEE-BRAISED PULLED PORK SANDWICHES

BEEF & POTATO SOUP

3. Cover and cook on low for 8-10 hours or until meat is tender. When cool enough to handle, shred meat. Skim fat from cooking juices. Strain cooking juices, discarding the vegetables, cinnamon stick and bay leaf.

4. Spoon about ½ cup pork onto each bun; top with cheese. Serve with cooking juices.

Beef & Potato Soup

At our house, this lightened-up soup is an after-church tradition. We all arrive home to enjoy a relaxing meal...even the cook!

—SHEILA HOLDERMAN BERTHOLD, ND

PREP: 30 MIN. • **COOK:** 6½ HOURS
MAKES: 10 SERVINGS (3 QUARTS)

- 1½ **pounds lean ground beef (90% lean)**
- ¾ **cup chopped onion**
- ½ **cup all-purpose flour**
- 2 **cans (14½ ounces each) reduced-sodium chicken broth, divided**
- 5 **medium potatoes, peeled and cubed**
- 5 **medium carrots, chopped**
- 3 **celery ribs, chopped**
- 3 **teaspoons dried basil**
- 2 **teaspoons dried parsley flakes**
- 1 **teaspoon garlic powder**
- ½ **teaspoon pepper**
- 12 **ounces reduced-fat process cheese (Velveeta), cubed**
- 1½ **cups 2% milk**
- ½ **cup reduced-fat sour cream**

1. In a large skillet, cook beef and onion over medium heat until meat is no longer pink; drain. Combine flour and 1 can of broth until smooth. Add to beef mixture. Bring to a boil; cook and stir for 2 minutes or until thickened.

2. Transfer to a 5-qt. slow cooker. Stir in the potatoes, carrots, celery, seasonings and remaining broth. Cover and cook on low for 6-8 hours or until vegetables are tender.

3. Stir in cheese and milk. Cover and cook 30 minutes longer or until cheese is melted. Just before serving, stir in the sour cream.

Cioppino

If you're looking for a great seafood recipe to create in your slow cooker, this classic fish stew is just the ticket. It's full to the brim with clams, crab, fish and shrimp, and is fancy enough to serve as an elegant meal to guests.

—**LISA MORIARTY** WILTON, NH

PREP: 20 MIN. • **COOK:** 4½ HOURS
MAKES: 8 SERVINGS (2½ QUARTS)

- 1 can (28 ounces) diced tomatoes, undrained
- 2 medium onions, chopped
- 3 celery ribs, chopped
- 1 bottle (8 ounces) clam juice
- 1 can (6 ounces) tomato paste
- ½ cup white wine or vegetable broth
- 5 garlic cloves, minced
- 1 tablespoon red wine vinegar
- 1 tablespoon olive oil
- 1 to 2 teaspoons Italian seasoning
- ½ teaspoon sugar
- 1 bay leaf
- 1 pound haddock fillets, cut into 1-inch pieces
- 1 pound uncooked small shrimp, peeled and deveined
- 1 can (6 ounces) lump crabmeat, drained
- 1 can (6 ounces) chopped clams
- 2 tablespoons minced fresh parsley or 2 teaspoons dried parsley flakes

In a 4- or 5-qt. slow cooker, combine the first twelve ingredients. Cover and cook on low for 4-5 hours. Stir in the haddock, shrimp, crabmeat and clams. Cover and cook 30 minutes longer or until fish flakes easily with a fork and shrimp turn pink. Stir in parsley. Discard bay leaf.

CIOPPINO

GARY FENSKI'S
SLOW-COOKED CANNELLINI TURKEY SOUP

Slow-Cooked Cannellini Turkey Soup

All you have to do is add the ingredients to the slow cooker and let them cook! Nothing could be simpler.

—**GARY FENSKI** HURON, SD

PREP: 20 MIN. • **COOK:** 5 HOURS • **MAKES:** 4 SERVINGS

- 2 cans (15 ounces each) white kidney or cannellini beans, rinsed and drained
- 2 cups cubed cooked turkey
- 1 can (14½ ounces) chicken broth
- 1 can (10 ounces) diced tomatoes and green chilies, undrained
- 1 cup salsa
- ½ teaspoon ground cumin
- ¼ teaspoon curry powder
- ¼ teaspoon ground ginger
- ¼ teaspoon paprika

In a 3-qt. slow cooker, combine all ingredients. Cover and cook on low for 5-6 hours or until heated through.

Mint Lamb Stew

The lamb here isn't just tender, it melts in your mouth! This recipe is an adaptation of a stew my mother used to make while I was growing up in England. Now I like to round it out with root vegetables grown locally.

—**MAUREEN EVANS** RANCHO CUCAMONGA, CA

PREP: 40 MIN. • **COOK:** 7 HOURS • **MAKES:** 6 SERVINGS

- ½ cup all-purpose flour
- ½ teaspoon salt
- ¼ teaspoon pepper
- 1½ pounds lamb stew meat, cubed
- 2 shallots, sliced
- 2 tablespoons olive oil
- ½ cup red wine
- 2 cans (14½ ounces each) beef broth
- 2 medium potatoes, cubed
- 1 large sweet potato, peeled and cubed
- 2 large carrots, cut into 1-inch pieces
- 2 medium parsnips, peeled and cubed
- 1 garlic clove, minced
- 1 tablespoon mint jelly
- 4 bacon strips, cooked and crumbled

1. In a large resealable plastic bag, combine the flour, salt and pepper. Add the meat, a few pieces at a time, and shake to coat. In a large skillet, brown the meat and shallots in oil in batches.

2. Transfer to a 5- or 6-qt. slow cooker. Add the wine to the skillet, stirring to loosen browned bits from pan. Bring to a boil. Reduce heat; simmer, uncovered, for 1-2 minutes. Add to slow cooker.

3. Stir in the broth, potatoes, sweet potato, carrots, parsnips and garlic. Cover and cook on low for 7-9 hours or until meat is tender. Stir in jelly; sprinkle with bacon.

Satay-Style Pork Stew

Thai cuisine features flavors that are hot and sour, salty and sweet. This one-dish pork satay balances all of them using ginger and red pepper flakes, rice vinegar, garlic, lime juice and creamy peanut butter. You'll want to try this one.

—**NICOLE WERNER** ANN ARBOR, MI

PREP: 25 MIN. • **COOK:** 8 HOURS • **MAKES:** 6 SERVINGS

- 1 boneless pork shoulder butt roast (3 to 4 pounds), cut into 1½ inch cubes
- 2 medium parsnips, peeled and sliced
- 1 small sweet red pepper, thinly sliced
- 1 cup chicken broth
- ¼ cup reduced-sodium teriyaki sauce
- 2 tablespoons rice vinegar
- 1 tablespoon minced fresh gingerroot
- 1 tablespoon honey
- 2 garlic cloves, minced
- ½ teaspoon crushed red pepper flakes
- ¼ cup creamy peanut butter
  Hot cooked rice, optional
- 2 green onions, chopped
- 2 tablespoons chopped dry roasted peanuts

In a 3-qt. slow cooker, combine the first 10 ingredients. Cover and cook on low for 8-10 hours or until pork is tender. Skim fat; stir in peanut butter. Serve with rice if desired; top with onions and peanuts.

SATAY-STYLE PORK STEW

"Brining the chicken overnight helps it taste exceptionally good and makes it so tender, it literally melts in your mouth."
—RACHEL KUNKEL SCHELL CITY, MO

BBQ CHICKEN SLIDERS

BBQ Chicken Sliders

PREP: 25 MIN. + BRINING • **COOK:** 4 HOURS
MAKES: 8 SERVINGS (2 SLIDERS EACH)

BRINE
- 1½ quarts water
- ¼ cup packed brown sugar
- 2 tablespoons salt
- 1 tablespoon liquid smoke
- 2 garlic cloves, minced
- ½ teaspoon dried thyme

CHICKEN
- 2 pounds boneless skinless chicken breast halves
- ⅓ cup liquid smoke
- 1½ cups hickory smoke-flavored barbecue sauce
- 16 slider buns or dinner rolls, split and warmed

1. In a large bowl, mix the brine ingredients, stirring to dissolve brown sugar. Reserve 1 cup brine for cooking chicken; cover and refrigerate.

2. Place chicken in a large resealable bag; add remaining brine. Seal bag, pressing out as much air as possible; turn to coat chicken. Place in a large bowl; refrigerate 18-24 hours, turning occasionally.

3. Remove chicken from brine and transfer to a 3-qt. slow cooker; discard brine in bag. Add reserved 1 cup brine and ⅓ cup liquid smoke to chicken. Cook, covered, on low 4-5 hours or until chicken is tender.

4. Remove chicken; cool slightly. Discard cooking juices. Shred chicken with two forks and return to slow cooker. Stir in barbecue sauce; heat through. Serve on buns.

Lentil Stew

When you want a break from meat, try my hearty vegetarian stew. Adding the cream at the end gives it a smoother texture.
—**MICHELLE COLLINS** SUFFOLK, VA

PREP: 45 MIN. • **COOK:** 6 HOURS
MAKES: 8 SERVINGS (2¾ QUARTS)

- 2 large onions, thinly sliced, divided
- 2 tablespoons canola oil
- 2 tablespoons minced fresh gingerroot
- 3 garlic cloves, minced
- 8 plum tomatoes, chopped
- 2 teaspoons ground coriander
- 1½ teaspoons ground cumin
- ¼ teaspoon cayenne pepper
- 3 cups vegetable broth
- 2 cups water
- 2 cups dried lentils, rinsed
- 1 can (4 ounces) chopped green chilies
- ¾ cup heavy whipping cream
- 2 tablespoons butter
- 1 teaspoon cumin seeds
- 6 cups hot cooked basmati or jasmine rice
   Sliced green onions or minced fresh cilantro, optional

1. In a large skillet, saute half of the onions in oil until tender. Add the ginger and garlic; saute for 1 minute. Add the tomatoes, coriander, cumin and cayenne; cook and stir 5 minutes longer.

2. In a 4- or 5-qt. slow cooker, combine the vegetable broth, water, lentils, green chilies, tomato mixture and remaining onion. Cover and cook on low for 6-8 hours or until the lentils are tender.

3. Just before serving, stir cream into slow cooker. In a small skillet, heat the butter over medium heat. Add the cumin seeds; cook and stir for 1-2 minutes or until golden brown. Add to the lentil mixture.

4. To serve, spoon over the rice. Sprinkle with green onions or cilantro if desired.

Mulligatawny Soup

I learned to cook and bake from my mom and grandmother, and always try to use fresh fruits, vegetables and herbs. This is a delicious and satisfying soup that I make with leftover chicken, turkey and sometimes beef, pork or lamb.

—**MARY ANN MARINO** WEST PITTSBURGH, PA

PREP: 20 MIN. • **COOK:** 6 HOURS
MAKES: 8 SERVINGS (2 QUARTS)

1 carton (32 ounces) chicken broth
1 can (14½ ounces) diced tomatoes
2 cups cubed cooked chicken
1 large tart apple, peeled and chopped
¼ cup finely chopped onion
¼ cup chopped carrot
¼ cup chopped green pepper
1 tablespoon minced fresh parsley
2 teaspoons lemon juice
1 teaspoon salt
1 teaspoon curry powder
½ teaspoon sugar
¼ teaspoon pepper
2 whole cloves

In a 3- or 4-qt. slow cooker, combine all ingredients. Cover and cook on low for 6-8 hours or until vegetables are tender. Discard cloves.

MULLIGATAWNY SOUP

Vegetarian Chili Ole!

I combine ingredients for this hearty chili the night before, start my trusty slow cooker in the morning and come home to a rich, spicy meal at night!

—**MARJORIE AU** HONOLULU, HI

PREP: 35 MIN. • **COOK:** 6 HOURS • **MAKES:** 7 SERVINGS

- 1 can (16 ounces) kidney beans, rinsed and drained
- 1 can (15 ounces) black beans, rinsed and drained
- 1 can (14½ ounces) diced tomatoes, undrained
- 1½ cups frozen corn
- 1 large onion, chopped
- 1 medium zucchini, chopped
- 1 medium sweet red pepper, chopped
- 1 can (4 ounces) chopped green chilies
- 1 ounce Mexican chocolate, chopped
- 1 cup water
- 1 can (6 ounces) tomato paste
- 1 tablespoon cornmeal
- 1 tablespoon chili powder
- ½ teaspoon salt
- ½ teaspoon dried oregano
- ½ teaspoon ground cumin
- ¼ teaspoon hot pepper sauce, optional

  Optional toppings: diced tomatoes, chopped green onions and crumbled queso fresco

1. In a 4-qt. slow cooker, combine the first nine ingredients. Combine the water, tomato paste, cornmeal, chili powder, salt, oregano, cumin and pepper sauce if desired until smooth; stir into slow cooker. Cover and cook on low for 6-8 hours or until vegetables are tender.

2. Serve with toppings of your choice.

VEGETARIAN CHILI OLE!

NAVY BEAN DINNER

Navy Bean Dinner

This is one of my favorite recipes because the chili simmers all day long. When your hungry clan comes home for dinner, you can ladle up steaming bowlfuls in a hurry.

—**LANA RUTLEDGE** SHEPHERDSVILLE, KY

PREP: 5 MIN. • **COOK:** 8 HOURS
MAKES: 12 SERVINGS (3 QUARTS)

- 2 medium onions, chopped
- 4 garlic cloves, minced
- 2 quarts water
- 3 pounds chicken breasts or thighs, skin removed
- 1 pound dried navy beans
- 2 cans (4 ounces each) chopped green chilies
- 1 tablespoon ground cumin
- 2 teaspoons dried oregano
- 1 teaspoon salt, optional
- ½ to 1 teaspoon cayenne pepper
- ½ teaspoon ground cloves
- 2 chicken bouillon cubes
  Shredded Monterey Jack cheese, optional
  Sour cream, optional
  Minced chives and crushed red pepper flakes

1. Place the onions and garlic in a 5-qt. slow cooker. Add the next 10 ingredients; do not stir. Cook on high for 8-10 hours.

2. Uncover and stir (the meat should fall off the bones). Remove bones. Stir to break up the meat. Spoon into bowls; top with cheese and sour cream if desired. Sprinkle with chives and red pepper flakes.

Hearty Split Pea Soup

We started a 39-day soup challenge to eat healthfully, figuring if TV's *Survivor* contestants could last for 39 days on little food, surely we could survive on soup! This was a family favorite.

—**DEBRA KEIL** OWASSO, OK

PREP: 30 MIN. • **COOK:** 7 HOURS
MAKES: 6 SERVINGS (2¼ QUARTS)

- 1 large onion, chopped
- 1 cup chopped celery
- 1 cup chopped fresh carrots
- 2 tablespoons olive oil
- 1 teaspoon dried thyme
- 1 package (16 ounces) dried green split peas, rinsed
- 4 cups vegetable broth
- 2 cups water
- 6 ounces Canadian bacon, chopped
- ¼ teaspoon pepper

1. In a large skillet, saute the onion, celery and carrots in oil until tender. Add thyme; cook 1 minute longer.
2. Transfer to a 5-qt. slow cooker. Add the peas, broth and water. Cover and cook on low for 7-8 hours or until the peas are tender.
3. Cool slightly. In a blender, process half of the soup until smooth. Return all to the slow cooker. Add the bacon and pepper; heat through.

Gyro Soup

If you're a fan of lamb, don't pass up this Greek-style soup. Seasoned with classic flavors of rosemary, marjoram and mint, it will transport you straight to the Mediterranean!

—**BRIDGET KLUSMAN** OTSEGO, MI

PREP: 25 MIN. • **COOK:** 6 HOURS •**MAKES:** 6 SERVINGS

- 2 pounds ground lamb
- 5 cups water
- 1 can (14½ ounces) diced tomatoes, undrained
- 1 medium onion, chopped
- ¼ cup red wine
- 3 tablespoons minced fresh mint or 1 tablespoon dried mint
- 6 garlic cloves, minced
- 1 tablespoon dried marjoram
- 1 tablespoon dried rosemary, crushed
- 2 teaspoons salt
- ½ teaspoon pepper
  Optional toppings: plain Greek yogurt and crumbled feta cheese

1. In a large skillet, cook lamb over medium heat until no longer pink; drain. Transfer to a 4- or 5-qt. slow cooker. Add the water, tomatoes, onion, wine, mint, garlic, marjoram, rosemary, salt and pepper. Cover and cook on low for 6-8 hours or until flavors are blended.
2. Serve with yogurt and feta cheese if desired.

HEARTY SPLIT PEA SOUP

Herbed Chicken & Spinach Soup

I love this dish because it combines some of my favorite ingredients, such as savory spices, kidney beans and fresh spinach. To create a hearty meal, I like to eat the chicken soup with a side of crusty bread slathered in butter.

—TANYA MACDONALD
ANTIGONISH COUNTY, NS

PREP: 20 MIN. • **COOK:** 4½ HOURS
MAKES: 4 SERVINGS

- 1 **pound boneless skinless chicken thighs, cut into ½-inch pieces**
- 1 **can (16 ounces) kidney beans, rinsed and drained**
- 1 **can (14½ ounces) chicken broth**
- 1 **medium onion, chopped**
- 1 **medium sweet red pepper, chopped**
- 1 **celery rib, chopped**
- 2 **tablespoons tomato paste**
- 3 **garlic cloves, minced**
- ½ **teaspoon minced fresh rosemary or ¼ teaspoon dried rosemary, crushed**
- ½ **teaspoon minced fresh thyme or ¼ teaspoon dried thyme**
- ½ **teaspoon dried oregano**
- ¼ **teaspoon salt**
- ¼ **teaspoon pepper**
- 3 **cups fresh baby spinach**
- ¼ **cup shredded Parmesan cheese**

In a 3-qt. slow cooker, combine the first 13 ingredients. Cover and cook on low for 4-5 hours or until chicken is tender. Stir in spinach; cook for 30 minutes longer or until spinach is wilted. Top with cheese.

SWEET & SAVORY SLOW-COOKED BEEF

Sweet & Savory Slow-Cooked Beef

There's plenty of sweet and a little heat from the chipotle pepper in this family-friendly shredded beef. Add your favorite barbecue sauce or stir things up every time you make it by varying the flavor to see which way you like it best.

—DAVID KLEIMAN NEW BEDFORD, MA

PREP: 20 MIN. • **COOK:** 8½ HOURS
MAKES: 16 SERVINGS

- 1 **beef top round roast (4 pounds)**
- 1 **bottle (18 ounces) barbecue sauce**
- ½ **cup water**
- ¼ **cup packed brown sugar**
- 1 **chipotle pepper in adobo sauce, chopped**
- 2 **tablespoons Worcestershire sauce**
- 2 **tablespoons steak sauce**
- 1½ **teaspoons reduced-sodium soy sauce**
- 1 **teaspoon celery salt**
- 1 **teaspoon garlic salt**
- 1 **teaspoon seasoned salt**
- 1 **teaspoon pepper**
- 16 **onion rolls, split**

1. Cut roast in half; place in a 6-qt. slow cooker. Combine the barbecue sauce, water, brown sugar, chipotle pepper, Worcestershire sauce, steak sauce, soy sauce and seasonings. Pour over meat.

2. Cover and cook on low for 8-10 hours or until meat is tender. Remove roast and cool slightly. Skim fat from cooking juices. Shred meat with two forks and return to slow cooker; heat through. Serve on rolls.

NOTE *Wear disposable gloves when cutting hot peppers; the oils can burn skin. Avoid touching your face.*

top tip Spicy Situation

Chipotle peppers are dried, smoked jalapeno peppers that lend a sweet and smoky flavor to recipes. When dried, the peppers look brown and leathery, but in the thin, tomato-based adobe sauce they have a reddish appearance.

TANYA MACDONALD'S
HERBED CHICKEN & SPINACH SOUP

Spring

DESSERTS

Slow cookers aren't just for savory dishes anymore! Check out this colorful selection of sweet treats featuring the season's freshest berries, fruits and more!

SHERRY NIESE'S RAISIN BREAD PUDDING

Raisin Bread Pudding

A homemade vanilla sauce goes together quickly on the stovetop and provides a yummy drizzle over warm servings of this old-fashioned-tasting treat. My sister gave me the recipe for the delicious bread pudding that's dotted with raisins. It's a big hit with everyone who's tried it.

—**SHERRY NIESE** MCCOMB, OH

PREP: 15 MIN. • **COOK:** 3 HOURS • **MAKES:** 6 SERVINGS

- 8 slices bread, cubed
- 4 eggs
- 2 cups milk
- ¼ cup sugar
- ¼ cup butter, melted
- ¼ cup raisins
- ½ teaspoon ground cinnamon

SAUCE
- 2 tablespoons butter
- 2 tablespoons all-purpose flour
- 1 cup water
- ¾ cup sugar
- 1 teaspoon vanilla extract

1. Place bread cubes in a greased 3-qt. slow cooker. In a large bowl, beat eggs and milk; stir in the sugar, butter, raisins and cinnamon. Pour over bread; stir.
2. Cover and cook on high for 1 hour. Reduce heat to low; cook for 3-4 hours or until a thermometer reads 160°.
3. Just before serving, melt butter in a saucepan. Stir in flour until smooth. Gradually add water, sugar and vanilla. Bring to a boil; cook and stir for 2 minutes or until thickened. Serve with warm bread pudding.

Butterscotch Apple Crisp

I give this classic dessert a rich twist with butterscotch pudding. The warm apple filling bubbles to perfection in a mini slow cooker.

—**JOLANTHE ERB** HARRISONBURG, VA

PREP: 10 MIN. • **COOK:** 2½ HOURS • **MAKES:** 3 SERVINGS

- 3 cups thinly sliced peeled tart apples (about 3 medium)
- ⅓ cup packed brown sugar
- ¼ cup all-purpose flour
- ¼ cup quick-cooking oats
- ⅓ cup cook-and-serve butterscotch pudding mix
- ½ teaspoon ground cinnamon
- ¼ cup cold butter, cubed
  Vanilla ice cream, optional

1. Place apples in a 1½-qt. slow cooker. In a small bowl, combine the brown sugar, flour, oats, pudding mix and cinnamon. Cut in butter until mixture resembles coarse crumbs. Sprinkle over apples.
2. Cover and cook on low for 2½ to 3½ hours or until apples are tender. Serve with ice cream if desired.

top tip Tasty Treatments

Don't be afraid to get creative with the recipe for Chocolate-Raspberry Fondue. Add in a drop of coconut extract or stir in a tablespoon of butterscotch ice cream topping. Replace the raspberry jam with strawberry. Or, if the combination of chocolate and orange is appealing, try some orange marmalade in the mixture instead.
—**JILL B.** MADISON, MI

⑤ INGREDIENTS Chunky Applesauce

Serve this warm classic standby with a scoop of ice cream for dessert. My mother gave me the recipe for the cinnamony apple delight. Simmering it in a slow cooker fills the house with a wonderful aroma.
—**LISA ROESSNER** FORT RECOVERY, OH

PREP: 5 MIN. • **COOK:** 6 HOURS • **MAKES:** 5 CUPS

- 8 to 10 large tart apples, peeled and cut into chunks
  Sugar substitute equivalent to ½ to 1 cup sugar
- ½ cup water
- 1 teaspoon ground cinnamon

Combine apples, sugar, water and cinnamon in a 3-qt. slow cooker; stir gently. Cover and cook on low for 6-8 hours or until apples are tender.

CHOCOLATE-RASPBERRY FONDUE

Chocolate-Raspberry Fondue

You don't need a fancy fondue pot to make this melt-in-your-mouth concoction—just grab your slow cooker! Folks of all ages adore the chocolate-raspberry combination.
—**HEATHER MAXWELL** FORT RILEY, KS

START TO FINISH: 15 MIN. • **MAKES:** 5 CUPS

- 1 package (14 ounces) caramels
- 2 cups (12 ounces) semisweet chocolate chips
- 1 can (12 ounces) evaporated milk
- ½ cup butter
- ½ cup seedless raspberry jam
  Frozen pound cake, thawed
  Assorted fresh fruit

1. In a large saucepan, combine the first five ingredients. Cook over low heat until caramels, chips and butter are melted, about 15 minutes. Stir until smooth.
2. Transfer to a 1½-qt. slow cooker. Serve warm with pound cake or fruit.

CHUNKY APPLESAUCE

TROPICAL COMPOTE DESSERT

Tropical Compote Dessert

To make a more adult version of this recipe, use brandy instead of the extra tropical fruit juice.

—**TASTE OF HOME TEST KITCHEN**

PREP: 15 MIN. • **COOK:** 2¼ HOURS
MAKES: 6 SERVINGS

- 1 **jar (24 ounces) mixed tropical fruit**
- 1 **jalapeno pepper, seeded and chopped**
- ¼ **cup sugar**
- 1 **tablespoon chopped crystallized ginger**
- ¼ **teaspoon ground cinnamon**
- 1 **can (15 ounces) mandarin oranges, drained**
- 1 **jar (6 ounces) maraschino cherries, drained**
- 1 **medium firm banana, sliced**
- 6 **individual round sponge cakes**
- 6 **tablespoons flaked coconut, toasted**

1. Drain tropical fruit, reserving ¼ cup liquid. Combine tropical fruit and jalapeno in a 1½-qt. slow cooker. Combine the sugar, ginger, cinnamon and reserved juice; pour over fruit. Cover and cook on low for 2 hours. Stir in the mandarin oranges, cherries and banana; cook 15 minutes longer.

2. Place sponge cakes on dessert plates; top with compote. Sprinkle with coconut.

NOTE *Wear disposable gloves when cutting hot peppers; the oils can burn skin. Avoid touching your face.*

Chocolate Malt Pudding Cake

When I make this warm, comforting cake, I "chop" the malted milk balls by putting them in a plastic bag and pounding it with a rubber mallet. It completely eliminates the mess.

—**SARAH SKUBINNA** CASCADE, MT

PREP: 25 MIN.
COOK: 2 HOURS + STANDING
MAKES: 8 SERVINGS

- ½ **cup 2% milk**
- 2 **tablespoons canola oil**
- ½ **teaspoon almond extract**
- 1 **cup all-purpose flour**
- ½ **cup packed brown sugar**
- 2 **tablespoons baking cocoa**
- 1½ **teaspoons baking powder**
- ½ **cup coarsely chopped malted milk balls**
- ½ **cup semisweet chocolate chips**
- ¾ **cup sugar**
- ¼ **cup malted milk powder**
- 1¼ **cups boiling water**
- 4 **ounces cream cheese, softened and cubed**
     Vanilla ice cream and sliced almonds

1. In a large bowl, combine milk, oil and extract. Combine flour, brown sugar, cocoa and baking powder; gradually beat into milk mixture until blended. Stir in malted milk balls and chocolate chips.

2. Spoon into a greased 3-qt. slow cooker. In a small bowl, combine sugar and milk powder; stir in water and cream cheese. Pour over batter (do not stir).

3. Cover and cook on high for 2-3 hours or until a toothpick inserted in center of cake comes out clean. Turn off heat. Let stand 15 minutes.

Serve warm with ice cream; sprinkle with almonds.

⑤ INGREDIENTS
Butterscotch Dip

If you like the sweetness of butterscotch chips, you'll enjoy this warm, rum-flavored fruit dip. I serve it with apple and pear wedges. It holds up for up to 2 hours in the slow cooker.

—**JEAUNE HADL VAN METER** LEXINGTON, KY

PREP: 5 MIN. • **COOK:** 45 MIN.
MAKES: ABOUT 3 CUPS

- 2 **packages (10 to 11 ounces each) butterscotch chips**
- ⅔ **cup evaporated milk**
- ⅔ **cup chopped pecans**
- 1 **tablespoon rum extract**
     Apple and pear wedges

In a 1½-qt. slow cooker, combine butterscotch chips and milk. Cover and cook on low for 45-50 minutes or until chips are softened; stir until smooth. Stir in pecans and extract. Serve warm with fruit.

BUTTERSCOTCH DIP

ELVIS' PUDDING CAKE

Bread Pudding with Bourbon Sauce

There's nothing I like better than this comforting bread pudding after a busy day. The bourbon sauce makes the dessert seem special, but you wouldn't believe how easy it is to prepare—the slow cooker does most of the work!

—HOPE JOHNSON YOUNGWOOD, PA

PREP: 20 MIN. • **COOK:** 3 HOURS
MAKES: 6 SERVINGS

- 3 eggs
- 1¼ cups 2% milk
- ½ cup sugar
- 3 teaspoons vanilla extract
- ½ teaspoon ground cinnamon
- ¼ teaspoon ground nutmeg
- ⅛ teaspoon salt
- 4½ cups cubed day-old brioche or egg bread
- 1¼ cups raisins

BOURBON SAUCE
- ¼ cup butter, cubed
- ½ cup sugar
- ¼ cup light corn syrup
- 3 tablespoons bourbon

1. In a large bowl, whisk the first seven ingredients; stir in bread and raisins. Transfer to a greased 4-qt. slow cooker. Cover and cook on low for 3 hours.

2. In a small saucepan, heat butter. Stir in sugar and corn syrup; bring to a boil. Reduce heat; cook and stir until sugar is dissolved. Remove from the heat; stir in bourbon. Serve warm with bread pudding.

BREAD PUDDING WITH BOURBON SAUCE

"I love the flavors of peanut butter and banana together, and this slow cooker pudding cake is just like eating an Elvis sandwich...only sweeter! Banana chips add a surprisingly crunchy texture—find them near the dried fruit in your grocery store."

—**LISA RENSHAW** KANSAS CITY, MO

Elvis' Pudding Cake

PREP: 10 MIN.
COOK: 3 HOURS + STANDING
MAKES: 12 SERVINGS

- 3 cups cold 2% milk
- 1 package (3.4 ounces) instant banana cream pudding mix
- 1 package banana cake mix (regular size)
- ½ cup creamy peanut butter
- 2 cups peanut butter chips
- 1 cup chopped dried banana chips

1. In a small bowl, whisk milk and pudding mix for 2 minutes. Let stand for 2 minutes or until soft-set. Transfer to a greased 5-qt. slow cooker.

2. Prepare cake mix batter according to package directions, adding peanut butter before mixing. Pour over the pudding. Cover and cook on low for 3 to 3½ hours or until a toothpick inserted near the center comes out with moist crumbs.

3. Sprinkle with peanut butter chips; cover and let stand for 15-20 minutes or until partially melted. Top with banana chips.

DESSERTS

Spring

Pink Grapefruit Cheesecake

Cheesecake from a slow cooker? It's true! I experimented a few times to turn this iconic dessert into a slow-cooker classic!

—**KRISTA LANPHIER** MILWAUKEE, WI

PREP: 20 MIN. • **COOK:** 2 HOURS + CHILLING
MAKES: 6 SERVINGS

- ¾ cup graham cracker crumbs
- 1 tablespoon plus ⅔ cup sugar, divided
- 1 teaspoon grated grapefruit peel
- ¼ teaspoon ground ginger
- 2½ tablespoons butter, melted
- 2 packages (8 ounces each) cream cheese, softened
- ½ cup sour cream
- 2 tablespoons pink grapefruit juice
- 2 eggs, lightly beaten

1. Place a greased 6-in. springform pan on a double thickness of heavy-duty foil (about 12-in. square.) Wrap foil securely around pan. Pour 1 in. of water into a 6-qt. slow cooker. Layer two 24-in. pieces of aluminum foil. Starting with a long side, fold up foil to create a 1-in. wide strip; roll into a coil. Place in slow cooker to form a rack for the cheesecake.

2. In a small bowl, mix cracker crumbs, 1 tablespoon sugar, peel and ginger; stir in butter. Press onto bottom and about 1 in. up sides of prepared pan.

3. In a large bowl, beat cream cheese and remaining sugar until smooth. Beat in sour cream and grapefruit juice. Add eggs and beat on low speed just until combined.
Pour into crust. Place springform pan on top of coil. Cover slow cooker with a double layer of paper towels; place lid securely over towels. Cook, covered, on high 2 hours. Do not remove lid; turn off slow cooker and let cheesecake stand, covered, in slow cooker 1 hour. Center of cheesecake will be just set and top will appear dull.

4. Carefully remove springform pan from slow cooker; remove foil from pan. Cool cheesecake on a wire rack for 1 hour. Loosen sides from pan with a knife. Refrigerate overnight, covering after completely cooled. Remove the rim from pan.

Rice Pudding

For an old-fashioned sweet treat just like Grandma made, try my rich and delicious rice pudding.

—**JENNIFER BENNETT** SALEM, IN

PREP: 15 MIN. • **COOK:** 3 HOURS + CHILLING
MAKES: 4 SERVINGS

- 1¼ cups 2% milk
- ½ cup sugar
- ½ cup uncooked converted rice
- ½ cup raisins
- 2 eggs, lightly beaten
- 1 teaspoon ground cinnamon
- 1 teaspoon butter, melted
- 1 teaspoon vanilla extract
- ¾ teaspoon lemon extract
- 1 cup heavy whipping cream, whipped
- Additional whipped cream and ground cinnamon, optional

1. In a 1½-qt. slow cooker, combine the first nine ingredients. Cover and cook on low for 2 hours; stir. Cover and cook 1-2 hours longer or until rice is tender.

2. Transfer to a small bowl; cool. Refrigerate until chilled.

3. Just before serving, fold in whipped cream. If desired, garnish with additional whipped cream and cinnamon.

RICE PUDDING

Granola Apple Crisp

Tender apple slices are tucked beneath a sweet crunchy topping in my comforting dessert. For variety, replace the apples with your favorite spring fruit.

—BARBARA SCHINDLER NAPOLEON, OH

PREP: 20 MIN. • **COOK:** 5 HOURS • **MAKES:** 6-8 SERVINGS

> 8 medium tart apples, peeled and sliced
> ¼ cup lemon juice
> 1½ teaspoons grated lemon peel
> 2½ cups granola with fruit and nuts
> 1 cup sugar
> 1 teaspoon ground cinnamon
> ½ cup butter, melted

1. In a large bowl, toss the apples, lemon juice and peel. Transfer to a greased 3-qt. slow cooker. Combine the granola, sugar and cinnamon; sprinkle over apples. Drizzle with butter.

2. Cover and cook on low for 5-6 hours or until the apples are tender. Serve warm.

CHOCOLATE BREAD PUDDING

GRANOLA APPLE CRISP

Chocolate Bread Pudding

I love chocolate and I love berries, so I was thrilled to come across this recipe that combines the two. I like to use egg bread when making this dessert.

—BECKY FOSTER UNION, OR

PREP: 5 MIN. • **COOK:** 2¼ HOURS • **MAKES:** 6-8 SERVINGS

> 6 cups cubed day-old bread (¾-inch cubes)
> 1½ cups semisweet chocolate chips
> 1 cup fresh raspberries
> 4 eggs
> ½ cup heavy whipping cream
> ½ cup milk
> ¼ cup sugar
> 1 teaspoon vanilla extract
> Whipped cream and additional raspberries, optional

1. In a greased 3-qt. slow cooker, layer half of the bread cubes, chocolate chips and raspberries. Repeat layers. In a bowl, whisk the eggs, cream, milk, sugar and vanilla. Pour over bread mixture.

2. Cover and cook on high for 2¼ to 2½ hours or until a thermometer reads 160°. Let stand for 5-10 minutes. Serve with whipped cream and additional raspberries if desired.

Pear-Blueberry Granola

Oatmeal fans will love this dish. It's a delicious dessert when served with vanilla ice cream, but the pears, blueberries and granola make a beautiful breakfast item, too.

—LISA WORKMAN BOONES MILL, VA

PREP: 15 MIN. • **COOK:** 3 HOURS • **MAKES:** 10 SERVINGS

- 5 medium pears, peeled and thinly sliced
- 2 cups fresh or frozen unsweetened blueberries
- ½ cup packed brown sugar
- ⅓ cup apple cider or unsweetend apple juice
- 1 tablespoon all-purpose flour
- 1 tablespoon lemon juice
- 2 teaspoons ground cinnamon
- 2 tablespoons butter
- 3 cups granola without raisins

In a 4-qt. slow cooker, combine the first seven ingredients. Dot with butter. Sprinkle granola over top. Cover and cook on low for 3-4 hours or until fruit is tender.

PEAR-BLUEBERRY GRANOLA

NUTTY APPLE STREUSEL DESSERT

Nutty Apple Streusel Dessert

Many people don't think of using a slow cooker to make dessert, but I like finishing up our dinner and having this hot, scrumptious treat waiting to be served up. I can start it in the morning and not think about it all day.

—JACKI EVERY ROTTERDAM, NY

PREP: 20 MIN. • **BAKE:** 6 HOURS • **MAKES:** 6-8 SERVINGS

- 6 cups sliced peeled tart apples
- 1¼ teaspoons ground cinnamon
- ¼ teaspoon ground allspice
- ¼ teaspoon ground nutmeg
- ¾ cup 2% milk
- 2 tablespoons butter, softened
- ¾ cup sugar
- 2 eggs
- 1 teaspoon vanilla extract
- ½ cup biscuit/baking mix

TOPPING
- 1 cup biscuit/baking mix
- ⅓ cup packed brown sugar
- 3 tablespoons cold butter
- ½ cup sliced almonds
   Ice cream or whipped cream, optional

1. In a large bowl, toss apples with cinnamon, allspice and nutmeg. Place in a greased 3-qt. slow cooker. In a small bowl, combine the milk, butter, sugar, eggs, vanilla and baking mix. Spoon over apples.

2. For topping, combine biscuit mix and brown sugar in a large bowl; cut in butter until crumbly. Add almonds; sprinkle over apples.

3. Cover and cook on low for 6-8 hours or until the apples are tender. Serve with ice cream or whipped cream if desired.

CHERRY COLA CHOCOLATE CAKE

Cherry Cola Chocolate Cake

For a truly different chocolate cake, think outside the box and inside the slow cooker! This dessert comes out warm, moist, fudgy and wonderful. Best of all, it won't heat up the kitchen.
—ELAINE SWEET DALLAS, TX

PREP: 30 MIN. + STANDING • **COOK:** 2 HOURS + STANDING
MAKES: 8 SERVINGS

- ½ **cup cola**
- ½ **cup dried tart cherries**
- 1½ **cups all-purpose flour**
- ½ **cup sugar**
- 2 **ounces semisweet chocolate, chopped**
- 2½ **teaspoons baking powder**
- ½ **teaspoon salt**
- 1 **cup chocolate milk**
- ½ **cup butter, melted**
- 2 **teaspoons vanilla extract**

TOPPING

- 1¼ **cups cola**
- ½ **cup sugar**
- ½ **cup packed brown sugar**
- 2 **ounces semisweet chocolate, chopped**
- ¼ **cup dark rum**
  Vanilla ice cream and maraschino cherries, optional

1. In a small saucepan, bring cola and dried cherries to a boil. Remove from the heat; let stand for 30 minutes.
2. In a large bowl, combine the flour, sugar, chocolate, baking powder and salt. Combine the chocolate milk, butter and vanilla; stir into dry ingredients just until moistened. Fold in cherry mixture. Pour into a 3-qt. slow cooker coated with cooking spray.
3. For topping, in a small saucepan, combine the cola, sugar and brown sugar. Cook and stir until sugar is dissolved. Remove from the heat; stir in chocolate and rum until smooth. Pour over batter; do not stir.
4. Cover and cook on high for 2 to 2½ hours or until set. Turn off heat; let stand, covered, for 30 minutes. Serve warm with ice cream and maraschino cherries if desired.
NOTE *This recipe does not use eggs.*

"The flavors of caramel, rum and walnut naturally complement fresh bananas in this classic dessert made easy!" **—CRYSTAL BRUNS** ILIFF, CO

Bananas Foster

PREP: 10 MIN. • **COOK:** 2 HOURS • **MAKES:** 5 SERVINGS

- 5 **medium firm bananas**
- 1 **cup packed brown sugar**
- ¼ **cup butter, melted**
- ¼ **cup rum**
- 1 **teaspoon vanilla extract**
- ½ **teaspoon ground cinnamon**
- ⅓ **cup chopped walnuts**
- ⅓ **cup flaked coconut**
  Vanilla ice cream or sliced pound cake

1. Cut bananas in half lengthwise, then widthwise; layer in the bottom of a 1½-qt. slow cooker. Combine the brown sugar, butter, rum, vanilla and cinnamon; pour over bananas. Cover and cook on low for 1½ hours or until heated through.
2. Sprinkle with walnuts and coconut; cook 30 minutes longer. Serve with ice cream or pound cake.

CRYSTAL BRUNS'
BANANAS FOSTER

ESTELLA PETERSON'S
PEPPERONI PIZZA SOUP
page 168

Summer

Keep the kitchen cool and family meals hot with this warm-weather selection of slow-cooked favorites. Whether entertaining in the backyard, contributing to a block party or just whipping up a weeknight dinner, these summertime recipes promise to spice up any menu!

Summer

APPETIZERS & BEVERAGES

Summer brings with it friendly barbecues, tailgates, church picnics and neighborhood parties. Thanks to these slow-cooked snacks, you can enjoy these get-togethers without much effort!

**LISA FRANCIS'
PEPPERONI PIZZA DIP**

Pepperoni Pizza Dip

This dip is so easy to make and transport. You won't have to worry about keeping it warm for long, because it'll be gone in a flash! It's a great appetizer for a backyard barbecue.
—**LISA FRANCIS** ELBA, AL

PREP: 20 MIN. • **COOK:** 2½ HOURS • **MAKES:** 5 CUPS

- 4 cups (16 ounces) shredded cheddar cheese
- 4 cups (16 ounces) shredded part-skim mozzarella cheese
- 1 cup mayonnaise
- 1 jar (6 ounces) sliced mushrooms, drained
- 2 cans (2¼ ounces each) sliced ripe olives, drained
- 1 package (3½ ounces) pepperoni slices, quartered
- 1 tablespoon dried minced onion
  Assorted crackers

1. In a 3-qt. slow cooker, combine the cheeses, mayonnaise, mushrooms, olives, pepperoni and onion.
2. Cover and cook on low for 1½ hours; stir. Cover and cook 1 hour longer or until heated through. Serve with crackers.

Slow-Cooked Italian Meatballs

What I love about these versatile meatballs is that they can be served as an appetizer right out of the slow cooker or alongside your favorite pasta. They also make a delicious sandwich.
—**JASON ROMANO** DOWNINGTOWN, PA

PREP: 50 MIN. • **COOK:** 3 HOURS • **MAKES:** ABOUT 5 DOZEN

- 2 tablespoons olive oil
- 1 small onion, finely chopped
- 3 garlic cloves, minced
- 1 cup Italian-style panko (Japanese) bread crumbs
- 2 eggs, lightly beaten
- ½ cup grated Parmesan cheese
- ½ cup minced fresh parsley
- ¼ cup water
- ¼ cup minced fresh basil
- 2 tablespoons Worcestershire sauce
- ½ teaspoon salt
- ½ teaspoon pepper
- 1 pound ground beef
- ½ pound ground pork
- ½ pound ground veal
- 4 cups spaghetti sauce

1. Preheat oven to 400°. In a small skillet, heat oil over medium heat. Add onion and garlic; cook 5-9 minutes or until onion is tender and golden brown. Cool slightly.
2. In a large bowl, combine bread crumbs, eggs, cheese, parsley, water and seasonings. Add ground meats; mix lightly but thoroughly. Shape into 1-in. balls. Place on greased racks in shallow baking pans. Bake 20-25 minutes or until browned.
3. Transfer meatballs to a 4- or 5-qt. slow cooker. Pour spaghetti sauce over top. Cook, covered, on low for 3-4 hours or until meatballs are cooked through.

Sunny Ambrosia Punch

Inspired by the spices in chai, this unique twist on basic spiced cider punch is a favorite. It's so easy to make and everyone seems wonderfully surprised by the summery apricot and peach flavors.

—**AYSHA SCHURMAN** AMMON, ID

PREP: 15 MIN. • **COOK:** 3 HOURS
MAKES: 10 SERVINGS (¾ CUP EACH)

- 3½ cups apple cider or juice
- 3 cups apricot nectar
- 1 cup peach nectar or additional apricot nectar
- ¼ cup water
- 3 tablespoons lemon juice
- ½ teaspoon ground cardamom
- ½ teaspoon ground nutmeg
- 2 cinnamon sticks (3 inches)
- 1 teaspoon finely chopped fresh gingerroot
- 1 teaspoon grated orange peel
- 8 whole cloves
  Lemon or orange slices, optional

1. In a 3- or 4-qt. slow cooker, combine the first seven ingredients. Place cinnamon sticks, ginger, orange peel and cloves on a double thickness of cheesecloth. Gather corners of cloth to enclose seasonings; tie securely with string. Place bag in slow cooker.

2. Cook, covered, on low 3-4 hours or until heated through. Remove and discard spice bag. If desired, serve with lemon slices.

GREEN OLIVE DIP

Green Olive Dip

Olive fans will love this dip. It's cheesy and full of beef and beans. I like to use it as a festive filling for taco shells, too.

—**BETH DUNAHAY** LIMA, OH

PREP: 30 MIN. • **COOK:** 3 HOURS • **MAKES:** 8 CUPS

- 1 pound ground beef
- 1 medium sweet red pepper, chopped
- 1 small onion, chopped
- 1 can (16 ounces) refried beans
- 1 jar (16 ounces) mild salsa
- 2 cups (8 ounces) shredded part-skim mozzarella cheese
- 2 cups (8 ounces) shredded cheddar cheese
- 1 jar (5¾ ounces) sliced green olives with pimientos, drained
  Tortilla chips

1. In a large skillet, cook the beef, pepper and onion over medium heat until meat is no longer pink; drain.

2. Transfer to a greased 3-qt. slow cooker. Add the beans, salsa, cheeses and olives. Cover and cook on low for 3-4 hours or until cheese is melted, stirring occasionally. Serve with chips.

SUNNY AMBROSIA PUNCH

½ cup finely chopped fresh carrot
½ cup finely chopped red onion
½ cup finely chopped celery
2 garlic cloves, minced
4 tablespoons olive oil, divided
1 can (14 ounces) water-packed
   artichoke hearts, rinsed, drained
   and chopped
1 package (6½ ounces) spreadable
   garlic and herb cream cheese
1 package (1.4 ounces) vegetable
   recipe mix (Knorr)
1 teaspoon garlic powder
½ teaspoon white pepper
⅛ to ¼ teaspoon cayenne pepper
¼ cup vegetable broth
¼ cup half-and-half cream
3 cups (12 ounces) shredded Italian
   cheese blend
½ cup minced fresh basil
1 package (9 ounces) fresh spinach,
   finely chopped
   Assorted crackers or baked pita
   chips

1. In a large skillet, saute the broccoli, cauliflower, carrot, onion, celery and garlic in 2 tablespoons oil until tender. Stir in the artichokes, cream cheese, vegetable recipe mix, garlic powder, white pepper and cayenne; set aside.
2. In a 3-qt. slow cooker, combine the broth, cream and remaining oil. Stir in the broccoli mixture, Italian cheese blend and basil. Fold in spinach. Cover and cook on low for 1-2 hours or until cheese is melted and spinach is tender. Serve with crackers or pita chips.

HOT CHILI DIP

(5) INGREDIENTS
Hot Chili Dip
I first made this yummy dip for my husband's birthday party. So many people asked for the recipe that I photocopied it to pass out.
—**NIKKI ROSATI** FRANKSVILLE, WI

PREP: 5 MIN. • **COOK:** 1 HOUR
MAKES: ABOUT 2 CUPS

1 jar (24 ounces) salsa
1 can (15 ounces) chili with beans
2 cans (2¼ ounces each) sliced ripe
   olives, drained
12 ounces process cheese (Velveeta),
   cubed
   Tortilla chips

In a 1½-qt. slow cooker, combine the salsa, chili and olives. Stir in cheese. Cover and cook on low for 1-2 hours or until cheese is melted, stirring halfway through. Serve with chips.

Loaded Veggie Dip
Packed with veggies and bursting with flavor, this chunky dip promises to be a hit at your next party. Serve it with thick crackers that can be used as scoops.
—**PATRICE SLAUGHTER** PALM BAY, FL

PREP: 1 HOUR • **COOK:** 1 HOUR
MAKES: 5 CUPS

¾ cup finely chopped fresh broccoli
½ cup finely chopped cauliflower

 **Smart Shopping**

When purchasing fresh cauliflower, look for a head with compact florets that are free of yellow or brown spots. The leaves should be crisp and green, not withered or discolored. Tightly wrap an unwashed head of cauliflower and refrigerate for up to 5 days. Before using, wash and remove the leaves at the base and trim the stem.

Moist & Tender Wings

These no-fuss appetizers are fall-off-the-bone tender. Chili sauce offers a bit of spice, while molasses lends a hint of sweetness. Serve them with a side of rice, and you have a meal.

—SHARON MORCILIO JOSHUA TREE, CA

PREP: 15 MIN. • **COOK:** 8 HOURS
MAKES: ABOUT 4 DOZEN

- 5 **pounds chicken wings (about 25 wings)**
- 1 **bottle (12 ounces) chili sauce**
- ¼ **cup lemon juice**
- ¼ **cup molasses**
- 2 **tablespoons Worcestershire sauce**
- 6 **garlic cloves, minced**
- 1 **tablespoon chili powder**
- 1 **tablespoon salsa**
- 1 **teaspoon garlic salt**
- 3 **drops hot pepper sauce**

1. Cut chicken wings into three sections; discard wing tips. Place the wings in a 5-qt. slow cooker.

2. In a small bowl, combine the remaining ingredients; pour over chicken. Stir to coat. Cover and cook on low for 6-8 hours or until the chicken is tender.

NOTE *Uncooked chicken wing sections (wingettes) may be substituted for whole chicken wings.*

MOIST & TENDER WINGS

Makeover Creamy Artichoke Dip

Folks are sure to gather around this ooey-gooey dip whenever it's placed on the buffet table. It's a lightened-up take on a treasured family favorite.

—**MARY SPENCER** GREENDALE, WI

PREP: 20 MIN. • **COOK:** 1 HOUR • **MAKES:** 5 CUPS

- 2 **cans (14 ounces each) water-packed artichoke hearts, rinsed, drained and coarsely chopped**
- 1 **package (8 ounces) reduced-fat cream cheese, cubed**
- ¾ **cup (6 ounces) plain yogurt**
- 1 **cup (4 ounces) shredded part-skim mozzarella cheese**
- 1 **cup reduced-fat ricotta cheese**
- ¾ **cup shredded Parmesan cheese, divided**
- ½ **cup shredded reduced-fat Swiss cheese**
- ¼ **cup reduced-fat mayonnaise**
- 2 **tablespoons lemon juice**
- 1 **tablespoon chopped seeded jalapeno pepper**
- 1 **teaspoon garlic powder**
- 1 **teaspoon seasoned salt**
  Tortilla chips

1. In a 3-qt. slow cooker, combine the artichokes, cream cheese, yogurt, mozzarella cheese, ricotta cheese, ½ cup Parmesan cheese, Swiss cheese, mayonnaise, lemon juice, jalapeno, garlic powder and seasoned salt. Cover and cook on low for 1 hour or until heated through.

2. Sprinkle with remaining Parmesan cheese. Serve with tortilla chips.

NOTE *Wear disposable gloves when cutting hot peppers; the oils can burn skin. Avoid touching your face.*

MAKEOVER CREAMY ARTICHOKE DIP

Mocha Mint Coffee

My doctored-up coffee benefits from hints of mint, cocoa and cinnamon. The marshmallows on top are a playful addition that brings out the youngster in anyone.
—**MINDIE HILTON** SUSANVILLE, CA

PREP: 10 MIN. • **COOK:** 2 HOURS • **MAKES:** 8 SERVINGS

- 6 **cups hot brewed coffee**
- 2 **packets instant hot cocoa mix**
- ½ **cup dulce de leche**
- ¼ **cup peppermint crunch baking chips or mint chocolate chips**
- 4 **teaspoons sugar**
- 1 **cup miniature marshmallows**
- ½ **teaspoon ground cinnamon**

1. In a 3-qt. slow cooker, combine the coffee, hot cocoa mix, dulce de leche, baking chips and sugar. Cover and cook on low for 2-3 hours or until hot.

2. Ladle into mugs. Top with marshmallows; sprinkle with cinnamon.

NOTE *This recipe was tested with Nestle dulce de leche. Look for it in the international foods section.*

Hawaiian Kielbasa

Savory sausage teams up with tangy pineapple for a winning combination that you can prep in a flash. The sweet barbecue-style sauce is a tasty way to tie them together.
—**LOUISE KLINE** CARROLLTOWN, PA

PREP: 15 MIN. • **COOK:** 3 HOURS • **MAKES:** 12 SERVINGS

- 2 **pounds smoked kielbasa or Polish sausage, cut into 1-inch pieces**
- 1 **can (20 ounces) unsweetened pineapple chunks, undrained**
- ½ **cup ketchup**
- 2 **tablespoons brown sugar**
- 2 **tablespoons yellow mustard**
- 1 **tablespoon cider vinegar**
- ¾ **cup lemon-lime soda**
- 2 **tablespoons cornstarch**
- 2 **tablespoons cold water**

1. Place sausage in a 3- or 4-qt. slow cooker. Drain pineapple, reserving ¾ cup juice; set pineapple aside. In a small bowl, whisk the ketchup, brown sugar, mustard and vinegar. Stir in soda and reserved pineapple juice. Pour over sausage; stir to coat. Cover and cook on low for 2-3 hours or until heated through.

2. Stir in pineapple. In a small bowl, combine cornstarch and water until smooth. Stir into slow cooker. Cover and cook 30 minutes longer or until sauce is thickened. Serve with toothpicks.

SLOW COOKER CHEESE DIP

⑤INGREDIENTS Slow Cooker Cheese Dip

I brought this slightly spicy cheese dip to a gathering with friends, and it was a huge hit. The pork sausage provides the zip!
—**MARION BARTONE** CONNEAUT, OH

PREP: 15 MIN. • **COOK:** 4 HOURS • **MAKES:** 2 QUARTS

- 1 **pound ground beef**
- ½ **pound bulk spicy pork sausage**
- 2 **pounds process cheese (Velveeta), cubed**
- 2 **cans (10 ounces each) diced tomatoes and green chilies**
  Tortilla chips

1. In a large skillet, cook beef and sausage over medium heat until no longer pink; drain. Transfer to a 3- or 4-qt. slow cooker. Stir in cheese and tomatoes.

2. Cover and cook on low for 4-5 hours or until cheese is melted, stirring occasionally. Serve with tortilla chips.

NOTE *If you're planning on serving Slow Cooker Cheese Dip at a family get-together, make it ahead and freeze it. Then all you need to do is thaw and reheat it.*

TONI MENARD'S
SLOW-COOKED SALSA

Slow-Cooked Salsa

I love the fresh taste of homemade salsa, but as a working mother, I don't have much time to prepare it. So I came up with this slow-cooked version that practically makes itself!

—**TONI MENARD** LOMPOC, CA

PREP: 15 MIN. • **COOK:** 2½ HOURS + COOLING
MAKES: ABOUT 2 CUPS

- 10 plum tomatoes
- 2 garlic cloves
- 1 small onion, cut into wedges
- 2 jalapeno peppers
- ¼ cup cilantro leaves
- ½ teaspoon salt, optional

1. Core tomatoes. Cut a small slit in two tomatoes; insert a garlic clove into each slit. Place tomatoes and onion in a 3-qt. slow cooker.
2. Cut stems off jalapenos; remove seeds if a milder salsa is desired. Place jalapenos in the slow cooker.
3. Cover and cook on high for 2½ to 3 hours or until vegetables are softened (some may brown slightly); cool.
4. In a blender, combine the tomato mixture, cilantro and salt if desired; cover and process until blended. Refrigerate leftovers.
NOTE *Wear disposable gloves when cutting hot peppers; the oils can burn skin. Avoid touching your face.*

Tomato Fondue

Both the young and young at heart will gobble up my cheesy tomato fondue when served alongside bread cubes or even sliced hot dogs.

—**MARLENE MUCKENHIRN** DELANO, MN

START TO FINISH: 20 MIN.
MAKES: ABOUT 1 CUP

- 1 garlic clove, halved
- ½ cup condensed tomato soup, undiluted
- 1½ teaspoons ground mustard
- 1½ teaspoons Worcestershire sauce
- 10 slices process American cheese (Velveeta), cubed
- ¼ to ⅓ cup milk
- 1 package (16 ounces) miniature hot dogs or smoked sausage, warmed Cubed French bread

1. Rub garlic clove over the bottom and sides of a small fondue pot or a 1½-qt. slow cooker; discard garlic and set fondue pot aside.
2. In a small saucepan, combine the tomato soup, mustard and Worcestershire sauce; heat through. Stir in cheese until melted. Stir in milk; heat through.
3. Transfer to prepared fondue pot and keep warm. Serve with hot dogs and bread cubes.

Bacon Cheese Dip

I've tried several appetizer recipes before, but this one is a surefire people-pleaser. The thick dip has lots of bacon flavor and keeps friends happily munching.

—**SUZANNE WHITAKER** KNOXVILLE, TN

PREP: 15 MIN. • **COOK:** 2 HOURS
MAKES: 4 CUPS

- 2 packages (8 ounces each) cream cheese, cubed
- 4 cups (16 ounces) shredded cheddar cheese
- 1 cup half-and-half cream
- 2 teaspoons Worcestershire sauce
- 1 teaspoon dried minced onion
- 1 teaspoon prepared mustard
- 16 bacon strips, cooked and crumbled Tortilla chips or French bread slices

1. In a 1½-qt. slow cooker, combine the first six ingredients. Cover and cook on low for 2-3 hours or until cheeses are melted, stirring occasionally.
2. Just before serving, stir in bacon. Serve warm with tortilla chips or French bread slices.

BACON CHEESE DIP

CHEESE-TRIO ARTICHOKE & SPINACH DIP

Cheese-Trio Artichoke & Spinach Dip

No appetizer spread is complete without at least one amazing dip, and this is it! Creamy and chock-full of veggies, it will quickly become your new go-to appetizer.

—DIANE SPEARE KISSIMMEE, FL

PREP: 20 MIN. • **COOK:** 2 HOURS • **MAKES:** 4 CUPS

- 1 **cup chopped fresh mushrooms**
- 1 **tablespoon butter**
- 2 **garlic cloves, minced**
- 1½ **cups mayonnaise**
- 1 **package (8 ounces) cream cheese, softened**
- 1 **cup plus 2 tablespoons grated Parmesan cheese, divided**
- 1 **cup (4 ounces) shredded part-skim mozzarella cheese, divided**

- 1 **can (14 ounces) water-packed artichoke hearts, rinsed, drained and chopped**
- 1 **package (10 ounces) frozen chopped spinach, thawed and squeezed dry**
- ¼ **cup chopped sweet red pepper**
  Toasted French bread baguette slices

1. In a large skillet, saute mushrooms in butter until tender. Add garlic; cook 1 minute longer.

2. In a large bowl, combine the mayonnaise, cream cheese, 1 cup Parmesan cheese and ¾ cup mozzarella cheese. Add the mushroom mixture, artichokes, spinach and red pepper.

3. Transfer to a 3-qt slow cooker. Sprinkle with remaining cheeses. Cover and cook on low for 2-3 hours or until heated through. Serve with baguette slices.

Chai Tea

PREP: 20 MIN. • **COOK:** 8 HOURS
MAKES: 12 SERVINGS (3 QUARTS)

- 3½ ounces fresh gingerroot, peeled and thinly sliced
- 25 whole cloves
- 15 cardamom pods, crushed
- 3 cinnamon sticks (3 inches)
- 3 whole peppercorns
- 3½ quarts water
- 8 individual black tea bags
- 1 can (14 ounces) sweetened condensed milk

1. Place the ginger, cloves, cardamom, cinnamon sticks and peppercorns on a double thickness of cheesecloth; bring up corners of cloth and tie with string to form a bag. Add spice bag and water to a 5- or 6-qt. slow cooker. Cover and cook on low for 8 hours.
2. Add tea bags; cover and steep for 3-5 minutes. Discard tea bags and spice bag. Stir in milk; heat through. Serve warm.

SLOW COOKER PARTY MIX

Slow Cooker Party Mix

A nicely seasoned snack mix is always a party-time favorite. It's so crunchy and satisfying. For variety, substitute cashews for the peanuts. Try it any time of year.
—**DANA HUGHES** GRESHAM, OR

PREP: 5 MIN. • **COOK:** 1 HOUR • **MAKES:** ABOUT 3 QUARTS

- 4 cups Wheat Chex
- 4 cups Cheerios
- 3 cups pretzel sticks
- 1 can (12 ounces) salted peanuts
- ¼ cup butter, melted
- 2 to 3 tablespoons grated Parmesan cheese
- 1 teaspoon celery salt
- ½ to ¾ teaspoon seasoned salt

In a 5-qt. slow cooker, combine cereals, pretzels and peanuts. Combine the butter, cheese, celery salt and seasoned salt; drizzle over cereal mixture and mix well. Cover and cook on low for 1 to 1½ hours, stirring every 20 minutes. Serve warm or at room temperature.

CHAI TEA

SWEET & SPICY PEANUTS

Slow-Cooked Crab Dip

Slow-cooked dips are ideal for entertaining since they don't need much hands-on attention. These leftovers are great on top of baked potatoes next day.

—SUSAN D'AMORE WEST CHESTER, PA

PREP: 20 MIN. • **COOK:** 2 HOURS
MAKES: 2⅓ CUPS

- 1 package (8 ounces) cream cheese, softened
- 2 green onions, chopped
- ¼ cup chopped sweet red pepper
- 2 tablespoons minced fresh parsley
- 2 tablespoons mayonnaise
- 1 tablespoon Dijon mustard
- 1 teaspoon Worcestershire sauce
- ¼ teaspoon salt
- ¼ teaspoon pepper
- 2 cans (6 ounces each) lump crabmeat, drained
- 2 tablespoons capers, drained
  Dash hot pepper sauce
  Assorted crackers

1. In a 1½-qt. slow cooker, combine the first nine ingredients; stir in crab.
2. Cover and cook on low for 1-2 hours. Stir in capers and pepper sauce; cook 30 minutes longer to allow flavors to blend. Serve with crackers.

Sweet & Spicy Peanuts

With a caramel-like coating, these crunchy peanuts have a touch of heat from the hot sauce. They make a tasty snack at picnics, tailgates and other summertime events.

—TASTE OF HOME TEST KITCHEN

PREP: 10 MIN.
COOK: 1½ HOURS + COOLING
MAKES: 4 CUPS

- 3 cups salted peanuts
- ½ cup sugar
- ⅓ cup packed brown sugar
- 2 tablespoons hot water
- 2 tablespoons butter, melted
- 1 tablespoon sriracha Asian hot chili sauce or hot pepper sauce
- 1 teaspoon chili powder

1. Place peanuts in a greased 1½-qt. slow cooker. In a small bowl, combine the sugars, water, butter, hot sauce and chili powder. Pour over peanuts. Cover and cook on high for 1½ hours, stirring once.
2. Spread on waxed paper to cool. Store in an airtight container.

Sweet Kahlua Coffee

Here's a fun way to dress up your morning coffee! Or simmer up a batch for an after-dinner treat when friends visit.

—RUTH GRUCHOW YORBA LINDA, CA

PREP: 10 MIN. • **COOK:** 3 HOURS
MAKES: 9 SERVINGS (2¼ QUARTS)

- 2 quarts hot water
- ½ cup Kahlua (coffee liqueur)
- ¼ cup creme de cacao
- 3 tablespoons instant coffee granules
- 2 cups heavy whipping cream
- ¼ cup sugar
- 1 teaspoon vanilla extract
- 2 tablespoons grated chocolate

1. In a 4-qt. slow cooker, combine the water, Kahlua, creme de cacao and coffee granules. Cover and cook on low for 3-4 hours or until heated through.
2. In a large bowl, beat cream until it begins to thicken. Add sugar and vanilla; beat until stiff peaks form.
3. Ladle coffee into mugs. Garnish with whipped cream and grated chocolate.

top tip — Keeping it Fresh

Don't let unused parsley go to waste! It's a breeze to keep it fresh in the refrigerator for several weeks. Simply wash the entire bunch in warm water and shake off all excess moisture. Next, wrap the parsley in a paper towel and seal it in a plastic storage bag.

If you need longer storage time, remove the paper towel and place the sealed bag in the freezer. Then simply break off and crumble the amount of parsley you need for dips, spreads, soups, stews or whatever other cooked dishes you're preparing.

SUSAN D'AMORE'S
SLOW-COOKED CRAB DIP

Summer

SIDE DISHES

Looking for something to serve alongside your grilled specialty? Need a quick contribution to the family reunion or church picnic? Your slow cooker has you covered! Consider these easy alternatives when you want to round out summer meals.

MELISSA MARZOLF'S
CHEESY POTATOES

Cheesy Potatoes

For a comforting side dish that feeds a crowd, try these saucy slow-cooked potatoes. A simple topping of buttered croutons covers the creamy combination.
—**MELISSA MARZOLF** MARYSVILLE, MI

PREP: 10 MIN. • **COOK:** 8 HOURS • **MAKES:** 10-12 SERVINGS

- 6 **medium potatoes, peeled and cut into ¼-inch strips**
- 2 **cups (8 ounces) shredded cheddar cheese**
- 1 **can (10¾ ounces) condensed cream of chicken soup, undiluted**
- 1 **small onion, chopped or 1 tablespoon dried minced onion**
- 7 **tablespoons butter, melted, divided**
- 1 **teaspoon salt**
- 1 **teaspoon pepper**
- 1 **cup (8 ounces) sour cream**
- 2 **cups seasoned stuffing cubes**

1. Toss the potatoes and cheese; place in a 5-qt. slow cooker. Combine soup, onion, 4 tablespoons butter, salt and pepper; pour over potato mixture.
2. Cover and cook on low for 8-10 hours or until potatoes are tender. Stir in sour cream. Toss stuffing cubes and remaining butter; sprinkle over potatoes.

Marmalade-Glazed Carrots

Here, baby carrots are simmered with orange marmalade and brown sugar. It's ideal when you'd like to serve your vegetables in a different way for a special get-together.
—**BARB RUDYK** VERMILION, AB

PREP: 10 MIN. • **COOK:** 5½ HOURS • **MAKES:** 6 SERVINGS

- 2 **pounds fresh baby carrots**
- ½ **cup orange marmalade**
- 3 **tablespoons cold water, divided**
- 2 **tablespoons brown sugar**
- 1 **tablespoon butter, melted**
- ½ **teaspoon ground cinnamon**
- ¼ **teaspoon salt**
- ¼ **teaspoon ground nutmeg**
- ⅛ **teaspoon pepper**
- 1 **tablespoon cornstarch**

1. In a 3-qt. slow cooker, combine the carrots, marmalade, 1 tablespoon water, brown sugar, butter and seasonings. Cover and cook on low for 5-6 hours or until the carrots are tender.
2. Combine the cornstarch and remaining water until smooth; stir into carrot mixture. Cover carrots and cook on high for 30 minutes or until thickened. Serve with a slotted spoon.

MAPLE BAKED BEANS

Maple Baked Beans

This recipe came from my mother and was always a hit. The chopped jalapeno pepper spices things up a bit. Best of all, the recipe is easy to remember—it's simply a half-cup of this and a half-cup of that!

—NADINE BRISSEY JENKS, OK

PREP: 15 MIN. • **COOK:** 6 HOURS • **MAKES:** 8 SERVINGS

- 3 cans (15 ounces each) pork and beans
- ½ cup finely chopped onion
- ½ cup chopped green pepper
- ½ cup ketchup
- ½ cup maple syrup
- 2 tablespoons finely chopped seeded jalapeno pepper
- ½ cup crumbled cooked bacon

In a 3-qt. slow cooker, combine the first six ingredients. Cover and cook on low for 6-8 hours or until vegetables are tender. Just before serving, stir in bacon.

NOTE *Wear disposable gloves when cutting hot peppers; the oils can burn skin. Avoid touching your face.*

top tip — Easy Entree

Turn leftover Maple Baked Beans into a main course by adding shredded cheese and salsa to taste. Heat the mixture through until the cheese melts, and stir until well combined. Using a slotted spoon, place the mixture in flour tortillas. Top with lettuce and additional salsa or cheese if desired. Roll up and enjoy!

Butternut Coconut Curry

I love my slow cooker because it's so easy to make dinner with one! This flavorful curry was first created for a potluck. Since then, I've often been asked for the recipe.
—JESS APFE BERKELEY, CA

PREP: 35 MIN. • **COOK:** 4 HOURS • **MAKES:** 9 SERVINGS

- 1 cup chopped carrots
- 1 small onion, chopped
- 1 tablespoon olive oil
- 1½ teaspoons brown sugar
- 1½ teaspoons curry powder
- 1 garlic clove, minced
- ½ teaspoon ground cinnamon
- ¼ teaspoon ground ginger
- ⅛ teaspoon salt
- 1 medium butternut squash (about 2½ pounds), cut into 1-inch cubes
- 2½ cups vegetable broth
- ¾ cup coconut milk
- ½ cup uncooked basmati or jasmine rice

1. In a large skillet, saute carrots and onion in oil until onion is tender. Add the brown sugar, curry, garlic, cinnamon, ginger and salt. Cook and stir 2 minutes longer.
2. In a 3- or 4-qt. slow cooker, combine the butternut squash, broth, coconut milk, rice and carrot mixture. Cover and cook on low for 4-5 hours or until rice is tender.

BUTTERNUT COCONUT CURRY

SLOW COOKER MUSHROOM RICE PILAF

Slow Cooker Mushroom Rice Pilaf

A few modifications to Great-Aunt Bernice's mushroom rice pilaf made this an always-requested dish for summer barbecues, potlucks and family get-togethers. It'll become a slow cooker favorite in your household, too!

—**AMY WILLIAMS** RIALTO, CA

PREP: 20 MIN. • **COOK:** 3 HOURS
MAKES: 6 SERVINGS

- 1 cup medium grain rice
- ¼ cup butter, cubed
- 6 green onions, chopped
- 2 garlic cloves, minced
- ½ pound sliced baby portobello mushrooms
- 2 cups warm water
- 4 teaspoons beef base

1. In a large skillet, saute rice in butter until lightly browned. Add green onions and garlic; cook and stir until tender. Stir in mushrooms.
2. Transfer to a 1½-qt. slow cooker. In a small bowl, whisk the water and beef base; pour over rice mixture. Cover and cook on low for 3 to 3½ hours or until rice is tender and the liquid is absorbed. Fluff with a fork.
NOTE *Look for beef base near the broth and bouillon.*

Slow Cooker Ratatouille

Try this classic side dish in the summer with your garden-fresh vegetables! It is wonderful alongside grilled meats, but it also makes a pretty addition to any entree you may be serving.

—**JOLENE WALTERS** NORTH MIAMI, FL

PREP: 20 MIN. + STANDING • **COOK:** 3 HOURS
MAKES: 10 SERVINGS

- 1 large eggplant, peeled and cut into 1-inch cubes
- 2 teaspoons salt, divided
- 3 medium tomatoes, chopped
- 3 medium zucchini, halved lengthwise and sliced
- 2 medium onions, chopped
- 1 large green pepper, chopped
- 1 large sweet yellow pepper, chopped
- 1 can (6 ounces) pitted ripe olives, drained and chopped
- 1 can (6 ounces) tomato paste
- ½ cup minced fresh basil
- 2 garlic cloves, minced
- ½ teaspoon pepper
- 2 tablespoons olive oil

1. Place eggplant in a colander over a plate; sprinkle with 1 teaspoon salt and toss. Let stand for 30 minutes. Rinse and drain well. Transfer to a 5-qt. slow cooker coated with cooking spray.
2. Stir in the tomatoes, zucchini, onions, green and yellow peppers, olives, tomato paste, basil, garlic, pepper and remaining salt. Drizzle with oil. Cover and cook on high for 3-4 hours or until the vegetables are tender.

STOVETOP RATATOUILLE *Increase olive oil to 3 tablespoons and substitute 1 can (14½ ounces) undrained diced tomatoes for the 3 tomatoes. Prepare eggplant as directed. In a Dutch oven, saute the eggplant, zucchini, onions and peppers in oil in batches until crisp-tender. Add the diced tomatoes, olives, tomato paste, basil, garlic, pepper and remaining salt. Bring to a boil. Reduce heat; cover and simmer for 15-20 minutes or until vegetables are tender, stirring occasionally.*

top tip Ideal Appetizer

Not only does ratatouille make a phenomenal side dish, but you can also serve it with sliced French bread for a warm appetizer!

—**JOLENE W.** NORTH MIAMI, FL

JOLENE WALTERS'
SLOW COOKER RATATOUILLE

SLOW-COOKED RANCH POTATOES

⑤INGREDIENTS

Jalapeno Creamed Corn

My version of creamed corn gets its spicy kick from jalapeno peppers. Try a chopped poblano or small red bell pepper for a more mild side dish.

—JUDY CARTY WICHITA, KS

PREP: 15 MIN. • **COOK:** 4 HOURS
MAKES: 8 SERVINGS

- 2 **packages (16 ounces each) frozen corn**
- 1 **package (8 ounces) cream cheese, softened and cubed**
- 4 **jalapeno peppers, seeded and finely chopped**
- ¼ **cup butter, cubed**
- 2 **tablespoons water**
- ½ **teaspoon salt**
- ¼ **teaspoon pepper**

In a 3-qt. slow cooker, combine all the ingredients. Cover and cook on low for 4-5 hours or until corn is tender, stirring occasionally.
NOTE *Wear disposable gloves when cutting hot peppers; the oils can burn skin. Avoid touching your face.*

top tip # Special Spuds

Have you ever wondered why red potatoes are so popular in slow-cooker recipes? There are a few reasons why this sensational spud finds itself simmering to perfection in slow cookers across the country.

One reason is that the skin of the red potato is very thin, allowing busy cooks to prepare dishes without having to peel the potatoes. What a time-saver!

In addition, red potatoes have a firm flesh that helps them hold their shape during slow cooking (as well as boiling).

Benefits like these make red potatoes a natural fit for salads, soups and casseroles regardless of how the recipe is prepared.

Slow-Cooked Ranch Potatoes

Even after seven years, my family still asks for this tasty potato and bacon dish. Try it once and I'll bet your family will be hooked, too.

—LYNN IRELAND LEBANON, WI

PREP: 15 MIN. • **COOK:** 7 HOURS
MAKES: 10 SERVINGS

- 6 **bacon strips, chopped**
- 2½ **pounds small red potatoes, cubed**
- 1 **package (8 ounces) cream cheese, softened**
- 1 **can (10¾ ounces) condensed cream of potato soup, undiluted**
- ¼ **cup 2% milk**
- 1 **envelope buttermilk ranch salad dressing mix**
- 3 **tablespoons thinly sliced green onions**

1. In a large skillet, cook bacon over medium heat until crisp, stirring occasionally. Remove with a slotted spoon; drain on paper towels. Drain drippings, reserving 1 tablespoon.
2. Place potatoes in a 3-qt. slow cooker. In a bowl, beat cream cheese, soup, milk, dressing mix and reserved drippings until blended; stir into potatoes. Sprinkle with bacon.
3. Cook, covered, on low 7-8 hours or until potatoes are tender. Top with green onions.

Hawaiian Barbecue Beans

The ingredient list is short but creative. Guests rave and wonder about the unique flavor—fresh ginger is the tasty surprise. It's a hit at every barbecue.

—**HELEN REYNOLDS** QUINCY, CA

PREP: 10 MIN. • **COOK:** 5 HOURS
MAKES: 9 SERVINGS

- **4 cans (15 ounces each) black beans, rinsed and drained**
- **1 can (20 ounces) crushed pineapple, drained**
- **1 bottle (18 ounces) barbecue sauce**
- **1½ teaspoons minced fresh gingerroot**
- **½ pound bacon strips, cooked and crumbled**

In a 4-qt. slow cooker, combine the beans, pineapple, barbecue sauce and ginger. Cover and cook on low for 5-6 hours. Stir in bacon before serving.

Stewed Zucchini and Tomatoes

Zucchini, tomatoes and green peppers star in my make-ahead specialty, which offers a fresh take on traditional vegetable side dishes. Bubbly cheddar cheese adds a down-home feel to this colorful dish.

—**BARBARA SMITH** SALEM, OR

PREP: 20 MIN. • **COOK:** 3½ HOURS
MAKES: 6 SERVINGS

- **3 medium zucchini, cut into ¼-inch slices**
- **1 teaspoon salt, divided**
- **½ teaspoon pepper, divided**
- **1 medium onion, thinly sliced**
- **1 medium green pepper, thinly sliced**
- **3 medium tomatoes, sliced**
- **⅔ cup condensed tomato soup, undiluted**
- **1 teaspoon dried basil**
- **1 cup (4 ounces) shredded cheddar cheese**

1. Place zucchini in a greased 3-qt. slow cooker. Sprinkle zucchini with ½ teaspoon salt and ¼ teaspoon pepper. Layer with onion, green pepper and tomatoes. In a small bowl, combine the soup, basil and remaining salt and pepper; spread over tomatoes.
2. Cover and cook on low for 3-4 hours or until vegetables are tender. Sprinkle with cheese. Cover; cook 30 minutes longer or until cheese is melted.

HAWAIIAN BARBECUE BEANS

JOYCE JOHNSON'S
CORN AND BROCCOLI IN CHEESE SAUCE

Corn and Broccoli in Cheese Sauce

Here's a dish that's a standby at our house. My daughter adds leftover ham to it. No one guesses it calls for lighter ingredients.

—JOYCE JOHNSON UNIONTOWN, OH

PREP: 10 MIN. • **COOK:** 3 HOURS
MAKES: 8 SERVINGS

- 1 package (16 ounces) frozen corn, thawed
- 1 package (16 ounces) frozen broccoli florets, thawed
- 4 ounces reduced-fat process cheese (Velveeta), cubed
- ½ cup shredded cheddar cheese
- 1 can (10¼ ounces) reduced-fat reduced-sodium condensed cream of chicken soup, undiluted
- ¼ cup fat-free milk

1. In a 4-qt. slow cooker, combine the corn, broccoli and cheeses. In a small bowl, combine soup and milk; pour over vegetable mixture.
2. Cover slow cooker and cook on low for 3-4 hours or until heated through. Stir before serving.

Vegetable Medley

Here's a wonderful side dish to make when summer vegetables are plentiful. You'll find it a great complement to any entree.

—TERRY MALY OLATHE, KS

PREP: 15 MIN. • **COOK:** 5 HOURS
MAKES: 8 SERVINGS

- 4 cups diced peeled potatoes
- 1½ cups frozen whole kernel corn or 1 can (15¼ ounces) whole kernel corn, drained
- 4 medium tomatoes, seeded and diced
- 1 cup sliced carrots
- ½ cup chopped onion
- ¾ teaspoon salt
- ½ teaspoon sugar
- ½ teaspoon dill weed
- ⅛ teaspoon pepper

In a 3-qt. slow cooker, combine all ingredients. Cover and cook on low for 5-6 hours or until vegetables are tender.

Brown Rice and Vegetables

This nutritious rice dish, full of big chunks of butternut squash and sweet potatoes, is a good combination of sweet and savory flavors.

—TASTE OF HOME TEST KITCHEN

PREP: 20 MIN. • **COOK:** 5 HOURS
MAKES: 12 SERVINGS

- 1 cup uncooked brown rice
- 1 medium butternut squash (about 3 pounds), cubed
- 2 medium apples, coarsely chopped
- 1 medium sweet potato, peeled and cubed
- 1 medium onion, chopped
- 1 teaspoon salt
- ½ teaspoon pepper
- 1 can (14½ ounces) reduced-sodium chicken broth
- ½ cup raisins
- 1 tablespoon minced fresh tarragon or 1 teaspoon dried tarragon

1. Place rice in a greased 4- or 5-qt. slow cooker. In a large bowl, combine the squash, apples, sweet potato, onion, salt and pepper; add to slow cooker. Pour broth over vegetables.
2. Cover and cook on low for 5-6 hours or until vegetables are tender. Stir in raisins and tarragon.

BROWN RICE AND VEGETABLES

Smoky Baked Beans

They'll be standing in line for this saucy bean dish full of campfire flavor. A variation on colorful calico beans, this great side goes well with all your cookout favorites.

—LYNNE GERMAN WOODLAND HILLS, CA

PREP: 25 MIN. • **COOK:** 7 HOURS
MAKES: 16 SERVINGS

- 1 **pound bulk spicy pork sausage**
- 1 **medium onion, chopped**
- 1 **can (31 ounces) pork and beans**
- 1 **can (16 ounces) kidney beans, rinsed and drained**
- 1 **can (16 ounces) butter beans, rinsed and drained**
- 1 **can (15½ ounces) navy beans, rinsed and drained**
- 1 **can (15 ounces) black beans, rinsed and drained**
- 1 **can (10 ounces) diced tomatoes and green chilies, drained**
- ½ **cup hickory smoke-flavored barbecue sauce**
- ½ **cup ketchup**
- ½ **cup packed brown sugar**
- 1 **teaspoon ground mustard**
- 1 **teaspoon steak seasoning**
- 1 **teaspoon Liquid Smoke, optional**

1. In a large skillet, cook sausage and onion over medium heat until meat is no longer pink; drain.

2. In a 5-qt. slow cooker, combine the beans, tomatoes and sausage mixture. In a small bowl, combine the barbecue sauce, ketchup, brown sugar, mustard, steak seasoning and Liquid Smoke if desired. Stir into bean mixture.

3. Cover and cook on low for 7-8 hours or until heated through.

NOTE *This recipe was tested with McCormick's Montreal Steak Seasoning. Look for it in the spice aisle.*

Scalloped Taters

My creamy and comforting side dish tastes wonderful with almost anything and is a snap to assemble with convenient frozen hash browns. This is a good way to make potatoes when your oven is busy with other items.

—LUCINDA WOLKER SOMERSET, PA

PREP: 10 MIN. • **COOK:** 4 HOURS
MAKES: 12 SERVINGS

- 1 **package (2 pounds) frozen cubed hash brown potatoes**
- 1 **can (10¾ ounces) condensed cream of chicken soup, undiluted**
- 1½ **cups whole milk**
- 1 **cup (4 ounces) shredded cheddar cheese**
- ½ **cup plus 1 tablespoon butter, melted, divided**
- ¼ **cup dried minced onion**
- ½ **teaspoon salt**
- ⅛ **teaspoon pepper**
- ¾ **cup crushed cornflakes**

1. In a large bowl, combine the hash browns, soup, milk, cheese, ½ cup butter, onion, salt and pepper. Pour into a greased 5-qt. slow cooker. Cover and cook on low for 4-5 hours or until potatoes are tender.

2. Just before serving, combine the cornflake crumbs and remaining butter in a pie plate. Bake at 350° for 4-6 minutes or until the crumbs are golden brown. Stir potatoes; sprinkle with crumb topping.

SMOKY BAKED BEANS

(5) INGREDIENTS
Creamed Corn

Five ingredients are all you'll need for my popular dinner accompaniment. It's wonderful no matter what the occasion is. Try it on a barbecue buffet.
—**BARBARA BRIZENDINE** HARRISONVILLE, MO

PREP: 10 MIN. • **COOK:** 3 HOURS
MAKES: 5 SERVINGS

- 2 packages (one 16 ounces, one 10 ounces) frozen corn
- 1 package (8 ounces) cream cheese, softened and cubed
- ¼ cup butter, cubed
- 1 tablespoon sugar
- ½ teaspoon salt

In a 3-qt. slow cooker coated with cooking spray, combine all ingredients. Cover and cook on low for 3 to 3½ hours or until cheese is melted and corn is tender. Stir just before serving.

Fiesta Corn and Beans

Bursting with Southwestern flavors, the zesty veggie medley here can be served as a side dish or a meatless entree. The dollop of yogurt is a cool finishing touch.
—**GERALD HETRICK** ERIE, PA

PREP: 25 MIN. • **COOK:** 3 HOURS
MAKES: 10 SERVINGS

- 1 large onion, chopped
- 1 medium green pepper, cut into 1-inch pieces
- 1 to 2 jalapeno peppers, seeded and sliced
- 1 tablespoon olive oil
- 1 garlic clove, minced
- 2 cans (16 ounces each) kidney beans, rinsed and drained
- 1 package (16 ounces) frozen corn
- 1 can (14½ ounces) diced tomatoes, undrained
- 1 teaspoon chili powder
- ¾ teaspoon salt
- ½ teaspoon ground cumin
- ½ teaspoon pepper
  Optional toppings: plain yogurt and sliced ripe olives

1. In a large skillet, saute onion and peppers in oil until tender. Add garlic; cook 1 minute longer. Transfer to a 4-qt. slow cooker. Stir in the beans, corn, tomatoes and seasonings.
2. Cover and cook on low for 3-4 hours or until heated through. Serve with yogurt and olives if desired.
NOTE *Wear disposable gloves when cutting hot peppers; the oils can burn skin. Avoid touching your face.*

HASH BROWNS WITH HAM

PREP: 15 MIN. • **COOK:** 5 HOURS
MAKES: 8 SERVINGS

- 7 cups cubed uncooked red potatoes
- 1 cup (8 ounces) 4% cottage cheese
- ½ cup sour cream
- ½ cup cubed process cheese (Velveeta)
- 1 tablespoon dried minced onion
- 2 garlic cloves, minced
- ½ teaspoon salt
  Paprika and minced chives, optional

1. Place the potatoes in a 3-qt. slow cooker. In a blender, puree cottage cheese and sour cream until smooth. Transfer to a large bowl; stir in the process cheese, onion, garlic and salt. Pour over potatoes and mix well.

2. Cover and cook on low for 5-6 hours or until potatoes are tender. Stir well before serving. Garnish with paprika and chives if desired.

Green Beans and New Potatoes

The beans and potatoes come out tender in my slow-cooked recipe. The beefy onion soup mix and seasonings add lots of flavor to the broth.

—**ANN BAKER** TEXARKANA, TX

PREP: 15 MIN. • **COOK:** 6 HOURS
MAKES: 10 SERVINGS

- 1 pound fresh green beans, trimmed
- 1 pound small red potatoes, quartered
- ½ pound medium fresh mushrooms, halved
- ½ cup thinly sliced sweet onion
- 2 cans (14½ ounces each) beef broth
- 2 tablespoons beefy onion soup mix
- 2 teaspoons Worcestershire sauce
- 1 teaspoon grated lemon peel
- ½ teaspoon salt
- ½ teaspoon pepper
- ¼ teaspoon garlic powder

In a 5-qt. slow cooker, layer the green beans, potatoes, mushrooms and onion. In a small bowl, combine the remaining ingredients; pour over vegetables. Cover and cook on low for 6-8 hours or until vegetables are tender. Serve with a slotted spoon.

Hash Browns with Ham

Convenient grocery store items like frozen hash browns and a can of chicken soup make this an easy-to-make dish. Both kids and adults love it because it's super tasty and chock-full of cheese.

—**LIGHTNINGBUG**
TASTE OF HOME ONLINE COMMUNITY

PREP: 15 MIN. • **COOK:** 3¼ HOURS
MAKES: 8 SERVINGS

- 1 package (32 ounces) frozen cubed hash brown potatoes, thawed
- 1 cup cubed fully cooked ham
- 1 small onion, chopped
- 2 cups (8 ounces) shredded cheddar cheese, divided
- 1 can (14¾ ounces) condensed cream of chicken soup, undiluted
- ½ cup butter, melted
- 1 cup (8 ounces) sour cream

1. In a 3-qt. slow cooker, combine the potatoes, ham, onion and 1 cup cheese. Combine soup and butter; pour over potato mixture. Cover and cook on low for 3-4 hours or until potatoes are tender.

2. Stir in sour cream. Sprinkle with remaining cheese. Cover and cook for 15 minutes or until cheese is melted.

Summer Side Dish

I use my slow cooker to make these tasty potatoes in a rich and creamy sauce. Be sure to stir them well before serving to help the cheese mixture thicken.

—**ELAINE RYAN** HOLLEY, NY

ANN BAKER'S
GREEN BEANS AND NEW POTATOES

Summer

ENTREES

Don't feel like standing over a hot grill all summer? Want to keep the oven off and the house cool? You've come to the right spot! Turn here for slow-cooked main dishes just perfect for steamy summer nights.

JACQUELINE CORREA'S ENCHILADA PIE

Enchilada Pie

Stacked with layers of beans, vegetables and cheese, this mile-high pie makes for a fun fiesta night with the family. Who would have guessed it all comes together in the slow cooker?

—**JACQUELINE CORREA** LANDING, NJ

PREP: 40 MIN. • **COOK:** 4 HOURS • **MAKES:** 8 SERVINGS

- 1 package (12 ounces) frozen vegetarian meat crumbles
- 1 cup chopped onion
- ½ cup chopped green pepper
- 2 teaspoons canola oil
- 1 can (16 ounces) kidney beans, rinsed and drained
- 1 can (15 ounces) black beans, rinsed and drained
- 1 can (10 ounces) diced tomatoes and green chilies, undrained
- ½ cup water
- 1½ teaspoons chili powder
- ½ teaspoon ground cumin
- ¼ teaspoon pepper
- 6 whole wheat tortillas (8 inches)
- 2 cups (8 ounces) shredded reduced-fat cheddar cheese

1. Cut three 25-in. x 3-in. strips of heavy-duty foil; crisscross so they resemble spokes of a wheel. Place strips on the bottom and up the sides of a 5-qt. slow cooker. Coat strips with cooking spray.

2. In a large saucepan, cook the meat crumbles, onion and green pepper in oil until vegetables are tender. Stir in both cans of beans, tomatoes, water, chili powder, cumin and pepper. Bring to a boil. Reduce heat; simmer, uncovered, for 10 minutes.

3. In prepared slow cooker, layer about a cup of bean mixture, one tortilla and ⅓ cup cheese. Repeat layers five times. Cover and cook on low for 4-5 hours or until heated through and cheese is melted.

4. Using foil strips as handles, remove the pie to a platter.

NOTE *Vegetarian meat crumbles are a nutritious pro source made from soy. Look for them in the natural foods freezer section.*

top tip) **Easy Ideas for Leftovers**

Have an opened package of tortillas in the refrigerator? Here are some ways to use them up:

- Brush the tortillas with butter and sprinkle with cinnamon-sugar. Bake on a cookie sheet until crisp.
- Make a breakfast burrito by spooning scrambled eggs and salsa down the center of the tortilla and rolling up.
- Spread peanut butter, apple butter and cream cheese on a tortilla and roll it up for a quick snack or no-fuss sandwich.

Jamaica-Me-Crazy Chicken Tropicale

PREP: 25 MIN. • **COOK:** 5 HOURS • **MAKES:** 4 SERVINGS

- 3 medium sweet potatoes, peeled and cut into 2-inch pieces
- 1 can (8 ounces) sliced water chestnuts, drained
- 1 cup dried cranberries
- 1 can (20 ounces) unsweetened pineapple tidbits
- 2 pounds bone-in chicken breast halves, skin removed
- 2 tablespoons Caribbean jerk seasoning
- ¼ cup dried minced onion
- 3 tablespoons minced fresh gingerroot
- 2 tablespoons Worcestershire sauce
- 1 tablespoon grated lime peel
- 1 teaspoon cumin seeds, crushed
- 3 fresh thyme sprigs
  Hot cooked rice

1. Place potatoes in a 4- or 5-qt. slow cooker. Add water chestnuts and cranberries. Drain pineapple, reserving juice; add pineapple to slow cooker. Top with chicken. Sprinkle jerk seasoning over chicken.

2. Combine the onion, ginger, Worcestershire sauce, lime peel, cumin seeds and reserved juice. Pour over the chicken. Top with thyme sprigs.

3. Cover and cook on low for 5-6 hours or until chicken and vegetables are tender. Serve with rice.

JAMAICA-ME-CRAZY CHICKEN TROPICALE

CHILI CONEY DOGS

Chili Coney Dogs

Everyone in our family, from the smallest kids to the oldest adults, loves these hot dogs! They're so easy to throw together and heat in the slow cooker.
—**MICHELE HARRIS** VICKSBURG, MI

PREP: 20 MIN. • **COOK:** 4 HOURS • **MAKES:** 8 SERVINGS

- 1 pound lean ground beef (90% lean)
- 1 can (15 ounces) tomato sauce
- ½ cup water
- 2 tablespoons Worcestershire sauce
- 1 tablespoon dried minced onion
- ½ teaspoon garlic powder
- ½ teaspoon ground mustard
- ½ teaspoon chili powder
- ½ teaspoon pepper
  Dash cayenne pepper
- 8 hot dogs
- 8 hot dog buns, split
  Shredded cheddar cheese, relish and chopped onion, optional

1. In a large skillet, cook beef over medium heat until no longer pink; drain. Stir in the tomato sauce, water, Worcestershire sauce, onion and spices.

2. Place hot dogs in a 3-qt. slow cooker; top with beef mixture. Cover and cook on low for 4-5 hours or until heated through. Serve on buns with cheese, relish and onion if desired.

CHICKEN THIGHS WITH SAUSAGE

Pork and Green Chile Stew

An easily adaptable stew, this dish is ready in 4 hours if cooked on high in a slow cooker, or in 8 hours if cooked low and slow.

—**PAUL SEDILLO** PLAINFIELD, IL

PREP: 40 MIN. • **COOK:** 7 HOURS
MAKES: 8 SERVINGS (2 QUARTS)

- 2 **pounds boneless pork shoulder butt roast, cut into ¾-inch cubes**
- 1 **large onion, cut into ½-in. pieces**
- 2 **tablespoons canola oil**
- 1 **teaspoon salt**
- 1 **teaspoon coarsely ground pepper**
- 4 **large potatoes, peeled and cut into ¾-inch cubes**
- 3 **cups water**
- 1 **can (16 ounces) hominy, rinsed and drained**
- 2 **cans (4 ounces each) chopped green chilies**
- 2 **tablespoons quick-cooking tapioca**
- 2 **garlic cloves, minced**
- ½ **teaspoon dried oregano**
- ½ **teaspoon ground cumin**
- 1 **cup minced fresh cilantro**
  Sour cream, optional

1. In a large skillet, brown pork and onion in oil in batches. Sprinkle with salt and pepper. Transfer to a 4-qt. slow cooker.

2. Stir in the potatoes, water, hominy, chilies, tapioca, garlic, oregano and cumin. Cover and cook on low for 7-9 hours or until meat is tender, stirring in cilantro during the last 30 minutes of cooking. Serve with sour cream if desired.

PORK AND GREEN CHILE STEW

Chicken Thighs with Sausage

Whether serving your family on a weeknight or hosting guests on the weekend, my entree hits the spot.

—**JOANNA IOVINO** KINGS PARK, NY

PREP: 25 MIN. • **COOK:** 6 HOURS
MAKES: 8 SERVINGS

- 2 **medium carrots, chopped**
- 2 **celery ribs, chopped**
- 1 **large onion, finely chopped**
- 8 **bone-in chicken thighs (about 3 pounds), skin removed**
- 1 **package (14 ounces) smoked turkey sausage, cut into ½-inch slices**
- ¼ **cup ketchup**
- 6 **garlic cloves, minced**
- 1 **tablespoon Louisiana-style hot sauce**
- 1 **teaspoon dried basil**
- 1 **teaspoon paprika**
- 1 **teaspoon dried thyme**
- ½ **teaspoon dried oregano**
- ½ **teaspoon pepper**
- ¼ **teaspoon ground allspice**
- 1 **teaspoon browning sauce, optional**

1. In a 4- or 5-qt. slow cooker, combine the carrots, celery and onion. Top with chicken and sausage.

2. In a small bowl, combine the ketchup, garlic, hot sauce, seasonings and, if desired, browning sauce. Spoon over meats. Cover and cook on low for 6-8 hours or until chicken is tender.

Slow-Cooked Pork and Beans

I like to get this entree started before leaving for work in the morning. When I get home, my supper's ready! It's a hearty slow cooker meal that is also good for a potluck. A generous helping of tender pork and beans is perfect alongside a slice of warm corn bread.

—**PATRICIA HAGER** NICHOLASVILLE, KY

PREP: 15 MIN. • **COOK:** 6 HOURS
MAKES: 12 SERVINGS

- 1 boneless pork loin roast (3 pounds)
- 1 medium onion, sliced
- 3 cans (15 ounces each) pork and beans
- 1½ cups barbecue sauce
- ¼ cup packed brown sugar
- 1 teaspoon garlic powder

1. Cut roast in half; place in a 5-qt. slow cooker. Top with onion. In a large bowl, combine the beans, barbecue sauce, brown sugar and garlic powder; pour over meat. Cover and cook on low for 6-8 hours or until meat is tender.
2. Remove roast; shred with two forks. Return meat to slow cooker; heat through.

Beer-Braised Stew

Friends and family will never guess that the secret ingredient in this wonderful stew is beer! What a nice meal to come home to: just cook the noodles and dinner is ready.
—**GERI FAUSTICH** APPLETON, WI

PREP: 20 MIN. • **COOK:** 6 HOURS
MAKES: 8 SERVINGS

- 3 bacon strips, diced
- 2 pounds beef stew meat, cut into 1-inch cubes
- ½ teaspoon pepper
- ¼ teaspoon salt
- 2 tablespoons canola oil
- 2 cups fresh baby carrots
- 1 medium onion, cut into wedges
- 1 teaspoon minced garlic
- 1 bay leaf
- 1 can (12 ounces) beer or nonalcoholic beer
- 1 tablespoon soy sauce
- 1 tablespoon Worcestershire sauce
- 1 teaspoon dried thyme
- 2 tablespoons all-purpose flour
- ¼ cup water
  Hot cooked noodles

1. In a large skillet, cook bacon over medium heat until crisp. Remove to paper towels; drain, discarding drippings. Sprinkle beef with pepper and salt. In the same skillet, brown beef in oil in batches; drain.
2. Transfer to a 5-qt. slow cooker. Add the carrots, bacon, onion, garlic and bay leaf. In a small bowl, combine the beer, soy sauce, Worcestershire sauce and thyme. Pour over beef mixture.
3. Cover and cook on low for 5½ to 6 hours or until meat and vegetables are tender.
4. In a small bowl, combine flour and water until smooth. Gradually stir into slow cooker. Cover and cook on high for 30 minutes or until thickened. Discard bay leaf. Serve beef with noodles.

BEER-BRAISED STEW

Italian Sausages with Provolone

Here's an easy recipe everyone will rave about. These sausages with their pepper-and-onion topping will disappear quickly. Better make a double batch!

—SHELLY BEVINGTON-FISHER HERMISTON, OR

PREP: 15 MIN. • **COOK:** 4 HOURS. • **MAKES:** 10 SERVINGS

- 10 **Italian sausage links (4 ounces each)**
- 1 **tablespoon canola oil**
- 1 **each small sweet red, yellow and orange peppers, cut into strips**
- 2 **medium onions, halved and sliced**
- 2 **cups Italian salad dressing**
- 10 **slices provolone cheese**
- 10 **brat buns**

1. In a large skillet, brown sausages in batches in oil. Drain. Transfer to a 5-qt. slow cooker. Add the peppers, onions and salad dressing. Cover and cook on low for 4-5 hours or until a thermometer reads 160° and vegetables are tender.

2. Place sausages and cheese in buns; using a slotted spoon, top with pepper mixture.

LOUISIANA RED BEANS AND RICE

ITALIAN SAUSAGES WITH PROVOLONE

Louisiana Red Beans and Rice

Smoked turkey sausage and red pepper flakes add zip to this saucy, slow-cooked version of the New Orleans classic. For extra heat, add red pepper sauce at the table.

—JULIA BUSHREE GEORGETOWN, TX

PREP: 20 MIN. • **COOK:** 8 HOURS. • **MAKES:** 9 SERVINGS

- 4 **cans (16 ounces each) kidney beans, rinsed and drained**
- 1 **can (14½ ounces) diced tomatoes, undrained**
- 1 **package (14 ounces) smoked turkey sausage, sliced**
- 1 **cup chicken broth**
- 3 **celery ribs, chopped**
- 1 **large onion, chopped**
- 1 **medium green pepper, chopped**
- 1 **small sweet red pepper, chopped**
- 6 **garlic cloves, minced**
- 1 **bay leaf**
- ½ **teaspoon crushed red pepper flakes**
- 2 **green onions, chopped**
  Hot cooked rice

1. In a 4-qt. slow cooker, combine the first 11 ingredients. Cover and cook on low for 8-10 hours or until vegetables are tender. Stir before serving. Discard bay leaf.

2. Sprinkle each serving with onions. Serve with rice.

Fiesta-Twisted Brunswick Stew

PREP: 20 MIN. • **COOK:** 5 HOURS • **MAKES:** 9 SERVINGS (3½ QUARTS)

- ½ pound uncooked chorizo or bulk spicy pork sausage
- 1 large potato, cubed
- 1 large onion, chopped
- 1 large green pepper, chopped
- 3 jalapeno peppers, seeded and chopped
- 1 can (28 ounces) crushed tomatoes
- 1 jar (26 ounces) marinara sauce
- 1 can (14¾ ounces) cream-style corn
- 1 tablespoon Cajun seasoning
- 1 garlic clove, minced
- ½ teaspoon sugar
- ½ teaspoon pepper
- ¼ teaspoon salt
- ⅓ cup all-purpose flour
- 1 can (14½ ounces) chicken broth

FIESTA-TWISTED BRUNSWICK STEW

- 4 bone-in chicken breast halves (8 ounces each), skin removed
- 1 cup cut fresh green beans
- 2 tablespoons minced fresh cilantro
  Shredded Asiago cheese

1. Crumble chorizo into a small skillet; cook over medium heat for 6-8 minutes or until fully cooked. Drain. Transfer to a 6-qt. slow cooker. Add the potato, onion, green pepper, jalapenos, tomatoes, marinara sauce, corn, Cajun seasoning, garlic, sugar, pepper and salt.

2. In a small bowl, combine flour and broth until smooth; stir into slow cooker. Add the chicken. Cover and cook on low for 5-6 hours or until chicken and vegetables are tender, adding green beans and cilantro during the last 2 hours of cooking.

3. Remove chicken from slow cooker. When cool enough to handle, remove meat from bones; discard bones. Cut meat into bite-size pieces and return to slow cooker; heat through. Sprinkle servings with cheese.

NOTE *Wear disposable gloves when cutting hot peppers; the oils can burn skin. Avoid touching your face.*

Bayou Gulf Shrimp Gumbo

This recipe skips the traditional hard-to-find spices and still delivers the true seafood flavor beloved in the Louisiana Bayou and beyond.

—**WOLFGANG HANAU** WEST PALM BEACH, FL

PREP: 35 MIN. • **COOK:** 5 HOURS • **MAKES:** 6 SERVINGS

- ½ pound bacon strips, chopped
- 3 celery ribs, chopped
- 1 medium onion, chopped
- 1 medium green pepper, chopped
- 2 garlic cloves, minced
- 2 bottles (8 ounces each) clam juice
- 1 can (14½ ounces) diced tomatoes, undrained
- 2 tablespoons Worcestershire sauce
- 1 teaspoon kosher salt
- 1 teaspoon dried marjoram
- 2 pounds uncooked large shrimp, peeled and deveined
- 2½ cups frozen sliced okra, thawed
  Hot cooked rice

1. In a large skillet, cook bacon over medium heat until crisp. Remove to paper towels with a slotted spoon; drain, reserving 2 tablespoons drippings. Saute the celery, onion, green pepper and garlic in drippings until tender.

2. Transfer to a 4-qt. slow cooker. Stir in the bacon, clam juice, tomatoes, Worcestershire sauce, salt and marjoram. Cover and cook on low for 4 hours.

3. Stir in shrimp and okra. Cover and cook 1 hour longer or until shrimp turn pink and okra is heated through. Serve with rice.

GERI LESCH'S
SWEET AND SPICY JERK RIBS

Sweet and Spicy Jerk Ribs

(5) INGREDIENTS

Here's a no-fuss ribs recipe that the whole family will love. The spicy rub and sweet sauce make it an instant summer favorite.

—GERI LESCH NEW PORT RICHEY, FL

PREP: 10 MIN. • **COOK:** 6 HOURS
MAKES: 5 SERVINGS

- 4½ pounds pork baby back ribs
- 3 tablespoons olive oil
- ⅓ cup Caribbean jerk seasoning
- 3 cups honey barbecue sauce
- 3 tablespoons apricot preserves
- 2 tablespoons honey

1. Cut ribs into serving-size pieces; brush with oil and rub with jerk seasoning. Place in a 5- or 6-qt. slow cooker. Combine the remaining ingredients; pour over ribs.
2. Cover and cook on low for 6-8 hours or until meat is tender. Skim fat from sauce before serving.

Southwest Chicken

Chicken is cooked until tender, and then it's combined with corn, beans and salsa for a delicious meal with Southwestern flair. The garnishes really complete it.

—MADDYMOO

TASTE OF HOME ONLINE COMMUNITY

PREP: 15 MIN. • **COOK:** 4 HOURS
MAKES: 6 SERVINGS

- 1 can (15¼ ounces) whole kernel corn, drained
- 1 can (15 ounces) black beans, rinsed and drained
- 1 jar (16 ounces) mild salsa
- 4 boneless skinless chicken breast halves (5 ounces each)
  Sweet red and yellow pepper strips, sour cream, shredded cheddar cheese and sliced green onions, optional

1. In a 3-qt. slow cooker, layer three-fourths each of the corn and beans and half of the salsa. Arrange chicken over salsa; top with remaining corn, beans and salsa. Cover and cook on low for 4-5 hours or until chicken is tender.
2. Shred chicken with two forks and return to the slow cooker; heat through. Top with the peppers, sour cream, cheese and onions if desired.

Slow-Roasted Chicken with Vegetables

The aroma of rosemary and garlic is mouthwatering, and this recipe could not be easier. Just a few minutes of prep and you'll come home to a delicious dinner. Even a beginner cook will find perfection in this entree.

—ANITA BELL HERMITAGE, TN

PREP: 15 MIN. • **COOK:** 6 HOURS + STANDING
MAKES: 6 SERVINGS

- 2 medium carrots, halved lengthwise and cut into 3-inch pieces
- 2 celery ribs, halved lengthwise and cut into 3-inch pieces
- 8 small red potatoes, quartered
- ¾ teaspoon salt, divided
- ⅛ teaspoon pepper
- 1 medium lemon, halved
- 2 garlic cloves, crushed
- 1 broiler/fryer chicken (3 to 4 pounds)
- 1 tablespoon dried rosemary, crushed
- 1 tablespoon lemon juice
- 1 tablespoon olive oil
- 2 teaspoons paprika

1. Place carrots, celery and potatoes in a 6-qt. slow cooker; toss with ¼ teaspoon salt and pepper. Place lemon halves and garlic in chicken cavity. Tuck wings under chicken; tie drumsticks together. Place chicken over vegetables in slow cooker, breast side up. Mix rosemary, lemon juice, oil, paprika and remaining salt; rub over chicken.
2. Cook, covered, on low 6-8 hours or until a thermometer inserted in thigh reads 180° and vegetables are tender.
3. Remove chicken to a serving platter; tent with foil. Let stand 15 minutes before carving. Serve with vegetables.

SLOW-ROASTED CHICKEN WITH VEGETABLES

MEXICAN PORK ROAST

Mexican Pork Roast

A friend who lives in Mexico shared this recipe with me years ago. They cooked the roast in a clay pot in a slow oven, but I found it works well in a slow cooker. The leftovers make great burritos and tacos.

—**CHUCK ALLEN** DANA POINT, CA

PREP: 15 MIN. • **COOK:** 8 HOURS
MAKES: 8 SERVINGS

- 2 **medium onions, sliced**
- 2 **medium carrots, sliced**
- 2 **jalapeno peppers, seeded and chopped**
- 2 **tablespoons olive oil**
- 3 **garlic cloves, minced**
- ½ **cup water**
- ½ **cup chicken broth**
- 1 **teaspoon ground coriander**
- ½ **teaspoon salt**
- ½ **teaspoon ground cumin**
- ½ **teaspoon dried oregano**
- ¼ **teaspoon pepper**
- 1 **boneless pork shoulder butt roast (3 pounds)**

1. In a large skillet, saute the onions, carrots and jalapenos in oil for 3 minutes. Add garlic; cook 1 minute longer. Transfer to a 5-qt. slow cooker; add water and broth.
2. In a small bowl, combine the coriander, salt, cumin, oregano and pepper; rub over roast. Cut roast in half; place in the slow cooker. Cover and cook on low for 8-9 hours or until meat is tender.
3. Transfer roast and vegetables to a serving platter; keep warm. Strain cooking juices and skim fat. Pour into a small saucepan. Bring to a boil; cook until liquid is reduced to about 1 cup. Serve with roast and vegetables.
NOTE *Wear disposable gloves when cutting hot peppers; the oils can burn skin. Avoid touching your face.*

Beef Osso Bucco

Our beef osso bucco boasts a thick, savory sauce complemented by the addition of gremolata, a chopped herb condiment made of lemon zest, garlic, and parsley.

—**TASTE OF HOME TEST KITCHEN**

PREP: 30 MIN. • **COOK:** 7 HOURS
MAKES: 6 SERVINGS

- ½ **cup all-purpose flour**
- ½ **teaspoon pepper**
- ¾ **teaspoon salt, divided**
- 6 **beef shanks (14 ounces each)**
- 2 **tablespoons butter**
- 1 **tablespoon olive oil**
- ½ **cup white wine or beef broth**
- 1 **can (14½ ounces) diced tomatoes, undrained**
- 1½ **cups beef broth**
- 2 **medium carrots, chopped**
- 1 **medium onion, chopped**
- 1 **celery rib, sliced**
- 1 **tablespoon dried thyme**
- 1 **tablespoon dried oregano**
- 2 **bay leaves**
- 3 **tablespoons cornstarch**
- ¼ **cup cold water**
- **GREMOLATA**
  - ⅓ **cup minced fresh parsley**
  - 1 **tablespoon grated lemon peel**
  - 1 **tablespoon grated orange peel**
  - 2 **garlic cloves, minced**

1. In a large resealable plastic bag, combine the flour, pepper and ½ teaspoon salt. Add beef, a few pieces at a time, and shake to coat.
2. In a large skillet, brown beef in butter and oil. Transfer meat and drippings to a 6-qt. slow cooker. Add wine to skillet, stirring to loosen browned bits from pan; pour over meat. Add the tomatoes, broth, carrots, onion, celery, thyme, oregano, bay leaves and remaining salt.
3. Cover and cook on low for 7-9 hours or until meat is tender. Discard bay leaves.
4. Skim fat from cooking juices; transfer juices to a large saucepan. Bring to a boil. Combine cornstarch and water until smooth; gradually stir into the pan. Bring to a boil; cook and stir for 2 minutes or until thickened.
5. In a small bowl, combine the gremolata ingredients. Serve beef with gremolata and sauce.

BEEF OSSO BUCCO

JAVA ROAST BEEF

Java Roast Beef

Coffee adds richness to my gravy, which is perfect to sop up with crusty bread or drape over mashed potatoes.

—**CHARLA SACKMANN** ORANGE CITY, IA

PREP: 10 MIN. • **COOK:** 8 HOURS
MAKES: 12 SERVINGS

- 5 garlic cloves, minced
- 1½ teaspoons salt
- ¾ teaspoon pepper
- 1 boneless beef chuck roast (3 to 3½ pounds)
- 1½ cups strong brewed coffee
- 2 tablespoons cornstarch
- ¼ cup cold water

1. Combine the garlic, salt and pepper; rub over beef. Transfer to a 4-qt. slow cooker. Pour coffee around meat. Cover and cook on low for 8-10 hours or until meat is tender.

2. Remove meat to a serving platter; keep warm. Skim fat from cooking juices; transfer to a small saucepan. Bring to a boil.

3. Combine cornstarch and water until smooth; gradually stir into the pan. Bring to a boil; cook and stir for 2 minutes or until thickened. Serve with meat.

Lime Chicken Tacos

Lime juice adds standout flavor to an easy taco filling that's surprisingly healthy. This fun recipe is great for a casual summer dinner with friends and family. Best of all, the chicken is a nice change from beef.

—**TRACY GUNTER** BOISE, ID

PREP: 10 MIN. • **COOK:** 5½ HOURS
MAKES: 12 TACOS

- 1½ pounds boneless skinless chicken breasts
- 3 tablespoons lime juice
- 1 tablespoon chili powder
- 1 cup frozen corn
- 1 cup chunky salsa
- 12 fat-free flour tortillas (6 inches), warmed
  Sour cream, shredded cheddar cheese and shredded lettuce, optional

1. Place the chicken in a 3-qt. slow cooker. Combine lime juice and chili powder; pour over chicken. Cover and cook on low for 5-6 hours or until chicken is tender.

2. Remove chicken; cool slightly. Shred meat with two forks and return to the slow cooker. Stir in corn and salsa.

3. Cover and cook on low for 30 minutes or until heated through. Serve in tortillas with sour cream, cheese and lettuce if desired.

LIME CHICKEN TACOS

Moroccan Vegetable Chicken Tagine

Take a trip to Morocco with this exotic, rich dish. A tagine is a North African slow-cooked stew that is named after the pot in which it is cooked.

—TASTE OF HOME TEST KITCHEN

PREP: 45 MIN. • **COOK:** 7½ HOURS
MAKES: 6 SERVINGS

- 1 medium butternut squash (about 3 pounds), peeled and cut into 1-inch cubes
- 2 medium red potatoes, cut into 1-inch cubes
- 1 medium sweet potato, peeled and cut into 1-inch cubes
- 1 large onion, halved and sliced
- 2 garlic cloves, minced
- 6 chicken leg quarters, skin removed
- ½ teaspoon salt
- ¼ teaspoon pepper
- ½ cup dried apricots, chopped
- ½ cup dried cranberries, chopped
- 2 tablespoons all-purpose flour
- 1 can (14¾ ounces) reduced-sodium chicken broth
- ¼ cup chili sauce
- 1 tablespoon minced fresh gingerroot
- 1 teaspoon curry powder
- ½ teaspoon ground cinnamon
- ½ teaspoon ground cumin
- 1 can (15 ounces) garbanzo beans or chickpeas, rinsed and drained
  Hot cooked couscous, optional

1. In a 6-qt. slow cooker, combine the squash, potatoes, onion and garlic. Sprinkle chicken with salt and pepper; place over vegetables. Top with apricots and cranberries.

2. In a small bowl, combine flour and broth until smooth. Stir in the chili sauce, ginger, curry, cinnamon and cumin. Pour over chicken. Cover and cook on low for 7-8 hours or until chicken and vegetables are tender.

3. Stir in garbanzo beans; cover and cook for 30 minutes or until heated through. Serve with couscous if desired.

MOROCCAN VEGETABLE CHICKEN TAGINE

LEMON CILANTRO CHICKEN

Glazed Lamb Shanks

Ideal on a night in for two, these slow-cooked shanks are packed with complex, grown-up flavors. The Guinness and honey nicely balance the lamb, while garlic lends zing.

—**ELIZABETH MITCHELL** COCHRANVILLE, PA

PREP: 30 MIN. + MARINATING
COOK: 6 HOURS • **MAKES:** 4 SERVINGS

- 4 lamb shanks
  (about 20 ounces each)
- 4 garlic cloves, thinly sliced
- 1 cup lemon juice
- 4 tablespoons olive oil, divided
- 1 tablespoon each minced fresh
  thyme, rosemary and parsley
- 1 teaspoon salt
- ½ teaspoon pepper

SAUCE
- 1 cup Guinness (dark beer)
- ¼ cup honey
- 3 fresh thyme sprigs
- 2 bay leaves
- 1 tablespoon Dijon mustard
- 2 garlic cloves, minced
- ½ teaspoon salt
- ¼ teaspoon pepper
- ⅛ teaspoon crushed red pepper
  flakes
- 2 pounds Yukon Gold potatoes,
  peeled and cut into chunks

1. Cut slits into each lamb shank; insert garlic slices. In a large resealable plastic bag, combine the lemon juice, 2 tablespoons oil, thyme, rosemary, parsley, salt and pepper. Add the lamb; seal bag and turn to coat. Refrigerate overnight.

2. Drain and discard marinade. In large skillet, brown shanks in remaining oil on all sides in batches. Place shanks in a 5- or 6-qt. slow cooker.

3. In the same skillet, combine the beer, honey, thyme, bay leaves, Dijon, garlic, salt, pepper and pepper flakes. Bring to a boil, stirring constantly. Pour over meat. Cover and cook on low for 6-8 hours or until meat and potatoes are tender, adding the potatoes during the last 2 hours of cooking.

4. Remove lamb and potatoes from slow cooker. Strain sauce and discard bay leaves. If desired, thicken sauce. Serve with lamb and potatoes.

Lemon Cilantro Chicken

This fall-off-the-bone chicken with lemony gravy is very easy to prepare and is a wonderful way to cook a whole chicken in the slow cooker.

—**TASTE OF HOME TEST KITCHEN**

PREP: 25 MIN.
COOK: 4 HOURS + STANDING
MAKES: 6 SERVINGS

- ½ cup chopped fresh cilantro
- 3 tablespoons canola oil, divided
- 2 tablespoons lemon juice
- 2 garlic cloves, minced
- 2 teaspoons salt
- 1 teaspoon grated lemon peel
- 1 broiler/fryer chicken
  (3 to 4 pounds)
- ½ teaspoon paprika
- ½ teaspoon pepper
- ½ cup white wine or chicken broth

1. In a small bowl, combine the cilantro, 2 tablespoons oil, lemon juice, garlic, salt and lemon peel. Loosen skin around the chicken breast, leg and thigh. Rub the cilantro mixture under and over the skin. Rub any remaining mixture into the cavity. Drizzle with remaining oil. Sprinkle with paprika and pepper.

2. Place in a 6- or 7-qt. slow cooker. Add wine to slow cooker. Cover and cook on low for 4-5 hours or until a meat thermometer reads 180°. Remove chicken to a serving platter; cover and let stand 15 minutes before carving. Skim fat and thicken juices if desired. Serve with chicken.

CARIBBEAN BEEF SHORT RIBS

Caribbean Beef Short Ribs

This is a fantastic change from a typical slow cooker stew. The combination of flavors makes it feel like an exotic dish.
—GARY CHIU IRVING, TX

PREP: 30 MIN. • **COOK:** 5½ HOURS
MAKES: 8 SERVINGS

- 3 **pounds boneless beef short ribs, cut into 1½-inch pieces**
- ¼ **cup olive oil**
- ⅔ **cup thawed pineapple juice concentrate**
- ⅔ **cup reduced-sodium soy sauce**
- ½ **cup water**
- ⅓ **cup rum**
- ⅓ **cup honey**
- 2 **tablespoons minced fresh gingerroot**
- 6 **garlic cloves, minced**
- 2 **teaspoons pepper**
- 1 **teaspoon ground allspice**
- ½ **teaspoon salt**
- 2 **large sweet red peppers, chopped**
- 2 **cups cubed fresh pineapple**
- 2 **cups cubed peeled mango**
- 6 **green onions, cut into 1-inch pieces**
- 2 **tablespoons cornstarch**
- 2 **tablespoons cold water**
  Lettuce leaves

1. In a large skillet, brown ribs in oil in batches on all sides. Transfer to a 4-qt. slow cooker.

2. Add the pineapple juice concentrate, soy sauce, water, rum, honey, ginger, garlic, pepper, allspice and salt to the skillet. Bring to a boil; reduce heat and simmer for 5 minutes. Pour over ribs.

3. Cover and cook on low for 5-6 hours or until meat is tender. Stir in red peppers. Top with the pineapple, mango and onions (do not stir). Cover and cook 30 minutes longer or until heated through.

4. Remove beef mixture to a large bowl; keep warm. Transfer cooking juices to a small saucepan. Combine cornstarch and cold water until smooth; gradually stir into pan. Bring to a boil; cook and stir for 2 minutes or until thickened. Serve beef mixture on lettuce; drizzle with gravy.

top tip
Keeping Color

When making the short ribs, leave the mangoes and pineapple on top of the beef, so their colors stay bright. When removing the mixture from the slow cooker, take out the fruit first and place in a separate bowl from the meat to avoid coating them with the with brown sauce.

Tempting Teriyaki Chicken Stew

PREP: 20 MIN. • **COOK:** 7 HOURS
MAKES: 6 SERVINGS

- 1 **tablespoon olive oil**
- 6 **bone-in chicken thighs (about 2 pounds)**
- 2 **medium sweet potatoes, cut into 1-inch pieces**
- 3 **medium carrots, cut into 1-inch pieces**
- 1 **medium parsnip, peeled and cut into 1-inch pieces**
- 1 **medium onion, sliced**
- 1 **cup apricot preserves**
- ½ **cup maple syrup**
- ½ **cup teriyaki sauce**
- ½ **teaspoon ground ginger**
- ⅛ **teaspoon cayenne pepper**
- 2 **tablespoons cornstarch**
- 2 **tablespoons cold water**

1. In a large skillet, heat oil over medium-high heat; brown chicken on both sides. Place vegetables in a 4-qt. slow cooker; add chicken. In a small bowl, mix the preserves, maple syrup, teriyaki sauce, ginger and cayenne; pour over chicken.

2. Cover and cook on low for 6-8 hours or until chicken is tender. Remove chicken and vegetables to a platter; keep warm.

3. Transfer cooking liquid to a small saucepan. Skim fat. Bring cooking liquid to a boil. In a small bowl, combine cornstarch and water until smooth; gradually stir into pan. Return to a boil, stirring constantly; cook and stir for 2 minutes or until thickened. Serve with chicken and vegetables.

AMY SIEGEL'S
TEMPTING TERIYAKI CHICKEN STEW

Brat Sauerkraut Supper

My stick-to-your-ribs German dish is sure to satisfy even the biggest appetites at your house. Sliced apple and apple juice lend mellowing sweetness to the tangy sauerkraut, flavorful bratwurst, red potatoes and bacon. It's perfect for late summer or early fall.

—ANN CHRISTENSEN MESA, AZ

PREP: 15 MIN. • **COOK:** 4 HOURS • **MAKES:** 6 SERVINGS

- 1 jar (32 ounces) sauerkraut, rinsed and well drained
- 2 medium red potatoes, peeled, halved and cut into thin slices
- 1 medium tart apple, peeled and cut into thick slices
- 1 small onion, chopped
- ½ cup apple juice
- ¼ cup water
- 2 tablespoons brown sugar
- 1 teaspoon chicken bouillon granules
- 1 teaspoon caraway seeds
- 1 garlic clove, minced
- 1 bay leaf
- 1 pound fully cooked bratwurst links
- 6 bacon strips, cooked and crumbled

In a 5-qt. slow cooker, combine the first 11 ingredients. Top with bratwurst. Cover and cook on high for 4-5 hours or until potatoes are tender. Discard bay leaf. Sprinkle with bacon.

SLOW COOKER SALMON LOAF

BRAT SAUERKRAUT SUPPER

Slow Cooker Salmon Loaf

I'm always looking for quick, easy recipes that can be prepared ahead of time. I also don't like to heat up my oven during our hot Georgia summers. I adapted this recipe from one I found in an old slow-cooker book of my grandma's. I serve it with macaroni and cheese and pinto beans.

—KELLY RITTER DOUGLASVILLE, GA

PREP: 10 MIN. • **COOK:** 4 HOURS • **MAKES:** 6 SERVINGS

- 2 eggs, lightly beaten
- 2 cups seasoned stuffing croutons
- 1 cup chicken broth
- 1 cup grated Parmesan cheese
- ¼ teaspoon ground mustard
- 1 can (14¾ ounces) salmon, drained, bones and skin removed

1. Cut three 20-in. x 3-in. strips of heavy duty foil; crisscross so they resemble spokes of a wheel. Place strips on the bottom and up the sides of a 3-qt. slow cooker coated with cooking spray.
2. In a large bowl, combine the first five ingredients. Add salmon and mix well. Gently shape mixture into a round loaf. Place in the center of the strips.
3. Cover and cook on low for 4-6 hours or until a thermometer reads 160°. Using foil strips as handles, remove the loaf to a platter.

Spicy Chicken and Rice

PREP: 20 MIN. • **COOK:** 5½ HOURS • **MAKES:** 8 SERVINGS

- 4 boneless skinless chicken breast halves (6 ounces each)
- 2 cans (14½ ounces each) diced tomatoes with mild green chilies, undrained
- 2 medium green peppers, chopped
- 1 medium onion, chopped
- 1 garlic clove, minced
- 1 teaspoon smoked paprika
- ¾ teaspoon salt
- ½ teaspoon ground cumin
- ½ teaspoon ground chipotle pepper
- 6 cups cooked brown rice
- 1 can (15 ounces) black beans, rinsed and drained
- ½ cup shredded cheddar cheese
- ½ cup reduced-fat sour cream

1. Place chicken in a 4- or 5-qt. slow cooker. In a large bowl, combine the tomatoes, green peppers, onion, garlic, paprika, salt, cumin and chipotle pepper; pour over chicken. Cover and cook on low for 5-6 hours or until chicken is tender.

2. Shred chicken with two forks and return to the slow cooker. Stir in rice and beans; heat through. Garnish with cheese and sour cream.

COLA BARBECUE RIBS

Cola Barbecue Ribs

Enjoy the smoky goodness of a summer barbecue all year long by preparing these moist and tender ribs in your slow cooker, inclement weather or not.

—**KAREN SHUCK** EDGAR, NE

PREP: 10 MIN. • **COOK:** 9 HOURS • **MAKES:** 4 SERVINGS

- ¼ cup packed brown sugar
- 2 garlic cloves, minced
- 1 teaspoon salt
- ½ teaspoon pepper
- 3 tablespoons Liquid Smoke, optional
- 4 pounds pork spareribs, cut into serving-size pieces
- 1 medium onion, sliced
- ½ cup cola
- 1½ cups barbecue sauce

1. In a small bowl, combine the brown sugar, garlic, salt, pepper and Liquid Smoke if desired; rub over ribs.

2. Layer ribs and onion in a greased 5- or 6-qt. slow cooker; pour cola over ribs. Cover and cook on low for 8-10 hours or until ribs are tender. Drain liquid. Pour sauce over ribs and cook 1 hour longer.

top tip Sparerib Secrets

Pork spareribs are curved ribs taken from the pork belly. While they are the least meaty of the ribs, they have a hearty flavor that folks adore. Because the ribs may be tough, slow cooking is a perfect method for this economical cut of pork.

SPICY CHICKEN AND RICE

LAURA POWELL'S
CHILI-LIME CHICKEN TOSTADAS

Chili-Lime Chicken Tostadas

Featuring a hint of lime, this flavorful chicken is simply sensational. It has just the right amount of heat to spice things up while keeping the dinner family friendly.

—**LAURA POWELL** SOUTH JORDAN, UT

PREP: 10 MIN. • **COOK:** 5 HOURS
MAKES: 5 SERVINGS

- 4 pounds bone-in chicken breast halves, skin removed
- 1 medium onion, chopped
- 1 can (4 ounces) chopped green chilies
- 3 tablespoons lime juice
- 4½ teaspoons chili powder
- 4 garlic cloves, minced
- 10 tostada shells
- 1 can (16 ounces) fat-free refried beans
  Optional ingredients: Shredded cabbage, shredded cheddar cheese, salsa, sour cream, sliced ripe olives and guacamole

1. In a 4-qt. slow cooker, combine chicken and onion. In a small bowl, combine the green chilies, lime juice, chili powder and garlic; pour over chicken. Cover and cook on low for 5-6 hours or until meat is tender.

2. Remove chicken; cool slightly. Set aside ⅔ cup cooking juices. Discard remaining juices. Shred chicken with two forks and return to slow cooker. Stir in reserved cooking juices.

3. Spread tostadas with refried beans; top with chicken. Layer with cabbage, cheese, salsa, sour cream, olives and guacamole if desired.

top tip — Menu Ideas

It's a snap to round out a meal that features Chili-Lime Chicken Tostadas. Serve the entree alongside canned refried beans easily warmed in the microwave, or grill up a few ears of corn. Consider lemonade, margaritas or white sangria for possible beverages, and cap off the meal with pineapple slices.

SIMPLE CHCKEN TAGINE

Simple Chicken Tagine

I like to sprinkle this with toasted almonds or cashews and serve it with hot couscous. Flavored with cinnamon and a touch of sweetness from the apricots, this stew tastes like you spent all day in the kitchen!

—**ANGELA BUCHANAN** LONGMONT, CO

PREP: 15 MIN. • **COOK:** 6 HOURS
MAKES: 6 SERVINGS

- 2¼ pounds bone-in chicken thighs, skin removed
- 1 large onion, chopped
- 2 medium carrots, sliced
- ¾ cup unsweetened apple juice
- 1 garlic clove, minced
- 1 teaspoon salt
- ½ teaspoon ground cinnamon
- ½ teaspoon pepper
- 1 cup chopped dried apricots
  Hot cooked couscous

1. Place the chicken, onion and carrots in a 3- or 4-qt. slow cooker coated with cooking spray. In a small bowl, combine the apple juice, garlic, salt, cinnamon and pepper; pour over vegetables.

2. Cover and cook on low for 6-8 hours or until chicken is tender.

3. Remove chicken from slow cooker; shred meat with two forks. Skim fat from cooking juices; stir in apricots. Return shredded chicken to slow cooker; heat though. Serve with couscous.

SLOW COOKER BUFFALO CHICKEN LASAGNA

Slow Cooker Buffalo Chicken Lasagna

When I make this tasty chicken lasagna at home, I use a whole bottle of buffalo wing sauce because my family likes it nice and spicy. Use less if you prefer, and just increase the pasta sauce.
—**HEIDI PEPIN** SYKESVILLE, MD

PREP: 25 MIN.
COOK: 4 HOURS + STANDING
MAKES: 8 SERVINGS

- 1½ pounds ground chicken
- 1 tablespoon olive oil
- 1 bottle (12 ounces) buffalo wing sauce
- 1½ cups meatless spaghetti sauce
- 1 carton (15 ounces) ricotta cheese
- 2 cups (8 ounces) shredded part-skim mozzarella cheese
- 9 no-cook lasagna noodles
- 2 medium sweet red peppers, chopped
- ½ cup crumbled blue cheese or feta cheese
  Chopped celery and additional crumbled blue cheese, optional

1. In a Dutch oven, cook chicken in oil over medium heat until no longer pink; drain. Stir in wing sauce and spaghetti sauce. In a small bowl, mix ricotta and mozzarella cheeses.
2. Spread 1 cup sauce onto the bottom of an oval 6-qt. slow cooker. Layer with three noodles (breaking noodles to fit), 1 cup sauce, a third of the peppers and a third of the cheese mixture. Repeat layers twice. Top with remaining sauce; sprinkle with blue cheese.
3. Cover and cook on low for 4-5 hours or until noodles are tender. Let stand 15 minutes before serving. Top with celery and additional blue cheese if desired.

Tropical Triple Pork

PREP: 25 MIN. • **COOK:** 5 HOURS
MAKES: 8 SERVINGS

- 1½ pounds boneless pork loin roast
- ¾ pound fully cooked andouille sausage links, sliced
- 1½ cups cubed fully cooked ham
- 1 can (28 ounces) diced tomatoes, undrained
- 2 medium mangoes, peeled and chopped
- 1 medium onion, chopped
- 1 cup roasted sweet red peppers, cut into strips
- 1 bay leaf
- 1 teaspoon salt
- ½ teaspoon pepper
  Hot cooked rice

1. Place roast in a 5-qt. slow cooker. Add sausage and ham. Stir in the tomatoes, mangoes, onion, red peppers, bay leaf, salt and pepper. Cover and cook on low for 5-6 hours or until meat is tender.
2. Remove roast to a plate. Discard bay leaf. Shred meat with two forks and return to slow cooker; heat through. Serve with rice.

MOIST TURKEY BREAST WITH WHITE WINE GRAVY

Moist Turkey Breast with White Wine Gravy

I modified a favorite dish for slow cooker ease. It's moist and tender each time and perfectly complemented by the white wine gravy. It's best made with drinking wine, not cooking wine.

—**TINA MACKISSOCK** MANCHESTER, NH

PREP: 20 MIN. • **COOK:** 6 HOURS
MAKES: 8 SERVINGS

- 1 cup white wine
- 1 medium apple, chopped
- ½ cup sliced fennel bulb
- ⅓ cup chopped celery
- ⅓ cup chopped carrot
- 3 garlic cloves, minced
- 1 teaspoon ground mustard
- 1 bay leaf
- ½ teaspoon dried rosemary, crushed
- ½ teaspoon dried thyme
- ½ teaspoon rubbed sage
- ¼ teaspoon pepper
- 1 package (3 pounds) frozen boneless turkey roast with gravy, thawed
- 2 tablespoons plus 1½ teaspoons cornstarch
- ½ cup half-and-half cream

1. In a 6-qt. slow cooker, combine the wine, apple, fennel, celery, carrot, garlic, mustard and bay leaf. In a small bowl, combine the rosemary, thyme, sage and pepper; rub over turkey. (Discard gravy packet or save for another use.) Add turkey to slow cooker. Cover and cook on low for 6-8 hours or until meat is tender.

2. Remove meat to a serving platter and keep warm. Strain drippings into a measuring cup to measure 1 cup. Skim fat. In a small saucepan, combine cornstarch and cream; stir until smooth. Gradually add drippings. Bring to a boil; cook and stir for 2 minutes or until thickened. Serve with turkey.

Lip Smackin' Ribs

No matter what time of year you eat them, these ribs taste like summer. It's truly feel-good food!

—**RON BYNAKER** LEBANON, PA

PREP: 20 MIN. • **COOK:** 6 HOURS
MAKES: 8 SERVINGS

- 3 tablespoons butter
- 3 pounds boneless country-style pork ribs
- 1 can (15 ounces) tomato sauce
- 1 cup packed brown sugar
- 1 cup ketchup
- ¼ cup prepared mustard
- 2 tablespoons honey
- 3 teaspoons pepper
- 2 teaspoons dried savory
- 1 teaspoon salt

In a large skillet, heat the butter over medium heat. Brown ribs in batches; transfer to a 5-qt. slow cooker. Add remaining ingredients. Cook, covered, on low 6-8 hours or until the meat is tender.

LIP-SMACKIN' RIBS

"Here, an economical whole chicken is cut up and simmered in a spicy tomato sauce. I serve it with crusty bread so we can mop up and enjoy every last drop of sauce."
—GILDA LESTER MILLSBORO, DE

Red, White and Brew Slow-Cooked Chicken

PREP: 25 MIN. • **COOK:** 6 HOURS
MAKES: 6 SERVINGS

- 1 can (14½ ounces) fire-roasted diced tomatoes, undrained
- 1 medium onion, chopped
- 1 jalapeno pepper, seeded and chopped
- 3 tablespoons brown sugar
- 3 tablespoons balsamic vinegar
- 1 tablespoon ground mustard
- 1 teaspoon dried basil
- ¼ teaspoon crushed red pepper flakes
- 1 cup beer or nonalcoholic beer
- 1 broiler/fryer chicken (3 to 4 pounds), cut up and skin removed
- 1 envelope (1¼ ounces) chili seasoning
  Hot cooked pasta

1. Place the first eight ingredients in a food processor; cover and process until pureed. Stir in beer; set aside.

2. Rub chicken pieces with chili seasoning. Place in a 5-qt. slow cooker. Pour tomato mixture over chicken. Cover and cook on low for 6-7 hours or until chicken is tender.

3. Thicken cooking liquid if desired. Serve chicken with pasta.

NOTE *Wear disposable gloves when cutting hot peppers; the oils can burn skin. Avoid touching your face.*

One-Dish Moroccan Chicken

Spices really work their magic on plain chicken in this exciting dish. Dried fruit and couscous add an exotic touch.
—KATHY MORGAN RIDGEFIELD, WA

PREP: 20 MIN. • **COOK:** 6 HOURS
MAKES: 4 SERVINGS

- 4 medium carrots, sliced
- 2 large onions, halved and sliced
- 1 broiler/fryer chicken (3 to 4 pounds), cut up, skin removed
- ½ teaspoon salt
- ½ cup chopped dried apricots
- ½ cup raisins
- 2 tablespoons all-purpose flour
- 1 can (14½ ounces) reduced-sodium chicken broth
- ¼ cup tomato paste
- 2 tablespoons lemon juice
- 2 garlic cloves, minced
- 1½ teaspoons ground ginger
- 1½ teaspoons ground cumin
- 1 teaspoon ground cinnamon
- ¾ teaspoon pepper
  Hot cooked couscous

1. Place carrots and onions in a greased 5-qt. slow cooker. Sprinkle chicken with salt; add to slow cooker. Top with apricots and raisins. In a small bowl, combine flour and broth until smooth; whisk in the tomato paste, lemon juice, garlic, ginger, cumin, cinnamon and pepper. Pour over chicken.

2. Cover and cook on low for 6 to 7 hours or until chicken is tender. Serve with couscous.

RED, WHITE AND BREW SLOW-COOKED CHICKEN

KATHY MORGAN'S
ONE-DISH MOROCCAN CHICKEN

SUNDAY DINNER BRISKET

Sunday Dinner Brisket

We loved how tender this brisket came out of the slow cooker. The sauce has a robust, beefy flavor with a slight tang from the balsamic vinegar, and the rich caramelized onions complete the hearty entree.

—TASTE OF HOME TEST KITCHEN

PREP: 45 MIN. • **COOK:** 8 HOURS • **MAKES:** 10 SERVINGS

- 4 **cups sliced onions (about 4 medium)**
- 3 **tablespoons olive oil, divided**
- 4 **garlic cloves, minced**
- 1 **tablespoon brown sugar**
- ⅓ **cup all-purpose flour**
- 1 **fresh beef brisket (4 to 5 pounds)**
- 1 **teaspoon salt**
- 1 **teaspoon coarsely ground pepper**
- ¼ **cup balsamic vinegar**
- 1 **can (14 ounces) reduced-sodium beef broth**
- 2 **tablespoons tomato paste**
- 2 **teaspoons Italian seasoning**
- 1 **teaspoon Worcestershire sauce**
- ½ **teaspoon paprika**
- 1 **tablespoon cornstarch**
- 2 **tablespoons cold water**

1. In a large skillet, saute onions in 1 tablespoon oil until softened. Sprinkle with garlic and brown sugar. Reduce heat to medium-low; cook for 10 minutes or until onions are golden brown, stirring occasionally. Transfer to a 4- or 5-qt. slow cooker.

2. Sprinkle flour over both sides of brisket; shake off excess. In the same skillet, brown beef in remaining oil on all sides. Remove from the heat; sprinkle with salt and pepper. Place beef on top of onions. Add balsamic vinegar to skillet; increase heat to medium-high. Cook, stirring to loosen browned bits from pan. Pour over beef.

3. In a small bowl, combine the broth, tomato paste, Italian seasoning, Worcestershire sauce and paprika; pour over beef. Cover and cook on low for 8-10 hours or until the meat is tender.

4. Remove roast to a serving platter; keep warm. Pour cooking juices into a small saucepan; skim fat and bring to a boil. In a small bowl, combine cornstarch and water until smooth; stir into cooking juices. Return to a boil; cook and stir for 1-2 minutes or until thickened. Thinly slice beef across the grain; serve with sauce.

NOTE *This is a fresh beef brisket, not corned beef.*

Sweet 'n' Tangy Chicken

My slow cooker comes in handy during the late-summer harvest season. We're so busy that if supper isn't prepared before I serve lunch, it doesn't seem to get done on time. This recipe is satisfying, delicious and fuss-free.

—**JOAN AIREY** RIVERS, MB

PREP: 15 MIN. • **COOK:** 4 HOURS • **MAKES:** 4 SERVINGS

- 1 medium onion, chopped
- 1½ teaspoons minced garlic
- 1 broiler/fryer chicken (3 pounds), cut up, skin removed
- ⅔ cup ketchup
- ⅓ cup packed brown sugar
- 1 tablespoon chili powder
- 1 tablespoon lemon juice
- 1 teaspoon dried basil
- ½ teaspoon salt
- ¼ teaspoon pepper
- ⅛ teaspoon hot pepper sauce
- 2 tablespoons cornstarch
- 3 tablespoons cold water

1. In a 3-qt. slow cooker, combine onion and garlic; top with chicken. In a small bowl, combine the ketchup, brown sugar, chili powder, lemon juice, basil, salt, pepper and pepper sauce; pour over chicken. Cover and cook on low for 4-5 hours or until meat is tender. Remove chicken to a serving platter; keep warm.

2. Skim fat from cooking juices; transfer to a small saucepan. Bring liquid to a boil. Combine cornstarch and water until smooth. Gradually stir into the pan. Bring to a boil; cook and stir for 2 minutes or until thickened. Serve with the chicken.

Greek Orzo Chicken

No one would suspect that this savory ethnic dish came from a slow cooker. Take your first bite and you'll be on a dinner-table tour of the sunny Greek Isles. Sprinkle lemon zest on top of the finished chicken to give it a little extra flair.

—**ANGELA BUCHANAN** LONGMONT, CO

PREP: 15 MIN. • **COOK:** 5½ HOURS • **MAKES:** 6 SERVINGS

- 6 bone-in chicken thighs, (about 2¼ pounds), skin removed
- 1 cup sliced fresh carrots
- 1 cup chicken broth
- ¼ cup lemon juice
- 1 garlic clove, minced
- 1 teaspoon dried oregano
- ½ teaspoon salt
- 1 cup uncooked orzo pasta
- ½ cup sliced pitted green olives
- ¼ cup golden raisins
- ½ cup minced fresh parsley
- ½ cup crumbled feta cheese

1. In a 3-qt. slow cooker, combine the chicken, carrots, broth, lemon juice, garlic, oregano and salt. Cover and cook on low for 5-6 hours or until chicken is tender.

2. Stir in the orzo, olives and raisins. Cover and cook 30 minutes longer or until pasta is tender.

3. Sprinkle with parsley and feta cheese.

top tip
Feta Facts

Feta is a white, salty, semi-firm cheese. Traditionally, it was made from sheep or goat's milk but it is now also made with cow's milk. After feta is formed in a special mold, it's sliced into large pieces, salted and soaked in brine. Although feta cheese is mostly associated with Greek cooking, "feta" comes from the Italian word "fette," meaning slice of food. Many slow cooker recipes instruct cooks to add feta at the very end of the cooking cycle.

SWEET 'N' TANGY CHICKEN

TENDER SALSA BEEF

Tender Salsa Beef

Here is my Mexican-style twist on comfort food. To keep it kid-friendly, use mild salsa.

—STACIE STAMPER NORTH WILKESBORO, NC

PREP: 15 MIN. • **COOK:** 8 HOURS
MAKES: 8 SERVINGS

- 1½ **pounds beef stew meat, cut into ¾-inch cubes**
- 2 **cups salsa**
- 1 **tablespoon brown sugar**
- 1 **tablespoon reduced-sodium soy sauce**
- 1 **garlic clove, minced**
- 4 **cups hot cooked brown rice**

In a 3-qt. slow cooker, combine the beef, salsa, brown sugar, soy sauce and garlic. Cover and cook on low for 8-10 hours or until meat is tender. Using a slotted spoon, serve beef with rice.

Tasty Chicken Marsala

A friend shared this company-worthy recipe with me. There's enough of the smooth, creamy sauce to dress both the meat and the noodles, should you choose to serve them.

—PATRICIA CAMPBELL VALENCIA, PA

PREP: 20 MIN. • **COOK:** 5 HOURS
MAKES: 6 SERVINGS

- ¾ **cup water**
- ¼ **cup butter, melted**
- 1 **teaspoon garlic salt**
- 1 **teaspoon dried basil**
- 1 **teaspoon dried oregano**
- 6 **boneless skinless chicken breast halves (5 ounces each)**
- 2 **cups sliced fresh mushrooms**
- 2 **cans (10¾ ounces each) condensed golden mushroom soup, undiluted**
- 1 **package (8 ounces) reduced-fat cream cheese, cubed**
- ¾ **cup Marsala wine**
  Hot cooked noodles, optional

In a greased 4- or 5-qt. slow cooker, combine the water, butter, garlic salt, basil and oregano. Add chicken and mushrooms. In a large bowl, combine the soup, cream cheese and wine; pour over chicken. Cover and cook on low for 5-6 hours or until chicken is tender. Serve with noodles if desired.

Cajun Chicken Lasagna

Destined to be a new favorite around the table, this zesty take on traditional Italian lasagna nods to the Gulf Coast. Increase the amount of Cajun seasoning if you like spicier fare.

—MARY LOU COOK WELCHES, OR

PREP: 20 MIN. • **COOK:** 3 HOURS
MAKES: 8 SERVINGS

- 2 **pounds ground chicken**
- 2 **celery ribs with leaves, chopped**
- 1 **medium green pepper, chopped**
- 1 **medium onion, chopped**
- 1 **can (28 ounces) crushed tomatoes, undrained**
- 1 **cup water**
- 1 **can (6 ounces) tomato paste**
- 3 **teaspoons Cajun seasoning**
- 1 **teaspoon sugar**
- 2 **cups (8 ounces) shredded part-skim mozzarella cheese**
- 1 **carton (15 ounces) ricotta cheese**
- 9 **uncooked lasagna noodles**

1. In a large skillet, cook chicken over medium heat until no longer pink. Add the celery, green pepper and onion; cook and stir 5 minutes longer or until tender. Stir in the tomatoes, water, tomato paste, Cajun seasoning and sugar. In a small bowl, combine cheeses.

2. Spread 1 cup meat sauce in a greased oval 5- or 6-qt. slow cooker. Layer with 3 noodles (breaking noodles if necessary to fit), a third of the remaining meat sauce and a third of the cheese mixture. Repeat layers twice. Cover and cook on low for 3-4 hours or until noodles are tender.

Slow-Cooked Pulled Pork with Mojito Sauce

This Cuban take on pulled pork will knock the socks off any man! Serve with rice and beans for a complete meal.

—**KRISTINA WILEY** JUPITER, FL

PREP: 15 MIN. + MARINATING
COOK: 9 HOURS
MAKES: 12 SERVINGS (1½ CUPS SAUCE)

- 2 **large onions, quartered**
- 12 **garlic cloves**
- 1 **bottle (18 ounces) Cuban-style mojo sauce and marinade**
- ½ **cup lime juice**
- ½ **teaspoon salt**
- ¼ **teaspoon pepper**
- 1 **bone-in pork shoulder butt roast (5 to 5¼ pounds)**

MOJITO SAUCE

- ¾ **cup canola oil**
- 1 **medium onion, finely chopped**
- 6 **garlic cloves, finely chopped**
- ⅓ **cup lime juice**
- ½ **teaspoon salt**
- ¼ **teaspoon pepper**
  Additional chopped onion and lime wedges, optional

1. Place onions and garlic in a food processor; process until finely chopped. Add mojo marinade, lime juice, salt and pepper; process until blended. Pour half of the marinade into a large resealable plastic bag. Cut roast into quarters; add to bag. Seal bag and turn to coat. Refrigerate 8 hours or overnight. Transfer remaining marinade to a small bowl; refrigerate, covered, while marinating meat.

2. Drain pork, discarding marinade in bag. Place pork in a 5-qt. slow cooker coated with cooking spray. Top with reserved marinade. Cook, covered, on low 8-10 hours or until meat is tender.

3. For sauce, in a small saucepan, heat oil over medium heat 2½ to 3 minutes or until a thermometer reads 200°. Carefully add onion; cook 2 minutes, stirring occasionally. Stir in garlic; remove from heat. Stir in lime juice, salt and pepper.

4. Remove pork from slow cooker; cool slightly. Skim fat from cooking juices. Remove meat from bone; discard bone. Shred pork with two forks. Return cooking juices and pork to slow cooker; heat through.

5. Using tongs, remove pork to a platter. Serve with chopped onion, lime wedges and mojito sauce, stirring just before serving.

SLOW-COOKED PULLED PORK WITH MOJITO SAUCE

SLOW COOKER
ROTISSERIE-STYLE CHICKEN

Slow Cooker Rotisserie-Style Chicken

You wouldn't believe this golden-brown chicken was made in the slow cooker. Packed with flavor, the meat is moist, the carrots are tender and the juices make a nice gravy.

—TASTE OF HOME TEST KITCHEN

PREP: 30 MIN. • **COOK:** 6 HOURS + STANDING
MAKES: 6 SERVINGS

- 4 teaspoons seasoned salt
- 4 teaspoons poultry seasoning
- 1 tablespoon paprika
- 1½ teaspoons onion powder
- 1½ teaspoons brown sugar
- 1½ teaspoons salt-free lemon-pepper seasoning
- ¾ teaspoon garlic powder
- 1 broiler/fryer chicken (4 pounds)
- 1 pound carrots, halved lengthwise and cut into 1½-inch lengths
- 2 large onions, chopped
- 2 tablespoons cornstarch

1. In a small bowl, combine the first seven ingredients. Carefully loosen the skin from the chicken breast; rub 1 tablespoon spice mixture under the skin. Rub remaining spice mixture over chicken. In another bowl, toss carrots and onions with cornstarch; transfer to a 5-qt. slow cooker. Place chicken on vegetables.

2. Cover and cook on low for 6-7 hours or until a thermometer inserted in thigh reads 180°. Remove chicken and vegetables to a serving platter; cover and let stand for 15 minutes before carving. Skim fat from cooking juices. Serve with chicken and vegetables.

top tip — Simple Solution

Out of poultry seasoning? When a recipe calls for the popular seasoning blend, simply combine ¾ teaspoon rubbed sage and ¼ teaspoon dried thyme or marjoram. This yields 1 teaspoon, so review your recipe and plan accordingly.

No-Fuss Pork Roast Dinner

Wow! Talk about an easy meal in one! This recipe results in the most tender pork you've ever tasted. You can cut it with a fork, and it's just as tender the next day...if there are any leftovers.

—JANE MONTGOMERY PIQUA, OH

PREP: 25 MIN. • **COOK:** 6 HOURS
MAKES: 8 SERVINGS

- 1 large onion, halved and sliced
- 1 boneless pork loin roast (2½ pounds)
- 4 medium potatoes, peeled and cubed
- 1 package (16 ounces) frozen sliced carrots
- 1 cup hot water
- ¼ cup sugar
- 3 tablespoons cider vinegar
- 2 tablespoons reduced-sodium soy sauce
- 1 tablespoon ketchup
- ½ teaspoon salt
- ½ teaspoon pepper
- ¼ teaspoon garlic powder
- ¼ teaspoon chili powder
- 2 tablespoons cornstarch
- 2 tablespoons cold water

1. Place onion in a 5-qt. slow cooker. Add the pork, potatoes and carrots. Whisk the hot water, sugar, vinegar, soy sauce, ketchup, salt, pepper, garlic powder and chili powder; pour over pork and vegetables. Cover and cook on low for 6-8 hours or until meat is tender.

2. Remove pork and vegetables to a serving platter; keep warm. Skim fat from cooking juices; transfer to a small saucepan. Bring liquid to a boil. Combine cornstarch and cold water until smooth. Gradually stir into the pan. Bring to a boil; cook and stir for 2 minutes or until thickened. Serve with meat and vegetables.

NO-FUSS PORK ROAST DINNER

Italian Sausage and Vegetables

Wonderful served with a slice of hot garlic bread, this one-pot meal is both healthy and delicious. I found the recipe in a magazine and made adjustments to suit my taste.

—GINNY STUBY ALTOONA, PA

PREP: 20 MIN. • **COOK:** 5½ HOURS • **MAKES:** 6 SERVINGS

- 1¼ pounds sweet or hot Italian turkey sausage links
- 1 can (28 ounces) diced tomatoes, undrained
- 2 medium potatoes, cut into 1-inch pieces
- 4 small zucchini, cut into 1-inch slices
- 1 medium onion, cut into wedges
- ½ teaspoon garlic powder
- ¼ teaspoon crushed red pepper flakes
- ¼ teaspoon dried oregano
- ¼ teaspoon dried basil
- 1 tablespoon dry bread crumbs
- ¾ cup shredded pepper jack cheese

1. In a nonstick skillet, brown sausages over medium heat. Place in a 5-qt. slow cooker. Add vegetables and seasonings. Cover and cook on low for 5½ to 6½ hours or until a thermometer reads 165°.

2. Remove sausages and cut into 1-in. pieces; return to slow cooker. Stir in bread crumbs. Serve in bowls; sprinkle with cheese.

SAVORY LEMONADE CHICKEN

Savory Lemonade Chicken

I don't know where this recipe originally came from, but my mother used to prepare it for our family when I was little. Now I love to make it! A sweet and tangy sauce nicely coats chicken that's ready to serve in just a few hours.

—JENNY COOK EAU CLAIRE, WI

PREP: 10 MIN. • **COOK:** 3 HOURS • **MAKES:** 6 SERVINGS

- 6 boneless skinless chicken breast halves (4 ounces each)
- ¾ cup thawed lemonade concentrate
- 3 tablespoons ketchup
- 2 tablespoons brown sugar
- 1 tablespoon cider vinegar
- 2 tablespoons cornstarch
- 2 tablespoons cold water

1. Place chicken in a 5-qt. slow cooker. In a small bowl, combine the lemonade concentrate, ketchup, brown sugar and vinegar; pour over chicken. Cover and cook on low for 2½ hours or until chicken is tender.

2. Remove chicken and keep warm. Combine cornstarch and water until smooth; gradually stir into cooking juices. Cover and cook on high for 30 minutes or until thickened. Return chicken to the slow cooker; heat through.

ITALIAN SAUSAGE AND VEGETABLES

top tip

Brown Sugar Basics

Brown sugar is a mixture of sugar and molasses, with dark brown sugar containing more molasses than light brown sugar. Light brown sugar has a delicate flavor, while dark brown has a stronger molasses flavor. They can be used interchangeably.

Pork Roast Cubano

PREP: 30 MIN. • **COOK:** 7 HOURS • **MAKES:** 8 SERVINGS

- 3 pounds boneless pork shoulder butt roast
- 2 tablespoons olive oil
- 1 can (15 ounces) black beans, rinsed and drained
- 1 medium sweet potato, cut into ½-inch cubes
- 1 small sweet red pepper, cubed
- 1 can (13.66 ounces) light coconut milk
- ½ cup salsa verde
- 1 teaspoon minced fresh gingerroot
- 2 green onions, thinly sliced
  Sliced papaya

1. In a large skillet, brown roast in oil on all sides. Transfer to a 5-qt. slow cooker. Add black beans, sweet potato and red pepper. In a small bowl, mix coconut milk, salsa and ginger; pour over top.
2. Cook, covered, on low 7-9 hours or until pork is tender. Sprinkle with green onions; serve with papaya.

PORK WITH PEACH SAUCE

Pork with Peach Sauce

When fresh peaches are in season, I cook up my pork ribs for family and friends. I love the recipe because I only need six ingredients, the slow cooker does the work for me and the ribs turn out tender every time!

—**CONNIE JENISTA** VALRICO, FL

PREP: 20 MIN. + CHILLING • **COOK:** 5½ HOURS
MAKES: 6 SERVINGS

- 2 pounds boneless country-style pork ribs
- 2 tablespoons taco seasoning
- ½ cup mild salsa
- ¼ cup peach preserves
- ¼ cup barbecue sauce
- 2 cups chopped fresh peeled peaches or frozen unsweetened sliced peaches, thawed and chopped

1. In a large bowl, toss ribs with taco seasoning. Cover and refrigerate overnight.
2. Place pork in a 3-qt. slow cooker. In a small bowl, combine the salsa, preserves and barbecue sauce. Pour over ribs. Cover and cook on low for 5-6 hours or until meat is tender.
3. Add peaches; cover and cook 30 minutes longer or until peaches are tender.

PORK ROAST CUBANO

TEX-MEX CHICKEN & RICE

Polynesian Roast Beef

A family favorite for years, this easy idea came from my sibling. Pineapple and peppers add a perfect contrast to the rich and savory beef. Serve it with rice.

—**ANNETTE MOSBARGER** PEYTON, CO

PREP: 15 MIN. • **COOK:** 7 HOURS
MAKES: 10-11 SERVINGS

- 1 beef top round roast (3¾ pounds)
- 2 tablespoons browning sauce, optional
- ¼ cup all-purpose flour
- 1 teaspoon salt
- ¼ teaspoon pepper
- 1 medium onion, sliced
- 1 can (8 ounces) unsweetened sliced pineapple
- ¼ cup packed brown sugar
- 2 tablespoons cornstarch
- ¼ teaspoon ground ginger
- ½ cup beef broth
- ¼ cup reduced-sodium soy sauce
- ½ teaspoon minced garlic
- 1 medium green pepper, sliced

1. Cut roast in half; brush with browning sauce if desired. Combine the flour, salt and pepper; rub over meat. Place onion in a 3-qt. slow cooker; top with roast.
2. Drain pineapple, reserving juice; refrigerate the pineapple. In a small bowl, combine the brown sugar, cornstarch and ginger; whisk in the broth, soy sauce, garlic and reserved pineapple juice until smooth. Pour over meat. Cover and cook on low for 6-8 hours.
3. Add pineapple and green pepper. Cook 1 hour longer or until meat is tender.

Lively Leftovers

I saute slices of leftover roast beef in butter with minced garlic until lightly browned. I then add a can of tomato sauce, a dash of Worcestershire sauce and a bit of ground mustard and serve it over noodles.

—**PAT D.** OMAHA, NE

Tex-Mex Chicken & Rice

Here's a delicious go-to recipe for busy days. My sister mostly cooks by throwing canned goods into a pot, so I created this dish for her to get the most out of her new slow cooker.

—**ELIZABETH DUMONT** BOULDER, CO

PREP: 15 MIN. • **COOK:** 7 HOURS
MAKES: 6 SERVINGS

- 6 chicken leg quarters, skin removed
- 1 envelope taco seasoning, divided
- 1 can (14½ ounces) Mexican diced tomatoes, undrained
- 1 can (10¾ ounces) condensed cream of chicken soup, undiluted
- 1 large onion, chopped
- 1 can (4 ounces) chopped green chilies
- 1 cup uncooked instant rice
- 1 cup canned black beans, rinsed and drained
- 1 container (8 ounces) sour cream
- 1 cup (4 ounces) shredded cheddar cheese
- 1½ cups crushed tortilla chips
  Minced fresh cilantro

1. Sprinkle chicken with 1 tablespoon taco seasoning; transfer to a 5- or 6-qt. slow cooker. In a large bowl, combine the tomatoes, soup, onion, chilies and remaining taco seasoning; pour over chicken. Cover and cook on low for 7-9 hours or until chicken is tender.
2. Prepare rice according to package directions. Stir in beans; heat through.
3. Remove chicken from cooking juices; stir sour cream into cooking juices. Serve chicken with rice mixture and sauce. Sprinkle servings with cheese, tortilla chips and cilantro.

ANNETTE MOSBARGER'S
POLYNESIAN ROAST BEEF

Summer

SOUPS & SANDWICHES

The classic pairing of a soup and sandwich is a hit any time of year! Here, you'll find soups featuring the season's freshest ingredients and hearty sandwiches ideal for all of the appetites at your table.

JUDY DAMES'
HAWAIIAN SAUSAGE SUBS

---

⑤ INGREDIENTS Hawaiian Sausage Subs

If you're looking for a different way to use kielbasa, you've come to the right place! The sweet and mildly spicy flavor of these sandwiches is a nice change of pace.
—**JUDY DAMES** BRIDGEVILLE, PA

PREP: 15 MIN. • **COOK:** 3 HOURS. • **MAKES:** 12 SERVINGS

- 3 pounds smoked kielbasa or Polish sausage, cut into 3-inch pieces
- 2 bottles (12 ounces each) chili sauce
- 1 can (20 ounces) pineapple tidbits, undrained
- ¼ cup packed brown sugar
- 12 hoagie buns, split

Place kielbasa in a 3-qt. slow cooker. Combine the chili sauce, pineapple and brown sugar; pour over kielbasa. Cover and cook on low for 3-4 hours or until heated through. Serve on buns.

Southwestern Chicken & Lima Bean Soup

I love to cook for my family and hear them say, "that was so good!" This simple soup is colorful and delicious—and it's good for you, too! Featuring beans, corn, onion, pepper and tomatoes, it's a tasty take on chicken soup you won't soon forget. The addition of cilantro is lovely, particularly when it's fresh from the herb garden.
—**PAM CORDER** MONROE, LA

PREP: 20 MIN. • **COOK:** 6 HOURS. • **MAKES:** 6 SERVINGS

- 4 bone-in chicken thighs (1½ pounds), skin removed
- 2 cups frozen lima beans
- 2 cups frozen corn
- 1 large green pepper, chopped
- 1 large onion, chopped
- 2 cans (14 ounces each) fire-roasted diced tomatoes, undrained
- ¼ cup tomato paste
- 3 tablespoons Worcestershire sauce
- 3 garlic cloves, minced
- 1½ teaspoons ground cumin
- 1½ teaspoons dried oregano
- ¼ teaspoon salt
- ¼ teaspoon pepper
  Chopped fresh cilantro or parsley

1. Place the first five ingredients in a 5-qt. slow cooker. In a large bowl, combine tomatoes, tomato paste, Worcestershire sauce, garlic and seasonings; pour over top.
2. Cook, covered, on low 6-8 hours or until chicken is tender. Remove chicken from slow cooker. When cool enough to handle, remove meat from bones; discard bones. Shred meat with two forks; return to slow cooker and heat through. If desired, sprinkle with cilantro.

Slow-Cooked Barbecued Pork Sandwiches

PREP: 20 MIN. • **COOK:** 7 HOURS • **MAKES:** 10 SERVINGS

- 1 medium onion, chopped
- 1 tablespoon butter
- 1 can (15 ounces) tomato puree
- ½ cup packed brown sugar
- ¼ cup steak sauce
- 2 tablespoons lemon juice
- ½ teaspoon salt
- 1 boneless pork shoulder butt roast (3 pounds)
- 10 hard rolls, split

1. In a large skillet, saute onion in butter until tender. Stir in the tomato puree, brown sugar, steak sauce, lemon juice and salt. Cook over medium heat until sugar is dissolved and heated through.

2. Place roast in a 5-qt. slow cooker; pour sauce over the top. Cover and cook on low for 7-9 hours or until meat is tender. Remove roast; cool slightly. Skim fat from cooking juices. Shred meat with two forks and return to the slow cooker. Heat through. Serve on rolls.

SLOW-COOKED BARBECUED PORK SANDWICHES

ZIPPY SPANISH RICE SOUP

Zippy Spanish Rice Soup

I created this recipe after ruining a dinner of Spanish rice. I tried to salvage the dish by adding green chiles, cilantro and more water. It was a hit with the whole family. It's hearty enough to be a main dish with the addition of a garden salad and some corn bread.

—MARILYN SCHETZ CUYAHOGA FALLS, OH

PREP: 20 MIN. • **COOK:** 4 HOURS. • **MAKES:** 8 SERVINGS (2 QUARTS)

- 1 pound lean ground beef (90% lean)
- 1 medium onion, chopped
- 3 cups water
- 1 jar (16 ounces) salsa
- 1 can (14½ ounces) diced tomatoes, undrained
- 1 jar (7 ounces) roasted sweet red peppers, drained and chopped
- 1 can (4 ounces) chopped green chilies
- 1 envelope taco seasoning
- 1 tablespoon dried cilantro flakes
- ½ cup uncooked converted rice

1. In a large skillet, cook beef and onion over medium heat until meat is no longer pink; drain.

2. Transfer to a 4- or 5-qt. slow cooker. Add the water, salsa, tomatoes, red peppers, chilies, taco seasoning and cilantro. Stir in rice. Cover and cook on low for 4-5 hours or until rice is tender.

CUBAN-STYLE PORK SANDWICHES

Cuban-Style Pork Sandwiches

Loaded with tangy flavor, this is a lighter version of a favorite restaurant-style sandwich. If you don't have a panini maker, tuck the sandwiches under the broiler until the bread is browned and the cheese melted.

—ROBIN HAAS CRANSTON, RI

PREP: 20 MIN.
COOK: 6 HOURS + STANDING
MAKES: 10 SERVINGS

- 1 **large onion, cut into wedges**
- ¾ **cup reduced-sodium chicken broth**
- 1 **cup minced fresh parsley**
- 7 **garlic cloves, minced and divided**
- 2 **tablespoons cider vinegar**
- 1 **tablespoon plus 1½ teaspoons lemon juice, divided**
- 2 **teaspoons ground cumin**
- 1 **teaspoon ground mustard**
- 1 **teaspoon dried oregano**
- ½ **teaspoon salt**
- ½ **teaspoon pepper**
- 1 **boneless pork shoulder butt roast (3 to 4 pounds)**

- 1¼ **cups fat-free mayonnaise**
- 2 **tablespoons Dijon mustard**
- 10 **whole wheat hamburger buns, split**
- 1¼ **cups (5 ounces) shredded reduced-fat Swiss cheese**
- 1 **medium onion, thinly sliced and separated into rings**
- 2 **whole dill pickles, sliced**

1. Place onion wedges and broth in a 5-qt. slow cooker. In a small bowl, combine the parsley, 5 garlic cloves, vinegar, 1 tablespoon lemon juice, cumin, mustard, oregano, salt and pepper; rub over pork. Add to slow cooker. Cover and cook on low for 6-8 hours or until meat is tender.
2. Remove the meat; let stand for 10 minutes before slicing. In another small bowl, combine the mayonnaise, mustard and remaining garlic and lemon juice; spread over buns. Layer bun bottoms with pork, cheese, sliced onion and pickles; replace tops.
3. Cook on a panini maker or indoor grill for 2-3 minutes or until buns are browned and cheese is melted.

Lime Chicken Chili

Lime juice gives this chili a zesty twist, while canned tomatoes and beans make preparation a breeze. I like to serve it with toasted tortilla strips and sour cream.

—DIANE RANDAZZO SINKING SPRING, PA

PREP: 25 MIN. • **COOK:** 4½ HOURS
MAKES: 6 SERVINGS

- 1 **medium onion, chopped**
- 1 **each medium sweet yellow, red and green pepper, chopped**
- 2 **tablespoons olive oil**
- 3 **garlic cloves, minced**
- 1 **pound ground chicken**
- 2 **cans (14½ ounces each) diced tomatoes, undrained**
- 1 **can (15 ounces) white kidney or cannellini beans, rinsed and drained**
- ¼ **cup lime juice**
- 1 **tablespoon all-purpose flour**
- 1 **tablespoon baking cocoa**
- 1 **tablespoon ground cumin**
- 1 **tablespoon chili powder**
- 2 **teaspoons ground coriander**
- 1 **teaspoon grated lime peel**
- ½ **teaspoon salt**
- ½ **teaspoon garlic pepper blend**
- ¼ **teaspoon pepper**
- 2 **flour tortillas (8 inches), cut into ¼-inch strips**
- 6 **tablespoons reduced-fat sour cream**

1. In a large skillet, saute onion and peppers in oil for 7-8 minutes or until crisp-tender. Add garlic; cook 1 minute longer. Add chicken; cook and stir over medium heat for 8-9 minutes or until meat is no longer pink.
2. Transfer to a 3-qt. slow cooker. Stir in the tomatoes, beans, lime juice, flour, cocoa, cumin, chili powder, coriander, lime peel, salt, garlic pepper and pepper.
3. Cover and cook on low for 4-5 hours or until heated through.
4. Place tortilla strips on a baking sheet coated with cooking spray. Bake at 400° for 8-10 minutes or until crisp. Serve chili with sour cream and tortilla strips.

DIANE RANDAZZO'S
LIME CHICKEN CHILI

SOUTHWEST PULLED PORK

Teriyaki Sandwiches

The meat for these sandwiches comes out of the slow cooker tender and flavorful. Living as we do in the foothills of the Cascades, we frequently have deer and elk in the freezer. I sometimes substitute that in this recipe, and it never tastes like game.

—**BERNICE MUILENBURG** MOLALLA, OR

PREP: 30 MIN. • **COOK:** 7 HOURS
MAKES: 8 SERVINGS

- 2 pounds beef boneless chuck steak
- ¼ cup soy sauce
- 1 tablespoon brown sugar
- 1 teaspoon ground ginger
- 1 garlic clove, minced
- 4 teaspoons cornstarch
- 2 tablespoons water
- 8 French rolls, split
- ¼ cup butter, melted
  Pineapple rings
  Chopped green onions

1. Cut steak into thin bite-size slices. In a 3-qt. slow cooker, combine the soy sauce, sugar, ginger and garlic. Add steak. Cover and cook on low for 7-9 hours or until meat is tender.
2. Remove meat with a slotted spoon; set aside. Carefully pour liquid into a 2-cup measuring cup; skim fat. Add water to liquid to measure 1½ cups.
3. Pour into a large saucepan. Combine cornstarch and water until smooth; add to pan. Cook and stir until thick and bubbly, about 2 minutes. Add meat and heat through.
4. Brush rolls with butter; broil 4-5 in. from the heat for 2-3 minutes or until lightly toasted. Fill with meat, pineapple and green onions.

TERIYAKI SANDWICHES

Southwest Pulled Pork

I made this one morning when friends called and said they planned to drop by in the afternoon. It makes a lot, and I was able to serve our friends a casual supper. The seasonings and green chilies give the meat a spicy kick. Try it for family reunions, block parties or any place where you need to feed a large group!

—**DEB LEBLANC** PHILLIPSBURG, KS

PREP: 20 MIN. • **COOK:** 8 HOURS
MAKES: 14 SERVINGS

- 1 boneless pork shoulder butt roast (4 pounds)
- 2 tablespoons chili powder
- 1 tablespoon brown sugar
- 1½ teaspoons ground cumin
- 1 teaspoon salt
- ½ teaspoon pepper
- ½ teaspoon cayenne pepper
- 1 large sweet onion, coarsely chopped
- 2 cans (4 ounces each) chopped green chilies
- 1 cup chicken broth
- 14 kaiser rolls, split

1. Cut roast in half. In a small bowl, combine the chili powder, brown sugar, cumin, salt, pepper and cayenne; rub over meat. Transfer to a 5-qt. slow cooker. Top with onion and chilies. Pour broth around meat.
2. Cover and cook on low for 8-10 hours or until tender. Remove roast; cool slightly. Skim fat from cooking juices. Shred pork with two forks and return to slow cooker; heat through. Serve on rolls.

Mango & Coconut Chicken Soup

I love preparing dinner in a slow cooker because it's carefree cooking. This chicken dish uses ingredients that I love, such as coconut milk, edamame and fresh ginger. The Asian-style entree is perfect for a summer potluck party.

—**ROXANNE CHAN** ALBANY, CA

PREP: 25 MIN. • **COOK:** 6 HOURS
MAKES: 6 SERVINGS

- 1 broiler/fryer chicken (3 to 4 pounds), skin removed and cut up
- 2 tablespoons canola oil
- 1 can (15 ounces) whole baby corn, drained
- 1 package (10 ounces) frozen chopped spinach, thawed
- 1 cup frozen shelled edamame, thawed
- 1 small sweet red pepper, chopped
- 1 can (13.66 ounces) light coconut milk
- ½ cup mango salsa
- 1 teaspoon minced fresh gingerroot
- 1 medium mango, peeled and chopped
- 2 tablespoons lime juice
- 2 green onions, chopped

1. In a large skillet, brown chicken in oil in batches. Transfer chicken and drippings to a 5-qt. slow cooker. Add the corn, spinach, edamame and red pepper. In a small bowl, combine the coconut milk, salsa and ginger; pour over vegetables.

2. Cover and cook on low for 6-8 hours or until chicken is tender. Remove chicken; cool slightly. When cool enough to handle, remove meat from bones; cut or shred meat into bite-size pieces. Return meat to slow cooker.

3. Just before serving, stir in mango and lime juice. Sprinkle servings with green onions.

MANGO & COCONUT CHICKEN SOUP

ALICE PEACOCK'S
VEGETABLE MINESTRONE

Vegetable Minestrone

My husband and I created this recipe to replicate the minestrone soup at our favorite Italian restaurant. It's nice to have this ready to eat for our evening meal on days when we have a hectic schedule.

—ALICE PEACOCK GRANDVIEW, MO

PREP: 15 MIN. • **COOK:** 6½ HOURS
MAKES: 8 SERVINGS (2½ QUARTS)

- 2 cans (14½ ounces each) beef broth
- 1 can (16 ounces) kidney beans, rinsed and drained
- 1 can (15 ounces) great northern beans, rinsed and drained
- 1 can (14½ ounces) Italian-style stewed tomatoes
- 1 large onion, chopped
- 1 medium zucchini, thinly sliced
- 1 medium carrot, shredded
- ¾ cup tomato juice
- 1 teaspoon dried basil
- ¾ teaspoon dried oregano
- ¼ teaspoon garlic powder
- 1 cup frozen cut green beans, thawed
- ½ cup frozen chopped spinach, thawed
- ½ cup small shell pasta
- ½ cup shredded Parmesan cheese

1. In a 4- or 5-qt. slow cooker, combine the first 11 ingredients. Cover and cook on low for 6-7 hours or until vegetables are tender.
2. Stir in the green beans, spinach and pasta. Cover and cook for 30 minutes or until heated through. Sprinkle with cheese.

Posole Verde

With fresh tomatillos, green chilies and hominy, this hearty, healthy soup nods to authentic Mexican fare. Family and friends frequently request it when they are invited over for dinner.

—GAYLE EHRENMAN WHITE PLAINS, NY

PREP: 30 MIN. • **COOK:** 8 HOURS
MAKES: 8 SERVINGS (3 QUARTS)

- 1 pork tenderloin (1 pound), cubed
- 1 package (12 ounces) fully cooked spicy chicken sausage links, sliced
- 8 tomatillos, husks removed and cut into 1-inch pieces
- 2 cans (14 ounces each) hominy, rinsed and drained
- 1 can (16 ounces) kidney beans, rinsed and drained
- 1 can (14½ ounces) chicken broth
- 3 cans (4 ounces each) chopped green chilies
- 1 large red onion, quartered and sliced
- 2 tablespoons brown sugar
- 3 garlic cloves, minced
- 1 tablespoon ground cumin
- 1 tablespoon chili powder
- 1 teaspoon dried oregano
  Minced fresh cilantro, optional

In a 6-qt. slow cooker, combine the first 13 ingredients. Cover and cook on low for 8-10 hours or until pork is tender. Sprinkle with cilantro.

Slow-Cooked Spicy Portuguese Cacoila

Here's a tasty take on a pulled pork sandwich that doesn't include barbecue sauce. Portuguese pulled pork is a spicy dish often served at our large family functions. Each cook generally adds his or her own touches that reflect their taste and Portuguese heritage. A mixture of beef roast and pork can also be used.

—MICHELE MERLINO EXETER, RI

PREP: 20 MIN. • **COOK:** 6 HOURS.
MAKES: 12 SERVINGS

- 4 pounds boneless pork shoulder butt roast, cut into 2-in. pieces
- 1½ cups dry red wine or reduced-sodium chicken broth
- 4 garlic cloves, minced
- 4 bay leaves
- 1 tablespoon salt
- 1 tablespoon paprika
- 2 to 3 teaspoons crushed red pepper flakes
- 1 teaspoon ground cinnamon
- 1 large onion, chopped
- ½ cup water
- 12 bolillos or hoagie buns, split, optional

1. Place pork in a large resealable bag; add wine, garlic and seasonings. Seal bag and turn to coat. Refrigerate overnight.
2. Transfer pork mixture to a 5- or 6-qt. slow cooker; add chopped onion and water.
3. Cook, covered, on low 6-8 hours or until meat is tender.
4. Skim fat. Remove bay leaves. Shred meat with two forks. If desired, serve with a slotted spoon on bolillos.

SLOW-COOKED SPICY PORTUGUESE CACOILA

"Sauerkraut gives these beer-simmered brats a big flavor boost, but it's the special chili sauce and melted cheese that truly make them winners! Top your favorite burger with some of the chili sauce; you won't be sorry!" —ALANA SIMMONS JOHNSTOWN, PA

Slow-Cooked Reuben Brats

PREP: 30 MIN. • **COOK:** 7¼ HOURS
MAKES: 10 SERVINGS

- 10 uncooked bratwurst links
- 3 cans (12 ounces each) light beer or nonalcoholic beer
- 1 large sweet onion, sliced
- 1 can (14 ounces) sauerkraut, rinsed and well drained
- ¾ cup mayonnaise
- ¼ cup chili sauce
- 2 tablespoons ketchup
- 1 tablespoon finely chopped onion
- 2 teaspoons sweet pickle relish
- 1 garlic clove, minced
- ⅛ teaspoon pepper
- 10 hoagie buns, split
- 10 slices Swiss cheese

1. In a large skillet, brown bratwurst in batches; drain. In a 5-qt. slow cooker, combine beer, sliced onion and sauerkraut; top with bratwurst. Cook, covered, on low 7-9 hours or until sausages are cooked through.

2. Preheat oven to 350°. In a small bowl, mix mayonnaise, chili sauce, ketchup, chopped onion, relish, garlic and pepper until blended. Spread over cut sides of buns; top with cheese, bratwurst and sauerkraut mixture. Place on an ungreased baking sheet. Bake 8-10 minutes or until cheese is melted.

SLOW-COOKED REUBEN BRATS

COUNTRY RIB SANDWICHES

Country Rib Sandwiches

Plum sauce, allspice and chili sauce are the "secret ingredients" behind my mouthwatering sandwiches.

—MARGARET LUCHSINGER JUPITER, FL

PREP: 30 MIN. • **COOK:** 6¼ HOURS
MAKES: 8 SERVINGS

- 1 large onion, chopped
- 2 pounds boneless country-style pork ribs
- ½ cup ketchup
- ¼ cup plum sauce
- ¼ cup chili sauce
- 2 tablespoons brown sugar
- 1 teaspoon celery seed
- 1 teaspoon garlic powder
- 1 teaspoon liquid smoke, optional
- ½ teaspoon ground allspice
- 8 kaiser rolls, split

1. Place onion in a 3-qt. slow cooker; top with ribs. Combine the ketchup, plum sauce, chili sauce, brown sugar, celery seed, garlic powder, liquid smoke if desired and allspice; pour over ribs.

2. Cover and cook on low for 6-7 hours or until meat is tender. Shred the meat with two forks and return to the slow cooker. Cover and cook for 15 minutes longer or until heated through. Serve on rolls.

SOUTHWESTERN CHICKEN SOUP

Southwestern Chicken Soup

Here's the perfect recipe for a busy week because the slow cooker does most of the work for you!

—HAROLD TARTAR WEST PALM BEACH, FL

PREP: 10 MIN. • **COOK:** 7 HOURS
MAKES: 10 SERVINGS (2½ QUARTS)

- 1¼ pounds boneless skinless chicken breasts, cut into thin strips
- 1 tablespoon canola oil
- 2 cans (14½ ounces each) reduced-sodium chicken broth
- 1 package (16 ounces) frozen corn, thawed
- 1 can (14½ ounces) diced tomatoes, undrained
- 1 medium onion, chopped
- 1 medium green pepper, chopped
- 1 medium sweet red pepper, chopped
- 1 can (4 ounces) chopped green chilies
- 1½ teaspoons seasoned salt, optional
- 1 teaspoon ground cumin
- ½ teaspoon garlic powder

1. In a large skillet, saute chicken in oil until lightly browned. Transfer to a 5-qt. slow cooker. Stir in the remaining ingredients.

2. Cover and cook on low for 7-8 hours or until chicken and vegetables are tender. Stir before serving.

VERY BEST BARBECUE BEEF SANDWICHES

Vegetable Beef Barley Soup

A host of garden-fresh vegetables and well-seasoned beef make this slow cooker soup taste just like home. Serve with a loaf of fresh bread or a crispy green salad and dinner is done!

—TARA MCDONALD KANSAS CITY, MO

PREP: 45 MIN. • **COOK:** 7 HOURS
MAKES: 8 SERVINGS (2¾ QUARTS)

- 1 teaspoon seasoned salt
- 1 teaspoon onion powder
- 1 teaspoon garlic powder
- 1½ pounds beef stew meat, cut into 1-inch cubes
- 2 tablespoons canola oil
- 3 cups water
- 3 medium potatoes, peeled and diced
- 1 cup sliced fresh carrots
- 1 cup chopped celery
- ½ cup chopped onion
- 1 teaspoon beef bouillon granules
- 1 can (15¼ ounces) whole kernel corn, drained
- 1 can (14½ ounces) diced tomatoes, undrained
- 1 can (8½ ounces) peas, drained
- 1 cup tomato juice
- ¾ cup medium pearl barley
- ½ teaspoon salt
- ¼ teaspoon pepper

1. In a large resealable plastic bag, combine the seasoned salt, onion powder and garlic powder. Add beef and toss to coat.
2. In a large skillet, brown beef in oil until meat is no longer pink; drain.
3. Transfer to a 5- or 6-qt. slow cooker. Add the water, potatoes, carrots, celery, onion and bouillon.
4. Cover and cook on low for 5-6 hours or until meat and vegetables are almost tender.
5. Add the corn, tomatoes, peas, tomato juice, barley, salt and pepper; cover and cook 2 hours longer or until barley is tender.

Very Best Barbecue Beef Sandwiches

Friends will beg for the recipe of these sweet and oh-so good sandwiches. Give the crowd-pleasers a try, and you'll see that they definitely live up to their name!

—TASTE OF HOME TEST KITCHEN

PREP: 20 MIN. • **COOK:** 8½ HOURS
MAKES: 12 SERVINGS

- 1 boneless beef chuck roast (3 to 4 pounds)
- 1½ cups ketchup
- 1 small onion, finely chopped
- ¼ cup packed brown sugar
- ¼ cup red wine vinegar
- 1 tablespoon Dijon mustard
- 1 tablespoon Worcestershire sauce
- 2 garlic cloves, minced
- ½ teaspoon salt
- ¼ teaspoon celery seed
- ¼ teaspoon paprika
- ¼ teaspoon pepper
- 2 tablespoons cornstarch
- 2 tablespoons cold water
- 12 kaiser rolls, split
  Dill pickle slices, optional

1. Cut roast in half. Place in a 5-qt. slow cooker. In a small bowl, combine the ketchup, onion, brown sugar, vinegar, mustard, Worcestershire sauce, garlic, salt, celery seed, paprika and pepper; pour over roast. Cover and cook on low for 8-10 hours or until meat is tender.
2. Remove meat. Skim fat from cooking juices; transfer to a large saucepan. Bring to a boil. Combine cornstarch and water until smooth; gradually stir into juices. Return to a boil; cook and stir for 2 minutes or until thickened.
3. When meat is cool enough to handle, shred with two forks. Return to slow cooker and stir in sauce mixture; heat through. Serve on rolls with pickle slices if desired.

TARA MCDONALD'S
VEGETABLE BEEF BARLEY SOUP

Pepperoni Pizza Soup

Once upon a time my husband and I owned a pizzeria, and this dish was always popular. We've since sold the restaurant, but I still make the soup for all kinds of potlucks and gatherings. It's always a big hit, and everyone asks for the recipe.

—**ESTELLA PETERSON** MADRAS, OR

PREP: 20 MIN. • **COOK:** 8 HOURS
MAKES: 6 SERVINGS (2¼ QUARTS)

　2　**cans (14½ ounces each) Italian stewed tomatoes, undrained**
　2　**cans (14½ ounces each) reduced-sodium beef broth**
　1　**small onion, chopped**
　1　**small green pepper, chopped**
　½　**cup sliced fresh mushrooms**
　½　**cup sliced pepperoni, halved**
1½　**teaspoons dried oregano**
　⅛　**teaspoon pepper**
　1　**package (9 ounces) refrigerated cheese ravioli**
　　Shredded part-skim mozzarella cheese and sliced ripe olives

1. In a 4-qt. slow cooker, combine the first eight ingredients. Cook, covered, on low 8-9 hours.
2. Stir in ravioli; cook, covered, on low 15-30 minutes or until pasta is tender. Top servings with cheese and olives.

PEPPERONI PIZZA SOUP

TEX-MEX BEEF SANDWICHES

Tex-Mex Beef Sandwiches

Cocoa is a surprise ingredient that adds a depth of flavor to my hearty beef bites. It's hard to identify, so I'm often asked, "What's that terrific flavor?"

—**BRENDA THEISEN** ADDISON, MI

PREP: 25 MIN. • **COOK:** 8 HOURS. • **MAKES:** 8 SERVINGS

1　**boneless beef chuck roast (3 pounds)**
1　**envelope burrito seasoning**
2　**tablespoons baking cocoa**
1　**large green pepper, coarsely chopped**
1　**large sweet red pepper, coarsely chopped**
1　**large onion, chopped**
1　**cup beef broth**
½　**cup ketchup**
8　**hoagie buns, split**

1. Cut roast in half. Combine burrito seasoning and cocoa; rub over meat. Place peppers and onion in a 3- or 4-qt. slow cooker; top with meat. Combine broth and ketchup; pour over meat.
2. Cover and cook on low for 8-10 hours or until meat is tender.
3. Skim fat. When cool enough to handle, shred meat with two forks and return to slow cooker; heat through. Using a slotted spoon, spoon ½ cup onto each bun.

Chicago-Style Beef Rolls

PREP: 20 MIN. • **COOK:** 8 HOURS • **MAKES:** 16 SERVINGS

- 1 boneless beef chuck roast (4 to 5 pounds)
- 1 tablespoon olive oil
- 3 cups beef broth
- 1 medium onion, chopped
- 1 package Italian salad dressing mix
- 3 garlic cloves, minced
- 1 tablespoon Italian seasoning
- ½ teaspoon crushed red pepper flakes
- 16 sourdough rolls, split
  Sliced pepperoncini and pickled red pepper rings, optional

1. Brown roast in oil on all sides in a large skillet; drain. Transfer beef to a 5-qt. slow cooker. Combine the broth, onion, dressing mix, garlic, Italian seasoning and pepper flakes in a large bowl; pour over roast.

2. Cover and cook on low for 8-10 hours or until tender. Remove meat; cool slightly. Skim fat from cooking juices. Shred beef with two forks and return to slow cooker; heat through. Place ½ cup on each roll using a slotted spoon. Serve with pepperoncini and pepper rings if desired.

EASY PHILLY CHEESESTEAKS

Easy Philly Cheesesteaks

Since we live in a rural area where there really aren't any restaurants to speak of, I thought it would be fun to come up with my take on this classic sandwich at home. They're so effortless and delicious! Grab a bottle of steak sauce to top them off for an extra bolt of flavor.
—LENETTE BENNETT COMO, CO

PREP: 20 MIN. • **COOK:** 6 HOURS • **MAKES:** 6 SERVINGS

- 2 medium onions, halved and sliced
- 2 medium sweet red or green peppers, halved and sliced
- 1 beef top sirloin steak (1½ pounds), cut into thin strips
- 1 envelope onion soup mix
- 1 can (14½ ounces) reduced-sodium beef broth
- 6 hoagie buns, split
- 12 slices provolone cheese, halved
  Pickled hot cherry peppers, optional

1. Place onions and red peppers in a 4- or 5-qt. slow cooker. Add beef, soup mix and broth. Cook, covered, on low for 6-8 hours or until meat is tender.

2. Arrange buns on a baking sheet, cut side up. Using tongs, place meat mixture on bun bottoms; top with cheese.

3. Broil 2-3 in. from heat 30-60 seconds or until cheese is melted and bun tops are toasted. If desired, serve with cherry peppers.

CHICAGO-STYLE BEEF ROLLS

MYRNA SIPPEL'S
ZESTY ITALIAN SOUP

Zesty Italian Soup

While visiting my sister-in-law, we had a delicious Italian soup at a local restaurant. We decided to duplicate it at home and came up with this version. Vary the seasonings and types of canned tomatoes to suit your family's tastes.

—**MYRNA SIPPEL** THOMPSON, IL

PREP: 15 MIN. • **COOK:** 7 HOURS
MAKES: 10 SERVINGS (3½ QUARTS)

- 1 pound bulk Italian sausage
- 3 cans (14½ ounces each) reduced-sodium chicken broth
- 1 can (15 ounces) black beans, rinsed and drained
- 1 can (15 ounces) pinto beans, rinsed and drained
- 1 can (14½ ounces) diced tomatoes and green chilies, undrained
- 1 can (14½ ounces) Italian diced tomatoes
- 1 large carrot, chopped
- 1 jalapeno pepper, seeded and chopped
- 1½ teaspoons Italian seasoning
- 1 teaspoon dried minced garlic
- 1½ cups cooked elbow macaroni

1. In a large skillet, cook sausage over medium heat until no longer pink; drain.
2. Transfer to a 5-qt. slow cooker. Stir in the broth, beans, tomatoes, carrot, jalapeno, Italian seasoning and garlic.
3. Cover and cook on low for 7-8 hours or until heated through. Just before serving, stir in macaroni.
NOTE *Wear disposable gloves when cutting hot peppers; the oils can burn skin. Avoid touching your face.*

top tip — Chop, Chop!

To chop carrots coarsely for soup, I peel the carrots and remove the ends. Next, I cut the carrots into quarters, and I then let the food processor do the chopping.
—**MARION K.** WATERLOO, IA

Spinach Bean Soup

This meatless dish is great for a busy weeknight supper after I get home from my job as a college nursing professor. The soup provides plenty of nutrients to keep me healthy as well.

—**BRENDA JEFFERS** OTTUMWA, IA

PREP: 20 MIN. • **COOK:** 6¼ HOURS
MAKES: 8 SERVINGS (2 QUARTS)

- 3 cans (14½ ounces each) vegetable broth
- 1 can (15½ ounces) great northern beans, rinsed and drained
- 1 can (15 ounces) tomato puree
- ½ cup finely chopped onion
- ½ cup uncooked converted long grain rice
- 2 garlic cloves, minced
- 1 teaspoon dried basil
- ½ teaspoon salt
- ¼ teaspoon pepper
- 1 package (6 ounces) fresh baby spinach, coarsely chopped
- ¼ cup shredded Parmesan cheese

1. In a 4-qt. slow cooker, combine the first nine ingredients. Cover and cook on low for 6-7 hours or until heated through.
2. Stir in spinach. Cover and cook for 15 minutes or until spinach is wilted. Sprinkle with cheese.

SPINACH BEAN SOUP

Summer

DESSERTS

You don't need a special occasion to enjoy dessert! Make summer a little sweeter with these slow-cooked treats that feature berries, bananas, coconut and more. What a tasty way to top off a meal!

KAREN JAROCKI'S
SLOW-COOKER BERRY COBBLER

Slow-Cooker Berry Cobbler

Even during warm weather, you can still enjoy the amazing flavor of homemade cobbler without heating up the kitchen.
—**KAREN JAROCKI** YUMA, AZ

PREP: 15 MIN. • **COOK:** 2 HOURS • **MAKES:** 8 SERVINGS

- 1¼ cups all-purpose flour, divided
- 2 tablespoons plus 1 cup sugar, divided
- 1 teaspoon baking powder
- ¼ teaspoon ground cinnamon
- 1 egg, lightly beaten
- ¼ cup fat-free milk
- 2 tablespoons canola oil
- ⅛ teaspoon salt
- 2 cups fresh or frozen raspberries, thawed
- 2 cups fresh or frozen blueberries, thawed
  Low-fat vanilla frozen yogurt, optional

1. In a large bowl, combine 1 cup flour, 2 tablespoons sugar, baking powder and cinnamon. Combine the egg, milk and oil; stir into dry ingredients just until moistened (batter will be thick). Spread batter evenly into a 5-qt. slow cooker coated with cooking spray.
2. In a large bowl, combine the salt and remaining flour and sugar; add berries and toss to coat. Spread over batter.
3. Cover and cook on high for 2 to 2½ hours or until a toothpick inserted into cobbler comes out clean. Serve with frozen yogurt if desired.

Caribbean Bread Pudding

A completely unexpected dessert from the slow cooker, my bread pudding offers tropical flavors—pineapple and coconut.
—**ELIZABETH DOSS** CALIFORNIA CITY, CA

PREP: 30 MIN. • **COOK:** 4 HOURS • **MAKES:** 16 SERVINGS

- 1 cup raisins
- 1 can (8 ounces) crushed pineapple, undrained
- 2 large firm bananas, halved
- 1 can (12 ounces) evaporated milk
- 1 can (10 ounces) frozen non-alcoholic pina colada mix
- 1 can (6 ounces) unsweetened pineapple juice
- 3 eggs
- ½ cup cream of coconut
- ¼ cup light rum, optional
- 1 loaf (1 pound) French bread, cut into 1-inch cubes
  Whipped cream and maraschino cherries, optional

1. In a small bowl, combine raisins and pineapple; set aside. In a blender, combine the bananas, milk, pina colada mix, pineapple juice, eggs, cream of coconut and rum if desired. Cover and process until smooth.
2. Place two-thirds of the bread in a greased 5- or 6-qt. slow cooker. Top with 1 cup raisin mixture. Layer with remaining bread and raisin mixture. Pour banana mixture into slow cooker. Cover and cook on low for 4-5 hours or until a knife inserted near the center comes out clean. Serve warm with whipped cream if desired.

Minty Hot Fudge Sundae Cake

The best part about dessert from the slow cooker is that when dinner's done, a hot treat is ready to serve. In this case, a chocolaty, gooey, minty dessert you can't get enough of!

—**TERRI MCKITRICK** DELAFIELD, WI

PREP: 15 MIN. • **COOK:** 4 HOURS • **MAKES:** 12 SERVINGS

1¾ cups packed brown sugar, divided
1 cup all-purpose flour
5 tablespoons baking cocoa, divided
2 teaspoons baking powder
½ teaspoon salt
½ cup evaporated milk
2 tablespoons butter, melted
½ teaspoon vanilla extract
⅛ teaspoon almond extract
1 package (4.67 ounces) mint Andes candies
1¾ cups boiling water
4 teaspoons instant coffee granules
 Vanilla ice cream, whipped cream and maraschino cherries

1. In a large bowl, combine 1 cup brown sugar, flour, 3 tablespoons cocoa, baking powder and salt. In another bowl, combine the milk, butter and extracts. Stir into dry ingredients just until moistened. Transfer to a 3-qt. slow cooker coated with cooking spray. Sprinkle with candies.
2. Combine the water, coffee granules and remaining brown sugar and cocoa; pour over batter (do not stir). Cover and cook on high for 4 to 4½ hours or until a toothpick inserted near the center of the cake comes out clean. Serve with ice cream, whipped cream and cherries.

AMARETTO CHERRIES WITH DUMPLINGS

Amaretto Cherries with Dumplings

You can't beat the flavor combination of almond and cherry. These light and fluffy dumplings are heavenly. Topped with the sauce and ice cream, they make for a scrumptious surprise.

—**TASTE OF HOME TEST KITCHEN**

PREP: 15 MIN. • **COOK:** 7¾ HOURS • **MAKES:** 5 SERVINGS

2 cans (14½ ounces each) pitted tart cherries
¾ cup sugar
¼ cup cornstarch
⅛ teaspoon salt
¼ cup amaretto
DUMPLINGS
1 cup all-purpose flour
¼ cup sugar
1 teaspoon baking powder
½ teaspoon grated lemon peel
⅛ teaspoon salt
⅓ cup 2% milk
3 tablespoons butter, melted
 Vanilla ice cream, optional

1. Drain cherries, reserving ¼ cup juice. Place cherries in a 3-qt. slow cooker.
2. In a small bowl, combine the sugar, cornstarch and salt. Stir in reserved juice until smooth. Add to slow cooker. Cover and cook on high for 7 hours. Drizzle amaretto over cherry mixture.
3. For dumplings, in a small bowl, combine the flour, sugar, baking powder, lemon peel and salt. Stir in milk and butter just until moistened. Drop by tablespoonfuls onto hot cherry mixture. Cover and cook for 45 minutes or until a toothpick inserted in a dumpling comes out clean. Serve warm with ice cream if desired.

MINTY HOT FUDGE SUNDAE CAKE

Cherry & Spice Rice Pudding

I live in Traverse City, the Cherry Capital of the World, and what better way to celebrate our wonderful orchards than by using plump, tart, dried cherries in my favorite desserts? This slow-cooked rice pudding recipe always turns out just wonderful.

—DEB PERRY TRAVERSE CITY, MI

PREP: 10 MIN. • **COOK:** 2 HOURS
MAKES: 12 SERVINGS

- 4 **cups cooked long grain rice**
- 1 **can (12 ounces) evaporated milk**
- 1 **cup 2% milk**
- ⅓ **cup sugar**
- ¼ **cup water**
- ¾ **cup dried cherries**
- 3 **tablespoons butter, softened**
- 2 **teaspoons vanilla extract**
- ½ **teaspoon ground cinnamon**
- ¼ **teaspoon ground nutmeg**

1. In a large bowl, combine the rice, evaporated milk, milk, sugar and water. Stir in the remaining ingredients. Transfer to a 3-qt. slow cooker coated with cooking spray.
2. Cover and cook on low for 2-3 hours or until mixture is thickened. Stir lightly before serving. Serve warm or cold. Refrigerate leftovers.

CHERRY & SPICE RICE PUDDING

FRUIT COMPOTE DESSERT

Fruit Compote Dessert

This is one of the first desserts I learned to make in the slow cooker, and it's the one guests still enjoy most. It tastes like it came from a fancy restaurant. Honey adds a lovely sweet touch to the pineapple, peaches, apples and banana.

—LAURA BRYANT GERMAN
WEST WARREN, MA

PREP: 15 MIN. • **COOK:** 3 HOURS
MAKES: 8 SERVINGS

- 2 **medium tart apples, peeled**
- 2 **medium peaches, peeled and cubed**
- 2 **cups unsweetened pineapple chunks**
- 1¼ **cups unsweetened pineapple juice**
- ¼ **cup honey**
- 2 **lemon slices (¼ inch)**
- 1 **cinnamon stick (3½ inches)**
- 1 **medium firm banana, thinly sliced Whipped cream, sliced almonds and maraschino cherries, optional**

1. Cut apples into ¼-in. slices and then in half; place in a 3-qt. slow cooker. Add the peaches, pineapple, pineapple juice, honey, lemon and cinnamon. Cover and cook on low for 3-4 hours.
2. Just before serving, stir in banana slices. Serve with a slotted spoon if desired. Garnish with whipped cream, almonds and cherries if desired.

Apple Granola Dessert

I would be lost without my slow cooker. Besides using it to prepare our evening meal, I often make desserts in it, including these tender apples that get a tasty treatment with granola cereal.

—**JANIS LAWRENCE** CHILDRESS, TX

PREP: 10 MIN. • **COOK:** 6 HOURS
MAKES: 4-6 SERVINGS

- **4 medium tart apples, peeled and sliced**
- **2 cups granola cereal with fruit and nuts**
- **¼ cup honey**
- **2 tablespoons butter, melted**
- **1 teaspoon ground cinnamon**
- **½ teaspoon ground nutmeg**
  Whipped topping, optional

In a 1½-qt. slow cooker, combine apples and cereal. In a small bowl, combine the honey, butter, cinnamon and nutmeg; pour over apple mixture and mix well. Cover and cook on low for 6-8 hours. Serve with whipped topping if desired.

top tip

Honey Hints

I freeze honey to keep it from crystallizing. It never freezes solid due to its low moisture content; but, it does become thick. When thawed to room temperature, it returns to its original consistency.

—**J.M.** WEST BEND, WI

APPLE GRANOLA DESSERT

CLEO GONSKE'S
BLUEBERRY GRUNT

Blueberry Grunt

PREP: 20 MIN. • **COOK:** 2½ HOURS
MAKES: 6 SERVINGS

- 4 **cups fresh or frozen blueberries**
- ¾ **cup sugar**
- ½ **cup water**
- 1 **teaspoon almond extract**

DUMPLINGS

- 2 **cups all-purpose flour**
- 4 **teaspoons baking powder**
- 1 **teaspoon sugar**
- ½ **teaspoon salt**
- 1 **tablespoon cold butter**
- 1 **tablespoon shortening**
- ¾ **cup 2% milk**
  Vanilla ice cream, optional

1. In a 3-qt. slow cooker, combine the blueberries, sugar, water and extract. Cover and cook on high for 2-3 hours or until bubbly.
2. For dumplings, in a small bowl, combine the flour, baking powder, sugar and salt. Cut in butter and shortening until crumbly. Add milk; stir just until moistened.
3. Drop by tablespoonfuls onto hot blueberry mixture. Cover and cook 30 minutes longer or until a toothpick inserted in a dumpling comes out clean. Serve warm with ice cream if desired.

MAPLE CREME BRULEE

Maple Creme Brulee

The slow cooker is the perfect cooking vessel for classic creme brulee. The crunchy brown sugar topping in this recipe is wonderful, and the custard is smooth and creamy.
—**TASTE OF HOME TEST KITCHEN**

PREP: 20 MIN. • **COOK:** 2 HOURS + CHILLING
MAKES: 3 SERVINGS

- 1⅓ **cups heavy whipping cream**
- 3 **egg yolks**
- ½ **cup packed brown sugar**
- ¼ **teaspoon ground cinnamon**
- ½ **teaspoon maple flavoring**

TOPPING

- 1½ **teaspoons sugar**
- 1½ **teaspoons brown sugar**

1. In a small saucepan, heat cream until bubbles form around sides of pan. In a small bowl, whisk the egg yolks, brown sugar and cinnamon. Remove cream from the heat; stir a small amount of hot cream into egg mixture. Return all to the pan, stirring constantly. Stir in maple flavoring.
2. Transfer to three 6-oz. ramekins or custard cups. Place in a 6-qt. slow cooker; add 1 in. of boiling water to slow cooker. Cover and cook on high for 2 to 2½ hours or until centers are just set (mixture will jiggle). Carefully remove cups from slow cooker; cool for 10 minutes. Cover and refrigerate for at least 4 hours.
3. For topping, combine sugar and brown sugar. If using a creme brulee torch, sprinkle custards with sugar mixture. Heat sugar with the torch until caramelized. Serve immediately.
4. If broiling the custards, place ramekins on a baking sheet; let stand at room temperature for 15 minutes. Sprinkle with sugar mixture. Broil 8 in. from the heat for 3-5 minutes or until sugar is caramelized. Refrigerate for 1-2 hours or until firm.

Chocolate Pecan Fondue

When our kids have friends sleep over, I like to surprise them with this chocolate treat. Our favorite dippers include fresh fruit, marshmallows, cookies and pound cake.

—**SUZANNE MCKINLEY** LYONS, GA

START TO FINISH: 15 MIN. • **MAKES:** 1⅓ CUPS

- ½ cup half-and-half cream
- 2 tablespoons honey
- 9 ounces semisweet chocolate, broken into small pieces
- ¼ cup finely chopped pecans
- 1 teaspoon vanilla extract
  Fresh fruit and shortbread cookies

1. In a heavy saucepan over low heat, combine cream and honey; heat until warm. Add chocolate; stir until melted. Stir in pecans and vanilla.

2. Transfer to a warmed fondue pot or a 1½-qt. slow cooker and keep warm. Serve with fruit and cookies.

top tip

Different Dippers

When it comes to dippers for this fondue, get creative! Consider bite-sized brownies or pieces of pound cake. Try your favorite cookie or sliced mango.

CHOCOLATE PECAN FONDUE

Strawberry Rhubarb Sauce

A neighbor shared the secrets behind this wonderful fruit sauce. It's a great way to use up a bumper crop of rhubarb. We like it over ice cream, pancakes and even fresh, hot biscuits.

—**NANCY COWLISHAW** BOISE, ID

PREP: 15 MIN. • **COOK:** 4¼ HOURS
MAKES: 4½ CUPS

- 6 **cups sliced fresh or frozen rhubarb, thawed**
- 1 **cup sugar**
- ½ **cup unsweetened apple juice**
- 3 **cinnamon sticks (3 inches)**
- ½ **teaspoon grated orange peel**
- ¼ **teaspoon ground ginger**
- 1 **pint fresh strawberries, halved**
  Vanilla ice cream

1. Place the rhubarb, sugar, juice, cinnamon sticks, orange peel and ginger in a 3-qt. slow cooker. Cover and cook on low for 4-5 hours or until rhubarb is tender.

2. Stir in strawberries; cover and cook 15 minutes longer or until heated through. Discard cinnamon sticks. Serve with ice cream.

STOVETOP STRAWBERRY RHUBARB SAUCE *Increase apple juice to 1 cup. In a Dutch oven, combine the first six ingredients. Bring to a boil. Reduce heat; simmer, uncovered, for 20-25 minutes or until rhubarb is tender. Stir in strawberries; heat through.*

BLUEBERRY COBBLER

⑤ INGREDIENTS

Blueberry Cobbler

This simple-to-make dessert comes together in a jiffy. If you like, you can substitute the blueberry pie filling with other flavors, such as apple or cherry.

—**NELDA CRONBAUGH** BELLE PLAINE, IA

PREP: 10 MIN. • **COOK:** 3 HOURS
MAKES: 6 SERVINGS

- 1 **can (21 ounces) blueberry pie filling**
- 1 **package (9 ounces) yellow cake mix**
- ¼ **cup chopped pecans**
- ¼ **cup butter, melted**
  Vanilla ice cream, optional

Place pie filling in a greased 1½-qt. slow cooker. Sprinkle with cake mix and pecans. Drizzle with butter. Cover and cook on high for 3 hours or until topping is golden brown. Serve warm with ice cream if desired.

STRAWBERRY RHUBARB SAUCE

1 teaspoon grated orange peel
Whipped cream or vanilla ice
cream, optional

1. In a large bowl, combine the flour, ¾ cup sugar, baking powder, salt, cinnamon and nutmeg. Combine the eggs, milk and oil; stir into dry ingredients just until moistened. Spread the batter evenly onto the bottom of a greased 5-qt. slow cooker.
2. In a large saucepan, combine the berries, water, orange peel and remaining sugar; bring to a boil. Remove from the heat; immediately pour over batter. Cover and cook on high for 2 to 2½ hours or until a toothpick inserted into the batter comes out clean.
3. Turn cooker off. Uncover and let stand for 30 minutes before serving. Serve with whipped cream or ice cream if desired.

Slow-Cooker Bread Pudding

A slow cooker turns day-old cinnamon rolls into a comforting, old-fashioned treat. It tastes fabulous topped with lemon or vanilla sauce or ice cream.

—EDNA HOFFMAN HEBRON, IN

PREP: 15 MIN. • **COOK:** 3 HOURS
MAKES: 6 SERVINGS

8 cups cubed day-old unfrosted
   cinnamon rolls
4 eggs
2 cups milk
¼ cup sugar
¼ cup butter, melted
½ teaspoon vanilla extract
¼ teaspoon ground nutmeg
1 cup raisins

Place cubed cinnamon rolls in a 3-qt. slow cooker. In a small bowl, whisk the eggs, milk, sugar, butter, vanilla and nutmeg. Stir in raisins. Pour over cinnamon rolls; stir gently. Cover and cook on low for 3 hours or until a knife inserted near the center comes out clean.
NOTE *Eight slices of cinnamon or white bread, cut into 1-inch cubes, may be substituted for the cinnamon rolls.*

BLACK AND BLUE COBBLER

Black and Blue Cobbler

It never occurred to me that I could bake a cobbler in my slow cooker until I saw some other recipes and decided to try it with my favorite fruity dessert. It took a bit of experimenting, but the tasty results are "berry" well worth it!

—MARTHA CREVELING ORLANDO, FL

PREP: 15 MIN.
COOK: 2 HOURS + STANDING
MAKES: 6 SERVINGS

1 cup all-purpose flour
1½ cups sugar, divided
1 teaspoon baking powder
¼ teaspoon salt
¼ teaspoon ground cinnamon
¼ teaspoon ground nutmeg
2 eggs, lightly beaten
2 tablespoons milk
2 tablespoons canola oil
2 cups fresh or frozen blackberries
2 cups fresh or frozen blueberries
¾ cup water

EDNA HOFFMAN'S
SLOW-COOKER BREAD PUDDING

TONYA SWAIN'S
OKTOBERFEST PORK ROAST
page 226

Autumn

For most, comfort food is at its best when the weather turns crisp, the nights become longer and harvest-fresh flavors abound. Enjoy the colors, aromas and flavors of autumn with all of the satisfying slow -cooked dishes found here.

Autumn

APPETIZERS & BEVERAGES

Harvest festivals...Halloween... Thanksgiving...these are just a few of the reasons to host an open house this fall. Brimming with heartwarming goodness, these slow-cooked favorites promise to help you build happy memories for years to come.

NOEL LICKENFELT'S
HOT SPICED WINE

Hot Spiced Wine

My friends, family and I often enjoy this spiced wine during crisp-weather gatherings. This warm drink is especially pleasing to those who like dry red wines.

—**NOEL LICKENFELT** BOLIVAR, PA

PREP: 15 MIN. • **COOK:** 4 HOURS • **MAKES:** 8 SERVINGS

- 2 cinnamon sticks (3 inches)
- 3 whole cloves
- 2 bottles (750 milliliters each) dry red wine
- 3 medium tart apples, peeled and sliced
- ½ cup sugar
- 1 teaspoon lemon juice

1. Place cinnamon sticks and cloves on a double thickness of cheesecloth; bring up corners of cloth and tie with string to form a bag.
2. In a 3-qt. slow cooker, combine the wine, apples, sugar and lemon juice. Add spice bag. Cover and cook on low for 4-5 hours or until heated through. Discard spice bag. Serve warm.

Creamy Onion Dip

Here, caramelized onions are teamed up with Gruyere cheese for a rich appetizer that's fit for a classic cocktail party.

—**BECKY WALCH** MANTECA, CA

PREP: 20 MIN. • **COOK:** 5 HOURS • **MAKES:** 5 CUPS

- 4 cups finely chopped sweet onions
- ¼ cup butter, cubed
- ¼ cup white wine or chicken broth
- 6 garlic cloves, minced
- 1 bay leaf
- 2 cups (8 ounces) shredded Gruyere or Swiss cheese
- 1 package (8 ounces) cream cheese, softened
- ¼ cup sour cream
  Assorted crackers or breadsticks

1. In a 3-qt. slow cooker, combine the onions, butter, wine, garlic and bay leaf. Cover and cook on low for 4-5 hours or until onions are tender and golden brown.
2. Discard bay leaf. Stir in the Gruyere cheese, cream cheese and sour cream. Cover and cook 1 hour longer or until cheese is melted. Serve warm with crackers.

top tip

Appetizing Offerings

An appetizer-and-beverage buffet is a fun twist on fall entertaining and lends itself to a less formal atmosphere than a traditional sit-down dinner. For an appetizer buffet that serves as the meal, offer five or six different appetizers (including some substantial selections) and plan on roughly 8-9 pieces per guest.

Chili Cheese Dip

After trying to create a Mexican soup, I ended up with this outstanding dip that eats like a meal. My husband and two young children love it! Now it's become popular for football game days and family gatherings.

—**SANDRA FICK** LINCOLN, NE

PREP: 20 MIN. • **COOK:** 4½ HOURS • **MAKES:** 8 CUPS

- 1 **pound lean ground beef (90% lean)**
- 1 **cup chopped onion**
- 1 **can (16 ounces) kidney beans, rinsed and drained**
- 1 **can (15 ounces) black beans, rinsed and drained**
- 1 **can (14½ ounces) diced tomatoes in sauce**
- 1 **cup frozen corn**
- ¾ **cup water**
- 1 **can (2¼ ounces) sliced ripe olives, drained**
- 3 **teaspoons chili powder**
- ½ **teaspoon dried oregano**
- ½ **teaspoon chipotle hot pepper sauce**
- ¼ **teaspoon garlic powder**
- ¼ **teaspoon ground cumin**
- 1 **package (16 ounces) reduced-fat process cheese (Velveeta), cubed**
  Corn chips

1. In a large skillet, cook beef and onion over medium heat until no longer pink; drain. Transfer to a 5-qt. slow cooker. Stir in the beans, tomatoes, corn, water, olives, chili powder, oregano, pepper sauce, garlic powder and cumin.
2. Cover and cook on low for 4-5 hours or until heated through; stir in cheese. Cover and cook for 30 minutes or until cheese is melted. Serve with corn chips.

CHILI CHEESE DIP

BUFFET MEATBALLS

(5) INGREDIENTS Buffet Meatballs

I need only 5 ingredients to fix these easy appetizers. Grape juice and apple jelly are the secrets behind the sweet yet tangy sauce that complements convenient packaged meatballs.

—**JANET ANDERSON** CARSON CITY, NV

PREP: 10 MIN. • **COOK:** 4 HOURS • **MAKES:** ABOUT 10½ DOZEN

- 1 **cup grape juice**
- 1 **cup apple jelly**
- 1 **cup ketchup**
- 1 **can (8 ounces) tomato sauce**
- 1 **package (64 ounces) frozen fully cooked Italian meatballs**

1. In a small saucepan, combine the juice, jelly, ketchup and tomato sauce. Cook and stir over medium heat until jelly is melted.
2. Place meatballs in a 5-qt. slow cooker. Pour sauce over the top and gently stir to coat. Cover and cook on low for 4-5 hours or until heated through.

GINNIE BUSAM'S
APRICOT-APPLE CIDER

Apricot-Apple Cider

Dried apricots give this comforting cider a deliciously new twist. Add cranberries, cinnamon, allspice and cloves, and you've got the perfect hot drink to sip on during frosty autumn nights.

—**GINNIE BUSAM** PEWEE VALLEY, KY

PREP: 20 MIN. • **COOK:** 3 HOURS
MAKES: 13 SERVINGS (2½ QUARTS)

- 8 cups unsweetened apple juice
- 1 can (12 ounces) ginger ale
- ½ cup dried apricots, halved
- ½ cup dried cranberries
- 2 cinnamon sticks (3 inches)
- 1 tablespoon whole allspice
- 1 tablespoon whole cloves

1. In a 5-qt. slow cooker, combine apple juice and ginger ale. Place the apricots, cranberries, cinnamon sticks, allspice and cloves on a double thickness of cheesecloth; bring up corners of cloth and tie with string to form a bag. Place in slow cooker.
2. Cover and cook on high for 3-4 hours or until heated through. Discard spice bag.

Sweet & Sour Turkey Meatballs

Here's a great way to use pomegranates, which seem to grow in popularity every year! The recipe is wonderful for potlucks or buffets at cool-weather events. It's seasonal, easy and delicious.

—**CHRISTINE WENDLAND** BROWNS MILLS, NJ

PREP: 30 MIN. • **COOK:** 2¼ HOURS
MAKES: ABOUT 5½ DOZEN

- 4 thick-sliced peppered bacon strips
- 1 egg, beaten
- ½ cup seasoned bread crumbs
- 3 tablespoons minced fresh cilantro
- 1 teaspoon salt
- 1 teaspoon white pepper
- 2 pounds ground turkey
- 1 jar (18 ounces) apricot preserves
- 1 can (14½ ounces) diced tomatoes, undrained
- 1 bottle (8 ounces) taco sauce
- ½ cup pomegranate juice

1. Place bacon in a food processor; cover and process until finely chopped. In a large bowl, combine the egg, bread crumbs, cilantro, salt and pepper. Crumble turkey and bacon over mixture and mix well. Shape into 1-in. balls.
2. Place in two ungreased 15-in. x 10-in. x 1-in. baking pans. Bake at 400° for 8-10 minutes or until no longer pink.
3. In a 4-qt. slow cooker, combine the preserves, tomatoes, taco sauce and juice. Stir in the meatballs. Cover and cook on high for 2-3 hours or until heated through.

Spiced Coffee

Even people who don't usually drink coffee will find this special blend with a hint of chocolate appealing. I keep a big batch ready to serve at fall parties.

—**JOANNE HOLT** BOWLING GREEN, OH

PREP: 10 MIN. • **COOK:** 2 HOURS
MAKES: 8 SERVINGS

- 8 cups brewed coffee
- ⅓ cup sugar
- ¼ cup chocolate syrup
- ½ teaspoon anise extract
- 4 cinnamon sticks (3 inches)
- 1½ teaspoons whole cloves
  Additional cinnamon sticks, optional

1. In a 3-qt. slow cooker, combine coffee, sugar, chocolate syrup and extract. Place cinnamon sticks and cloves on a double thickness of cheesecloth. Gather corners of cloth to enclose spices; tie securely with string. Add to slow cooker. Cook, covered, on low 2-3 hours.
2. Discard spice bag. Ladle coffee into mugs. If desired, serve with cinnamon sticks.

SPICED COFFEE

EASY HOT SPICED CIDER

Taco Joe Dip

My daughter was the first to try this recipe. She thought it was so good that she passed it on to me. My husband and I both agree that it's terrific—and great for parties or busy days.
—**LANG SECREST** SIERRA VISTA, AZ

PREP: 5 MIN. • **COOK:** 5 HOURS
MAKES: ABOUT 7 CUPS

- 1 can (16 ounces) kidney beans, rinsed and drained
- 1 can (15¼ ounces) whole kernel corn, drained
- 1 can (15 ounces) black beans, rinsed and drained
- 1 can (14½ ounces) stewed tomatoes, undrained
- 1 can (8 ounces) tomato sauce
- 1 can (4 ounces) chopped green chilies, drained
- 1 envelope taco seasoning
- ½ cup chopped onion
  Tortilla chips

In a 5-qt. slow cooker, combine the first eight ingredients. Cover and cook on low for 5-6 hours. Serve with tortilla chips.
NOTE *To make Taco Joe Soup, add a 29-ounce can of tomato sauce to the slow cooker. It will serve 6-8.*

top tip · Easy Extras

Leftovers from Taco Joe Dip (if there are any) aren't a problem! Not only do the extras freeze well for a future party, but you can use them for dinner the next night. Stuff them into taco shells or tortillas for a meatless main course. Or, you could also warm up the leftover dip and spoon it over cooked chicken breast for a no-fuss meal

Easy Hot Spiced Cider

It's such a treat to enjoy this warm, comforting cider after a day of raking leaves or picking pumpkins!
—**TRINDA HEINRICH** LAKEMOOR, IL

PREP: 5 MIN. • **COOK:** 2 HOURS
MAKES: 3 SERVINGS

- 2½ cups apple cider or unsweetened apple juice
- ⅔ cup orange juice
- ⅓ cup sugar
- 2 tablespoons lemon juice
- ¼ teaspoon ground nutmeg
- 1 cinnamon stick (3 inches)
- 12 whole cloves

1. In a 1½-qt. slow cooker, combine the first five ingredients. Place cinnamon stick and cloves on a double thickness of cheesecloth; bring up corners of cloth and tie with string to form a bag. Place bag in slow cooker.
2. Cover and cook on low for 1 hour. Discard spice bag; continue to cook 1-2 hours or until heated through.

Hot Wing Dip

Since I usually have all the ingredients on hand, this is a great go-to recipe whenever unexpected guests show up at my door. The hot sauce warms them up, while the other ingredients create a familiar flavor that folks crave.

—**COLEEN CORNER** GROVE CITY, PA

PREP: 10 MIN. • **COOK:** 1 HOUR
MAKES: 4½ CUPS

- 2 cups shredded cooked chicken
- 1 package (8 ounces) cream cheese, cubed
- 2 cups (8 ounces) shredded cheddar cheese
- 1 cup ranch salad dressing
- ½ cup Louisiana-style hot sauce
  Tortilla chips and/or celery sticks
  Minced fresh parsley, optional

In a 3-qt. slow cooker, combine the chicken, cream cheese, cheddar cheese, salad dressing and hot sauce. Cover and cook on low for 1-2 hours or until cheese is melted. Serve with chips and/or celery. Sprinkle with parsley if desired.

⑤ INGREDIENTS

Butterscotch Mulled Cider

Five minutes of preparation results in this grown-up slow cooker drink. You'll love the sweet taste of the butterscotch combined with the cinnamon.

—**KAREN MACK** WEBSTER, NY

PREP: 5 MIN. • **COOK:** 3 HOURS
MAKES: 18 SERVINGS (1 CUP EACH)

BUTTERSCOTCH MULLED CIDER

- 1 gallon apple cider or juice
- 2 cups butterscotch schnapps liqueur
- 8 cinnamon sticks (3 inches)

In a 6-qt. slow cooker, combine all ingredients. Cover and cook on low for 3-4 hours or until heated through.

HOT WING DIP

HOT SPICED CHERRY SIPPER

"This is the dish I am always asked to bring to events. It is so yummy! It can also be baked in the oven at about 400 degrees for 30 minutes or until it's all hot and bubbly."

—**NOELLE MYERS** GRAND FORKS, ND

Five-Cheese Spinach & Artichoke Dip

PREP: 20 MIN. • **COOK:** 2½ HOURS
MAKES: 16 SERVINGS (¼ CUP EACH)

- 1 jar (12 ounces) roasted sweet red peppers
- 1 jar (6½ ounces) marinated quartered artichoke hearts
- 1 package (10 ounces) frozen chopped spinach, thawed and squeezed dry
- 8 ounces fresh mozzarella cheese, cubed
- 1½ cups (6 ounces) shredded Asiago cheese
- 2 packages (3 ounces each) cream cheese, softened and cubed
- 1 cup (4 ounces) crumbled feta cheese
- ⅓ cup shredded provolone cheese
- ⅓ cup minced fresh basil
- ¼ cup finely chopped red onion
- 2 tablespoons mayonnaise
- 2 garlic cloves, minced
  Assorted crackers

1. Drain the peppers, reserving 1 tablespoon liquid; chop them. Drain artichokes, reserving 2 tablespoons liquid; coarsely chop artichokes.
2. In a 3-qt. slow cooker coated with cooking spray, combine spinach, cheeses, basil, onion, mayonnaise, garlic, artichoke hearts and peppers. Stir in reserved pepper and artichoke liquids. Cook, covered, on high 2 hours. Stir dip; cook, covered, 30-60 minutes longer. Stir before serving; serve with crackers.

⑤ INGREDIENTS

Hot Spiced Cherry Sipper

This cider is great to have simmering in the slow cooker after being out in brisk autumn weather—and oh, the aroma!
—**MARLENE WICZEK** LITTLE FALLS, MN

PREP: 5 MIN. • **COOK:** 4 HOURS
MAKES: 4 QUARTS

- 1 gallon apple cider or juice
- 2 cinnamon sticks (3 inches)
- 2 packages (3 ounces each) cherry gelatin

Place cider in a 6-qt. slow cooker; add cinnamon sticks. Cover and cook on high for 3 hours. Stir in gelatin; cook for 1 hour longer. Discard cinnamon sticks before serving.

top tip **Simple Swap**

If you enjoyed the Hot Spiced Cherry Sipper, feel free to mix things up with a different flavor. Try orange juice and orange gelatin, or simmer up a combination of lemonade and lemon gelatin. You could even try a combo of different juices and gelatins for a unique flavor.

NOELLE MYERS'
FIVE-CHEESE SPINACH & ARTICHOKE DIP

SLOW-COOKED APPLE CRANBERRY CIDER

Brown Sugar Fix

There's no need to run to the store if you're out of brown sugar—you can substitute 1 cup granulated sugar or 2 cups sifted confectioners' sugar for 1 cup brown sugar. It's important to sift the confectioners' sugar before measuring to make an equal substitution.

(5) INGREDIENTS

Slow-Cooked Smokies

I like to include these little sausages smothered in barbecue sauce on all my party menus. They're popular with both children and adults.

—SUNDRA HAUCK BOGALUSA, LA

PREP: 5 MIN. • **COOK:** 6 HOURS
MAKES: 8 SERVINGS

- 1 package (1 pound) miniature smoked sausages
- 1 bottle (28 ounces) barbecue sauce
- 1¼ cups water
- 3 tablespoons Worcestershire sauce
- 3 tablespoons steak sauce
- ½ teaspoon pepper

In a 3-qt. slow cooker, combine all ingredients. Cover and cook on low for 5-6 hours or until heated through. Serve with a slotted spoon.

SLOW-COOKED SMOKIES

(5) INGREDIENTS ## Slow-Cooked Apple Cranberry Cider

Buffets are my favorite way to feed a crowd. This cider can be made ahead, then kept warm in a slow cooker so guests can serve themselves on the buffet line.

—KATHY WELLS BRODHEAD, WI

PREP: 5 MIN. • **COOK:** 2 HOURS
MAKES: 11 CUPS

- 3 cinnamon sticks (3 inches), broken
- 1 teaspoon whole cloves
- 2 quarts apple cider or juice
- 3 cups cranberry juice
- 2 tablespoons brown sugar

1. Place cinnamon sticks and cloves on a double thickness of cheesecloth; bring up corners of cloth and tie with string to form a bag.

2. In a 5-qt. slow cooker, combine the cider, cranberry juice and brown sugar add spice bag. Cover and cook on high for 2 hours or until cider reaches desired temperature. Discard the spice bag.

TANGY BARBECUE WINGS

Tangy Barbecue Wings

When I took these savory chicken wings to work, they were gone before I even got a bite! Spicy ketchup, vinegar, molasses and honey create a sauce that's lip-smacking good.

—SHERRY PITZER TROY, MO

PREP: 1½ HOURS • **COOK:** 3 HOURS • **MAKES:** ABOUT 4 DOZEN

- 5 pounds chicken wings
- 2½ cups hot and spicy ketchup
- ⅔ cup white vinegar
- ½ cup plus 2 tablespoons honey
- ½ cup molasses
- 1 teaspoon salt
- 1 teaspoon Worcestershire sauce
- ½ teaspoon onion powder
- ½ teaspoon chili powder
- ½ to 1 teaspoon liquid smoke, optional

1. Cut chicken wings into three sections; discard wing tip sections. Place chicken wings in two greased 15-in. x 10-in. x 1-in. baking pans. Bake, uncovered, at 375° for 30 minutes; drain. Turn wings; bake 20-25 minutes longer or until juices run clear.

2. Meanwhile, in a large saucepan, combine the ketchup, vinegar, honey, molasses, salt, Worcestershire sauce, onion powder and chili powder. Add liquid smoke if desired. Bring to a boil. Reduce heat; simmer, uncovered, for 25-30 minutes.

3. Drain wings; place a third of them in a 5-qt. slow cooker. Top with about 1 cup sauce. Repeat layers twice. Cover and cook on low for 3-4 hours. Stir before serving.

NOTE *Uncooked chicken wing sections (wingettes) may be substituted for whole chicken wings.*

AMY WARREN'S CREAMY CRANBERRY MEATBALLS
SUE BAYLESS' SWEET & SPICY CHICKEN WINGS

5 INGREDIENTS Creamy Cranberry Meatballs

Extras from tonight's rich and juicy appetizers can become tomorrow's entree. Simply serve them over a bed of noodles or rice—if there are any left!

—AMY WARREN MAINEVILLE, OH

PREP: 10 MIN. • **COOK:** 3 HOURS
MAKES: ABOUT 5 DOZEN

- 2 envelopes (0.87 ounce each) brown gravy mix
- 1 package (32 ounces) frozen fully cooked Swedish meatballs
- ⅔ cup jellied cranberry sauce
- 2 teaspoons Dijon mustard
- ¼ cup heavy whipping cream

Prepare gravy mix according to package directions. In a 4-qt. slow cooker, combine the meatballs, cranberry sauce, mustard and gravy. Cover and cook on low for 3-4 hours or until heated through, adding cream during the last 30 minutes of cooking.

Sweet & Spicy Chicken Wings

The meat literally falls off the bones of these wings! Spice lovers will get a kick out of the big sprinkling of red pepper flakes.

—SUE BAYLESS PRIOR LAKE, MN

PREP: 25 MIN. • **COOK:** 5 HOURS
MAKES: ABOUT 1 DOZEN

- 3 pounds chicken wings
- 1½ cups ketchup
- 1 cup packed brown sugar
- 1 small onion, finely chopped
- ¼ cup finely chopped sweet red pepper
- 2 tablespoons chili powder
- 2 tablespoons Worcestershire sauce
- 1½ teaspoons crushed red pepper flakes
- 1 teaspoon ground mustard
- 1 teaspoon dried basil
- 1 teaspoon dried thyme
- 1 teaspoon pepper

Cut wings into three sections; discard wing tip sections. Place chicken in a 4-qt. slow cooker. In a small bowl, combine the remaining ingredients. Pour over chicken; stir until coated. Cover and cook on low for 5-6 hours or until chicken juices run clear.

NOTE *Uncooked chicken wing sections (wingettes) may be substituted for whole chicken wings.*

Mulled Dr Pepper

When neighbors or friends visit us on chilly evenings, I often serve this warming beverage with ham sandwiches.

—BERNICE MORRIS MARSHFIELD, MO

PREP: 10 MIN. • **COOK:** 2 HOURS
MAKES: 8-10 SERVINGS

- 8 cups Dr Pepper
- ¼ cup packed brown sugar
- ¼ cup lemon juice
- ½ teaspoon ground allspice
- ½ teaspoon whole cloves
- ¼ teaspoon salt
- ¼ teaspoon ground nutmeg
- 3 cinnamon sticks (3 inches)

1. In a 3-qt. slow cooker, combine all ingredients.
2. Cover and cook on low for 2 hours or until heated through. Discard cloves and cinnamon sticks.

MULLED DR PEPPER

Autumn

SIDE DISHES

When it's time to round out menus, nothing satisfies like Coconut-Pecan Sweet Potatoes, Slow Cooked-Sausage Dressing, Mushroom Wild Rice and other fall favorites. Turn here for all of those comforting dishes that are ideal for cozy meals.

MARY ANN JONNS'
WARM FRUIT SALAD

⑤ INGREDIENTS Warm Fruit Salad

I use canned goods and my slow cooker to whip up this old-fashioned side dish that's loaded with sweet fruits. It makes a heartwarming accompaniment to holiday menus.
—**MARY ANN JONNS** MIDLOTHIAN, IL

PREP: 10 MIN. • **COOK:** 2 HOURS • **MAKES:** 14-18 SERVINGS

- 2 cans (29 ounces each) sliced peaches, drained
- 2 cans (29 ounces each) pear halves, drained and sliced
- 1 can (20 ounces) pineapple chunks, drained
- 1 can (15¼ ounces) apricot halves, drained and sliced
- 1 can (21 ounces) cherry pie filling

In a 5-qt. slow cooker, combine the peaches, pears, pineapple and apricots. Top with pie filling. Cover and cook on high for 2 hours or until heated through. Serve with a slotted spoon.

Cheesy Sausage Gravy

Looking for make-ahead convenience? A friend shared this breakfast dish many years ago. I've served it often to overnight guests, and they never fail to ask for the recipe.
—**P.J. PRUSIA** RAYMORE, MO

PREP: 15 MIN. • **COOK:** 7 HOURS • **MAKES:** 8 SERVINGS

- 1 pound bulk pork sausage
- ¼ cup butter, cubed
- ¼ cup all-purpose flour
- ¼ teaspoon pepper
- 2½ cups milk
- 2 cans (10¾ ounces each) condensed cheddar cheese soup, undiluted
- 6 hard-cooked eggs, chopped
- 1 jar (4½ ounces) sliced mushrooms, drained
  Warm biscuits

1. In a large skillet, cook sausage over medium heat until no longer pink; drain and remove sausage. In the same skillet, melt butter. Stir in flour and pepper until smooth. Gradually whisk in milk. Bring to a boil; cook and stir for 2 minutes or until thickened and bubbly.
2. Stir in soup until blended. Stir in eggs, mushrooms and sausage. Transfer to a 3-qt. slow cooker. Cover and cook on low for 7-8 hours. Stir; serve over biscuits.

top tip Great Gravy

In our house, it's a family tradition to make Tomato Sausage Gravy. In the same skillet that you cooked the sausage in the recipe above, simply whisk in tomato juice instead of milk. The tomato gravy is a delicious change of pace at breakfast.
—**ANNE C.** MILAN, TN

Spiced Acorn Squash

Working a full-time job, I found I didn't always have time to cook the meals my family loved. So I re-created many of our favorites for the slow cooker. This treatment for squash is one of them.

—**CAROL GRECO** CENTEREACH, NY

PREP: 10 MIN. • **COOK:** 4 HOURS • **MAKES:** 4 SERVINGS

- ¾ cup packed brown sugar
- 1 teaspoon ground cinnamon
- 1 teaspoon ground nutmeg
- 2 small acorn squash, halved and seeded
- ¾ cup raisins
- 4 tablespoons butter
- ½ cup water

1. In a small bowl, combine the brown sugar, cinnamon and nutmeg; spoon into squash halves. Sprinkle with raisins. Top each with 1 tablespoon of butter. Wrap each squash half individually in heavy-duty foil; seal tightly.
2. Pour water into a 5-qt. slow cooker. Place the squash, cut side up, in slow cooker (packets may be stacked). Cover and cook on high for 4 hours or until the squash is tender. Open foil packets carefully to allow steam to escape.

CORN SPOON BREAD

SPICED ACORN SQUASH

Corn Spoon Bread

My spoon bread is moister then corn pudding made in the oven, and the cream cheese makes a nice addition. It goes great with Thanksgiving turkey or Christmas ham.

—**TAMARA ELLEFSON** FREDERIC, WI

PREP: 15 MIN. • **COOK:** 3 HOURS • **MAKES:** 8 SERVINGS

- 1 package (8 ounces) cream cheese, softened
- ⅓ cup sugar
- 1 cup 2% milk
- 2 eggs
- 2 tablespoons butter, melted
- 1 teaspoon salt
- ¼ teaspoon ground nutmeg
  Dash pepper
- 2⅓ cups frozen corn, thawed
- 1 can (14¾ ounces) cream-style corn
- 1 package (8½ ounces) corn bread/muffin mix

1. In a large bowl, beat cream cheese and sugar until smooth. Gradually beat in milk. Beat in the eggs, butter, salt, nutmeg and pepper until blended. Stir in corn and cream-style corn. Stir in corn bread mix just until moistened.
2. Pour into a greased 3-qt. slow cooker. Cover and cook on high for 3-4 hours or until center is almost set.

SLOW-COOKED SAUSAGE DRESSING

Chuck Wagon Beans

My inspiration for these savory beans came from the cooks of the Old West's cattle ranches. Sweet and smoky, the beans are extra hearty with sausage.
—**NANCY MOORE** BUCKLIN, KS

PREP: 15 MIN. • **COOK:** 8 HOURS
MAKES: 24 SERVINGS (⅔ CUP EACH)

- 2 **cans (28 ounces each) baked beans**
- 3 **cans (16 ounces each) kidney beans, rinsed and drained**
- 2 **cans (15 ounces each) pinto beans, rinsed and drained**
- 1 **pound smoked kielbasa or Polish sausage, sliced**
- 1 **jar (12 ounces) pickled jalapeno slices, drained**
- 1 **medium onion, chopped**
- 1 **cup barbecue sauce**
- ½ **cup spicy brown mustard**
- ¼ **cup steak seasoning**

In a greased 6-qt. slow cooker, combine all ingredients. Cover and cook on low for 8-10 hours or until heated through.
NOTE *This recipe was tested with McCormick's Montreal Steak Seasoning. Look for it in the spice aisle.*

Dressed-Up Dishes

There are several easy ways to jazz up any baked bean recipe. Try laying strips of cooked bacon over the top of the bean mixture as it simmers in the slow cooker. Add a few dashes of your favorite dried herbs, or stir in a couple of bay leaves. (Just remember to remove the leaves before serving.) Also, a little soy sauce, Worcestershire sauce or honey goes a long way when flavoring beans. Or, you can also try sprinkling finely crushed gingersnaps over the warm beans right before serving.

Slow-Cooked Sausage Dressing

This dressing is so delicious, no one will guess it's lower in fat. And best of all, it cooks effortlessly in the slow cooker, so the stove and oven are free for other dishes during the busy holidays.
—**RAQUEL HAGGARD** EDMOND, OK

PREP: 20 MIN. • **COOK:** 3 HOURS
MAKES: 8 CUPS

- ½ **pound reduced-fat bulk pork sausage**
- 2 **celery ribs, chopped**
- 1 **large onion, chopped**
- 7 **cups seasoned stuffing cubes**
- 1 **can (14½ ounces) reduced-sodium chicken broth**
- 1 **medium tart apple, chopped**
- ⅓ **cup chopped pecans**
- 2 **tablespoons reduced-fat butter, melted**
- 1½ **teaspoons rubbed sage**
- ½ **teaspoon pepper**

1. In a large nonstick skillet, cook the sausage, celery and onion over medium heat until meat is no longer pink; drain. Transfer to a large bowl; stir in the remaining ingredients.
2. Place in a 5-qt. slow cooker coated with cooking spray. Cover and cook on low for 3-4 hours or until heated through and the apple is tender, stirring once.
NOTE *This recipe was tested with Land O'Lakes light stick butter.*

NANCY MOORE'S
CHUCK WAGON BEANS

Coconut-Pecan Sweet Potatoes

Here, coconut gives a classic dish new mouthwatering flavor. The delicious sweet potatoes cook effortlessly in the slow cooker, letting you tend to other things.

—RAQUEL HAGGARD EDMOND, OK

PREP: 15 MIN. • **COOK:** 4 HOURS
MAKES: 12 SERVINGS

- 4 **pounds sweet potatoes, peeled and cut into chunks**
- ½ **cup chopped pecans**
- ½ **cup flaked coconut**
- ⅓ **cup sugar**
- ⅓ **cup packed brown sugar**
- ¼ **cup reduced-fat butter, melted**
- ½ **teaspoon ground cinnamon**
- ¼ **teaspoon salt**
- ½ **teaspoon coconut extract**
- ½ **teaspoon vanilla extract**

1. Place sweet potatoes in a 5-qt. slow cooker coated with cooking spray. Combine the pecans, coconut, sugar, brown sugar, butter, cinnamon and salt; sprinkle over potatoes.

2. Cover and cook on low for 4 hours or until potatoes are tender. Stir in the extracts.

NOTE *This recipe was tested with Land O'Lakes light stick butter.*

Sweet Potato Secrets

Two varieties of sweet potatoes are readily available. One has a pale skin with a light yellow flesh and dry mealy texture. The other has dark skin with a dark orange flesh that cooks to a moist texture. This variety is often commonly known as a yam. Yams and sweet potatoes are interchangeable in most recipes.

COCONUT-PECAN SWEET POTATOES

Applesauce Sweet Potatoes

Sweet potatoes are a must on our special family menus, and this no-fuss version will have everyone thinking you spent hours in the kitchen. It's great for parties, holidays and other events.

—**PAMELA ALLEN** MARYSVILLE, OH

PREP: 15 MIN. • **COOK:** 4 HOURS
MAKES: 8 SERVINGS

- 2 pounds sweet potatoes, peeled and sliced
- 1½ cups unsweetened applesauce
- ⅔ cup packed brown sugar
- 3 tablespoons butter, melted
- 1 teaspoon ground cinnamon
- ½ cup chopped glazed pecans, optional

Place sweet potatoes in a 4-qt. slow cooker. Combine the applesauce, brown sugar, butter and cinnamon; pour over sweet potatoes. Cover and cook on low for 4-5 hours or until potatoes are tender. Sprinkle with pecans if desired. Serve with a slotted spoon.

Cranberry Apple Topping

A generous spoonful of this sweet-tart sauce makes a tasty addition to chicken, turkey or pork. The ruby-red color lends a festive look to meals.

—**LISE ODE** DELRAY BEACH, FL

PREP: 15 MIN. • **COOK:** 3½ HOURS + COOLING
MAKES: 3¾ CUPS

- 4 cups fresh or frozen cranberries, thawed
- 2 medium tart apples, peeled and chopped
- 1¼ cups sugar
- ¼ cup orange juice
- 2 teaspoons grated orange peel
- ½ teaspoon ground cinnamon
- 2 tablespoons cornstarch
- 2 tablespoons cold water

1. In a 3-qt. slow cooker, combine the first six ingredients. Cover and cook on low for 3-4 hours or until bubbly.
2. In a small bowl, combine cornstarch and water until smooth; stir into cranberry mixture. Cover and cook 30 minutes longer or until thickened. Transfer to a serving bowl; cool. Serve with turkey, chicken or pork.

Easy Squash Stuffing

My friends rave about this creamy side dish. It jazzes up a stuffing mix with fresh summer squash, carrots and onion.

—**PAMELA THORSON** HOT SPRINGS, AR

PREP: 15 MIN. • **COOK:** 4 HOURS
MAKES: 8 SERVINGS

- ¼ cup all-purpose flour
- 1 can (10¾ ounces) condensed cream of chicken soup, undiluted
- 1 cup (8 ounces) sour cream
- 2 medium yellow summer squash, cut into ½-inch slices
- 1 small onion, chopped
- 1 cup shredded carrots
- 1 package (8 ounces) stuffing mix
- ½ cup butter, melted

1. In a large bowl, combine the flour, soup and sour cream. Add the vegetables and gently stir to coat.
2. Combine stuffing mix and butter; sprinkle half into a 3-qt. slow cooker. Top with vegetable mixture and remaining stuffing mixture. Cover and cook on low for 4-5 hours or until the vegetables are tender.

Potluck Candied Sweet Potatoes

It's hard to go wrong with candied sweet potatoes when it comes to pleasing a crowd. To make it easier to bring this traditional Southern staple to a potluck or gathering, I updated the recipe so that it can be cooked in a slow cooker.

—**DEIRDRE COX** KANSAS CITY, KS

PREP: 20 MIN. • **COOK:** 5 HOURS
MAKES: 12 SERVINGS (¾ CUP EACH)

- 1 **cup packed brown sugar**
- 1 **cup sugar**
- 8 **medium sweet potatoes, peeled and cut into ½-inch slices**
- ¼ **cup butter, melted**
- 2 **teaspoons vanilla extract**
- ¼ **teaspoon salt**
- 2 **tablespoons cornstarch**
- 2 **tablespoons cold water**
   Minced fresh parsley, optional

1. In a small bowl, combine sugars. In a greased 5-qt. slow cooker, layer a third of the sweet potatoes; sprinkle with a third of the sugar mixture. Repeat layers twice. In a small bowl, combine the butter, vanilla and salt; drizzle over potatoes. Cover and cook on low for 5-6 hours or until the sweet potatoes are tender.

2. Using a slotted spoon, transfer potatoes to a serving dish; keep warm. Pour cooking juices into a small saucepan; bring to a boil. In a small bowl, combine cornstarch and water until smooth; stir into pan. Return to a boil, stirring constantly; cook and stir for 1-2 minutes or until thickened. Spoon over sweet potatoes.

3. Sprinkle with parsley if desired.

FALL GARDEN MEDLEY

POTLUCK CANDIED SWEET POTATOES

Fall Garden Medley

I like to make this recipe in the fall and winter for special occasions because it's very colorful, tasty and healthy. It's a hearty side dish that complements many different entrees.

—**KRYSTINE KERCHER** LINCOLN, NE

PREP: 20 MIN. • **COOK:** 5 HOURS • **MAKES:** 8 SERVINGS

- 4 **large carrots, cut into 1½-inch pieces**
- 3 **fresh beets, peeled and cut into 1½-inch pieces.**
- 2 **medium sweet potatoes, peeled and cut into 1½-inch pieces**
- 2 **medium onions, peeled and quartered**
- ½ **cup water**
- 2 **teaspoons salt**
- ½ **teaspoon pepper**
- ¼ **teaspoon dried thyme**
- 1 **tablespoon olive oil**
   Fresh parsley or dried parsley flakes, optional

1. Place the carrots, beets, sweet potatoes, onions and water in a greased 3-qt. slow cooker. Sprinkle with salt, pepper and thyme. Drizzle with olive oil. Cover and cook on low for 5-6 hours or until tender.

2. Stir vegetables and sprinkle with parsley if desired.

Saucy Scalloped Potatoes

For appealing old-fashioned flavor, try these scalloped potatoes. They cook up tender, creamy and comforting. Chopped ham adds a hearty touch.

—ELAINE KANE KEIZER, OR

PREP: 15 MIN. • **COOK:** 7 HOURS • **MAKES:** 8 SERVINGS

- 4 cups thinly sliced peeled potatoes (about 2 pounds)
- 1 can (10¾ ounces) condensed cream of celery soup or mushroom soup, undiluted
- 1 can (12 ounces) evaporated milk
- 1 large onion, sliced
- 2 tablespoons butter
- ½ teaspoon salt
- ¼ teaspoon pepper
- 1½ cups chopped fully cooked ham

In a 3-qt. slow cooker, combine the first seven ingredients. Cover and cook on high for 1 hour. Stir in ham. Reduce heat to low; cook 6-8 hours longer or until potatoes are tender.

SAUCY SCALLOPED POTATOES

BOB MALCHOW'S
MUSHROOM WILD RICE

Mushroom Wild Rice

This is one of my favorite recipes from my mother. With only seven ingredients, it's quick to assemble in the morning before I leave for work. By the time I get home, mouthwatering aromas have filled the entire house!

—**BOB MALCHOW** MONON, IN

PREP: 5 MIN. • **COOK:** 7 HOURS
MAKES: 12-16 SERVINGS

- 2¼ cups water
- 1 can (10½ ounces) condensed beef consomme, undiluted
- 1 can (10½ ounces) condensed French onion soup, undiluted
- 3 cans (4 ounces each) mushroom stems and pieces, drained
- ½ cup butter, melted
- 1 cup uncooked brown rice
- 1 cup uncooked wild rice

In a 3-qt. slow cooker, combine all ingredients. Cover and cook on low for 7-8 hours or until rice is tender.

Butternut Squash with Whole Grain Pilaf

Fresh thyme really shines in this hearty slow-cooked side dish featuring tender butternut squash, nutritious whole grain pilaf and vitamin-packed baby spinach.

—**TASTE OF HOME TEST KITCHEN**

PREP: 15 MIN. • **COOK:** 4 HOURS
MAKES: 12 SERVINGS (¾ CUP EACH)

- 1 cup Kashi whole grain pilaf
- 1 medium butternut squash (about 3 pounds), cut into ½-inch cubes
- 1 can (14½ ounces) vegetable broth
- 1 medium onion, chopped
- ½ cup water
- 3 garlic cloves, minced
- 2 teaspoons minced fresh thyme or ½ teaspoon dried thyme
- ½ teaspoon salt
- ¼ teaspoon pepper
- 1 package (6 ounces) fresh baby spinach

Place pilaf in a 4-qt slow cooker. In a large bowl, combine the squash, broth, onion, water, garlic, thyme, salt and pepper. Cover and cook on low for 4-5 hours or until the pilaf is tender, adding spinach during the last 30 minutes of cooking.

STUFFING FROM THE SLOW COOKER

Stuffing From the Slow Cooker

If you're hosting a big Thanksgiving dinner, add this simple slow-cooked stuffing to your menu to ease entertaining. The recipe also comes in handy when you run out of oven space at large family gatherings. I use it often.

—**DONALD SEILER** MACON, MS

PREP: 30 MIN. • **COOK:** 3 HOURS
MAKES: 12 SERVINGS

- 1 cup chopped onion
- 1 cup chopped celery
- ¼ cup butter
- 6 cups cubed day-old white bread
- 6 cups cubed day-old whole wheat bread
- 1 teaspoon salt
- 1 teaspoon poultry seasoning
- 1 teaspoon rubbed sage
- ½ teaspoon pepper
- 1 can (14½ ounces) reduced-sodium chicken broth or vegetable broth
- ½ cup egg substitute

1. In a small nonstick skillet over medium heat, cook onion and celery in butter until tender.
2. In a large bowl, combine the bread cubes, salt, poultry seasoning, sage and pepper. Stir in onion mixture. Combine broth and egg substitute; add to bread mixture and toss to coat.
3. Transfer to a 3-qt. slow cooker coated with cooking spray. Cover and cook on low for 3-4 hours or until heated through.

RICH & CREAMY MASHED POTATOES

Rich & Creamy Mashed Potatoes

It's a cinch to jazz up instant mashed potatoes with sour cream and cream cheese, then cook and serve them from a slow cooker. For a special touch, sprinkle the perfect-for-party-time potatoes with chopped fresh chives, canned French-fried onions or fresh grated Parmesan cheese.

—DONNA BARDOCZ HOWELL, MI

PREP: 15 MIN. • **COOK:** 2 HOURS • **MAKES:** 10 SERVINGS

- 3¾ cups boiling water
- 1½ cups 2% milk
- 1 package (8 ounces) cream cheese, softened
- ½ cup butter, cubed
- ½ cup sour cream
- 4 cups mashed potato flakes
- 1 teaspoon garlic salt
- ¼ teaspoon pepper
  Minced fresh parsley, optional

In a greased 4-qt. slow cooker, whisk the boiling water, milk, cream cheese, butter and sour cream until smooth. Stir in the potato flakes, garlic salt and pepper. Cover and cook on low for 2-3 hours or until heated through. Sprinkle with parsley if desired.

⑤INGREDIENTS Ginger Applesauce

This is my favorite way to prepare applesauce. It's so simple to do and makes the whole house smell like autumn.

—RENEE PAJESTKA BRUNSWICK, OH

PREP: 25 MIN. • **COOK:** 4 HOURS • **MAKES:** ABOUT 5 CUPS

- 4 pounds apples (about 12 medium), peeled and cubed
- ¼ cup water
- 2 tablespoons brown sugar
- 2 teaspoons ground cinnamon
- 2 teaspoons minced fresh gingerroot
- 2 teaspoons vanilla extract

1. Place all ingredients in a 4-qt. slow cooker; stir until combined.
2. Cover and cook on low for 4-5 hours or until apples are tender. Mash if desired. Refrigerate leftovers.

⑤INGREDIENTS Lazy-Day Cranberry Relish

This no-fuss condiment simmers away while I make other holiday preparations. It's especially delicious served with turkey.

—JUNE FORMANEK BELLE PLAINE, IA

PREP: 5 MIN. • **COOK:** 6 HOURS + CHILLING • **MAKES:** 3 CUPS

- 2 cups sugar
- 1 cup orange juice
- 1 teaspoon grated orange peel
- 4 cups fresh or frozen cranberries

1. In a 1½ qt. slow cooker, combine sugar, orange juice and peel; stir until sugar is dissolved. Add the cranberries.
2. Cover and cook on low for 6 hours. Mash the mixture. Transfer to a small bowl; cool. Refrigerate until chilled.

⑤INGREDIENTS All-Day Apple Butter

I make several batches of this simple and delicious apple butter to freeze in jars. Depending on the sweetness of the apples used, you can adjust the sugar to taste.

BETTY RUENHOLL SYRACUSE, NE

PREP: 20 MIN. • **COOK:** 11 HOURS • **MAKES:** 4 PINTS

- 5½ pounds apples, peeled and finely chopped
- 4 cups sugar
- 2 to 3 teaspoons ground cinnamon
- ¼ teaspoon ground cloves
- ¼ teaspoon salt

1. Place apples in a 3-qt. slow cooker. Combine sugar, cinnamon, cloves and salt; pour over apples and mix well. Cover and cook on high for 1 hour.
2. Reduce heat to low; cover and cook for 9-11 hours or until thickened and dark brown, stirring occasionally (stir more frequently as it thickens to prevent sticking).
3. Uncover and cook on low 1 hour longer. If desired, stir with a wire whisk until smooth. Spoon into freezer containers, leaving ½-in. headspace. Cover and refrigerate or freeze.

Sweet Potato Stuffing

Mom always likes to make sure there will be enough stuffing to satisfy our large family. For our holiday gatherings, she slow-cooks this tasty sweet potato dressing in addition to the traditional stuffing cooked inside the turkey.

—**KELLY POLLOCK** LONDON, ON

PREP: 15 MIN. • **COOK:** 4 HOURS • **MAKES:** 10 SERVINGS

- ¼ **cup butter, cubed**
- ½ **cup chopped celery**
- ½ **cup chopped onion**
- ½ **cup chicken broth**
- ½ **teaspoon salt, optional**
- ½ **teaspoon rubbed sage**
- ½ **teaspoon poultry seasoning**
- ½ **teaspoon pepper**
- 6 **cups dry bread cubes**
- 1 **large sweet potato, cooked, peeled and finely chopped**
- ¼ **cup chopped pecans**

1. In a Dutch oven, heat butter over medium-high heat. Add celery and onion; cook and stir until tender. Stir in broth and seasonings. Add remaining ingredients; toss to combine.

2. Transfer to a greased 3-qt. slow cooker. Cook, covered, on low 4 hours or until heated through.

SWEET POTATO STUFFING

Autumn

ENTREES

It's time to dig into flavor with these satisfying fall dinners. From hearty roasts to stick-to-your ribs ethnic favorites, the main courses shared here lend heartwarming appeal to crisp autumn nights.

LINDA SOUTH'S
STACK OF BONES RIBS

Stack of Bones Ribs

My husband devours these delicious ribs until there's nothing left but a stack of bones! Perfect for Halloween fun, they're prepared in a slow cooker so they turn out tender every time.
—**LINDA SOUTH** PINEVILLE, NC

PREP: 15 MIN. • **COOK:** 4 HOURS • **MAKES:** 4 SERVINGS

- 1 cup chili sauce
- 2 green onions, chopped
- 2 tablespoons brown sugar
- 2 tablespoons balsamic vinegar
- 1 tablespoon Dijon mustard
- 1 tablespoon Worcestershire sauce
- 1 tablespoon soy sauce
- 1 teaspoon ground ginger
- ¼ teaspoon crushed red pepper flakes
- ½ teaspoon liquid smoke, optional
- 4 pounds pork baby back ribs

In a large bowl, combine the first 10 ingredients. Cut ribs into individual pieces; dip each into sauce. Transfer to a 5-qt. slow cooker; top with remaining sauce. Cover and cook on low for 4-5 hours or until meat is tender.

Family-Friendly Pizza

This slow cooker casserole has lots of cheese and pepperoni, so it's family- and kid-friendly. It makes a lot, is easy to prepare and has all the wonderful flavors of pizza!
—**HOLLIE CLARK** AMES, IA

PREP: 30 MIN. • **COOK:** 3 HOURS • **MAKES:** 8 SERVINGS

- 6 cups uncooked egg noodles
- 1½ pounds ground beef
- 1 medium onion, chopped
- 1 medium green pepper, chopped
- 2 cans (15 ounces each) pizza sauce
- 1 can (4 ounces) mushroom stems and pieces, drained
- 2 cups (8 ounces) shredded cheddar cheese
- 2 cups (8 ounces) shredded part-skim mozzarella cheese
- 1 package (3½ ounces) sliced pepperoni

1. Cook noodles according to package directions; drain. Meanwhile, in a large skillet, cook the beef, onion and green pepper over medium heat until meat is no longer pink; drain. Stir in pizza sauce and mushrooms.
2. In a greased 5-qt. slow cooker, layer half of the noodles, meat sauce, cheese and pepperoni. Repeat layers. Cover and cook on low for 3-4 hours or until heated through.

top tip Swift Move

I've found that a melon baller works great to scoop out the seeds and membranes from green peppers. —**CHARLINE S.** SAN DIEGO, CA

Green Chili Beef Burritos

This recipe gets rave reviews every time I make it. The shredded beef has a luscious slow-cooked flavor that you can't get anywhere else.

—**JENNY FLAKE** NEWPORT BEACH, CA

PREP: 30 MIN. • **COOK:** 9 HOURS • **MAKES:** 12 SERVINGS

- 1 boneless beef chuck roast (3 pounds)
- 1 can (14½ ounces) beef broth
- 2 cups green enchilada sauce
- 1 can (4 ounces) chopped green chilies
- ½ cup Mexican-style hot tomato sauce
- ½ teaspoon salt
- ½ teaspoon garlic powder
- ½ teaspoon pepper
- 12 flour tortillas (12 inches)
   Optional toppings: shredded lettuce, chopped tomatoes, shredded cheddar cheese and sour cream

1. Cut roast in half and place in a 3- or 4-qt. slow cooker. Add broth. Cover and cook on low for 8-9 hours or until meat is tender.

2. Remove beef. When cool enough to handle, shred meat with two forks. Skim fat from cooking liquid; reserve ½ cup liquid. Return shredded beef and reserved liquid to the slow cooker. Stir in the enchilada sauce, green chilies, tomato sauce, salt, garlic powder and pepper.

3. Cover and cook on low for 1 hour or until heated through. Spoon beef mixture down the center of tortillas; add toppings of your choice. Roll up.

NOTE *This recipe was tested with El Pato brand Mexican-style hot tomato sauce. If you cannot find Mexican-style hot tomato sauce, you may substitute ½ cup tomato sauce, 1 teaspoon hot pepper sauce, ⅛ teaspoon onion powder and ⅛ teaspoon chili powder.*

GREEN CHILI BEEF BURRITOS

CRANBERRY TURKEY BREAST WITH GRAVY

⑤ INGREDIENTS

Cranberry Turkey Breast with Gravy

This is wonderful served for a holiday meal because it's so convenient. The turkey turns out tender and moist. You can use additional slow cookers to prepare side dishes such as homemade stuffing.

—**SHIRLEY WELCH** TULSA, OK

PREP: 15 MIN. • **COOK:** 5 HOURS
MAKES: 12 SERVINGS (3 CUPS GRAVY)

- 1 bone-in turkey breast (5 to 6 pounds)
- 1 can (14 ounces) whole-berry cranberry sauce
- ¼ cup orange juice
- 1 envelope onion soup mix
- ¼ teaspoon salt
- ¼ teaspoon pepper
- 3 to 4 teaspoons cornstarch
- 1 tablespoon water

1. Place turkey in a 5-qt. slow cooker. In a small bowl, combine the cranberry sauce, orange juice, onion soup mix, salt and pepper; pour over turkey. Cover and cook on low for 5-6 hours or until tender.

2. Remove turkey to a serving platter; keep warm. Skim fat from cooking juices; transfer to a small saucepan. Bring to a boil. Combine cornstarch and water until smooth. Gradually stir into the pan. Bring to a boil; cook and stir for 2 minutes or until thickened. Serve with turkey.

SLOW COOKER SAUERBRATEN

Blue Cheese and Apple Pork Chops

Tangy apple wedges and smoky bacon create a yummy topping for my popular pork chops. Try this entree alongside mashed potatoes for an especially comforting supper.

—**NICOLE EPPERSON** SARASOTA, FL

PREP: 25 MIN. • **COOK:** 5 HOURS
MAKES: 4 SERVINGS

- 4 **bone-in pork loin chops (8 ounces each)**
- ½ **teaspoon salt**
- ¼ **teaspoon pepper**
- 1 **tablespoon olive oil**
- 2 **large tart apples, peeled and cut into wedges**
- 2 **medium onions, chopped**
- 6 **maple-flavored bacon strips, cooked and crumbled**
- 2 **tablespoons all-purpose flour**
- 1 **tablespoon sugar**
- 1 **can (14½ ounces) chicken broth**
- 1 **cup unsweetened apple juice**
- 1 **cup (4 ounces) crumbled blue cheese**

1. Sprinkle pork with salt and pepper. In a large skillet, brown pork chops in oil in batches.
2. In a 5-qt. slow cooker, combine the apples, onions and bacon. In a large bowl, combine the flour, sugar, broth and apple juice; pour over apple mixture. Top with pork chops. Cover and cook on low for 5-6 hours or until meat is tender.
3. Remove pork from slow cooker. Using a slotted spoon, remove the apples; serve with pork. Sprinkle with blue cheese.

Savory Strategy

I like to keep a little cooked and crumbled bacon in the freezer. Before cooking the bacon, I always cut the strips into small pieces so they cook faster.

—**K.K.M** MAPLEWOOD, MN

Slow Cooker Sauerbraten

My family is of German-Lutheran descent, and although we enjoy traditional sauerbraten, I never liked the amount of time and fuss it takes to make it. This recipe is so good and oh-so-easy. It's great served with dumplings, spaetzle, veggies or a green salad.

—**NORMA ENGLISH** BADEN, PA

PREP: 20 MIN. • **COOK:** 6 HOURS
MAKES: 10 SERVINGS

- 1 **boneless beef chuck roast or rump roast (3 to 4 pounds)**
- 4 **cups water**
- 1 **bottle (14 ounces) ketchup**
- 1 **large onion, chopped**
- ¾ **cup packed brown sugar**
- ¾ **cup cider vinegar**
- 1 **tablespoon mixed pickling spices**
- 3 **bay leaves**
- 1½ **cups crushed gingersnap cookies (about 30 cookies)**

GRAVY
- 2 **tablespoons cornstarch**
- ¼ **cup cold water**

1. Cut roast in half. Place in a 5-qt. slow cooker; add water. In a large bowl, combine the ketchup, onion, brown sugar and vinegar; pour over roast.
2. Place pickling spices and bay leaves on a double thickness of cheesecloth; bring up corners of cloth and tie with string to form a bag. Add spice bag and cookie crumbs to slow cooker.
3. Cover and cook on low for 6-8 hours or until meat is tender.
4. Remove roast and keep warm. Discard spice bag. Strain cooking juices; transfer 4 cups to a large saucepan. Combine cornstarch and water until smooth; stir into cooking juices. Bring to a boil; cook and stir for 2 minutes or until thickened. Slice roast; serve with gravy.

Mandarin Turkey Tenderloin

My husband grew up in an area with lots of turkey farms, so he learned to love dishes that use turkey. Here's a tasty meal-in-one dinner that requires no fuss. I like to serve it when I have company over.

—LORIE MINER KAMAS, UTAH

PREP: 15 MIN. • **COOK:** 4½ HOURS
MAKES: 8 SERVINGS

- **8 turkey breast tenderloins (4 ounces each)**
- **½ teaspoon ground ginger**
- **½ teaspoon crushed red pepper flakes**
- **1 can (11 ounces) mandarin oranges, drained**
- **1 cup sesame ginger marinade**
- **½ cup chicken broth**
- **1 package (16 ounces) frozen stir-fry vegetable blend, thawed**
- **1 tablespoon sesame seeds, toasted**
- **1 green onion, sliced Hot cooked rice, optional**

1. Place turkey in a 3-qt. slow cooker. Sprinkle with ginger and pepper flakes. Top with oranges. In a small bowl, combine marinade and broth; pour over turkey. Cover and cook on low for 4-5 hours or until a meat thermometer reads 170°.

2. Stir vegetables into the slow cooker. Cover and cook 30 minutes longer or until vegetables are heated through.

3. Sprinkle with sesame seeds and green onion. Serve with rice if desired.

MANDARIN TURKEY TENDERLOIN

SLOW COOKER TAMALE PIE

3. In a small bowl, combine muffin mix and eggs; spoon over meat mixture. Cover and cook 1 hour longer or until a toothpick inserted near the center comes out clean.
4. Sprinkle with cheese; cover and let stand for 5 minutes. Serve with sour cream and additional cilantro if desired.

Chicken & Vegetables with Mustard-Herb Sauce

Here's an almost effortless recipe that makes a simply delicious, comforting chicken dinner.
—MARIE RIZZIO INTERLOCHEN, MI

PREP: 20 MIN. • **COOK:** 6 HOURS • **MAKES:** 4 SERVINGS

- 4 medium red potatoes, quartered
- 3 medium parsnips, cut into 1-inch pieces
- 2 medium leeks (white portion only), thinly sliced
- ¾ cup fresh baby carrots
- 4 chicken leg quarters (about 2 pounds), skin removed
- 1 can (10¾ ounces) condensed cream of chicken soup with herbs, undiluted
- 2 tablespoons minced fresh parsley
- 1 tablespoon snipped fresh dill or 1 teaspoon dill weed
- 1 tablespoon Dijon mustard

1. In a 5- or 6-qt. slow cooker, place the potatoes, parsnips, leeks, carrots and chicken; pour soup over top. Cover and cook on low for 6-8 hours or until chicken is tender.
2. Remove chicken and vegetables; cover and keep warm. Stir the parsley, dill and mustard into cooking juices; serve with chicken and vegetables.

CHICKEN & VEGETABLES WITH MUSTARD-HERB SAUCE

Slow Cooker Tamale Pie

Canned beans and corn bread mix speed up the prep on this crowd-pleasing main dish. It's perfect for busy evenings and carry-in dinners.
—JILL POKRIVKA YORK, PA

PREP: 25 MIN. • **COOK:** 7 HOURS • **MAKES:** 8 SERVINGS

- 1 pound ground beef
- 1 teaspoon ground cumin
- ½ teaspoon salt
- ½ teaspoon chili powder
- ¼ teaspoon pepper
- 1 can (15 ounces) black beans, rinsed and drained
- 1 can (14½ ounces) diced tomatoes with mild green chilies, undrained
- 1 can (11 ounces) whole kernel corn, drained
- 1 can (10 ounces) enchilada sauce
- 2 green onions, chopped
- ¼ cup minced fresh cilantro
- 1 package (8½ ounces) corn bread/muffin mix
- 2 eggs
- 1 cup (4 ounces) shredded Mexican cheese blend
  Sour cream and additional minced fresh cilantro, optional

1. In a large skillet, cook beef over medium heat until no longer pink; drain. Stir in the cumin, salt, chili powder and pepper.
2. Transfer to a 4-qt. slow cooker; stir in the beans, tomatoes, corn, enchilada sauce, onions and cilantro. Cover and cook on low for 6-8 hours or until heated through.

PORK CHOP CACCIATORE

Pork Chop Cacciatore

It's hard to believe that the wonderful flavor of these tender chops could come from such an easy recipe! Serve with buttered noodles and a simple green salad, and dinner is done.
—TRACY HIATT GRICE SOMERSET, WI

PREP: 30 MIN. • **COOK:** 8 HOURS • **MAKES:** 6 SERVINGS

- 6 bone-in pork loin chops (7 ounces each)
- ¾ teaspoon salt, divided
- ¼ teaspoon pepper
- 1 tablespoon olive oil
- 1 cup sliced fresh mushrooms
- 1 small onion, chopped
- 1 celery rib, chopped
- 1 small green pepper, chopped
- 2 garlic cloves, minced
- 1 can (14½ ounces) diced tomatoes
- ½ cup water, divided
- ½ teaspoon dried basil
- 2 tablespoons cornstarch
- 4½ cups cooked egg noodles

1. Sprinkle chops with ½ teaspoon salt and pepper. In a large skillet, brown chops in oil in batches. Transfer to a 4- or 5-qt. slow cooker coated with cooking spray. Saute the mushrooms, onion, celery and green pepper in drippings until tender. Add garlic; cook 1 minute longer. Stir in the tomatoes, ¼ cup water, basil and remaining salt; pour over chops.

2. Cover and cook on low for 8-10 hours or until pork is tender. Remove meat to a serving platter; keep warm. Skim fat from cooking juices if necessary; transfer to a small saucepan. Bring liquid to a boil. Combine cornstarch and remaining water until smooth. Gradually stir into the pan. Bring to a boil; cook and stir for 2 minutes or until thickened. Serve with meat and noodles.

GINGERED SHORT RIBS WITH GREEN RICE

honey, vinegar, ginger and garlic. Pour over top. Cover and cook on low for 8-10 hours or until meat is tender.

2. Meanwhile, cook the rice according to package directions. Stir in the green onions, cilantro, jalapenos and lime peel.

3. Remove ribs to a serving platter; keep warm. Skim fat from cooking juices; transfer to a small saucepan. Bring to a boil. Combine cornstarch and water until smooth; gradually stir into the cooking liquid. Bring to a boil; cook and stir for 2 minutes or until thickened. Serve with ribs and rice.

Pork Roast Dinner

I am single and love to cook, so I often invite friends over who either don't cook or work nights. They love to try new dishes, and this was one of their favorites. The leftover meat makes great barbecue pork sandwiches the next day.

—LISA CHAMBERLAIN ST. CHARLES, IL

PREP: 30 MIN. + MARINATING
COOK: 8 HOURS
MAKES: 8 SERVINGS

- 2 **teaspoons minced garlic**
- 2 **teaspoons fennel seed, crushed**
- 1½ **teaspoons dried rosemary, crushed**
- 1 **teaspoon dried oregano**
- 1 **teaspoon paprika**
- ¾ **teaspoon salt**
- ¼ **teaspoon pepper**
- 1 **boneless whole pork loin roast (3 to 4 pounds)**
- 1½ **pounds medium potatoes, peeled and cut into chunks**
- 1½ **pounds large sweet potatoes, peeled and cut into chunks**
- 2 **large sweet onions, cut into eighths**
- ½ **cup chicken broth**

1. Combine the garlic, fennel, rosemary, oregano, paprika, salt and pepper; rub over pork. Cover and refrigerate for 8 hours.

2. Place potatoes and onions in a 5-qt. slow cooker. Top with pork. Pour broth over meat. Cover and cook on low for 8-10 hours or until the meat and vegetables are tender.

3. Let meat stand 10-15 minutes before slicing.

Gingered Short Ribs with Green Rice

I love the exotic flavors of Korean cooking, so I altered this one-dish recipe for slow cooker convenience.

—LILY JULOW GAINESVILLE, FL

PREP: 25 MIN. • **COOK:** 8 HOURS
MAKES: 6 SERVINGS

- 4 **medium carrots, chopped**
- 2 **medium onions, chopped**
- 3 **pounds bone-in beef short ribs**
- ½ **teaspoon salt**
- ½ **teaspoon pepper**
- ½ **cup reduced-sodium beef broth**
- ⅓ **cup sherry or additional reduced-sodium beef broth**
- ¼ **cup reduced-sodium soy sauce**
- 3 **tablespoons honey**
- 1 **tablespoon rice vinegar**
- 1 **tablespoon minced fresh gingerroot**
- 3 **garlic cloves, minced**
- 3 **cups uncooked instant brown rice**
- 3 **green onions, thinly sliced**
- 3 **tablespoons minced fresh cilantro**
- 2 **tablespoons chopped pickled jalapenos**
- ¾ **teaspoon grated lime peel**
- 4½ **teaspoons cornstarch**
- 4½ **teaspoons cold water**

1. In a 5-qt. slow cooker, layer the carrots, onions and ribs; sprinkle with salt and pepper. In a small bowl, combine the broth, sherry, soy sauce,

LISA CHAMBERLAIN'S
PORK ROAST DINNER

Sweet and Saucy Chicken

I can't remember where this recipe came from, but I've been making it for several years. Everyone who tries it enjoys it. When the chicken is done cooking, it's so tender it falls off the bone.

—PATRICIA WEIR CHILLIWACK, BC

PREP: 30 MIN. • **COOK:** 6 HOURS • **MAKES:** 6 SERVINGS

- 1 broiler/fryer chicken (4 pounds), cut up and skin removed
- ¾ cup packed brown sugar
- ¼ cup all-purpose flour
- ⅔ cup water
- ⅓ cup white vinegar
- ⅓ cup reduced-sodium soy sauce
- 2 tablespoons ketchup
- 1 tablespoon dried minced onion
- 1 teaspoon prepared mustard
- ¼ teaspoon garlic powder
- ¼ teaspoon salt
- ¼ teaspoon pepper
  Hot cooked rice or egg noodles, optional

1. Place chicken in a 3-qt. slow cooker. In a small saucepan, combine brown sugar and flour. Stir in the water, vinegar and soy sauce. Add the ketchup, onion, mustard, garlic powder, salt and pepper. Bring to a boil; cook and stir for 1-2 minutes or until thickened.

2. Pour over chicken. Cover and cook on low for 6-8 hours or until chicken juices run clear. Serve with rice or noodles if desired.

ZESTY SAUSAGE & BEANS

Zesty Sausage & Beans

You will love this hearty dish when it comes time to feed your hungry bunch. Packed with sausage, beans and bacon, it's guaranteed to satisfy even the heftiest appetites.

—MELISSA JUST MINNEAPOLIS, MN

PREP: 30 MIN. • **COOK:** 5 HOURS • **MAKES:** 10 SERVINGS

- 2 pounds smoked kielbasa or Polish sausage, halved and sliced
- 2 cans (15 ounces each) black beans, rinsed and drained
- 1 can (15 ounces) great northern beans, rinsed and drained
- 1 can (15 ounces) thick and zesty tomato sauce
- 1 medium green pepper, chopped
- 1 medium onion, chopped
- 5 bacon strips, cooked and crumbled
- 3 tablespoons brown sugar
- 2 tablespoons cider vinegar
- 3 garlic cloves, minced
- ¼ teaspoon dried thyme
- ¼ teaspoon dried marjoram
- ¼ teaspoon cayenne pepper
  Hot cooked rice

In a large skillet, brown the sausage. Transfer to a 4-qt. slow cooker; add the beans, tomato sauce, green pepper, onion, bacon, brown sugar, vinegar, garlic, thyme, marjoram and cayenne. Cover and cook on low for 5-6 hours or until vegetables are tender. Serve with rice.

SWEET AND SAUCY CHICKEN

Apple-Cinnamon Pork Loin

I love making this slow-cooked dish for chilly fall dinners. The heartwarming apple-cinnamon aroma fills our whole house. I think that the roast tastes best when it is served with homemade mashed potatoes.

—RACHEL SCHULTZ LANSING, MI

PREP: 20 MIN. • **COOK:** 6 HOURS • **MAKES:** 6 SERVINGS

- 1 boneless pork loin roast (2 to 3 pounds)
- ½ teaspoon salt
- ¼ teaspoon pepper
- 1 tablespoon canola oil
- 3 medium apples, peeled and sliced, divided
- ¼ cup honey
- 1 small red onion, halved and sliced
- 1 tablespoon ground cinnamon
  Minced fresh parsley, optional

1. Sprinkle roast with salt and pepper. In a large skillet, brown roast in oil on all sides; cool slightly. With a paring knife, cut about sixteen 3-in. deep slits in sides of roast; insert one apple slice into each slit.

2. Place half of the remaining apples in a 4-qt. slow cooker. Place roast over apples. Drizzle with honey; top with onion and remaining apples. Sprinkle with cinnamon.

3. Cover and cook on low for 6-8 hours or until meat is tender. Remove pork and apple mixture; keep warm.

4. Transfer cooking juices to a small saucepan. Bring to a boil; cook until liquid is reduced by half. Serve with pork and apple mixture. Sprinkle with parsley if desired.

APPLE-CINNAMON PORK LOIN

SAUSAGE-STUFFED FLANK STEAK

Sausage-Stuffed Flank Steak

As part of a prize I won for a recipe contest, I received a slow cooker. I hadn't used one in years, so I had no recipes on hand. This tasty beef was my first creation and is now a family favorite.

—JULIE MERRIMAN COLD BROOK, NY

PREP: 35 MIN. • **COOK:** 6 HOURS • **MAKES:** 4 SERVINGS

- ¼ cup dried cherries
- ¾ cup dry red wine or beef broth, divided
- 1 beef flank steak (1½ pounds)
- ¾ teaspoon salt, divided
- ½ teaspoon pepper, divided
- 1 medium onion, finely chopped
- 3 tablespoons olive oil, divided
- 4 garlic cloves, minced
- ½ cup seasoned bread crumbs
- ¼ cup pitted Greek olives, halved
- ¼ cup grated Parmesan cheese
- ¼ cup minced fresh basil
- ½ pound bulk hot Italian sausage
- 1 jar (24 ounces) marinara sauce
  Hot cooked pasta

1. In a small bowl, combine cherries and ¼ cup wine; let stand 10 minutes. Meanwhile, cut steak into four serving-size pieces; flatten to ¼-in. thickness. Sprinkle both sides with ½ teaspoon salt and ¼ teaspoon pepper.

2. In a large skillet, saute onion in 1 tablespoon oil until tender. Add garlic; cook 1 minute longer. Transfer to a large bowl; stir in bread crumbs, olives, cheese, basil, cherry mixture and remaining salt and pepper. Crumble sausage over mixture and mix well.

3. Spread ½ cup sausage mixture over each steak piece. Roll up jelly-roll style, starting with a long side; tie with kitchen string.

4. In the same skillet, brown meat in remaining oil on all sides. Transfer to a greased 3-qt. slow cooker. Top with marinara sauce and remaining wine. Cover and cook on low for 6-8 hours or until beef is tender. Serve with pasta.

TANGY TOMATO PORK CHOPS

Mushroom Chicken Florentine

Here's a simple way to prepare an elegant dish. The rich flavors of portobello mushrooms, fresh spinach and herbes de Provence make a delicious backdrop for the succulent chicken.

—NANCY SWAIN ST. AUGUSTINE, FL

PREP: 20 MIN. • **COOK:** 4 HOURS
MAKES: 4 SERVINGS

- 1 can (10¾ ounces) condensed cream of mushroom soup, undiluted
- ½ cup white wine or chicken broth
- ½ cup sour cream
- 1 teaspoon herbes de Provence
- 1½ pounds boneless skinless chicken breasts, cut into 2-inch pieces
- 1¾ cups sliced baby portobello mushrooms
- 6 cups fresh spinach
  Hot cooked egg noodles

In a 3-qt. slow cooker, combine the soup, wine, sour cream and herbes de Provence. Stir in the chicken and mushrooms. Fold in spinach. Cover and cook on low for 4-5 hours or until chicken is tender. Serve with noodles.
NOTE *Look for herbes de Provence in the spice aisle.*

Portobello Pointers

With their large size and meaty texture, portobello mushrooms are well suited for a slow cooker as well as for grilling and broiling. Their meaty texture makes them popular in vegetarian burgers and other meat-free dishes.

The recipe for Mushroom Chicken Florentine calls for baby portobello mushrooms. These mushrooms are sometimes labeled as cremini mushrooms. They can be used instead of white mushrooms for a flavor boost in most recipes.

Tangy Tomato Pork Chops

These tender chops are smothered in a delightfully rich sauce. I've used a chuck roast instead of pork loin chops, stewed tomatoes instead of diced, and served it over rice for a change. It's always good!
—LEA ANN SCHALK GARFIELD, AR

PREP: 20 MIN. • **COOK:** 8 HOURS
MAKES: 6 SERVINGS

- 6 bone-in pork loin chops (8 ounces each)
- 1 tablespoon canola oil
- 1 large onion, sliced
- 1 large sweet red pepper, sliced
- 1 jar (4½ ounces) sliced mushrooms, drained
- 1 can (28 ounces) diced tomatoes, undrained
- 1 tablespoon brown sugar
- 1 tablespoon balsamic vinegar
- 2 teaspoons Worcestershire sauce
- ¼ teaspoon salt
- ¼ teaspoon pepper
  Hot cooked egg noodles, optional

1. In a large skillet, brown pork chops in oil. Transfer to a 5-qt. slow cooker. Layer onion, red pepper and mushrooms over pork chops.
2. In a large bowl, combine the tomatoes, brown sugar, vinegar, Worcestershire sauce, salt and pepper; pour over pork and vegetables.
3. Cover and cook on low for 8-9 hours or until pork is tender. Serve with noodles if desired.

Bavarian Pot Roast

I grew up eating pot roast but never really liked it until I got this delightful recipe and changed a few ingredients to suit my taste. Now my child especially loves the seasoned apple gravy.

—**PATRICIA GASMUND** ROCKFORD, IL

PREP: 10 MIN. • **COOK:** 7 HOURS
MAKES: 6 SERVINGS

- 1 **beef top round roast (2 pounds)**
- 1 **cup unsweetened apple juice**
- ½ **cup tomato sauce**
- 1 **small onion, chopped**
- 1 **tablespoon white vinegar**
- 1½ **teaspoons minced fresh gingerroot**
- 1 **teaspoon salt**
- 1 **teaspoon ground cinnamon**
- 2 **tablespoons cornstarch**
- ¼ **cup water**

1. In a large skillet coated with cooking spray, brown roast on all sides. Transfer to a 3-qt. slow cooker.

2. In a small bowl, combine the juice, tomato sauce, onion, vinegar, ginger, salt and cinnamon; pour over roast. Cover and cook on low for 6 hours.

3. In a small bowl, combine the cornstarch and water until smooth; stir into the cooking juices until well combined.

4. Cover and cook 1 hour longer or until the meat is tender and gravy begins to thicken.

BAVARIAN POT ROAST

MATTHEW LAMAN'S
CREOLE CHICKEN THIGHS

Creole Chicken Thighs

Cajun seasoning adds loads of flavor and spice to this easy-to-assemble meal. The slow cooker does most of the work so you don't have to!

—**MATTHEW LAMAN** HUMMELSTOWN, PA

PREP: 30 MIN. • **COOK:** 7 HOURS
MAKES: 8 SERVINGS

- 8 bone-in chicken thighs (about 3 pounds), skin removed
- 3 tablespoons Cajun seasoning, divided
- 1 tablespoon canola oil
- 3½ cups chicken broth
- 1 can (16 ounces) red beans, rinsed and drained
- 1½ cups uncooked converted rice
- 2 medium tomatoes, finely chopped
- 1 medium green pepper, chopped
- 2 tablespoons minced fresh parsley

1. Sprinkle chicken with 1 tablespoon Cajun seasoning. In a large skillet, brown chicken in oil.
2. In a 5-qt. slow cooker, combine the broth, beans, rice, tomatoes, green pepper, parsley and remaining Cajun seasoning. Top with chicken. Cover and cook on low for 7-8 hours or until chicken is tender.

Spicy Goulash

Ground cumin, chili powder and a can of Mexican diced tomatoes jazz up my goulash recipe. Even the macaroni is prepared in the slow cooker.

—**MELISSA POLK** WEST LAFAYETTE, IN

PREP: 25 MIN. • **COOK:** 5½ HOURS
MAKES: 12 SERVINGS

SPICY GOULASH

CRANBERRY PORK ROAST

- 1 pound lean ground beef (90% lean)
- 4 cans (14½ ounces each) Mexican diced tomatoes, undrained
- 2 cans (16 ounces each) kidney beans, rinsed and drained
- 2 cups water
- 1 medium onion, chopped
- 1 medium green pepper, chopped
- ¼ cup red wine vinegar
- 2 tablespoons chili powder
- 1 tablespoon Worcestershire sauce
- 2 teaspoons beef bouillon granules
- 1 teaspoon dried basil
- 1 teaspoon dried parsley flakes
- 1 teaspoon ground cumin
- ¼ teaspoon pepper
- 2 cups uncooked elbow macaroni

1. In a large skillet, cook beef over medium heat until no longer pink; drain. Transfer to a 5-qt. slow cooker. Stir in the tomatoes, beans, water, onion, green pepper, vinegar, chili powder, Worcestershire sauce, bouillon and seasonings. Cover and cook on low for 5-6 hours or until heated through.
2. Stir in macaroni; cover and cook for 30 minutes longer or until the macaroni is tender.

Cranberry Pork Roast

I love to serve guests this moist, flavorful pork. You don't have to slave away in the kitchen to prepare it, yet it tastes like a gourmet meal!

—**KIMBERLEY SCASNY** DOUGLASVILLE, GA

PREP: 5 MIN. • **COOK:** 4 HOURS + STANDING
MAKES: 6-8 SERVINGS

- 1 boneless rolled pork loin roast (2½ to 3 pounds)
- ½ teaspoon salt
- ¼ teaspoon pepper
- 1 can (14 ounces) whole-berry cranberry sauce
- ¼ cup honey
- 1 teaspoon grated orange peel
- ⅛ teaspoon ground cloves
- ⅛ teaspoon ground nutmeg

Cut roast in half and place in a 3-qt. slow cooker; sprinkle with salt and pepper. Combine the remaining ingredients; pour over roast. Cover and cook on low for 4-5 hours or until a thermometer reads 160°. Let stand 10 minutes before slicing.

Moroccan Chicken

PREP: 25 MIN. • **COOK:** 6 HOURS • **MAKES:** 8 SERVINGS

- 1½ pounds butternut squash, peeled, seeded and cut into 2-inch cubes
- 1 can (15 ounces) garbanzo beans or chickpeas, rinsed and drained
- 1 medium onion, chopped
- 1 cup chicken broth
- ⅓ cup raisins
- 2 garlic cloves, minced
- 2 teaspoons ground coriander
- 2 teaspoons ground cumin
- ½ teaspoon ground cinnamon
- ½ teaspoon salt
- ¼ teaspoon pepper
- 8 bone-in chicken thighs (about 3 pounds), skin removed

- 2 medium tomatoes, chopped
- ½ cup pitted green olives
- 1 tablespoon cornstarch
- 1 tablespoon cold water
  Hot cooked couscous

1. In a 6-qt. slow cooker, place the squash, beans, onion, broth, raisins and garlic. Combine the coriander, cumin, cinnamon, salt and pepper; rub over chicken. Place in slow cooker.

2. Cover and cook on low for 6-8 hours or until chicken is tender, adding tomatoes and olives during the last 20 minutes of cooking.

3. Remove chicken and vegetables to a serving platter; keep warm. Skim fat from cooking juices; transfer to a small saucepan. Bring to a boil. Combine cornstarch and water until smooth; gradually stir into cooking juices. Return to a boil; cook and stir for 2 minutes or until thickened. Serve with chicken, vegetables and couscous.

Favorite Beef Chimichangas

Feeding a hungry crowd? Turn to these mouthwatering chimichangas that feature slow-roasted beef and melted cheese inside a crispy tortilla. Everyone will want the recipe!
—JUDY SANCHEZ RACINE, WI

PREP: 1 HOUR • **COOK:** 7½ HOURS • **MAKES:** 16 SERVINGS

- 1 boneless beef chuck roast (3½ pounds)
- 2 cups chopped peeled potatoes
- 1½ cups water
- 1 tablespoon reduced-sodium soy sauce
- 2 teaspoons garlic salt with parsley
- ¾ teaspoon pepper
- 2 cans (4 ounces each) chopped green chilies
- 2 tablespoons all-purpose flour
- 2 tablespoons taco seasoning
- 16 flour tortillas (10 inches), warmed
- 4 cups (16 ounces) shredded cheddar cheese
- ⅓ cup canola oil
  Optional toppings: guacamole, salsa or sour cream

1. Cut roast in half; place in a 4- or 5-qt. slow cooker. Arrange potatoes around the roast; pour water over potatoes. Drizzle meat with soy sauce. Sprinkle with garlic salt and pepper. Top with green chilies. Cover and cook on low for 7-9 hours or until meat is very tender.

2. Remove roast to a platter. Shred meat with two forks and return to the slow cooker. Combine flour and taco seasoning; stir into meat mixture. Cover and cook 30 minutes longer or until juices are thickened.

3. To assemble chimichangas, using a slotted spoon, spoon ½ cup meat mixture off-center on each tortilla. Sprinkle with ¼ cup cheese. Fold up edge nearest filling; fold in both sides and roll up.

4. In a large skillet, fry chimichangas, folded side down, in oil in batches for 2-3 minutes on each side or until golden brown. Drain on paper towels. Serve with toppings if desired.

MOROCCAN CHICKEN

Cajun-Style Pot Roast

I often make this well-seasoned beef roast when hosting a dinner party. It gives me time to visit, and guests always enjoy it—even my friend who's a chef. If I have leftovers, I simply remove the vegetables and freeze the meat for future meals. It's a wonderful time-saver on extra-busy nights!

—GINGER MENZIES OAK CREEK, CO

PREP: 15 MIN. • **COOK:** 6 HOURS • **MAKES:** 6 SERVINGS

- 1 boneless beef chuck roast (2 to 3 pounds)
- 2 tablespoons Cajun seasoning
- 1 tablespoon olive oil
- 2 cans (10 ounces each) diced tomatoes and green chilies
- 1 medium sweet red pepper, chopped
- 1½ cups chopped celery
- ¾ cup chopped onion
- ¼ cup quick-cooking tapioca
- 1½ teaspoons minced garlic
- 1 teaspoon salt
  Hot cooked rice

1. Cut roast in half; sprinkle with Cajun seasoning. In a large skillet, brown roast in oil on all sides.
2. Transfer roast to a 5-qt. slow cooker. Combine the tomatoes, red pepper, celery, onion, tapioca, garlic and salt; pour over roast.
3. Cover and cook on low for 6-8 hours or until meat is tender. Serve with rice.

CREAMY CELERY BEEF STROGANOFF

Creamy Celery Beef Stroganoff

Cream of celery soup adds rich flavor to this family-favorite Stroganoff. Besides its delicious taste, I love the ease that's involved in preparing this entree.

—KIM WALLACE DENNISON, OH

PREP: 20 MIN. • **COOK:** 8 HOURS • **MAKES:** 6 SERVINGS

- 2 pounds beef stew meat, cut into 1-inch cubes
- 1 can (10¾ ounces) condensed cream of celery soup, undiluted
- 1 can (10¾ ounces) condensed cream of mushroom soup, undiluted
- 1 medium onion, chopped
- 1 jar (6 ounces) sliced mushrooms, drained
- 1 envelope onion soup mix
- ½ teaspoon pepper
- 1 cup (8 ounces) sour cream
  Hot cooked noodles

In a 3-qt. slow cooker, combine the first seven ingredients. Cover and cook on low for 8 hours or until beef is tender. Stir in sour cream. Serve with noodles.

CAJUN-STYLE POT ROAST

BEEF & TORTELLINI MARINARA

⑤ INGREDIENTS

Carnitas Tacos

My house smells fantastic all day when I'm making this. The tacos have so much flavor, you'd never guess they use just five ingredients. I love that they're ready when you need them at the end of the day.

—**MARY WOOD** MAIZE, KS

PREP: 15 MIN. • **COOK:** 6 HOURS
MAKES: 12 SERVINGS

- 1 **boneless pork shoulder butt roast (3 to 4 pounds)**
- 1 **envelope taco seasoning**
- 1 **can (10 ounces) diced tomatoes and green chilies, undrained**
- 12 **flour tortillas (8 inches), warmed**
- 2 **cups (8 ounces) shredded Colby-Monterey Jack cheese**
  Sour cream, optional

1. Cut roast in half; place in a 4- or 5-qt. slow cooker. Sprinkle with taco seasoning. Pour tomatoes over top. Cover and cook on low for 6-8 hours or until meat is tender.
2. Remove meat from slow cooker; shred with two forks. Skim fat from cooking juices. Return meat to slow cooker; heat through. Using a slotted spoon, place ½ cup on each tortilla; top with cheese. Serve with sour cream if desired.

Beef & Tortellini Marinara

My hearty pasta dish, made with green beans, is a meal in itself. It's great served with crusty Italian bread to dip into the sauce and a nice big green salad.

—**JOYCE FREY** MACKSVILLE, KS

PREP: 30 MIN. • **COOK:** 6½ HOURS
MAKES: 11 SERVINGS

- 1 **pound beef stew meat**
- 2 **tablespoons olive oil**
- 2 **garlic cloves, minced**
- 1 **jar (26 ounces) marinara or spaghetti sauce**
- 2 **cups dry red wine or beef broth**
- 1 **pound fresh green beans, trimmed**
- 1 **can (14½ ounces) Italian diced tomatoes, undrained**
- ½ **pound small fresh mushrooms**
- 2 **envelopes thick and zesty spaghetti sauce mix**
- 2 **tablespoons minced fresh parsley**
- 1 **tablespoon dried minced onion**
- 2 **teaspoons minced fresh rosemary**
- 1 **teaspoon coarsely ground pepper**
- ¼ **teaspoon salt**
- 1 **package (9 ounces) refrigerated cheese tortellini**

1. In a large skillet, brown beef in oil until no longer pink. Add garlic; cook 1 minute longer. Transfer to a 5- or 6-qt. slow cooker.
2. Stir in the marinara sauce, wine, green beans, tomatoes, mushrooms, sauce mix, parsley, onion, rosemary, pepper and salt. Cover and cook on low for 6-8 hours or until meat is tender.
3. Stir in tortellini. Cover and cook on high for 30 minutes or until tortellini are heated through.

CARNITAS TACOS

Mom's Spaghetti Sauce

Mom made this when we were kids, and it was always my first choice for birthday dinners. Now I do the prep work in the morning and just let it simmer all day. When I get home, all I have to do is boil the spaghetti, brown some garlic bread and dinner is on! Best of all, this recipe makes a lot, and any leftover sauce freezes well for future nights when I'm swamped.

—KRISTY HAWKES SOUTH OGDEN, UTAH

PREP: 20 MIN. **• COOK:** 4 HOURS
MAKES: 10-12 SERVINGS

- 1 **pound ground beef**
- 1 **medium onion, chopped**
- 1 **medium green pepper, chopped**
- 8 **to 10 fresh mushrooms, sliced**
- 3 **celery ribs, chopped**
- 1½ **teaspoons minced garlic**
- 2 **cans (14½ ounces each) Italian stewed tomatoes**
- 1 **jar (26 ounces) spaghetti sauce**
- ½ **cup ketchup**
- 2 **teaspoons brown sugar**
- 1 **teaspoon sugar**
- 1 **teaspoon salt**
- 1 **teaspoon dried oregano**
- 1 **teaspoon chili powder**
- 1 **teaspoon prepared mustard**
  Hot cooked spaghetti

1. In a large skillet, cook the beef, onion, green pepper, mushrooms and celery over medium heat until meat is no longer pink. Add garlic; cook 1 minute longer. Drain.

2. In a 3-qt. slow cooker, combine the tomatoes, spaghetti sauce, ketchup, sugars, salt, oregano, chili powder and mustard. Stir in the beef mixture.

3. Cover and cook on low for 4-5 hours or until heated through. Serve immediately with spaghetti.

Oktoberfest Pork Roast

This recipe was adapted from one my mom used to make when I was growing up. It has all of our favorite "fall" flavors, such as apples, pork roast, sauerkraut and potatoes. I often coat the slow cooker insert with cooking spray to prevent the potatoes and meat from sticking.

—TONYA SWAIN SEVILLE, OH

PREP: 35 MIN. • **COOK:** 8 HOURS
MAKES: 8 SERVINGS

- 16 **small red potatoes**
- 1 **can (14 ounces) sauerkraut, rinsed and well drained**
- 2 **large tart apples, peeled and cut into wedges**
- 1 **pound smoked kielbasa or Polish sausage, cut into 16 slices**
- 2 **tablespoons brown sugar**
- 1 **teaspoon caraway seeds**
- 1 **teaspoon salt, divided**
- 1 **teaspoon pepper, divided**
- 1 **boneless pork loin roast (3 pounds)**
- 3 **tablespoons canola oil**

1. Place potatoes in a greased 6-qt. slow cooker. Top with sauerkraut, apples and kielbasa. Sprinkle with brown sugar, caraway seeds, 1/2 teaspoon salt and 1/2 teaspoon pepper.
2. Cut roast in half; sprinkle with remaining salt and pepper. In a large skillet, brown meat in oil on all sides. Transfer to slow cooker.
3. Cover and cook on low for 8-10 hours or until meat and vegetables are tender. Skim fat and thicken cooking liquid if desired.

"This festive and spicy main dish is wonderful for entertaining or for weeknight family meals"

—JUDY ARMSTRONG PRAIRIEVILLE, LA

Cranberry-Ginger Pork Ribs

PREP: 20 MIN. • **COOK:** 5 HOURS
MAKES: 8 SERVINGS

- 1 **can (14 ounces) whole-berry cranberry sauce**
- 2 **habanero peppers, seeded and minced**
- 4 1/2 **teaspoons minced grated gingerroot**
- 3 **garlic cloves, minced**
- 2 1/2 **pounds boneless country-style pork ribs**
- 1/2 **teaspoon salt**
- 1/2 **teaspoon cayenne pepper**
- 1/2 **teaspoon pepper**
- 2 **tablespoons olive oil**
  Hot cooked rice

1. In a small bowl, combine the cranberry sauce, habanero peppers, ginger and garlic. Sprinkle ribs with salt and peppers. In a large skillet, brown ribs in oil on all sides; drain.
2. Transfer meat to a 3-qt. slow cooker; pour cranberry mixture over ribs. Cover and cook on low for 5-6 hours or until meat is tender. Skim the fat from cooking juices. Serve with pork and rice.
NOTE *Wear disposable gloves when cutting hot peppers; the oils can burn skin. Avoid touching your face.*

OKTOBERFEST PORK ROAST

JUDY ARMSTRONG'S
CRANBERRY-GINGER PORK RIBS

Simple Sparerib & Sauerkraut Supper

This recipe simplifies our busy lives and lets us celebrate family time with a hearty meal that is on the table fast.

—**DONNA HARP** CINCINNATI, OH

PREP: 30 MIN. • **COOK:** 6 HOURS • **MAKES:** 4 SERVINGS

- 1   pound fingerling potatoes
- 1   medium onion, chopped
- 1   medium Granny Smith apple, peeled and chopped
- 3   slices thick-sliced bacon strips, cooked and crumbled
- 1   jar (16 ounces) sauerkraut, undrained
- 2   pounds pork spareribs
- ½   teaspoon salt
- ¼   teaspoon pepper
- 1   tablespoon vegetable oil
- 3   tablespoons brown sugar
- ¼   teaspoon caraway seeds
- ½   pound smoked Polish sausage, cut into 1-inch slices
- 1   cup beer

1. In a 6-qt. slow cooker, place the potatoes, onion, apple and bacon. Drain sauerkraut, reserving ⅓ cup of the liquid; add sauerkraut and reserved liquid to slow cooker.
2. Cut spareribs into serving-size portions; sprinkle with salt and pepper. In a large skillet, heat oil over medium-high heat; brown ribs in batches. Transfer to slow cooker; sprinkle with brown sugar and caraway seeds.
3. Add sausage; pour in beer. Cover and cook on low for 6-7 hours or until ribs are tender.

SIMPLE SPARERIB & SAUERKRAUT SUPPER

SLOW-COOKED HERBED TURKEY

Slow-Cooked Herbed Turkey

When it's time to harvest herbs from my garden, I prepare this entree. The turkey stays moist in the slow cooker and is bursting with herb flavors. When I served this to my Bible study group, everyone wanted the recipe!

—**SUE JURACK** MEQUON, WI

PREP: 15 MIN. + MARINATING • **COOK:** 4 HOURS + STANDING
MAKES: 14-16 SERVINGS

- 2   cans (14½ ounces each) chicken broth
- 1   cup lemon juice
- ½   cup packed brown sugar
- ½   cup minced fresh sage
- ½   cup minced fresh thyme
- ½   cup lime juice
- ½   cup cider vinegar
- ½   cup olive oil
- 2   envelopes onion soup mix
- ¼   cup Dijon mustard
- 2   tablespoons minced fresh marjoram
- 3   teaspoons paprika
- 2   teaspoons garlic powder
- 2   teaspoons pepper
- 1   teaspoon salt
- 2   boneless skinless turkey breast halves (3 pounds each)

1. In a blender, combine the first 15 ingredients; cover and process until blended. Place turkey breasts in a gallon-size resealable plastic bag; add half of marinade. Seal bag and turn to coat; seal and refrigerate overnight. Pour remaining marinade into a bowl; cover and refrigerate.
2. Drain and discard marinade from turkey. Transfer turkey breasts to a 5-qt. slow cooker. Add reserved marinade; cover and cook on high for 4-5 hours or until a thermometer reads 170°. Let stand for 10 minutes before slicing.

ENTREES

Autumn

"No more standing and stirring at the stove. This creamy Stroganoff preps in a skillet, then cooks all day while you're away."
—SARAH VASQUES MILFORD, NH

Beef Stroganoff

PREP: 20 MIN. • **COOK:** 6 HOURS • **MAKES:** 7 SERVINGS

- 2 **pounds beef top sirloin steak, cut into thin strips**
- 3 **tablespoons olive oil**
- 1 **cup water**
- 1 **envelope (1½ ounces) beef Stroganoff seasoning for the slow cooker**
- 1 **pound sliced baby portobello mushrooms**
- 1 **small onion, chopped**
- 3 **tablespoons butter**
- ¼ **cup port wine or beef broth**
- 2 **teaspoons ground mustard**
- 1 **teaspoon sugar**
- 1½ **cups (12 ounces) sour cream**
  Hot cooked egg noodles
  Minced fresh parsley, optional

BEEF STROGANOFF

1. In a large skillet, brown meat in oil. Add water and seasoning mix, stirring to loosen browned bits from pan. Transfer meat and drippings to a 3-qt. slow cooker.
2. In the same skillet, saute mushrooms and onion in butter until tender. Combine the wine, mustard and sugar; stir into the mushroom mixture. Add to slow cooker; stir to combine.
3. Cover and cook on low for 6-8 hours or until meat is tender. Stir in sour cream. Serve with noodles. Sprinkle with parsley if desired.

Over-the-Top Baked Ziti

I adapted a ziti recipe to remove ingredients my kids did not like, such as ground beef, garlic and onions. This revision was not only a success with my family, but it was a hit at potlucks, too. It is also very versatile. You can use jarred sauce or easily double or triple the recipe—and you can freeze any leftovers, as well.
—KIMBERLEY PITMAN SMYRNA, DE

PREP: 20 MIN. + 4 HOURS SIMMERING • **BAKE:** 20 MIN.
MAKES: 8 SERVINGS

- 2 **cans (29 ounces each) tomato puree**
- 1 **can (12 ounces) tomato paste**
- 1 **medium onion, chopped**
- ¼ **cup minced fresh parsley**
- 2 **tablespoons dried oregano**
- 4 **teaspoons sugar**
- 3 **garlic cloves, minced**
- 1 **tablespoon dried basil**
- 1 **teaspoon salt**
- ½ **teaspoon pepper**

ZITI
- 1 **package (16 ounces) ziti**
- 1 **egg, beaten**
- 1 **carton (15 ounces) reduced-fat ricotta cheese**
- 2 **cups (8 ounces) shredded part-skim mozzarella cheese, divided**
- ¾ **cup grated Parmesan cheese**
- ¼ **cup minced fresh parsley**
- ½ **teaspoon salt**
- ¼ **teaspoon pepper**

1. In a 3- or 4-qt. slow cooker, combine the first 10 ingredients. Cover and cook on low for 4 hours.
2. Cook ziti according to package directions. In a large bowl, combine the egg, ricotta cheese, 1 cup mozzarella, Parmesan, parsley, salt, pepper and 5 cups of sauce. Drain ziti; stir into cheese mixture.
3. Transfer to a 13-in. x 9-in. baking dish coated with cooking spray. Pour remaining sauce over the top; sprinkle with remaining mozzarella cheese. Bake at 350° for 20-25 minutes or until bubbly.

"Pepper steak is one of my favorite dishes, but I was always disappointed with beef that was too tough. This recipe solves that problem! The slow cooker keeps things simple and makes the meat very tender. I've frozen leftovers in one big zip-top bag and also in individual portions for quick lunches."

—**JULIE RHINE** ZELIENOPLE, PA

Pepper Steak

PREP: 30 MIN. • **COOK:** 6 HOURS
MAKES: 12 SERVINGS

- 1 **beef top round roast (3 pounds)**
- 1 **large onion, sliced**
- 1 **large green pepper, sliced**
- 1 **large sweet red pepper, sliced**
- 4 **garlic cloves, minced**
- 1 **cup water**
- ⅓ **cup cornstarch**
- ½ **cup reduced-sodium soy sauce**
- 2 **teaspoons sugar**
- 2 **teaspoons ground ginger**
- 8 **cups hot cooked brown rice**

1. In a 5-qt. slow cooker, combine the first six ingredients. Cook, covered, on low 6-8 hours or until meat is tender.
2. Remove roast; tent with foil. Let stand 10 minutes before slicing. Strain cooking juices. Reserve vegetables. Pour cooking juices into a large saucepan; skim fat. Bring to a boil.
3. In a small bowl, mix cornstarch, soy sauce, sugar and ginger until smooth; stir into saucepan. Return to a boil, stirring constantly; cook and stir 1-2 minutes or until thickened. Serve with roast, reserved vegetables and rice.

Turkey with Cranberry Sauce

Here's a tasty and easy way to cook turkey breast in the slow cooker. Ideal for Thanksgiving potlucks, large family get-togethers or holiday open houses, the sweet cranberry sauce complements the turkey very well. Most important, people will think you fussed!

—**MARIE RAMSDEN** FAIRGROVE, MI

PREP: 15 MIN. • **COOK:** 4 HOURS
MAKES: 15 SERVINGS

- 2 **boneless skinless turkey breast halves (3 pounds each)**
- 1 **can (14 ounces) jellied cranberry sauce**
- ½ **cup plus 2 tablespoons water, divided**
- 1 **envelope onion soup mix**
- 2 **tablespoons cornstarch**

1. Place turkey breasts in a 5-qt. slow cooker. In a large bowl, combine the cranberry sauce, ½ cup water and the soup mix. Pour over turkey. Cover and cook on low for 4-6 hours or until meat is tender. Remove turkey and keep warm.
2. Transfer cooking juices to a large saucepan. Combine the cornstarch and remaining water until smooth. Bring cranberry mixture to a boil; gradually stir in cornstarch mixture until smooth. Cook and stir for 2 minutes or until thickened.
3. Slice turkey; serve with cranberry sauce. Leftovers may be frozen for up to 3 months.

TURKEY WITH CRANBERRY SAUCE

Super Short Ribs

This idea started with an old recipe my mom had for short ribs. I added a few ingredients to her original to suit my taste, and I prepare it in the slow cooker!

—**COLEEN CARTER** MALONE, NY

PREP: 20 MIN. • **COOK:** 8 HOURS
MAKES: 6 SERVINGS

- 3 medium onions, cut into wedges
- 3 to 3½ pounds bone-in beef short ribs
- 1 bay leaf
- 1 bottle (12 ounces) light beer or nonalcoholic beer
- 2 tablespoons brown sugar
- 2 tablespoons Dijon mustard
- 2 tablespoons tomato paste
- 2 teaspoons dried thyme
- 2 teaspoons beef bouillon granules
- 1 teaspoon salt
- ¼ teaspoon pepper
- 3 tablespoons all-purpose flour
- ½ cup cold water
  Hot cooked noodles

1. Place onions in a 5-qt. slow cooker; add ribs and bay leaf. Combine the beer, brown sugar, mustard, tomato paste, thyme, bouillon, salt and pepper. Pour over meat. Cover and cook on low for 8-10 hours or until meat is tender.

2. Remove meat and vegetables to a serving platter; keep warm. Discard bay leaf. Skim fat from cooking juices; transfer juices to a small saucepan. Bring liquid to a boil.

3. Combine flour and water until smooth. Gradually stir into the pan. Bring to a boil; cook and stir for 2 minutes or until thickened.

4. Serve with meat and noodles.

LINDA BAUMANN'S
ZESTY CHICKEN MARINARA

Zesty Chicken Marinara

A friend served this delicious Italian-style chicken before a church social, and I fell in love with it. My husband says it tastes like something you'd get at a restaurant.
—**LINDA BAUMANN** RICHFIELD, WI

PREP: 15 MIN. • **COOK:** 4 HOURS
MAKES: 4 SERVINGS

- 4 **bone-in chicken breast halves (12 to 14 ounces each), skin removed**
- 2 **cups marinara sauce**
- 1 **medium tomato, chopped**
- ½ **cup Italian salad dressing**
- 1½ **teaspoons Italian seasoning**
- 1 **garlic clove, minced**
- ½ **pound uncooked angel hair pasta**
- ½ **cup shredded part-skim mozzarella cheese**

1. Place chicken in a 4-qt. slow cooker. In a small bowl, combine the marinara sauce, tomato, salad dressing, Italian seasoning and garlic; pour over chicken. Cover and cook on low for 4-5 hours or until chicken is tender.
2. Cook pasta according to package directions; drain. Serve chicken and sauce with pasta; sprinkle with cheese.

Autumn Pot Roast

This is one of my all-time-favorite slow cooker recipes. When the weather turns chilly, it's always comforting to come home to a warm, home-cooked meal like this one.
—**MARY HANKINS** KANSAS CITY, MO

PREP: 30 MIN. • **COOK:** 6 HOURS
MAKES: 6 SERVINGS

- 1 **boneless beef chuck roast (3 pounds)**
- 1 **teaspoon salt, divided**
- ½ **teaspoon pepper, divided**
- 1 **tablespoon olive oil**
- 1½ **pounds sweet potatoes, cut into 1-inch pieces**
- 2 **medium parsnips, cut into ½ inch pieces**
- 1 **large sweet onion, cut into chunks**
- ⅓ **cup sun-dried tomatoes (not packed in oil)**
- 3 **garlic cloves, minced**
- 1 **teaspoon dried thyme**
- 2 **bay leaves**
- 1 **can (14½ ounces) reduced-sodium beef broth**
- ¾ **cup dry red wine or additional reduced-sodium beef broth**

1. Cut roast in half; sprinkle with ½ teaspoon salt and ¼ teaspoon pepper. In a large skillet, brown meat in oil on all sides; drain.
2. Transfer to a 5-qt. slow cooker. Top with sweet potatoes, parsnips, onion, sun-dried tomatoes, garlic, thyme, bay leaves and remaining salt and pepper. Combine broth and wine; pour over vegetables.
3. Cover and cook on low for 6-8 hours or until meat and vegetables are tender. Skim fat. Discard bay leaves. If desired, thicken cooking juices.

Tips for Carving

You shouldn't have to do much carving of slow cooked meats, but if you do need to carve arm or blade chuck roasts, first separate the individual muscles by cutting around each muscle. Carve each muscle across the grain of the meat to desired thickness.

AUTUMN POT ROAST

PORTOBELLO BEEF BURGUNDY

Portobello Beef Burgundy

Rely on the convenience of your slow cooker for a meal that boasts all the hearty, stick-to-your-ribs goodness your family craves. These tender cubes of beef—loaded with a fantastic mushroom flavor and draped in a rich, Burgundy sauce—are sure to have them all asking for seconds!

—**MELISSA GALINAT** LAKELAND, FL

PREP: 30 MIN. • **COOK:** 7½ HOURS
MAKES: 6 SERVINGS

- ¼ **cup all-purpose flour**
- ½ **teaspoon salt**
- ½ **teaspoon seasoned salt**
- 1½ **teaspoons minced fresh thyme or ½ teaspoon dried thyme**
- ¾ **teaspoon minced fresh marjoram or ¼ teaspoon dried thyme**
- ½ **teaspoon pepper**
- 2 **pounds beef sirloin tip steak, cubed**
- 2 **bacon strips, diced**
- 3 **tablespoons canola oil**
- 1 **garlic clove, minced**
- 1 **cup Burgundy wine or beef broth**
- 1 **teaspoon beef bouillon granules**
- 1 **pound sliced baby portobello mushrooms**
  Hot cooked noodles, optional

1. In a large resealable plastic bag, combine the first six ingredients. Add beef, a few pieces at a time, and shake to coat.

2. In a large skillet, cook bacon over medium heat until crisp. Remove to paper towels with a slotted spoon; drain. In same skillet, brown beef in oil in batches, adding garlic to last batch; cook 1-2 minutes longer. Drain.

3. Transfer to a 4-qt. slow cooker. Add wine to skillet, stirring to loosen browned bits from pan. Add bouillon; bring to a boil. Stir into slow cooker. Stir in reserved bacon. Cover and cook on low for 7-9 hours or until the meat is tender.

4. Stir in mushrooms. Cover and cook on high 30-45 minutes longer or until mushrooms are tender and the sauce is slightly thickened. Serve with noodles if desired.

Tangy Venison Stroganoff

Tender chunks of venison and chopped onion are topped with a silky sour-cream sauce in this change-of-pace dish that's just perfect for autumn dinners.

—**ELLEN SPES** CARO, MI

PREP: 10 MIN. • **COOK:** 3¼ HOURS
MAKES: 4 SERVINGS

- 1½ **pounds boneless venison steak, cubed**
- 1 **medium onion, sliced**
- 1 **can (10½ ounces) condensed beef broth, undiluted**
- 1 **tablespoon Worcestershire sauce**
- 1 **tablespoon ketchup**
- 1 **teaspoon curry powder**
- ½ **teaspoon ground ginger**
- ½ **teaspoon salt**
- ¼ **teaspoon pepper**
- 4½ **teaspoons cornstarch**
- ½ **cup sour cream**
- 2 **tablespoons prepared horseradish**
  Hot cooked noodles

1. Place venison and onion in a 3-qt. slow cooker. Combine the next seven ingredients; pour over venison. Cover and cook on high for 3 to 3½ hours or until meat is tender.

2. In a small bowl, combine the cornstarch, sour cream and horseradish. Gradually stir into venison mixture. Cover and cook 15 minutes longer or until sauce is thickened. Serve with noodles.

TANGY VENISON STROGANOFF

MUSHROOM POT ROAST

Mushroom Pot Roast

Wow! The wine-warmed flavors in this recipe are amazing! Packed with wholesome veggies and tender beef, this is one company-special dish all ages will like. Serve with mashed potatoes to enjoy every last drop of the rich, beefy gravy.

—**ANGIE STEWART** TOPEKA, KS

PREP: 25 MIN. • **COOK:** 6 HOURS
MAKES: 10 SERVINGS

- 1 boneless beef chuck roast (3 to 4 pounds)
- ½ teaspoon salt
- ¼ teaspoon pepper
- 1 tablespoon canola oil
- 1½ pounds sliced fresh shiitake mushrooms
- 2½ cups thinly sliced onions
- 1½ cups reduced-sodium beef broth
- 1½ cups dry red wine or additional reduced-sodium beef broth
- 1 can (8 ounces) tomato sauce
- ¾ cup chopped peeled parsnips
- ¾ cup chopped celery
- ¾ cup chopped carrots
- 8 garlic cloves, minced
- 2 bay leaves
- 1½ teaspoons dried thyme
- 1 teaspoon chili powder
- ¼ cup cornstarch
- ¼ cup water
  Mashed potatoes

1. Sprinkle roast with salt and pepper. In a Dutch oven, brown roast in oil on all sides. Transfer to a 6-qt. slow cooker. Add the mushrooms, onions, broth, wine, tomato sauce, parsnips, celery, carrots, garlic, bay leaves, thyme and chili powder. Cover and cook on low for 6-8 hours or until meat is tender.

2. Remove meat and vegetables to a serving platter; keep warm. Discard bay leaves. Skim fat from cooking juices; transfer to a small saucepan. Bring liquid to a boil. Combine cornstarch and water until smooth; gradually stir into the pan. Bring to a boil; cook and stir for 2 minutes or until thickened. Serve with mashed potatoes, meat and vegetables.

CORN BREAD-TOPPED CHICKEN CHILI

Coffee-Braised Short Ribs

When the leaves start falling, I crave comfort foods like hearty slow-cooked stews and braised meats. I love this recipe because short ribs that cook until tender not only smell and taste impressive, but are so easy to prepare!

—MELISSA TURKINGTON
CAMANO ISLAND, WA

PREP: 25 MIN. • **COOK:** 6 HOURS
MAKES: 8 SERVINGS

- 4 **pounds bone-in beef short ribs**
- 1½ **teaspoons salt, divided**
- 1 **teaspoon ground coriander**
- ½ **teaspoon pepper**
- 2 **tablespoons olive oil**
- 1½ **pounds small red potatoes, cut in half**
- 1 **medium onion, chopped**
- 1 **cup reduced-sodium beef broth**
- 1 **whole garlic bulb, cloves separated, peeled and slightly crushed**
- 4 **cups strong brewed coffee**
- 2 **teaspoons red wine vinegar**
- 3 **tablespoons butter**

1. Sprinkle ribs with 1 teaspoon salt, coriander and pepper. In a large skillet, brown ribs in oil in batches. Using tongs, transfer ribs to a 6-qt. slow cooker. Add potatoes and onion.
2. Add broth to the skillet, stirring to loosen browned bits. Bring to a boil; cook until liquid is reduced by half. Stir in garlic and remaining salt; add to slow cooker. Pour coffee over top. Cover and cook on low for 6-8 hours or until meat is tender.
3. Remove ribs and potatoes to a serving platter; keep warm. Strain cooking juices into a small saucepan; skim fat. Bring to a boil; cook until liquid is reduced by half. Stir in vinegar. Remove from the heat; whisk in butter. Serve with ribs and potatoes.

Corn Bread-Topped Chicken Chili

After seeing a recipe for a slow cooker chicken potpie, I knew I had to try it. I loved the idea of a no-fuss chicken casserole, but wanted a Southwestern taste. I added peppers, spices and a crust that is more like a corn bread topping.

—NICOLE FILIZETTI GRAND MARAIS, MI

PREP: 20 MIN. • **COOK:** 4 HOURS
MAKES: 6 SERVINGS

- 1 **can (16 ounces) kidney beans, rinsed and drained**
- 2 **cans (2¼ ounces each) sliced ripe black olives, drained**
- 1 **cup frozen whole kernel corn, thawed and drained**
- 1 **cup tomato juice**
- 1 **can (4 ounces) chopped green chilies, drained**
- 2 **tablespoons minced fresh cilantro**
- 1 **tablespoon chili powder**
- ½ **teaspoon ground chipotle pepper**
- 1 **small onion, finely chopped**
- 1 **small sweet red pepper, chopped**
- 2 **tablespoons canola oil, divided**
- 2 **garlic cloves, minced**
- 1¼ **pounds boneless skinless chicken breasts, cubed**
- 2 **tablespoons cornstarch**
- ½ **teaspoon salt, divided**
- 1 **cup cornmeal**
- 2 **teaspoons baking powder**
- ½ **teaspoon baking soda**
- ½ **cup 2% milk**

1. In a 4-qt. slow cooker, combine the first eight ingredients. In a large skillet, saute onion and red pepper in 1 tablespoon oil until tender. Add garlic; cook 1 minute longer. Transfer to slow cooker. In a small bowl, toss chicken with cornstarch and ¼ teaspoon salt; stir into bean mixture. Cover and cook on low for 3-4 hours or until chicken is tender.
2. In a small bowl, combine the cornmeal, baking powder, baking soda and remaining salt. Stir in milk and remaining oil. Drop by tablespoonfuls over chicken mixture. Cover and cook 1 hour longer or until a toothpick inserted in center of topping comes out clean.

MELISSA TURKINGTON'S
COFFEE-BRAISED SHORT RIBS

Autumn
SOUPS, STEWS & SANDWICHES

Savory beef stews, juicy pulled-meat sandwiches and steaming soups topped with homemade dumplings...these are just a few of the fall classics shared here. Simmer up a favorite today for a meal that's sure to warm the soul.

CONSTANCE SULLIVAN'S MUSHROOM BARLEY SOUP

Mushroom Barley Soup

Here's a hearty fall soup that is packed with nutritious vegetables. I like to eat it with warm bread smothered in butter.
—**CONSTANCE SULLIVAN** OCEANSIDE, CA

PREP: 25 MIN. + SOAKING • **COOK:** 5 HOURS
MAKES: 12 SERVINGS (3 QUARTS)

- ½ cup dried great northern beans
- 1 pound sliced fresh mushrooms
- 2 cups chopped onions
- 1 medium leek (white portion only), sliced
- 2 tablespoons butter
- 1 to 2 garlic cloves, minced
- 2 cartons (32 ounces each) chicken broth
- 3 celery ribs, thinly sliced
- 3 large carrots, chopped
- ½ cup medium pearl barley
- 2 teaspoons dried parsley flakes
- 1½ teaspoons salt
- 1 bay leaf
- ¼ teaspoon white pepper

1. Soak beans according to package directions. In a large skillet, cook the mushrooms, onions and leek in butter over medium heat until tender. Add garlic; cook 1 minute longer.
2. Transfer to a 6-qt. slow cooker. Drain and rinse beans, discarding liquid. Add the beans, broth, celery, carrots, barley, parsley, salt, bay leaf and pepper. Cover and cook on low for 5-6 hours or until beans and vegetables are tender. Discard bay leaf.

Italian Venison Sandwiches

The slow cooker makes easy work of these satisfying sandwiches. The meat always turns out tender and tasty.
—**ANDREW HENSON** MORRISON, IL

PREP: 10 MIN. • **COOK:** 8 HOURS • **MAKES:** 10-12 SERVINGS

- 2 cups water
- 1 envelope onion soup mix
- 1 tablespoon dried basil
- 1 tablespoon dried parsley flakes
- 1 teaspoon beef bouillon granules
- ½ teaspoon celery salt
- ¼ teaspoon garlic powder
- ¼ teaspoon cayenne pepper
- ¼ teaspoon pepper
- 1 boneless venison roast (3 to 4 pounds), cut into 1-inch cubes
- 10 to 12 sandwich rolls, split
   Green pepper rings, optional

In a 3-qt. slow cooker, combine the first nine ingredients. Add venison and stir. Cover and cook on low for 8 hours or until meat is tender. Using a slotted spoon, spoon into rolls. Top with pepper rings if desired.

"This healthy, hearty stew is one of my husband's favorite meals. I always use fresh mushrooms, and I toss low-sodium bouillon cubes right into the roaster."

—**PATRICIA KILE** ELIZABETHTOWN, PA

Beef & Veggie Stew

PREP: 25 MIN. • **COOK:** 4 HOURS • **MAKES:** 8 SERVINGS

- ¼ **cup all-purpose flour**
- 2 **pounds boneless beef chuck roast, trimmed and cut into 1-inch cubes**
- 2 **tablespoons canola oil**
- 1 **can (10¾ ounces) condensed tomato soup, undiluted**
- 1 **cup water or red wine**
- 2 **reduced-sodium beef bouillon cubes**
- 3 **teaspoons Italian seasoning**
- 1 **bay leaf**
- ½ **teaspoon coarsely ground pepper**
- 6 **white onions or yellow onions, quartered**
- 4 **medium potatoes, cut into 1½-inch slices**
- 3 **medium carrots, cut into 1-inch slices**
- 12 **large fresh mushrooms**
- ½ **cup sliced celery**

1. Place flour in a large resealable plastic bag. Add beef, a few pieces at a time, and shake to coat.
2. In a large skillet, brown meat in oil in batches; drain. Transfer to a 5-qt. slow cooker. Combine the tomato soup, water or wine, bouillon and seasonings; pour over beef. Add the onions, potatoes, carrots, mushrooms and celery.
3. Cover and cook on low for 4-5 hours or until meat is tender. Discard bay leaf. Serve with noodles or French bread.

BEEF & VEGGIE STEW

PASTA E FAGIOLI

Pasta e Fagioli

This is my favorite soup to make because it's so tasty, hearty and healthy. I have served the dish to guests and received many compliments. The soup is thick and delicious.

—**PENNY NOVY** BUFFALO GROVE, IL

PREP: 30 MIN. • **COOK:** 7½ HOURS • **MAKES:** 8 SERVINGS (2½ QUARTS)

- 1 **pound ground beef**
- 1 **medium onion, chopped**
- 1 **carton (32 ounces) chicken broth**
- 2 **cans (14½ ounces each) diced tomatoes, undrained**
- 1 **can (15 ounces) white kidney or cannellini beans, rinsed and drained**
- 2 **medium carrots, chopped**
- 1½ **cups finely chopped cabbage**
- 1 **celery rib, chopped**
- 2 **tablespoons minced fresh basil or 2 teaspoons dried basil**
- 2 **garlic cloves, minced**
- ½ **teaspoon salt**
- ½ **teaspoon pepper**
- 1 **cup ditalini or other small pasta**
  Grated Parmesan cheese, optional

1. In a large skillet, cook beef and onion over medium heat until beef is no longer pink and onion is tender; drain.
2. Transfer to a 4- or 5-qt. slow cooker. Stir in the broth, tomatoes, beans, carrots, cabbage, celery, basil, garlic, salt and pepper. Cover and cook on low for 7-8 hours or until vegetables are tender.
3. Stir in pasta. Cover and cook on high 30 minutes longer or until pasta is tender. Sprinkle with cheese if desired.

SOUTHWESTERN PORK AND SQUASH SOUP

Curried Turkey Soup

What a delight to dish up this colorful soup the day after Thanksgiving! Best of all, it comes together in the slow cooker, allowing you time to get started on some of that early holiday shopping.

—**HOLLY BAUER** WEST BEND, WI

PREP: 40 MIN. • **COOK:** 8 HOURS
MAKES: 6 SERVINGS (2½ QUARTS)

- 4½ cups chicken broth
- 1 can (14½ ounces) diced tomatoes, undrained
- 2 medium carrots, chopped
- 2 celery ribs, chopped
- 1 medium onion, chopped
- 1 medium green pepper, chopped
- 1 medium tart apple, peeled and chopped
- 1 tablespoon curry powder
- ½ teaspoon salt
- ½ teaspoon pepper
- ¼ cup all-purpose flour
- ½ cup unsweetened apple juice or additional chicken broth
- 3 cups cubed cooked turkey
- 3 cups hot cooked rice

1. Combine the first 10 ingredients in a 4- or 5-qt. slow cooker. Cover and cook on low for 7-8 hours or until vegetables are tender. Mix flour and apple juice until smooth; stir into soup. Cover and cook on high for 30 minutes or until soup is thickened.

2. Stir in turkey; heat through. Serve with rice.

CURRIED TURKEY SOUP

Southwestern Pork and Squash Soup

I adapted a pork and squash stew recipe, using tomatoes and Southwestern-style seasonings. My husband and sons loved it, and the leftovers were even better the next day! Try this with fresh corn muffins.

—**MOLLY NEWMAN** PORTLAND, OR

PREP: 20 MIN. • **COOK:** 4 HOURS
MAKES: 6 SERVINGS

- 1 pound pork tenderloin, cut into 1-inch cubes
- 1 medium onion, chopped
- 1 tablespoon canola oil
- 3 cups reduced-sodium chicken broth
- 1 medium butternut squash, peeled and cubed
- 2 medium carrots, sliced
- 1 can (14½ ounces) diced tomatoes with mild green chilies, undrained
- 1 tablespoon chili powder
- 1 teaspoon ground cumin
- 1 teaspoon dried oregano
- ½ teaspoon pepper
- ¼ teaspoon salt

In a large skillet, brown pork and onion in oil; drain. Transfer to a 4- or 5-qt. slow cooker. Stir in the remaining ingredients. Cover and cook on low for 4-5 hours or until meat is tender.

French Dip au Jus

I created this sandwich because so many French Dip recipes seem bland or rely on a mix. Mine is simple to make and better than any restaurant version I've had.

—LINDSAY EBERT OREM, UTAH

PREP: 30 MIN. • **COOK:** 8 HOURS
MAKES: 8 SERVINGS

- 1½ teaspoons beef base
- 1 teaspoon dried thyme
- 1 beef rump roast or bottom round roast (3 pounds), cut in half
- 1 medium onion, quartered
- ½ cup reduced-sodium soy sauce
- 2 garlic cloves, minced
- 1 bay leaf
- ½ teaspoon pepper
- 8 cups water
- 2 tablespoons Dijon mustard
- 2 loaves French bread (1 pound each), split and toasted
- 12 slices part-skim mozzarella cheese
- 1 jar (4½ ounces) sliced mushrooms, drained

1. Combine beef base and thyme; rub over roast and place in a 5-qt. slow cooker. Combine the onion, soy sauce, garlic, bay leaf and pepper; pour over roast. Add water.

2. Cover and cook on low for 8-9 hours or until meat is tender. Remove roast to a cutting board; cool slightly. Strain cooking juices, reserving onion; skim fat from juices. Discard bay leaf. Thinly slice meat.

3. To assemble sandwiches, spread mustard over bread. Top each bottom with three slices cheese; layer with beef, remaining cheese, mushrooms and reserved onion. Replace tops. Cut each loaf into four slices; serve with reserved juices.

NOTE *Look for beef base near the broth and bouillon in your supermarket.*

Cranberry BBQ Pulled Pork

Cranberry sauce adds a yummy twist on traditional pulled pork in this sandwich that my family can't get enough of! The pork cooks to tender perfection in the slow cooker, which also makes this dish conveniently portable.

—CARRIE WIEGAND MT. PLEASANT, IA

PREP: 20 MIN. • **COOK:** 9 HOURS • **MAKES:** 14 SERVINGS

- 1 boneless pork shoulder roast (4 to 6 pounds)
- ⅓ cup cranberry juice
- 1 teaspoon salt

SAUCE
- 1 can (14 ounces) whole-berry cranberry sauce
- 1 cup ketchup
- ⅓ cup cranberry juice
- 3 tablespoons brown sugar
- 4½ teaspoons chili powder
- 2 teaspoons garlic powder
- 1 teaspoon onion powder
- ½ teaspoon salt
- ¼ teaspoon ground chipotle pepper
- ½ teaspoon liquid smoke, optional
- 14 hamburger buns, split

1. Cut roast in half. Place in a 4-qt. slow cooker. Add cranberry juice and salt. Cover and cook on low for 8-10 hours or until meat is tender.

2. Remove roast and set aside. In a small saucepan, combine the cranberry sauce, ketchup, cranberry juice, brown sugar, seasonings and liquid smoke if desired. Cook and stir over medium heat for 5 minutes or until slightly thickened.

3. Skim fat from cooking juices; set aside ½ cup juices. Discard remaining juices. When cool enough to handle, shred pork with two forks and return to slow cooker.

4. Stir in sauce mixture and reserved cooking juices. Cover and cook on low for 1 hour or until heated through. Serve on buns.

CRANBERRY BBQ PULLED PORK

MEXICAN BEEF & BEAN SUPPER

Mexican Beef & Bean Supper

I like that this is super-easy to toss together, and the leftovers reheat well. The healthy beans and veggies taste great, and the stew warms me up on cold, autumn days.

—TACY FLEURY CLINTON, SC

PREP: 20 MIN. • **COOK:** 8 HOURS • **MAKES:** 10 SERVINGS (2½ QUARTS)

- 1 cup all-purpose flour
- ¼ teaspoon salt
- ⅛ teaspoon pepper
- 1 pound beef stew meat, cut into 1-inch cubes
- 2 tablespoons canola oil
- 1 can (16 ounces) kidney beans, rinsed and drained
- 1 can (15¼ ounces) whole kernel corn, drained
- 2 medium potatoes, cubed
- 2 small carrots, sliced
- 2 celery ribs, sliced
- 1 small onion, chopped
- 2 cans (15 ounces each) tomato sauce
- 1 cup water
- 1 envelope taco seasoning
- ½ teaspoon ground cumin
   Tortilla chips and shredded cheddar cheese

1. Combine the flour, salt and pepper in a large resealable plastic bag. Add the beef, a few pieces at a time, and shake to coat.

2. Brown meat in batches in oil in a large skillet; drain. Transfer to a 5-qt. slow cooker. Add the beans, corn, potatoes, carrots, celery and onion.

3. Whisk the tomato sauce, water, taco seasoning and cumin; pour over top. Cover and cook on low for 8-10 hours or until meat is tender. Serve with tortilla chips and cheese.

Lentil and Pasta Stew

PREP: 25 MIN. • **COOK:** 8 HOURS • **MAKES:** 8 SERVINGS

- ½ pound smoked kielbasa or Polish sausage, chopped
- 3 tablespoons olive oil
- 3 tablespoons butter
- 1 cup cubed peeled potatoes
- ¾ cup sliced fresh carrots
- 1 celery rib, sliced
- 1 small onion, finely chopped
- 5 cups beef broth
- 1 cup dried lentils, rinsed
- 1 cup canned diced tomatoes
- 1 bay leaf
- 1 teaspoon coarsely ground pepper
- ¼ teaspoon salt
- 1 cup uncooked ditalini or other small pasta
  Shredded Romano cheese

1. Brown kielbasa in oil and butter in a large skillet. Add the potatoes, carrots, celery and onion. Cook and stir for 3 minutes over medium heat. Transfer to a 4- or 5-qt. slow cooker. Stir in the broth, lentils, tomatoes, bay leaf, pepper and salt.

2. Cover and cook on low for 8-10 hours or until lentils are tender. Meanwhile, cook pasta according to package directions; drain. Stir pasta into slow cooker. Discard bay leaf. Sprinkle servings with cheese.

LENTIL AND PASTA STEW

SPICY SHREDDED BEEF SANDWICHES

Spicy Shredded Beef Sandwiches

If you like your shredded beef with a little kick, then this recipe is for you! For an even zestier version, add another jar of jalapenos or use hot peppers instead of the pepperoncinis.

—**KRISTEN LANGMEIER** FARIBAULT, MN

PREP: 15 MIN. • **COOK:** 8 HOURS • **MAKES:** 12 SERVINGS

- 1 boneless beef chuck roast (4 to 5 pounds)
- 2 medium onions, coarsely chopped
- 1 jar (16 ounces) sliced pepperoncini, undrained
- 1 jar (8 ounces) pickled jalapeno slices, drained
- 1 bottle (12 ounces) beer or nonalcoholic beer
- 1 envelope onion soup mix
- 5 garlic cloves, minced
- ½ teaspoon pepper
- 12 kaiser rolls, split
- 12 slices provolone cheese

1. Cut roast in half; place in a 4- or 5-qt. slow cooker. Add the onions, pepperoncini, jalapenos, beer, soup mix, garlic and pepper.

2. Cover and cook on low for 8-10 hours or until the meat is tender.

3. Remove meat. Skim fat from cooking liquid. When cool enough to handle, shred meat with two forks and return to slow cooker; heat through. Serve ½ cup meat mixture on each roll with a slice of cheese.

NOTE *Look for pepperoncinis (pickled peppers) in the pickle and olive section of your grocery store.*

STEPHANIE RABBITT-SCHAPP'S
MOMMA'S TURKEY STEW WITH DUMPLINGS

Momma's Turkey Stew with Dumplings

My mother used to make turkey stew every year with our Thanksgiving leftovers. It is simple and really celebrates the natural flavors of good, simple ingredients. To this day, it remains one of my favorite meals.

—STEPHANIE RABBITT-SCHAPP
CINCINNATI, OH

PREP: 20 MIN. • **COOK:** 6½ HOURS
MAKES: 6 SERVINGS

- 3 **cups shredded cooked turkey**
- 1 **large sweet onion, chopped**
- 1 **large potato, peeled and cubed**
- 2 **large carrots, chopped**
- 2 **celery ribs, chopped**
- 2 **bay leaves**
- 1 **teaspoon salt**
- ½ **teaspoon poultry seasoning**
- ½ **teaspoon dried thyme**
- ¼ **teaspoon pepper**
- 1 **carton (32 ounces) chicken broth**
- ⅓ **cup cold water**
- 3 **tablespoons cornstarch**
- ½ **cup frozen corn, thawed**
- ½ **cup frozen peas, thawed**
- 1 **cup biscuit/baking mix**
- ⅓ **cup 2% milk**

1. In a 6-qt. slow cooker, combine the first 10 ingredients; stir in broth. Cover and cook on low for 6-7 hours.

2. Remove bay leaves. In a small bowl, mix water and cornstarch until smooth; stir into turkey mixture. Add corn and peas. Cover and cook on high until mixture reaches a simmer.

3. Meanwhile, in a small bowl, mix baking mix and milk just until moistened. Drop by rounded tablespoonfuls on top of the simmering liquid.

4. Reduce heat to low; cover and cook for 20-25 minutes or until a toothpick inserted in a dumpling comes out clean.

All-Day Meatball Stew

Frozen meatballs and convenient jarred mushrooms along with cans of tomato sauce and beef broth simplify this homey stew that simmers all day. Each bite boasts lots of fresh veggie flavor and a comforting rich gravy. It smells so good while it cooks, it's hard to resist!

—ANITA HOFFMAN HOLLAND, PA

PREP: 20 MIN. • **COOK:** 8½ HOURS
MAKES: 8 SERVINGS (3 QUARTS)

- 2 **packages (12 ounces each) frozen fully cooked Italian meatballs**
- 5 **medium potatoes, peeled and cubed**
- 1 **pound fresh baby carrots**
- 1 **medium onion, halved and sliced**
- 1 **jar (4½ ounces) sliced mushrooms, drained**
- 2 **cans (8 ounces each) tomato sauce**
- 1 **can (10½ ounces) condensed beef broth, undiluted**
- ¾ **cup water**
- ¾ **cup dry red wine or beef broth**
- ½ **teaspoon garlic powder**
- ¼ **teaspoon pepper**
- 2 **tablespoons all-purpose flour**
- ½ **cup cold water**

Place the meatballs, potatoes, carrots, onion and mushrooms in a 5- or 6-qt. slow cooker. In a large bowl, combine the tomato sauce, broth, water, wine, garlic powder and pepper; pour over top. Cover and cook on low for 8-10 hours or until vegetables are tender.

5. Combine flour and water until smooth; gradually stir into stew. Cover and cook on high for 30 minutes or until sauce is thickened.

ALL-DAY MEATBALL STEW

Slow Cooker Beef Vegetable Stew

Come home to warm comfort food! This is based on my mom's wonderful recipe, though I tweaked it for the slow cooker. Add a sprinkle of Parmesan to each bowl for a nice finishing touch.

—MARCELLA WEST WASHBURN, IL

PREP: 20 MIN. • **COOK:** 6½ HOURS
MAKES: 8 SERVINGS (3 QUARTS)

- 1½ **pounds boneless beef chuck roast, cut into 1-inch cubes**
- 3 **medium potatoes, peeled and cubed**
- 3 **cups hot water**
- 1½ **cups fresh baby carrots**
- 1 **can (10¾ ounces) condensed tomato soup, undiluted**
- 1 **medium onion, chopped**
- 1 **celery rib, chopped**
- 2 **tablespoons Worcestershire sauce**
- 1 **tablespoon browning sauce, optional**
- 2 **teaspoons beef bouillon granules**
- 1 **garlic clove, minced**
- 1 **teaspoon sugar**
- ¾ **teaspoon salt**
- ¼ **teaspoon pepper**
- ¼ **cup cornstarch**
- ¾ **cup cold water**
- 2 **cups frozen peas**

1. Place the roast, potatoes, hot water, carrots, soup, onion, celery, Worcestershire sauce, browning sauce if desired, bouillon granules, garlic, sugar, salt and pepper in a 5- or 6-qt. slow cooker. Cover and cook on low for 6-8 hours or until meat is tender.

2. Combine cornstarch and cold water in a small bowl until smooth; gradually stir into stew. Add peas; cover and cook on low for 30 minutes or until thickened.

SLOW COOKER BEEF VEGETABLE STEW

SWEET-AND-SOUR BEEF STEW

Sweet-and-Sour Beef Stew

This chunky meal in a bowl makes terrific use of nutrient-packed vegetables. It has a deliciously sweet and tangy taste.
—**FRANCES CONKLIN** GRANGEVILLE, ID

PREP: 25 MIN. • **COOK:** 8 HOURS • **MAKES:** 8 SERVINGS

- 2 pounds beef top round steak, cut into 1-inch cubes
- 2 tablespoons olive oil
- 1 can (15 ounces) tomato sauce
- 2 large onions, chopped
- 4 medium carrots, thinly sliced
- 1 large green pepper, cut into 1-inch pieces
- 1 cup canned pineapple chunks, drained
- ½ cup cider vinegar
- ¼ cup packed brown sugar
- ¼ cup light corn syrup
- 2 teaspoons chili powder
- 2 teaspoons paprika
- ½ teaspoon salt
  Hot cooked rice, optional

1. In a large skillet, brown beef in oil in batches; drain. Transfer to a 4- or 5-qt. slow cooker.
2. In a large bowl, combine the tomato sauce, onions, carrots, green pepper, pineapple, vinegar, brown sugar, corn syrup, chili powder, paprika and salt; pour over beef.
3. Cover and cook on low for 8-10 hours or until beef is tender. Serve with rice if desired.

Harvest Butternut & Pork Stew

Cure your craving for something different with a savory stew that's scrumptious with warm bread. Edamame adds a tasty protein-packed touch to the slow-cooked comfort food.
—**ERIN CHILCOAT** CENTRAL ISLIP, NY

PREP: 20 MIN. • **COOK:** 8½ HOURS
MAKES: 6 SERVINGS (2 QUARTS)

- ⅓ cup plus 1 tablespoon all-purpose flour, divided
- 1 tablespoon paprika
- 1 teaspoon salt
- 1 teaspoon ground coriander
- 1½ pounds boneless pork shoulder butt roast, cut into 1-inch cubes
- 1 tablespoon canola oil
- 2¾ cups cubed peeled butternut squash
- 1 can (14½ ounces) diced tomatoes, undrained
- 1 cup frozen corn, thawed
- 1 medium onion, chopped
- 2 tablespoons cider vinegar
- 1 bay leaf
- 2½ cups reduced-sodium chicken broth
- 1⅔ cups frozen shelled edamame, thawed

1. In a large resealable plastic bag, combine ⅓ cup flour, paprika, salt and coriander. Add pork, a few pieces at a time, and shake to coat.
2. In a large skillet, brown pork in oil in batches; drain. Transfer to a 5-qt. slow cooker. Add the squash, tomatoes, corn, onion, vinegar and bay leaf. In a small bowl, combine broth and remaining flour until smooth; stir into slow cooker.
3. Cover and cook on low for 8-10 hours or until pork and vegetables are tender. Stir in edamame; cover and cook 30 minutes longer. Discard bay leaf.

HARVEST BUTTERNUT & PORK STEW

Autumn Pumpkin Chili

I've prepared this chili often, and everyone loves it— even the most finicky of my grandchildren. It has also earned a thumbs-up from family and friends in other states who've tried it. The recipe's a definite "keeper" in my book!

—**KIMBERLY NAGY** PORT HADLOCK, WA

PREP: 20 MIN. • **COOK:** 7 HOURS
MAKES: 4 SERVINGS

- 1 **medium onion, chopped**
- 1 **small green pepper, chopped**
- 1 **small sweet yellow pepper, chopped**
- 1 **tablespoon canola oil**
- 1 **garlic clove, minced**
- 1 **pound ground turkey**
- 1 **can (15 ounces) solid-pack pumpkin**
- 1 **can (14½ ounces) diced tomatoes, undrained**
- 4½ **teaspoons chili powder**
- ¼ **teaspoon pepper**
- ¼ **teaspoon salt**
  Optional toppings: shredded cheddar cheese, sour cream and sliced green onions

1. Saute the onion and the green and yellow peppers in oil in a large skillet until tender. Add garlic; cook 1 minute longer. Crumble turkey into skillet. Cook over medium heat until meat is no longer pink.
2. Transfer to a 3-qt. slow cooker. Stir in the pumpkin, tomatoes, chili powder, pepper and salt. Cover and cook on low for 7-9 hours. Serve with toppings of your choice.

top tip
Earthy Addition

A can of solid-pack pumpkin is a wonderful addition to lots of fall favorites—whether made in the slow cooker or not. Stir a can into your favorite spaghetti sauce or sloppy joe mixture. You can also add a few tablespoons to prepared pudding, ice cream or frozen whipped topping.

STEPHANIE'S SLOW COOKER STEW

Stephanie's Slow Cooker Stew

Start this warming one-pot meal before you head out on a crisp autumn day. By the time you get home, the well-seasoned meat will be tender and ready to eat.

—**STEPHANIE RABBITT-SCHAPP**
CINCINNATI, OH

PREP: 20 MIN. • **COOK:** 7½ HOURS
MAKES: 5 SERVINGS

- 1 **pound beef stew meat**
- 2 **medium potatoes, peeled and cubed**
- 1 **can (14½ ounces) beef broth**
- 1 **can (11½ ounces) V8 juice**
- 2 **celery ribs, chopped**
- 2 **medium carrots, chopped**
- 1 **medium sweet onion, chopped**
- 3 **bay leaves**
- ½ **teaspoon salt**
- ½ **teaspoon dried thyme**
- ½ **teaspoon chili powder**
- ¼ **teaspoon pepper**
- 2 **tablespoons cornstarch**
- 1 **tablespoon cold water**
- ½ **cup frozen corn**
- ½ **cup frozen peas**

1. In a 3-qt. slow cooker, combine the first 12 ingredients. Cover and cook on low for 7-8 hours or until the meat is tender. Discard bay leaves.
2. In a small bowl, combine the cornstarch and water until smooth; stir into stew. Add corn and peas. Cover and cook on high for 30 minutes or until thickened.

KIMBERLY NAGY'S
AUTUMN PUMPKIN CHILI

Beef Stew with Ghoulish Mashed Potatoes

Big and little goblins alike will be delighted with the seasonal flavors of this hearty beef stew that includes mushrooms and parsnips. Rich mashed potato "ghosts" are piped onto each bowl for a no-fuss flair that's sure to steal smiles.

—TASTE OF HOME TEST KITCHEN

PREP: 30 MIN. • **COOK:** 8 HOURS
MAKES: 6 SERVINGS

- 2 pounds beef stew meat, cut into 1-inch cubes
- 1 pound fresh mushrooms, halved
- 2 cups fresh baby carrots
- 2 medium parsnips, peeled, halved lengthwise and sliced
- 2 medium onions, chopped
- 1½ cups beef broth
- 3 tablespoons tomato paste
- 1 tablespoon Worcestershire sauce
- 2 garlic cloves, minced
- ½ teaspoon ground cloves
- ¼ teaspoon pepper
- 8 medium potatoes (2⅓ pounds), peeled and cubed
- ⅔ cup sour cream
- 6 tablespoons butter, cubed
- 1 teaspoon salt, divided
- 1 cup frozen peas
- 2 tablespoons all-purpose flour
- 2 tablespoons water

1. In a 5-qt. slow cooker, combine the first 11 ingredients. Cover and cook on low for 8-9 hours or until beef and vegetables are tender.
2. About 30 minutes before serving, place potatoes in a large saucepan and cover with water. Bring to a boil. Reduce heat; cover and simmer for 15-20 minutes or until tender. Drain. Return potatoes to pan; add the sour cream, butter and ½ teaspoon salt. Mash until smooth.
3. Set aside 12 peas for garnish. Add remaining peas to the slow cooker. Increase heat to high. In a bowl, whisk the flour, water and remaining salt until smooth; stir into stew. Cover and cook for 5 minutes or until thickened.
4. Divide stew among six bowls. Place mashed potatoes in large resealable plastic bag; cut a 2-in. hole in one corner. Pipe ghost potatoes onto stew; garnish with reserved peas for eyes.

"Here's a real stick-to-your-ribs soup. I've also used chuck roast, rump roast and London broil that's been cut into bite-size pieces with tremendous success."
—JANE MCMILLAN DANIA BEACH, FL

Beef Barley Soup

PREP: 20 MIN. • **COOK:** 8½ HOURS
MAKES: 8 SERVINGS (2 QUARTS)

- 1½ pounds beef stew meat, cut into ½-inch cubes
- 1 tablespoon canola oil
- 1 carton (32 ounces) beef broth
- 1 bottle (12 ounces) beer or nonalcoholic beer
- 1 small onion, chopped
- ½ cup medium pearl barley
- 3 garlic cloves, minced
- 1 teaspoon dried oregano
- 1 teaspoon dried parsley flakes
- 1 teaspoon Worcestershire sauce
- ½ teaspoon crushed red pepper flakes
- ½ teaspoon pepper
- ¼ teaspoon salt
- 1 bay leaf
- 2 cups frozen mixed vegetables, thawed

1. In a large skillet, brown beef in oil; drain. Transfer to a 3-qt. slow cooker.
2. Add the broth, beer, onion, barley, garlic, oregano, parsley, Worcestershire sauce, pepper flakes, pepper, salt and bay leaf. Cover and cook on low for 8-10 hours.
3. Stir in vegetables; cover and cook 30 minutes longer or until meat is tender and vegetables are heated through. Discard bay leaf.

BEEF STEW WITH GHOULISH MASHED POTATOES

Pulled Turkey Tenderloin

Not your ordinary pulled turkey sandwich, this one shines thanks to its unique yogurt sauce. Serve the turkey by itself or stack on extra sweet pickle slices and jalapenos to echo the dressing.

—**SHANA CONRADT** GREENVILLE, WI

PREP: 15 MIN. • **COOK:** 6 HOURS
MAKES: 5 SERVINGS

- 1 **package (20 ounces) turkey breast tenderloins**
- 2 **cups water**
- ½ **cup sweet pickle juice**
- 1 **envelope onion soup mix**
- 2 **tablespoons canned diced jalapeno peppers**
- ½ **cup fat-free plain Greek yogurt**
- 1 **tablespoon yellow mustard**
- ⅛ **teaspoon pepper**
- 5 **kaiser rolls, split**

1. Place turkey in a 3-qt. slow cooker. In a small bowl, combine the water, pickle juice, soup mix and jalapeno peppers; pour over turkey. Cover and cook on low for 6-8 hours or until the meat is tender. Remove turkey and shred with two forks. Transfer to a small bowl.

2. Strain cooking juices, reserving ½ cup juices. In another small bowl, combine the yogurt, mustard, pepper and reserved cooking juices. Pour over turkey; toss to coat. Serve on rolls.

Butternut Squash Soup

The golden color, smooth and velvety texture, and wonderful taste of this soup make it welcome on chilly fall days. It has a slightly tangy flavor from the cream cheese, and the cinnamon really comes through nicely.

—**JACKIE CAMPBELL** STANHOPE, NJ

PREP: 30 MIN. • **COOK:** 6¼ HOURS
MAKES: 14 SERVINGS (2½ QUARTS)

- 1 **medium onion, chopped**
- 2 **tablespoons butter**
- 1 **medium butternut squash (about 4 pounds), peeled and cubed**
- 3 **cans (14½ ounces each) vegetable broth**
- 1 **tablespoon brown sugar**
- 1 **tablespoon minced fresh gingerroot**
- 1 **garlic clove, minced**
- 1 **cinnamon stick (3 inches)**
- 1 **package (8 ounces) cream cheese, softened and cubed**

1. In a small skillet, saute onion in butter until tender. Transfer to a 5-or 6-quart slow cooker; add squash. Combine the broth, brown sugar, ginger, garlic and cinnamon; pour over squash. Cover and cook on low for 6-8 hours or until squash is tender.

2. Cool slightly. Discard cinnamon stick. In a blender, process soup in batches until smooth. Return all to slow cooker. Whisk in cream cheese; cover and cook 15 minutes longer or until cheese is melted.

MARCIA O'NEIL'S
PUMPKIN HARVEST BEEF STEW

Pumpkin Harvest Beef Stew

By the time this stew is finished simmering and a loaf of fresh bread baked, the aromas in the house are wonderful!

—**MARCIA O'NEIL** CEDAR CREST, NM

PREP: 25 MIN. • **COOK:** 6½ HOURS
MAKES: 6 SERVINGS

- 1 tablespoon canola oil
- 1 beef top round steak (1½ pounds), cut into 1-inch cubes
- 1½ cups cubed peeled pie pumpkin or sweet potatoes
- 3 small red potatoes, peeled and cubed
- 1 cup cubed acorn squash
- 1 medium onion, chopped
- 2 cans (14½ ounces each) reduced-sodium beef broth
- 1 can (14½ ounces) diced tomatoes, undrained
- 2 bay leaves
- 2 garlic cloves, minced
- 2 teaspoons reduced-sodium beef bouillon granules
- ½ teaspoon chili powder
- ½ teaspoon pepper
- ¼ teaspoon ground allspice
- ¼ teaspoon ground cloves
- ¼ cup water
- 3 tablespoons all-purpose flour

1. In a large skillet, heat oil over medium-high heat. Brown beef in batches; remove with a slotted spoon to a 4- or 5-qt. slow cooker. Add the pumpkin, potatoes, squash and onion. Stir in the broth, tomatoes and seasonings. Cover and cook on low for 6-8 hours or until meat is tender.

2. Remove bay leaves. In a small bowl, mix water and flour until smooth; gradually stir into stew. Cover and cook on high for 30 minutes or until liquid is thickened.

Pumpkin Picking

Pie pumpkins should be picked when fully ripened—the color will be deep orange, and the stem will easily break loose.

SUNDAY STEW

Sunday Stew

We had an aunt who served this stew on every special occasion that we all got together. It brings back wonderful family memories. The cinnamon adds a unique and unexpected flavor.

—**JEANETTE LAZARY** ROCHESTER, NY

PREP: 25 MIN. • **COOK:** 6 HOURS
MAKES: 6 SERVINGS

- ⅓ cup all-purpose flour
- ¾ teaspoon salt
- ¾ teaspoon ground cinnamon
- ½ teaspoon pepper
- 2 pounds beef stew meat, cut into 1-inch cubes
- 2 tablespoons canola oil
- 1 package (14 ounces) frozen pearl onions
- 1 cup dry red wine or beef broth
- ¾ cup water
- 2 tablespoons red wine vinegar
- 2 tablespoons tomato paste
- 1 tablespoon honey
- 2 bay leaves
- 1 garlic clove, minced

1. In a large resealable plastic bag, combine the flour, salt, cinnamon and pepper. Add beef, a few pieces at a time, and shake to coat. In a large skillet, brown beef in oil. Transfer to a 3-qt. slow cooker. Stir in the remaining ingredients.

2. Cover and cook on low for 6-8 hours or until beef and onions are tender. Discard bay leaves.

Autumn

DESSERTS

Fall is a great time to get cozy with warm, aromatic desserts. Bubbling with heartwarming flavor, treats such as Pumpkin Pie Pudding, Caramel-Pecan Stuffed Apples and Fudgy Peanut Butter Cake make lovely finales to autumn dinners.

ANDREA SCHAAK'S
PUMPKIN PIE PUDDING

Pumpkin Pie Pudding

My husband loves anything pumpkin, and this creamy, comforting dessert is one of his favorites. Although we make the super-easy pudding all year long, it's especially nice in the fall.
—ANDREA SCHAAK BLOOMINGTON, MN

PREP: 10 MIN. • **COOK:** 6 HOURS • **MAKES:** 6 SERVINGS

- 1 can (15 ounces) solid-pack pumpkin
- 1 can (12 ounces) evaporated milk
- ¾ cup sugar
- ½ cup biscuit/baking mix
- 2 eggs, beaten
- 2 tablespoons butter, melted
- 2½ teaspoons pumpkin pie spice
- 2 teaspoons vanilla extract
  Whipped topping, optional

1. In a large bowl, combine the first eight ingredients. Transfer to a 3-qt. slow cooker coated with cooking spray.
2. Cover and cook on low for 6-7 hours or until a thermometer reads 160°. Serve in bowls with whipped topping if desired.

Old-Fashioned Tapioca

My family enjoys old-fashioned tapioca, but I don't always have the time to make it. That's why I developed this simple recipe that let's us enjoy the yummy dessert without the fuss.
—RUTH PETERS BEL AIR, MD

PREP: 10 MIN. • **COOK:** 4½ HOURS • **MAKES:** 18 SERVINGS

- 8 cups 2% milk
- 1 cup pearl tapioca
- 1 cup plus 2 tablespoons sugar
- ⅛ teaspoon salt
- 4 eggs
- 1½ teaspoons vanilla extract
  Sliced fresh strawberries and whipped cream, optional

1. In a 4- to 5-qt. slow cooker, combine the milk, tapioca, sugar and salt. Cover and cook on low for 4-5 hours.
2. In a large bowl, beat the eggs; stir in a small amount of hot tapioca mixture. Return all to the slow cooker, stirring to combine. Cover and cook 30 minutes longer or until a thermometer reads 160°. Stir in vanilla.
3. Serve with strawberries and whipped cream if desired.

(top tip) Savvy Storage

According to the American Egg Board, fresh eggs can be stored in their carton in the refrigerator for 4 to 5 weeks beyond the pack date. Unpeeled hard-cooked eggs will stay fresh in the refrigerator for up to 1 week. Once shelled, the eggs should be used right away.

Apple Betty with Almond Cream

PREP: 15 MIN. • **COOK:** 3 HOURS • **MAKES:** 8 SERVINGS

- 3 pounds tart apples, peeled and sliced
- 10 slices cinnamon-raisin bread, cubed
- ¾ cup packed brown sugar
- ½ cup butter, melted
- 1 teaspoon almond extract
- ½ teaspoon ground cinnamon
- ¼ teaspoon ground cardamom
- ⅛ teaspoon salt

WHIPPED CREAM

- 1 cup heavy whipping cream
- 2 tablespoons sugar
- 1 teaspoon grated lemon peel
- ½ teaspoon almond extract

1. Place apples in an ungreased 4- or 5-qt. slow cooker. In a large bowl, combine the bread, brown sugar, butter, extract, cinnamon, cardamom and salt; spoon over apples. Cover and cook on low for 3-4 hours or until apples are tender.
2. In a small bowl, beat cream until it begins to thicken. Add the sugar, lemon peel and extract; beat until soft peaks form. Serve with apple mixture.

APPLE BETTY WITH ALMOND CREAM

FUDGY PEANUT BUTTER CAKE

Fudgy Peanut Butter Cake

Clipped from a newspaper years ago, this recipe fills our house with a wonderful aroma while it's cooking. My husband and son enjoy the warm cake with ice cream and nuts on top.
—**BONNIE EVANS** NORCROSS, GA

PREP: 10 MIN. • **COOK:** 1½ HOURS • **MAKES:** 4 SERVINGS

- ⅓ cup milk
- ¼ cup peanut butter
- 1 tablespoon canola oil
- ½ teaspoon vanilla extract
- ¾ cup sugar, divided
- ½ cup all-purpose flour
- ¾ teaspoon baking powder
- 2 tablespoons baking cocoa
- 1 cup boiling water
  Vanilla ice cream

1. In a large bowl, beat the milk, peanut butter, oil and vanilla until well blended. In a small bowl, combine ¼ cup sugar, flour and baking powder; gradually beat into milk mixture until blended. Spread into a 1½-qt. slow cooker coated with cooking spray.
2. In a small bowl, combine cocoa and remaining sugar; stir in boiling water. Pour into slow cooker (do not stir).
3. Cover and cook on high for 1½ to 2 hours or until a toothpick inserted near the center comes out clean. Serve warm with ice cream.
NOTE *Reduced-fat peanut butter is not recommended for this recipe.*

CRUNCHY CANDY CLUSTERS

Glazed Cinnamon Apples

If you're seeking comfort food that's on the sweet side, this warm dessert, made with cinnamon and nutmeg, fits the bill.

—**MEGAN MAZE** OAK CREEK, WI

PREP: 20 MIN. • **COOK:** 3 HOURS
MAKES: 7 SERVINGS

- 6 **large tart apples**
- 2 **tablespoons lemon juice**
- ½ **cup packed brown sugar**
- ½ **cup sugar**
- 2 **tablespoons all-purpose flour**
- 1 **teaspoon ground cinnamon**
- ¼ **teaspoon ground nutmeg**
- 6 **tablespoons butter, melted**
  Vanilla ice cream

Peel, core and cut each apple into eight wedges; transfer to a 3-qt. slow cooker. Drizzle with lemon juice. Combine the sugars, flour, cinnamon and nutmeg; sprinkle over apples. Drizzle with butter. Cover and cook on low for 3-4 hours or until apples are tender. Serve with ice cream.

Caramel Pears

The crystallized ginger and cinnamon add a yummy flavor to this decadent desert made with fresh pears.

—**TASTE OF HOME TEST KITCHEN**

PREP: 15 MIN. • **COOK:** 2 HOURS
MAKES: 6 SERVINGS

- 6 **medium pears, peeled and sliced**
- ¾ **cup packed brown sugar**
- ¼ **cup heavy whipping cream**
- 2 **teaspoons lemon juice**
- 2 **tablespoons butter, melted**
- 1 **tablespoon chopped crystallized ginger**
- 1 **teaspoon cornstarch**
- ½ **teaspoon ground cinnamon**
  Grilled pound cake, whipped topping and sliced almonds

In a 1½-qt. slow cooker, combine the first eight ingredients. Cover and cook on low for 2-3 hours or until heated through. Serve warm over pound cake. Top with whipped topping; sprinkle with almonds. .

Crunchy Candy Clusters

Before I retired, I took these yummy peanut butter bites to work for special occasions. They're so simple. I still make them for holidays because my family always looks forward to the coated cereal-and-marshmallow clusters.

—**FAYE O'BRYAN** OWENSBORO, KY

PREP: 15 MIN. • **COOK:** 1 HOUR
MAKES: 6½ DOZEN

- 2 **pounds white candy coating, coarsely chopped**
- 1½ **cups peanut butter**
- ½ **teaspoon almond extract, optional**
- 4 **cups Cap'n Crunch cereal**
- 4 **cups crisp rice cereal**
- 4 **cups miniature marshmallows**

1. Place candy coating in a 5-qt. slow cooker. Cover and cook on high for 1 hour. Add peanut butter. Stir in extract if desired.

2. In a large bowl, combine the cereals and marshmallows. Stir in the peanut butter mixture until well-coated. Drop by tablespoonfuls onto waxed paper. Let stand until set. Store at room temperature.

MEGAN MAZE'S
GLAZED CINNAMON APPLES

"This irresistible dessert is slow-cooker easy. Warm and comforting, the tender apples are filled with chewy pecans and caramel topping."

—**PAM KAISER** MANSFIELD, MO

Caramel-Pecan Stuffed Apples

PREP: 20 MIN. • **COOK:** 3 HOURS
MAKES: 6 SERVINGS

- 6 large tart apples
- 2 teaspoons lemon juice
- ⅓ cup chopped pecans
- ¼ cup chopped dried apricots
- ¼ cup packed brown sugar
- 3 tablespoons butter, melted
- ¾ teaspoon ground cinnamon
- ¼ teaspoon ground nutmeg
  Granola and caramel ice cream topping, optional

1. Core apples and peel top third of each; brush peeled portions with lemon juice. Place in a 6-qt. slow cooker.

2. Combine the pecans, apricots, brown sugar, butter, cinnamon and nutmeg. Place a heaping tablespoonful of mixture in each apple. Pour 2 cups water around apples.

3. Cover and cook on low for 3-4 hours or until apples are tender. Serve with granola and caramel topping if desired.

CARAMEL-PECAN STUFFED APPLES

CHOCOLATE-COVERED CHERRY PUDDING CAKE

Chocolate-Covered Cherry Pudding Cake

Growing up, I remember my grandfather cherishing the chocolate-covered cherries we'd bring him. He passed away this past year, and I came up with this rich recipe in his honor. It's delicious served with whipped topping.
—**MEREDITH COE** CHARLOTTESVILLE, VA

PREP: 20 MIN. • **COOK:** 2 HOURS + STANDING
MAKES: 8 SERVINGS

- ½ cup reduced-fat sour cream
- 2 tablespoons canola oil
- 1 tablespoon butter, melted
- 2 teaspoons vanilla extract
- 1 cup all-purpose flour
- ¼ cup sugar
- ¼ cup packed brown sugar
- 3 tablespoons baking cocoa
- 2 teaspoon baking powder
- ½ teaspoon ground cinnamon
- ⅛ teaspoon salt
- 1 cup fresh or frozen pitted dark sweet cherries, thawed
- 1 cup fresh or frozen pitted tart cherries, thawed
- ⅓ cup 60% cacao bittersweet chocolate baking chips

PUDDING
- ½ cup packed brown sugar
- 2 tablespoons baking cocoa
- 1¼ cups hot water

1. In a large bowl, beat the sour cream, oil, butter and vanilla until blended. Combine the flour, sugars, cocoa, baking powder, cinnamon and salt. Add to sour cream mixture just until combined. Stir in cherries and chips. Pour into a 3-qt. slow cooker coated with cooking spray.

2. In a small bowl, combine brown sugar and cocoa. Stir in hot water until blended. Pour over the batter (do not stir). Cover and cook on high for 2 to 2½ hours or until set. Let stand for 15 minutes. Serve warm.

⑤INGREDIENTS Minister's Delight

You'll need just a few ingredients to simmer up this warm dessert. A friend gave me the recipe several years ago, saying that a minister's wife fixed it every Sunday so she named it accordingly.
—**MARY ANN POTTER** BLUE SPRINGS, MO

PREP: 5 MIN. • **COOK:** 2 HOURS • **MAKES:** 10-12 SERVINGS

- 1 can (21 ounces) cherry or apple pie filling
- 1 package yellow cake mix (regular size)
- ½ cup butter, melted
- ⅓ cup chopped walnuts, optional

Place pie filling in a 1½-qt. slow cooker. Combine cake mix and butter (mixture will be crumbly); sprinkle over filling. Sprinkle with walnuts if desired. Cover and cook on low for 2-3 hours. Serve in bowls.

MINISTER'S DELIGHT

Fruit Dessert Topping

You'll quickly warm up to the old-fashioned taste of this fruit topping! I like to spoon it over vanilla ice cream or buttery slices of pound cake.

—**DORIS HEATH** FRANKLIN, NC

PREP: 10 MIN. • **COOK:** 3½ HOURS • **MAKES:** ABOUT 6 CUPS

- 3 medium tart apples, peeled and sliced
- 3 medium pears, peeled and sliced
- 1 tablespoon lemon juice
- ½ cup packed brown sugar
- ½ cup maple syrup
- ¼ cup butter, melted
- ½ cup chopped pecans
- ¼ cup raisins
- 2 cinnamon sticks (3 inches)
- 1 tablespoon cornstarch
- 2 tablespoons cold water
  Pound cake or ice cream

1. In a 3-qt. slow cooker, toss apples and pears with lemon juice. Combine the brown sugar, maple syrup and butter; pour over fruit. Stir in the pecans, raisins and cinnamon sticks. Cover and cook on low for 3-4 hours.

2. Combine cornstarch and water until smooth; gradually stir into slow cooker. Cover and cook on high for 30-40 minutes or until thickened. Discard cinnamon sticks. Serve with pound cake or ice cream.

FRUIT DESSERT TOPPING

BUTTERSCOTCH PEARS

Butterscotch Pears

This grand finale simmers during dinner and impresses as soon as you bring it to the table. Serve as is, or with vanilla ice cream. Leftover pear nectar is heavenly when added to sparkling wine or enjoyed on ice with breakfast.

—**THERESA KREYCHE** TUSTIN, CA

PREP: 20 MIN. • **COOK:** 2 HOURS • **MAKES:** 8 SERVINGS

- 4 large firm pears
- 1 tablespoon lemon juice
- ¼ cup packed brown sugar
- 3 tablespoons butter, softened
- 2 tablespoons all-purpose flour
- ½ teaspoon ground cinnamon
- ¼ teaspoon salt
- ½ cup chopped pecans
- ½ cup pear nectar
- 2 tablespoons honey

1. Cut pears in half lengthwise; remove cores. Brush pears with lemon juice. In a small bowl, combine the brown sugar, butter, flour, cinnamon and salt; stir in pecans. Spoon into pears; place in 4-qt. slow cooker.

2. Combine pear nectar and honey; drizzle over pears. Cover and cook on low for 2-3 hours or until heated through. Serve warm.

HOT FUDGE CAKE

Hot Fudge Cake

A cake baked in a slow cooker may seem unusual, but smiles around the dinner table prove just how tasty it is. Sometimes, for a change of pace, I substitute butterscotch chips for chocolate.
—**MARLEEN ADKINS** PLACENTIA, CA

PREP: 20 MIN. • **COOK:** 4 HOURS • **MAKES:** 8 SERVINGS

- 1¾ cups packed brown sugar, divided
- 1 cup all-purpose flour
- 6 tablespoons baking cocoa, divided
- 2 teaspoons baking powder
- ½ teaspoon salt
- ½ cup 2% milk
- 2 tablespoons butter, melted
- ½ teaspoon vanilla extract
- 1½ cups semisweet chocolate chips
- 1¾ cups boiling water
  Vanilla ice cream

1. In a small bowl, combine 1 cup brown sugar, flour, 3 tablespoons cocoa, baking powder and salt. Combine the milk, butter and vanilla; stir into dry ingredients just until combined.

2. Spread into a 3-qt. slow cooker coated with cooking spray. Sprinkle with chocolate chips. In another bowl, combine the remaining brown sugar and cocoa; stir in boiling water. Pour over batter (do not stir).

3. Cover and cook on high for 4 to 4½ hours or until a toothpick inserted near center of cake comes out clean. Serve warm with ice cream.

NOTE *This recipe does not use eggs.*

JUDITH BUCCIARELLI'S
PUMPKIN CRANBERRY BREAD PUDDING

Pumpkin Cranberry Bread Pudding

Savor your favorite fall flavors with this scrumptious bread pudding served warm with a sweet vanilla sauce. Yum!

—JUDITH BUCCIARELLI JOHNSON, NY

PREP: 15 MIN. • **COOK:** 3 HOURS
MAKES: 8 SERVINGS (1⅓ CUPS SAUCE)

- 8 slices cinnamon bread, cut into 1-inch cubes
- 4 eggs, beaten
- 2 cups 2% milk
- 1 cup canned pumpkin
- ¼ cup packed brown sugar
- ¼ cup butter, melted
- 1 teaspoon vanilla extract
- ½ teaspoon ground cinnamon
- ¼ teaspoon ground nutmeg
- ½ cup dried cranberries

SAUCE

- 1 cup sugar
- ⅔ cup water
- 1 cup heavy whipping cream
- 2 teaspoons vanilla extract

1. Place bread in a greased 3- or 4-qt. slow cooker. In a large bowl, combine the eggs, milk, pumpkin, brown sugar, butter, vanilla, cinnamon and nutmeg; stir in cranberries. Pour over bread cubes. Cover and cook on low for 3-4 hours or until a knife inserted near the center comes out clean.

2. For sauce, in a large saucepan, bring sugar and water to a boil over medium heat. Cook until sugar is dissolved and mixture turns a golden amber color, about 20 minutes.

3. Gradually stir in cream until smooth. Remove from the heat; stir in vanilla. Serve warm with the bread pudding.

top tip Jazz Up Dessert

For a fun switch, try this the next time you make bread pudding. Swap out the bread cubes for pieces of angel food cake!

—JOYCE W. HOUSTON, TX

---

⑤ INGREDIENTS

Easy Chocolate Clusters

You can use this simple recipe to make a big batch of chocolate candy without a lot of fuss. I've sent these clusters to my husband's office a number of times...and passed the recipe along as well.

—DORIS REYNOLDS MUNDS PARK, AZ

PREP: 10 MIN. + STANDING
COOK: 2 HOURS
MAKES: 3½ DOZEN

- 2 pounds white candy coating, broken into small pieces
- 2 cups (12 ounces) semisweet chocolate chips
- 4 ounces German sweet chocolate, chopped
- 1 jar (24 ounces) dry roasted peanuts

1. In a 3-qt. slow cooker, combine candy coating, chocolate chips and German chocolate. Cover and cook on high for 1 hour. Reduce heat to low; cover and cook 1 hour longer or until melted, stirring every 15 minutes.

2. Stir in the peanuts. Drop by teaspoonfuls onto waxed paper. Let stand until set. Then store at room temperature.

EASY CHOCOLATE CLUSTERS

HEIDI FLEEK'S
EASY SLOW COOKER MAC & CHEESE
page 281

Winter

Jack Frost has blown into town, and that means it's time to get cozy and enjoy many of your favorite comfort foods. Put your slow cooker to good use this season, and you'll have no trouble preparing those heartwarming delights you've craved all year long.

Winter

APPETIZERS & BEVERAGES

Winter is a great time to gather with friends and family. Whether celebrating the holidays, cheering on your favorite football team or warming up after a day of skiing, hostessing is a snap with help from this colorful section.

LISA CASTELLI'S
CRANBERRY SAUERKRAUT
MEATBALLS

---

⑤ INGREDIENTS

Cranberry Sauerkraut Meatballs

I tried these meatballs at a friend's birthday party, and now I make them all the time. They're perfect for a potluck!
—**LISA CASTELLI** PLEASANT PRAIRIE, WI

PREP: 15 MIN. • **COOK:** 4 HOURS • **MAKES:** ABOUT 5 DOZEN

- 1 can (14 ounces) whole-berry cranberry sauce
- 1 can (14 ounces) sauerkraut, rinsed and well drained
- 1 bottle (12 ounces) chili sauce
- ¾ cup packed brown sugar
- 1 package (32 ounces) frozen fully cooked homestyle meatballs, thawed

In a 4-qt. slow cooker, combine the cranberry sauce, sauerkraut, chili sauce and brown sugar. Stir in meatballs. Cover and cook on low for 4-5 hours or until heated through.

---

⑤ INGREDIENTS ## Hot Cocoa for a Crowd

This is a simple, delicious and comforting hot cocoa with a hint of cinnamon. It has just the right amount of sweetness.
—**DEBORAH CANADAY** MANHATTAN, KS

PREP: 10 MIN. • **COOK:** 3 HOURS • **MAKES:** 12 SERVINGS (1 CUP EACH)

- 5 cups nonfat dry milk powder
- ¾ cup sugar
- ¾ cup baking cocoa
- 1 teaspoon vanilla extract
- ¼ teaspoon ground cinnamon
- 11 cups water
  Miniature marshmallows and peppermint candy sticks, optional

1. In a 5- or 6-qt. slow cooker, combine the milk powder, sugar, cocoa, vanilla and cinnamon; gradually whisk in water until smooth. Cover and cook on low for 3-4 hours or until heated through.
2. Garnish with marshmallows and use peppermint sticks for stirrers if desired.

---

⑤ INGREDIENTS ## Make-Ahead Eggnog

Homemade eggnog is a tradition in many families during the holiday season. Our slow cooker version of this classic beverage shaves off calories and time spent preparing the festive drink.
—**TASTE OF HOME TEST KITCHEN**

PREP: 10 MIN. • **COOK:** 2 HOURS • **MAKES:** 9 SERVINGS (¾ CUP EACH)

- 6 cups whole milk
- 1 cup egg substitute
- ⅔ cup sugar
- 2 teaspoons rum extract
- 1½ teaspoons pumpkin pie spice
  French vanilla whipped topping, optional

In a 3-qt. slow cooker, combine the first five ingredients. Cover and cook on low for 2-3 hours or until heated through. Serve in mugs; dollop with whipped topping if desired.

WARM CHRISTMAS PUNCH

Caramel Apple Fondue

I like to serve this warm caramel dip with sliced apples while we're watching football games on Sunday afternoons. It really warms us up.

—**KATIE KOZIOLEK** HARTLAND, MN

PREP/TOTAL TIME: 25 MIN. • **MAKES:** 3½ CUPS

- ½ cup butter, cubed
- 2 cups packed brown sugar
- 1 can (14 ounces) sweetened condensed milk
- 1 cup light corn syrup
- 2 tablespoons water
- 1 teaspoon vanilla extract
  Apple slices

1. In a heavy 3-qt. saucepan, combine the butter, brown sugar, milk, corn syrup and water; bring to a boil over medium heat. Cook and stir until a candy thermometer reads 230° (thread stage), about 8-10 minutes. Remove from the heat; stir in vanilla.

2. Transfer to a small fondue pot or 1½-qt. slow cooker; keep warm. Serve with apple slices.

NOTE *We recommend that you test your candy thermometer before each use by bringing water to a boil; the thermometer should read 212°. Adjust your recipe temperature up or down based on your test.*

CARAMEL APPLE FONDUE

"Red Hots add rich color and spiciness to this festive punch, and the cranberry juice gives it a little tang."
—**JULIE STERCHI** JACKSON, MO

⑤ INGREDIENTS Warm Christmas Punch

PREP: 5 MIN. • **COOK:** 2 HOURS • **MAKES:** 8 SERVINGS (2 QUARTS)

- 1 bottle (32 ounces) cranberry juice
- 5 cans (6 ounces each) unsweetened pineapple juice
- ⅓ cup Red Hots
- 1 cinnamon stick (3½ inches)
  Additional cinnamon sticks, optional

1. In a 3-qt. slow cooker, combine juices, Red Hots and cinnamon stick. Cover and cook on low for 2-4 hours or until heated through and candies are dissolved.

2. Discard cinnamon stick before serving. Use additional cinnamon sticks as stirrers if desired.

MARGARET HARMS'
WASSAIL BOWL PUNCH

TANGY PORK MEATBALLS

Tangy Pork Meatballs

Yuletide buffet "grazers" stampede for these meatballs! The mouthwatering morsels go so fast, I often make several batches at once. Barbecue sauce adds a nice bite to the mildly seasoned ground pork.
—**KATIE KOZIOLEK** HARTLAND, MINNESOTA

PREP/TOTAL TIME: 30 MIN. • **MAKES:** 7½ DOZEN

- 2 eggs, lightly beaten
- ⅔ cup dry bread crumbs
- 2 tablespoons dried minced onion
- 2 teaspoons seasoned salt
- 2 pounds ground pork

SAUCE
- 1½ cups ketchup
- 1 can (8 ounces) tomato sauce
- 3 tablespoons Worcestershire sauce
- 2 to 3 tablespoons cider vinegar
- 2 teaspoons liquid smoke, optional

1. In a large bowl, combine the eggs, bread crumbs, onion and salt. Crumble pork over mixture and mix well. Shape into ¾-in. balls.
2. Place meatballs on a greased rack in a shallow baking pan. Bake at 400° for 15 minutes or until a thermometer reads 160°; drain.
3. Meanwhile, in a large saucepan, combine sauce ingredients. Simmer, uncovered, for 10 minutes, stirring occasionally. Add meatballs. Serve in a 5-qt. slow cooker or chafing dish.

Wassail Bowl Punch

All ages will enjoy this warming punch. The blend of spice, fruit and citrus flavors is scrumptious! You can assemble it before heading out for a winter activity and sip away the chill when you return. It's ready whenever you are.
—**MARGARET HARMS** JENKINS, KY

PREP: 10 MIN. • **COOK:** 1 HOUR • **MAKES:** 3½ QUARTS

- 4 cups hot brewed tea
- 4 cups cranberry juice
- 4 cups unsweetened apple juice
- 2 cups orange juice
- 1 cup sugar
- ¾ cup lemon juice
- 3 cinnamon sticks (3 inches)
- 12 whole cloves

1. In a 5-qt. slow cooker, combine the first six ingredients. Place the cinnamon sticks and cloves on a double thickness of cheesecloth; bring up corners of cloth and tie with string to form a bag. Add to slow cooker.
2. Cover and cook on high for 1 hour or until punch begins to boil. Discard spice bag. Serve warm.

Cheesy Pizza Fondue

I keep these dip ingredients on hand for spur-of-the-moment gatherings. Folks can't seem to resist the chewy bread cubes coated with a savory sauce.
—**NEL CARVER** MOSCOW, ID

PREP: 10 MIN. • **COOK:** 4 HOURS • **MAKES:** 4 CUPS

- 1 jar (29 ounces) meatless spaghetti sauce
- 2 cups (8 ounces) shredded part-skim mozzarella cheese
- ¼ cup shredded Parmesan cheese
- 2 teaspoons dried oregano
- 1 teaspoon dried minced onion
- ¼ teaspoon garlic powder
  Cubed Italian bread

1. In a 1½-qt. slow cooker, combine the spaghetti sauce, cheeses, oregano, onion and garlic powder.
2. Cover and cook on low for 4-6 hours or until heated through and cheese is melted. Serve with bread cubes.

CHEESY PIZZA FONDUE

SPICED POMEGRANATE SIPPER

1. In a 3- or 4-qt. slow cooker, combine the cranberry juice, pineapple juice and sugar. Place cinnamon and cloves on a double thickness of cheesecloth; bring up corners of cloth and tie with string to form a bag. Place in slow cooker.
2. Cover and cook on low for 2-3 hours or until heated through. Discard spice bag. Serve warm in mugs.

Warm Broccoli Cheese Dip

Whenever my family gathers for a party, this flavorful, creamy dip is served. Everyone loves the spicy bite of the jalapeno pepper and the fresh crunch of the broccoli.

—**BARBARA MAIOL** CONYERS, GA

PREP: 15 MIN. • **COOK:** 2½ HOURS
MAKES: 5½ CUPS

- 2 jars (8 ounces each) process cheese sauce
- 1 can (10-¾ ounces) condensed cream of chicken soup, undiluted
- 3 cups frozen chopped broccoli, thawed and drained
- ½ pound fresh mushrooms, chopped
- 2 tablespoons chopped seeded jalapeno pepper
  Assorted fresh vegetables

In a 1½-qt. slow cooker, combine cheese sauce and soup. Cover and cook on low for 30 minutes or until cheese is melted, stirring occasionally. Stir in the broccoli, mushrooms and jalapeno. Cover and cook on low for 2-3 hours or until vegetables are tender. Serve with assorted fresh vegetables.

NOTE *Wear disposable gloves when cutting hot peppers; the oils can burn skin. Avoid touching your face.*

Spiced Pomegranate Sipper

This warm and festive beverage fills the entire house with the wonderful aroma of spices and simmering fruit juices. Kids and adults both love this spirit-warming sipper!

—**LISA RENSHAW** KANSAS CITY, MO

PREP: 10 MIN. • **COOK:** 1 HOUR
MAKES: 16 SERVINGS (ABOUT 3 QUARTS)

- 1 bottle (64 ounces) cranberry-apple juice
- 2 cups unsweetened apple juice
- 1 cup pomegranate juice
- ⅔ cup honey
- ½ cup orange juice
- 3 cinnamon sticks (3 inches)
- 10 whole cloves
- 2 tablespoons grated orange peel

In a 5-qt. slow cooker, combine first five ingredients. Place the cinnamon sticks, cloves and orange peel on a double thickness of cheesecloth; bring up corners of cloth and tie with string to form a bag. Add to slow cooker. Cover and cook on low for 1-2 hours. Discard spice bag.

(5)INGREDIENTS

Cranberry Punch

My mom used to serve this concoction every Thanksgiving and Christmas. To this day, whenever I smell it, I can't help but think of the holidays.

—**HANNAH SIMPSON** TUPELO, AR

PREP: 10 MIN. • **COOK:** 2 HOURS
MAKES: 9 SERVINGS

- 1 bottle (32 ounces) cranberry juice
- 3 cups unsweetened pineapple juice
- ½ cup sugar
- 1 cinnamon stick (3 inches)
- 12 whole cloves

WARM BROCCOLI CHEESE DIP

Barbecued Party Starters

These sweet and tangy bites are sure to tide everyone over until dinner. At the buffet, set out some pretty party toothpicks to make for easy nibbling.
—**ANASTASIA WEISS** PUNXSUTAWNEY, PA

PREP: 30 MIN. • **COOK:** 2 HOURS
MAKES: 18 SERVINGS (⅓ CUP EACH)

- 1 **pound ground beef**
- ¼ **cup finely chopped onion**
- 1 **package (16 ounces) miniature hot dogs, drained**
- 1 **jar (12 ounces) apricot preserves**
- 1 **cup barbecue sauce**
- 1 **can (20 ounces) pineapple chunks, drained**

1. In a small bowl, combine beef and onion. Shape into 1-in. balls. In a large skillet, cook meatballs in batches until no longer pink; drain.

2. Transfer to a 3-qt. slow cooker; add the hot dogs, preserves and barbecue sauce. Cover and cook on high for 2-3 hours or until heated through. Stir in pineapple; heat through.

Hot Mulled Wine

For a festive holiday drink, you'll love this warm wine. It's also fun to simmer up a batch to cap off a casual day at home.
—**TASTE OF HOME TEST KITCHEN**

PREP: 15 MIN. • **COOK:** 4 HOURS
MAKES: 5 SERVINGS

- 2 **cinnamon sticks (3 inches)**
- 6 **whole cloves**
- 1 **fresh rosemary sprig**
- 1 **bottle (750 milliliters) cabernet sauvignon or other dry red wine**
- 1 **cup fresh or frozen cranberries**
- ⅔ **cup sugar**
- ⅓ **cup bourbon**
- ⅓ **cup orange juice**
- 4 **teaspoons grated orange peel**

1. Place cinnamon sticks, cloves and rosemary on a double thickness of cheesecloth; bring up corners of cloth and tie with string to form a bag.

2. In a 1½-qt. slow cooker, combine the wine, cranberries, sugar, bourbon, orange juice and peel. Add spice bag. Cover and cook on low for 4-5 hours or until heated through. Discard spice bag. Serve warm.

top tip Cranberry Basics

Fresh cranberries are in season from early fall through December. When buying, look for packages with shiny, bright red (light or dark) berries. Avoid berries that are bruised, shriveled or have brown spots. Ripe cranberries should bounce when dropped. Refrigerate fresh unwashed cranberries for about 1 month.

BARBECUED PARTY STARTERS

BEER CHEESE FONDUE

PREP: 10 MIN. • **COOK:** 2 HOURS
MAKES: 2½ QUARTS

- 2 **quarts apple cider or juice**
- 1 **cup pineapple juice**
- 1 **cup orange juice**
- 1 **tablespoon brown sugar**
- 1 **tablespoon lemon juice**
- ⅛ **teaspoon salt**
- 8 **whole cloves**
- 4 **unpeeled fresh orange slices (¼ inch thick)**
- 4 **cinnamon sticks (3 inches)**
  Additional orange slices and cinnamon sticks

1. In a 5-qt. slow cooker, combine the first six ingredients. Push two cloves through each orange slice. Push a cinnamon stick through the center of each orange slice; add to cider mixture.
2. Cover and cook on low for 2-4 hours or until heated through. Discard oranges, cloves and cinnamon sticks. Stir cider before serving. Use additional oranges and cinnamon sticks to make orange twist garnishes.

Pepperoni Extreme Dip

Set it and forget it! With just 10 minutes of prep time and some assistance from a slow cooker, you'll be ready to serve this cheesy appetizer. Let the party begin!
—LAURA STONESIFER HOULTON, WI

PREP: 10 MIN. • **COOK:** 3 HOURS
MAKES: 2¼ QUARTS

- 4 **cups (16 ounces) shredded cheddar cheese**
- 3½ **cups spaghetti sauce**
- 2 **cups mayonnaise**
- 1 **package (8 ounces) sliced pepperoni, chopped**
- 1 **can (6 ounces) pitted ripe olives, chopped**
- 1 **jar (5¾ ounces) sliced green olives with pimientos, drained and chopped**
  Tortilla chips

Combine the first six ingredients in a 4-qt. slow cooker coated with cooking spray. Cover and cook on low for 1½ hours; stir. Cover and cook 1½ hours longer or until cheese is melted. Serve with tortilla chips.

Beer Cheese Fondue

This thick fondue originated in my kitchen when I didn't have all of the ingredients I needed to make the recipe I initially planned to prepare. Served with bread cubes, it has since become a staple, particularly while we watch football.
—CHRYSTIE WEAR GREENSBORO, NC

PREP/TOTAL TIME: 15 MIN.
MAKES: 3 CUPS

- 1 **loaf (1 pound) French bread, cubed**
- ¼ **cup chopped onion**
- 1 **tablespoon butter**
- 1 **teaspoon minced garlic**
- 1 **cup beer or nonalcoholic beer**
- 4 **cups (16 ounces) shredded cheddar cheese**
- 1 **tablespoon all-purpose flour**
- 2 **to 4 tablespoons half-and-half cream**

1. Place bread cubes in a single layer in an ungreased 15-in. x 10-in. x 1-in. baking pan. Bake at 450° for 5-7 minutes or until lightly crisp, stirring twice.
2. Meanwhile, in a small saucepan, saute onion in butter until tender. Add garlic; cook 1 minute longer. Stir in beer. Bring to a boil; reduce heat to medium-low. Toss cheese and flour; stir into saucepan until melted. Stir in 2 tablespoons cream.
3. Transfer to a 1½-qt. slow cooker. Keep warm; add additional cream if fondue thickens. Serve with toasted bread cubes.

Hot Cider with Orange Twists

I first tasted a steaming mug of this comforting beverage on a frigid evening. It's still a family favorite on wintry days.
—CATHERINE ALLAN TWIN FALLS, ID

LAURA STONESIFER'S
PEPPERONI EXTREME DIP

⑤ INGREDIENTS

Christmas Punch

I originally got the recipe for this colorful punch from a co-worker who brought it to our office Christmas party.

—**PATRICIA DICK** ANDERSON, IN

PREP: 15 MIN. • **COOK:** 3 HOURS
MAKES: 22 SERVINGS (¾ CUP EACH)

- 1 **quart brewed tea**
- 1 **quart unsweetened apple juice**
- 1 **quart orange juice**
- 1 **quart unsweetened pineapple juice**
- 1 **package (9 ounces) Red Hots**

In a 6-qt. slow cooker, combine all ingredients. Cover and cook on low for 3-4 hours or until candies are melted, stirring occasionally.

Chili Beef Dip

No last-minute party prep is needed for this warm, creamy dip. Put it together hours before the gathering and let a slow cooker do the work until your group is ready to dig in.

—**PAT HABIGER** SPEARVILLE, KS

PREP: 25 MIN. • **COOK:** 2 HOURS
MAKES: 8 CUPS

- 2 **pounds lean ground beef (90% lean)**
- 1 **large onion, chopped**
- 1 **jalapeno pepper, seeded and chopped**
- 2 **packages (8 ounces each) cream cheese, cubed**
- 2 **cans (8 ounces each) tomato sauce**
- 1 **can (4 ounces) chopped green chilies**
- ½ **cup grated Parmesan cheese**
- ½ **cup ketchup**
- 2 **garlic cloves, minced**
- 1½ **teaspoons chili powder**
- 1 **teaspoon dried oregano**
  Tortilla chips

1. In a large skillet, brown the beef, onion and jalapeno until meat is no longer pink; drain. Transfer to a 3- or 4-qt. slow cooker. Stir in the cream cheese, tomato sauce, chilies, Parmesan cheese, ketchup, garlic, chili powder and oregano.
2. Cover and cook on low for 2-3 hours or until heated through. Stir; serve with chips.

NOTE *Wear disposable gloves when cutting hot peppers; the oils can burn skin. Avoid touching your face.*

CHRISTMAS PUNCH

Holiday Smokies

This warm appetizer is so simple to make but so tasty! Cherry pie filling, chunks of pineapple and a little brown sugar create a fruity sauce that's just perfect for mini sausage links.

—DEBI HETLAND ROCHELLE, IL

PREP: 5 MIN. • **COOK:** 4 HOURS • **MAKES:** 16-20 SERVINGS

- 2 packages (16 ounces each) miniature smoked sausages
- 2 cans (21 ounces each) cherry pie filling
- 1 can (20 ounces) pineapple chunks, drained
- 3 tablespoons brown sugar

Place sausages in a 3-qt. slow cooker. In a small bowl, combine the pie filling, pineapple and brown sugar; pour over sausages. Cover and cook on low for 3-4 hours or until heated through. Keep warm.

Cranberry Hot Wings

Chicken wings get special treatment from cranberry sauce, honey and a touch of hot sauce in this no-fuss recipe. The wings are a tangy way to heat up a winter night.

—ROBIN HAAS CRANSTON, RI

PREP: 50 MIN. • **COOK:** 2 HOURS
MAKES: ABOUT 1 DOZEN

- 1 can (14 ounces) jellied cranberry sauce, cubed
- 2 tablespoons ground mustard
- 2 tablespoons hot pepper sauce
- 2 tablespoons reduced-sodium soy sauce
- 2 tablespoons honey
- 1 tablespoon cider vinegar
- 2 teaspoons garlic powder
- 1 teaspoon grated orange peel
- 3 pounds chicken wings
  Blue cheese salad dressing and celery ribs

1. In a 5-qt. slow cooker, combine the first eight ingredients. Cover and cook on low for 45 minutes or until the cranberry sauce is melted.
2. Meanwhile, cut wings into three sections; discard wing tip sections. Place wings on a greased broiler pan. Broil 4-6 in. from the heat for 15-20 minutes or until lightly browned, turning occasionally.
3. Transfer wings to slow cooker; toss to coat. Cover and cook on high for 2-3 hours or until tender. Serve wings with salad dressing and celery ribs.
NOTE *Uncooked chicken wing sections (wingettes) may be substituted for whole chicken wings.*

Sweet 'n' Spicy Meatballs

You'll usually find a batch of these meatballs in my freezer. The slightly sweet sauce nicely complements the spicy pork sausage.

—GENIE BROWN ROANOKE, VA

PREP: 25 MIN. • **BAKE:** 15 MIN.
MAKES: ABOUT 4 DOZEN

- 2 pounds bulk spicy pork sausage
- 1 egg, lightly beaten
- 1 cup packed brown sugar
- 1 cup red wine vinegar
- 1 cup ketchup
- 1 tablespoon soy sauce
- 1 teaspoon ground ginger

1. In a large bowl, combine sausage and egg. Shape into 1-in. balls. Place on a greased rack in a shallow baking pan. Bake at 400° for 15-20 minutes or until a thermometer reads 160°; drain.
2. Meanwhile, in a small saucepan, combine the remaining ingredients. Bring to a boil. Reduce heat; simmer, uncovered, until sugar is dissolved.
3. Transfer meatballs to a 3-qt. slow cooker. Add the sauce and stir gently to coat. Cover and keep warm on low until serving.

SWEET 'N' SPICY MEATBALLS

SLOW COOKER
CARAMEL APPLE CIDER

Slow Cooker Caramel Apple Cider

Spiced with cinnamon sticks, allspice and caramel, this pretty warm-you-up sipper is sure to chase away winter's chill. Serve brimming mugs of the hot beverage alongside a platter of festive cookies at your next holiday gathering.

—TASTE OF HOME TEST KITCHEN

PREP: 5 MIN. • **COOK:** 2 HOURS
MAKES: 12 SERVINGS (¾ CUP EACH)

- 8 cups apple cider or juice
- 1 cup caramel flavoring syrup
- ¼ cup lemon juice
- 1 vanilla bean
- 2 cinnamon sticks (3 inches)
- 1 tablespoon whole allspice
  Whipped cream, hot caramel ice cream topping and cinnamon sticks (3 inches), optional

1. In a 3-qt. slow cooker, combine the apple cider, caramel syrup and lemon juice. Split vanilla bean and scrape seeds; add seeds to cider mixture. Place the bean, cinnamon sticks and allspice on a double thickness of cheesecloth; bring up corners of cloth and tie with string to form a bag. Add to cider mixture.

2. Cover and cook on low for 2-3 hours or until heated through. Discard spice bag. Pour cider into mugs; garnish with whipped cream, caramel topping and additional cinnamon sticks if desired.

NOTE *This recipe was tested with Torani brand flavoring syrup. Look for it in the coffee section.*

Crab & Artichoke Dip

Whenever my girlfriends and I get together, this rich and creamy dip always accompanies our favorite bottle of wine. Because the recipe relies on the convenience of a slow cooker, it's a great addition to winter gatherings!

—CONNIE MCKINNEY MARSHALL, MO

PREP: 20 MIN. • **COOK:** 2 HOURS • **MAKES:** 3½ CUPS

- 3 cups fresh baby spinach
- 1 can (14 ounces) water-packed artichoke hearts, rinsed, drained and chopped
- 1 package (8 ounces) cream cheese, softened
- 2 cups (8 ounces) shredded Havarti cheese
- 1 can (6 ounces) lump crabmeat, drained
- ½ cup sour cream
- ⅛ teaspoon salt
- ⅛ teaspoon pepper
  Assorted crackers

1. In a large saucepan, bring ½ in. of water to a boil. Add spinach; cover and boil for 3-5 minutes or until wilted. Drain.

2. In a 1½-qt. slow cooker, combine the artichokes, cheeses, crabmeat, sour cream, salt, pepper and spinach. Cover and cook on low for 2-3 hours or until cheese is melted. Serve with crackers.

Cheddar Fondue

This cheesy blend, sparked with mustard and Worcestershire sauce, is yummy! It's the perfect way to treat yourself during those gray, cold-weather months.

—**NORENE WRIGHT** MANILLA, IN

START TO FINISH: 15 MIN. • **MAKES:** 2½ CUPS

- ¼ cup butter
- ¼ cup all-purpose flour
- ½ teaspoon salt, optional
- ¼ teaspoon ground mustard
- ¼ teaspoon pepper
- ¼ teaspoon Worcestershire sauce
- 1½ cups milk
- 2 cups (8 ounces) shredded cheddar cheese
  Bread cubes, ham cubes, bite-size sausage and or broccoli florets

1. In a small saucepan, melt butter; stir in flour, salt if desired, mustard, pepper and Worcestershire sauce until smooth. Gradually add milk. Bring to a boil; cook and stir for 2 minutes or until thickened. Reduce heat. Add the cheese; cook and stir until cheese is melted.

2. Transfer to a fondue pot or 1½-qt. slow cooker; keep warm. Serve with bread, ham, sausage and/or broccoli.

CHEDDAR FONDUE

Mini Hot Dogs 'n' Meatballs

Hot appetizers don't come much easier than this. The recipe is so popular that I usually double it and use a larger slow cooker. You can vary the meats to suit your own family's tastes, or increase the heat factor with a spicier barbecue or spaghetti sauce. Serve with fancy party picks.

—**ANDREA CHAMBERLAIN** MACEDON, NEW YORK

PREP: 5 MIN. • **COOK:** 3 HOURS • **MAKES:** 8 CUPS

- 1 **package (12 ounces) frozen fully cooked Italian meatballs**
- 1 **package (16 ounces) miniature hot dogs or smoked sausages**
- 1 **package (3½ ounces) sliced pepperoni**
- 1 **jar (24 ounces) meatless spaghetti sauce**
- 1 **bottle (18 ounces) barbecue sauce**
- 1 **bottle (12 ounces) chili sauce**

In a 5-qt. slow cooker, combine all ingredients. Cover and cook on low for 3-4 hours or until heated through.

SLOW COOKER HOT CRAB DIP

MINI HOT DOGS 'N' MEATBALLS

Slow Cooker Hot Crab Dip

This appetizer goes so quickly in my family, that I often make two batches. Bits of sweet onion give the creamy dip a bit of a crunch.

—**TERRI PERRIER** SIMONTON, TX

PREP: 10 MIN. • **COOK:** 2 HOURS • **MAKES:** 2 CUPS

- 1 **package (8 ounces) cream cheese, softened**
- ½ **cup finely chopped sweet onion**
- ¼ **cup grated Parmesan cheese**
- ¼ **cup mayonnaise**
- 2 **garlic cloves, minced**
- 2 **teaspoons sugar**
- 1 **can (6 ounces) crabmeat, drained, flaked and cartilage removed**
  Assorted crackers

In a 1½-qt. slow cooker, combine the first six ingredients; stir in crab. Cover and cook on low for 2-3 hours or until heated through. Serve with crackers.

Mulled Merlot

This mulled wine recipe is sure to warm up your adult guests when they come in from the cold.
—TASTE OF HOME TEST KITCHEN

PREP: 10 MIN. • **COOK:** 1 HOUR • **MAKES:** 9 SERVINGS

- 4 **cinnamon sticks (3 inches)**
- 4 **whole cloves**
- 2 **bottles (750 milliliters each) merlot**
- ½ **cup sugar**
- ½ **cup orange juice**
- ½ **cup brandy**
- 1 **medium orange, thinly sliced**

1. Place cinnamon sticks and cloves on a double thickness of cheesecloth; bring up corners of cloth and tie with string to form a bag.
2. In a 3-qt. slow cooker, combine the wine, sugar, orange juice, brandy and orange slices. Add spice bag. Cover and cook on high for 1 hour or until heated through. Discard spice bag and orange slices. Serve warm. .

POMEGRANATE-GLAZED TURKEY MEATBALLS

Pomegranate-Glazed Turkey Meatballs

A splash of pomegranate juice turns ordinary meatballs into something extraordinary. I love the light, sweet glaze combined with the ground turkey, herbs and spices.
—DANIELLE D'AMBROSIO BRIGHTON, MA

PREP: 30 MIN. • **COOK:** 10 MIN. • **MAKES:** 3 DOZEN

- 1 **egg, beaten**
- ½ **cup soft bread crumbs**
- ½ **cup minced fresh parsley**
- 1 **teaspoon salt**
- 1 **teaspoon smoked paprika**
- 1 **teaspoon coarsely ground pepper**
- ¼ **teaspoon garlic salt**
- 1¼ **pounds ground turkey**
- 3 **cups plus 1 tablespoon pomegranate juice, divided**
- ½ **cup sugar**
- 1 **tablespoon cornstarch**

1. In a large bowl, combine the egg, bread crumbs, parsley, salt, paprika, pepper and garlic salt. Crumble turkey over mixture and mix well. Shape into 1-in. balls.
2. Divide between two ungreased 15-in. x 10-in. x 1-in. baking pans. Bake at 375° for 10-15 minutes or until a thermometer reads 165° and juices run clear.
3. Meanwhile, in a large skillet, combine 3 cups pomegranate juice and sugar. Bring to a boil; cook until liquid is reduced to about 1 cup. Combine cornstarch and remaining juice; stir into skillet. Cook and stir for 1 minute or until thickened.
4. Gently stir in meatballs and heat through. Serve in a slow cooker or chafing dish.

MULLED MERLOT

Winter

SIDE DISHES

When it's time to complete your meal, let your slow cooker do the work! Dishes such as Jazzed-Up Green Bean Casserole, Vegetable-Stuffed Peppers and Moist Poultry Dressing are easy additions to any winter menu.

SUE LIVERMORE'S SLOW-COOKED BACON & BEANS

Slow-Cooked Bacon & Beans

Bacon adds a subtle smokiness to this hearty side dish that's loaded with flavor. Brown sugar, vinegar and a hint of molasses make the sauce irresistible.

—**SUE LIVERMORE** DETROIT LAKES, MN

PREP: 25 MIN. • **COOK:** 6 HOURS
MAKES: 12 SERVINGS (¾ CUP EACH)

- 1 package (1 pound) sliced bacon, chopped
- 1 cup chopped onion
- 2 cans (15 ounces each) pork and beans, undrained
- 1 can (16 ounces) kidney beans, rinsed and drained
- 1 can (16 ounces) butter beans, rinsed and drained
- 1 can (15¼ ounces) lima beans, rinsed and drained
- 1 can (15 ounces) black beans, rinsed and drained
- 1 cup packed brown sugar
- ½ cup cider vinegar
- 1 tablespoon molasses
- 2 teaspoons garlic powder
- ½ teaspoon ground mustard

1. In a large skillet, cook bacon and onion over medium heat until bacon is crisp. Remove to paper towels to drain.
2. In a 4-qt. slow cooker, combine the remaining ingredients; stir in bacon mixture. Cover and cook on low for 6-8 hours or until heated through.

Maple-Almond Butternut Squash

A heartwarming dinner addition, especially on chilly days, Maple-Almond Butternut Squash is a cinch to prepare, making it a good choice for any weeknight. It's impressive enough for company, too.

—**JUDY LAWSON** DEXTER, MI

PREP: 30 MIN. • **COOK:** 5½ HOURS • **MAKES:** 9 SERVINGS

- 1 medium butternut squash (about 4 pounds), peeled, seeded and cut into 2-inch cubes
- 4 garlic cloves, minced
- 1 teaspoon salt
- ½ teaspoon pepper
- ½ cup butter, melted
- ½ cup maple syrup
- ½ cup heavy whipping cream
- ¼ cup sliced almonds
- ¼ cup shredded Parmesan cheese

1. Place squash in a 4-qt. slow cooker. Sprinkle with garlic, salt and pepper. Add butter and maple syrup; stir to coat. Cover and cook on low for 5-6 hours or until the squash is tender.
2. Stir in cream. Cover and cook 30 minutes longer or until heated through. Sprinkle with almonds and cheese.

Easy Slow Cooker Mac & Cheese

PREP: 25 MIN. • **COOK:** 1 HOUR • **MAKES:** 8 SERVINGS

- 2 **cups uncooked elbow macaroni**
- 1 **can (10¾ ounces) condensed cheddar cheese soup, undiluted**
- 1 **cup 2% milk**
- ½ **cup sour cream**
- ¼ **cup butter, cubed**
- ½ **teaspoon onion powder**
- ¼ **teaspoon white pepper**
- ⅛ **teaspoon salt**
- 1 **cup (4 ounces) shredded cheddar cheese**
- 1 **cup (4 ounces) shredded fontina cheese**
- 1 **cup (4 ounces) shredded provolone cheese**

1. Cook macaroni according to package directions for al dente. Meanwhile, in a large saucepan, combine soup, milk, sour cream, butter and seasonings; cook and stir over medium-low heat until blended. Stir in cheeses until melted.

2. Drain pasta; transfer to a greased 3-qt. slow cooker. Stir in cheese mixture. Cook, covered, on low 1-2 hours or until heated through.

EASY SLOW COOKER MAC & CHEESE

OLD-FASHIONED DRESSING

Old-Fashioned Dressing

Remember Grandma's delicious turkey dressing? Taste it once again with the flavorful herbs and veggies in this classic family-favorite dressing. You'll love that you can make it in your slow cooker, particularly during the busy holidays.
—**SHERRY VINK** LACOMBE, AB

PREP: 35 MIN. • **COOK:** 3 HOURS • **MAKES:** 8 SERVINGS

- ½ **cup butter, cubed**
- 2 **celery ribs, chopped**
- 1 **cup sliced fresh mushrooms**
- 1 **medium onion, chopped**
- ½ **cup minced fresh parsley**
- 2 **teaspoons rubbed sage**
- 2 **teaspoons dried marjoram**
- 1 **teaspoon dried thyme**
- 1 **teaspoon poultry seasoning**
- ½ **teaspoon pepper**
- ¼ **teaspoon salt**
- 6 **cups cubed day-old white bread**
- 6 **cups cubed day-old whole wheat bread**
- 1 **can (14½ ounces) chicken broth**

1. In a large skillet, melt butter. Add the celery, mushrooms and onion; saute until tender. Stir in the seasonings. Place bread cubes in a large bowl. Stir in vegetable mixture. Add broth; toss to coat.

2. Transfer to a 3-qt. slow cooker coated with cooking spray. Cover and cook on low for 3-4 hours or until heated through.

Jazzed-Up Green Bean Casserole

After trying many variations of this old standby, I decide to give it a little extra kick. The crunchy texture, cheesy goodness and bacon make it a hit at any holiday get-together.

—SCOTT RUGH PORTLAND, OR

PREP: 20 MIN. • **COOK:** 5½ HOURS
MAKES: 10 SERVINGS

- 2 packages (16 ounces each) frozen cut green beans, thawed
- 2 cans (10¾ ounces each) condensed cream of mushroom soup, undiluted
- 1 can (8 ounces) sliced water chestnuts, drained
- 1 cup 2% milk
- 6 bacon strips, cooked and crumbled
- 1 teaspoon pepper
- ⅛ teaspoon paprika
- 4 ounces process cheese (Velveeta), cubed
- 1 can (2.8 ounces) French-fried onions

In a 4-qt. slow cooker, combine the green beans, soup, water chestnuts, milk, bacon, pepper and paprika. Cover and cook on low for 5-6 hours or until beans are tender; stir in cheese. Cover and cook for 30 minutes or until cheese is melted. Sprinkle with onions.

Broccoli-Cheddar Hash Browns

Need a new go-to comfort food? Hash browns will fit the bill. This gooey combo of tender potatoes and broccoli pairs well with a wide variety of entrees.

—DEBORAH BIGGS OMAHA, NE

PREP: 20 MIN. • **COOK:** 4½ HOURS
MAKES: 8 SERVINGS

- 1 package (30 ounces) frozen shredded hash brown potatoes
- 2 cups frozen broccoli florets
- 1¼ cups (5 ounces) shredded sharp cheddar cheese, divided
- 2 green onions, chopped
- 2 tablespoons butter
- 2 tablespoons all-purpose flour
- ½ cup whole milk
- 1 can (10¾ ounces) condensed cream of broccoli soup, undiluted
- ½ teaspoon salt
- ½ teaspoon Dijon mustard

1. In a greased 4- or 5-qt. slow cooker, combine the hash browns, broccoli, ¾ cup cheese and onions.
2. In a small saucepan, melt butter. Stir in flour until smooth; gradually add milk. Bring to a boil; cook and stir for 1 minute or until thickened. Stir in the soup, salt and mustard. Pour over potato mixture; stir to combine.
3. Cover and cook on low for 4-5 hours or until potatoes are tender. Sprinkle with remaining cheese. Cover and cook 30 minutes longer or until cheese is melted.

Easy Sweet Potato Casserole

It takes only a few ingredients to create this sweet potato side dish—and what a great way to free up the oven for other items! Granola adds unexpected crunch.

—TASTE OF HOME TEST KITCHEN

PREP: 20 MIN. • **COOK:** 5 HOURS
MAKES: 6 SERVINGS

- 2¼ pounds sweet potatoes, peeled and cubed
- ¾ teaspoon salt
- ⅛ teaspoon pepper
- 1 cup peach pie filling
- 2 tablespoons butter, melted
- ¼ teaspoon ground cinnamon
- ½ cup granola without raisins, optional

Place potatoes in a 3-qt. slow cooker coated with cooking spray. Toss with salt and pepper. Top with pie filling and drizzle with butter. Sprinkle with cinnamon. Cover and cook on low for 5-7 hours or until potatoes are tender. Sprinkle with granola if desired.

JAZZED-UP GREEN BEAN CASSEROLE

FOUR-BEAN MEDLEY

Four-Bean Medley

This bean side dish always draws compliments. Because it's easy to fix ahead and simmer in the slow cooker, it's convenient to take to potlucks and church meals any time of the year.

—SUSANNE WASSON MONTGOMERY, NY

PREP: 40 MIN. • **COOK:** 6 HOURS
MAKES: 8-10 SERVINGS

- 8 bacon strips, diced
- 2 medium onions, quartered and sliced
- ¾ cup packed brown sugar
- ½ cup cider vinegar
- 1 teaspoon salt
- 1 teaspoon ground mustard
- ½ teaspoon garlic powder
- 1 can (16 ounces) baked beans, undrained
- 1 can (16 ounces) kidney beans, rinsed and drained
- 1 can (16 ounces) butter beans, rinsed and drained
- 1 can (14½ ounces) cut green beans, drained

1. In a large skillet, cook bacon until crisp. Drain, reserving 2 tablespoons drippings; set bacon aside. Saute onions in drippings until tender. Stir in brown sugar, vinegar, salt, mustard and garlic powder.

2. Simmer, uncovered, for 15 minutes or until onions are golden brown. Place the beans in a 3-qt. slow cooker. Add onion mixture and bacon; stir to combine. Cover and cook on low for 6-7 hours or until heated through. Serve with a slotted spoon.

 **Holiday Helper**

We feed a lot of people at Thanksgiving and Christmas dinners, so my sisters and I always set up a big buffet on the kitchen counter. We put the side dishes in slow cookers (mashed potatoes, scalloped corn, squash, gravy and so forth) to keep everything warm. Guests bring the breads, rolls, salads and pies. If someone arrives late, they can still have a hot delicious meal.

—MARLA C. SMYRNA, NY

SANDRA ALLEN'S
VEGETABLE-STUFFED PEPPERS

Vegetable-Stuffed Peppers

This recipe came with my slow cooker. I fill green peppers with a flavorful combination of cooked rice, kidney beans, corn and onions. In addition to a change-of-pace side dish, this recipe makes a great meatless entree that we enjoy regularly.
—**SANDRA ALLEN** AUSTIN, TX

PREP: 10 MIN. • **COOK:** 8¼ HOURS
MAKES: 6 SERVINGS

- 2 **cans (14½ ounces each) diced tomatoes, undrained**
- 1 **can (16 ounces) kidney beans, rinsed and drained**
- 1½ **cups cooked rice**
- 2 **cups (8 ounces) shredded cheddar cheese, divided**
- 1 **package (10 ounces) frozen corn, thawed**
- ¼ **cup chopped onion**
- 1 **teaspoon Worcestershire sauce**
- ¾ **teaspoon chili powder**
- ½ **teaspoon pepper**
- ¼ **teaspoon salt**
- 6 **medium green peppers**

1. In a large bowl, combine the tomatoes, beans, rice, 1½ cups cheese, corn, onion, Worcestershire sauce, chili powder, pepper and salt. Remove and discard tops and seeds of green peppers. Fill each pepper with about 1 cup vegetable mixture. Place in a 5-qt. slow cooker. Cover and cook on low for 8 hours.
2. Sprinkle with remaining cheese. Cover and cook 15 minutes longer or until peppers are tender and cheese is melted.

(5)INGREDIENTS Slow-Cooked Applesauce

My sweet applesauce is perfect alongside main dishes or served as a snack. Because it's prepared in the slow cooker, you can set it before you head out for winter fun.
—**SUSANNE WASSON** MONTGOMERY, NY

PREP: 20 MIN. • **COOK:** 6 HOURS
MAKES: 12 CUPS

- 6 **pounds apples (about 18 medium), peeled and sliced**
- 1 **cup sugar**
- 1 **cup water**
- 1 **teaspoon salt**
- 1 **teaspoon ground cinnamon**
- ¼ **cup butter, cubed**
- 2 **teaspoons vanilla extract**

1. In a 5-qt. slow cooker, combine the apples, sugar, water, salt and cinnamon. Cover and cook on low for 6-8 hours or until tender.
2. Turn off heat; stir in the butter and vanilla. Mash if desired. Serve warm or cold.

(5)INGREDIENTS Creamy Red Potatoes

Here's a rich and creamy side dish that's easy to double, and I always receive compliments when I take it to potlucks.
—**SHELIA SCHMITT** TOPEKA, KS

PREP: 5 MIN. • **COOK:** 8 HOURS
MAKES: 4-6 SERVINGS

- 2 **pounds small red potatoes, quartered**
- 1 **package (8 ounces) cream cheese, softened**
- 1 **can (10¾ ounces) condensed cream of potato soup, undiluted**
- 1 **envelope ranch salad dressing mix**

Place potatoes in a 3-qt. slow cooker. In a small bowl, beat the cream cheese, soup and salad dressing mix until blended. Stir into potatoes. Cover and cook on low for 8 hours or until potatoes are tender.

CREAMY RED POTATOES

MOIST POULTRY DRESSING

Moist Poultry Dressing

Tasty mushrooms and onions complement the big herb flavor in my stuffing. This dressing stays so moist when cooked this way!

—**RUTH ANN STELFOX** RAYMOND, AB

PREP: 20 MIN. • **COOK:** 4 HOURS • **MAKES:** 12-16 SERVINGS

- 2 jars (4½ ounces each) sliced mushrooms, drained
- 4 celery ribs, chopped
- 2 medium onions, chopped
- ¼ cup minced fresh parsley
- ¾ cup butter, cubed
- 1½ pounds day-old bread, crusts removed and cubed (about 13 cups)
- 1½ teaspoons salt
- 1½ teaspoons rubbed sage
- 1 teaspoon poultry seasoning
- 1 teaspoon dried thyme
- ½ teaspoon pepper
- 2 eggs
- 1 can (14½ ounces) chicken broth or 14½ ounces vegetable broth

1. In a large skillet, saute the mushrooms, celery, onions and parsley in butter until the vegetables are tender. In a large bowl, toss the bread cubes with salt, sage, poultry seasoning, thyme and pepper. Add the mushroom mixture. Combine eggs and broth; add to the bread mixture and toss.

2. Transfer to 5-qt. slow cooker. Cover and cook on low for 4-5 hours or until a thermometer reads 160°.

Slow-Cooked Broccoli

This crumb-topped side dish is quick to assemble and full of flavor. Since it simmers in a slow cooker, it frees up my oven for other things. That's a great help when I'm preparing several items for a big meal at home.

—**CONNIE SLOCUM** ANTIOCH, TN

PREP: 10 MIN. • **COOK:** 2½ HOURS • **MAKES:** 8-10 SERVINGS

- 6 cups frozen chopped broccoli, partially thawed
- 1 can (10¾ ounces) condensed cream of celery soup, undiluted
- 1½ cups (6 ounces) shredded sharp cheddar cheese, divided
- ¼ cup chopped onion
- ½ teaspoon Worcestershire sauce
- ¼ teaspoon pepper
- 1 cup crushed butter-flavored crackers (about 25)
- 2 tablespoons butter

1. In a large bowl, combine the broccoli, soup, 1 cup cheese, onion, Worcestershire sauce and pepper. Pour into a greased 3-qt. slow cooker. Sprinkle crackers on top; dot with butter.

2. Cover and cook on high for 2½ to 3 hours. Sprinkle with remaining cheese. Cook 10 minutes longer or until the cheese is melted.

SLOW-COOKED BROCCOLI

MAKE-AHEAD MASHED POTATOES

Make-Ahead Mashed Potatoes

Sour cream and cream cheese add richness to these tasty time-saving potatoes. They're wonderful for entertaining because they don't require any last-minute mashing.
—**TRUDY VINCENT** VALLES MINES, MO

PREP: 20 MIN. • **COOK:** 2 HOURS • **MAKES:** 8-10 SERVINGS

- 1 package (3 ounces) cream cheese, softened
- ½ cup sour cream
- ¼ cup butter, softened
- 1 envelope ranch salad dressing mix
- 1 teaspoon dried parsley flakes
- 6 cups warm mashed potatoes (without added milk and butter)

In a large bowl, combine the cream cheese, sour cream, butter, salad dressing mix and parsley; stir in potatoes. Transfer to a 3-qt. slow cooker. Cover and cook on low for 2-3 hours.

NOTE *This recipe was tested with fresh potatoes (not instant) in a slow cooker with heating elements surrounding the unit, not only in the base.*

top tip
Lively Leftovers

I make a batch of mashed potatoes and freeze individual servings in muffin cups. Once frozen, I pop them out and store in resealable freezer bags. During the week, I pull out as many servings as I need and heat them in the microwave. —**GRETCHEN B.** SURPRISE, AZ

Winter Fruit Compote

You can make this colorful and easy fruit relish up to a week in advance. It makes a great accompaniment to turkey, chicken or pork throughout the holiday season.
—**ESTHER CHESNEY** CARTHAGE, MO

PREP: 10 MIN. • **COOK:** 1¼ HOURS + COOLING • **MAKES:** 2½ CUPS

- 1 package (12 ounces) fresh or frozen cranberries, thawed
- ⅔ cup packed brown sugar
- ¼ cup orange juice concentrate
- 2 tablespoons raspberry vinegar
- ½ cup chopped dried apricots
- ½ cup golden raisins
- ½ cup chopped walnuts, toasted

1. In a 1½-qt. slow cooker, combine the cranberries, brown sugar, orange juice concentrate and vinegar. Cover and cook on low for 1¼ to 1¾ hours or until cranberries pop and mixture is thickened.

2. Turn off the heat; stir in the apricots, raisins and walnuts. Cool to room temperature. Refrigerate leftovers.

Everything Stuffing

My husband and father both go crazy for this stuffing! It also freezes well so we can enjoy it anytime.
—**BETTE VOTRAL** BETHLEHEM, PA

PREP: 30 MIN. • **COOK:** 3 HOURS • **MAKES:** 9 SERVINGS

- ½ pound bulk Italian sausage
- 4 cups seasoned stuffing cubes
- 1½ cups crushed corn bread stuffing
- ½ cup chopped toasted chestnuts or pecans
- ½ cup minced fresh parsley
- 1 tablespoon minced fresh sage or 1 teaspoon rubbed sage
- ⅛ teaspoon salt
- ⅛ teaspoon pepper
- 1¾ cups sliced baby portobello mushrooms
- 1 package (5 ounces) sliced fresh shiitake mushrooms
- 1 large onion, chopped
- 1 medium apple, peeled and chopped
- 1 celery rib, chopped
- 3 tablespoons butter
- 1 can (14½ ounces) chicken broth

1. In a large skillet, cook sausage over medium heat until no longer pink; drain. Transfer to a large bowl. Stir in the stuffing cubes, corn bread stuffing, chestnuts, parsley, sage, salt and pepper.

2. In the same skillet, saute the mushrooms, onion, apple and celery in butter until tender. Stir into stuffing mixture. Add enough broth to reach desired moistness. Transfer to a 4-qt. slow cooker. Cover and cook on low for 3 hours, stirring once.

RANCH BEANS

Creamy Hash Browns

My mother often took this comforting side dish to social dinners because it was such a hit. Now I get the same compliments when I make it. Bacon and onion jazz up a creamy mixture that takes advantage of convenient frozen hash browns and canned soups.

—**DONNA DOWNES** LAS VEGAS, NV

PREP: 10 MIN. • **COOK:** 4 HOURS
MAKES: 14 SERVINGS

- 1 package (2 pounds) frozen cubed hash brown potatoes
- 2 cups (8 ounces) cubed process cheese (Velveeta)
- 2 cups (16 ounces) sour cream
- 1 can (10¾ ounces) condensed cream of celery soup, undiluted
- 1 can (10¾ ounces) condensed cream of chicken soup, undiluted
- 1 pound sliced bacon, cooked and crumbled
- 1 large onion, chopped
- ¼ cup butter, melted
- ¼ teaspoon pepper

Place potatoes in an ungreased 5-qt. slow cooker. In a large bowl, combine the remaining ingredients. Pour over potatoes and mix well. Cover and cook on low for 4-5 hours or until potatoes are tender and heated through.

Ranch Beans

This sweet and tangy side dish uses lots of convenient canned goods, so it's a snap to throw together. The recipe was sent to me by a friend. Its wide appeal makes it nice to serve at a potluck or charity event.

—**BARBARA GORDON** ROSWELL, GA

PREP: 10 MIN. • **COOK:** 3 HOURS
MAKES: 8-10 SERVINGS

- 1 can (16 ounces) kidney beans, rinsed and drained
- 1 can (15¾ ounces) pork and beans, undrained
- 1 can (15 ounces) lima beans, rinsed and drained
- 1 can (14½ ounces) cut green beans, drained
- 1 bottle (12 ounces) chili sauce
- ¾ cup packed brown sugar
- 1 small onion, chopped

In a 3-qt. slow cooker, combine all the ingredients. Cover and cook on high for 3-4 hours or until heated through. **NOTE** *This dish can be cooked in the oven instead. Cover and bake in a 350° oven for 40 minutes. Remove cover and cook 10 minutes longer.*

Italian Spaghetti Squash

Here's a unique and easy way to cook spaghetti squash. Be sure the squash is on the small or medium side so that it fits in the slow cooker after being cut in half.

—**MELISSA BROOKS** SPARTA, WI

PREP: 15 MIN. • **COOK:** 6¼ HOURS
MAKES: 4 SERVINGS

- 1 medium spaghetti squash
- 1 cup sliced fresh mushrooms
- 1 can (14½ ounces) diced tomatoes, undrained
- 1 teaspoon dried oregano
- 1 teaspoon salt
- ¼ teaspoon pepper
- ¾ cup shredded part-skim mozzarella cheese

1. Cut squash in half lengthwise; discard seeds. Place squash, cut side up, in a 6- or 7-qt. slow cooker. Layer with mushrooms, tomatoes, oregano, salt and pepper. Cover and cook on low for 6-8 hours or until squash is tender.
2. Sprinkle with cheese. Cover and cook for 15 minutes or until cheese is melted. When squash is cool enough to handle, use a fork to separate spaghetti squash strands.

 **Cheese "Whiz-ard"**

Process cheese is a blend of different cheeses that is similar in flavor to the natural cheese from which it's made. Generally, it is stable at room temperature and stays smooth and creamy when heated. The most common brand name of process American cheese is Velveeta. Be mindful that Velveeta's label reads "pasteurized prepared cheese product"—as that is the terminology sometimes used in articles, blogs, recipes and other culinary sources.

DONNA DOWNES'
CREAMY HASH BROWNS

Sausage Dressing

I first used this recipe one holiday when there was no room in the oven to bake stuffing. The results were fantastic—very moist and flavorful. Even family members who don't usually eat dressing enjoyed it.

—MARY KENDALL APPLETON, WI

PREP: 20 MIN. • **COOK:** 4 HOURS
MAKES: 12 SERVINGS

- 1 pound bulk pork sausage
- 1 large onion, chopped
- 2 celery ribs, chopped
- 1 package (14 ounces) seasoned stuffing croutons
- 1 can (14½ ounces) chicken broth
- 1 large tart apple, chopped
- 1 cup chopped walnuts or pecans
- ½ cup egg substitute
- ¼ cup butter, melted
- 1½ teaspoons rubbed sage
- ½ teaspoon pepper

1. In a large skillet, cook the sausage, onion and celery over medium heat until meat is no longer pink; drain. Transfer to a greased 5-qt. slow cooker. Stir in the remaining ingredients.

2. Cover and cook on low for 4-5 hours or until a thermometer reads 160°.

Praline Sweet Potatoes

I had a house full of relatives and was short on cooking space. So I used the basic idea behind traditional sweet potato casserole and adapted it for the slow cooker. My recipe's been a huge hit ever since!

—JOANNA STANFORTH SCOTT AFB, IL

PREP: 15 MIN. • **COOK:** 4 HOURS
MAKES: 6 SERVINGS

- 3 cups mashed sweet potatoes
- 1 cup sugar
- 3 eggs
- ½ cup 2% milk
- ¼ cup butter, melted
- 1 teaspoon salt
- 1 teaspoon vanilla extract

TOPPING

- ½ cup packed brown sugar
- ½ cup chopped pecans
- ¼ cup all-purpose flour
- 2 tablespoons cold butter

1. In a large bowl, combine the sweet potatoes, sugar, eggs, milk, butter, salt and vanilla. Transfer to a greased 1½-qt. slow cooker. Cover and cook on low for 3 hours.

2. In a small bowl, combine the brown sugar, pecans and flour; cut in butter until crumbly. Sprinkle over the sweet potatoes. Cover and cook 1-2 hours longer or until a thermometer reads 160°.

Light Spinach Casserole

This trimmed-down recipe was in an old slow cooker cookbook that I found. When I took the side dish to our church sewing circle, it was a big hit.

—VIODA GEYER UHRICHSVILLE, OH

PREP: 10 MIN. • **COOK:** 2½ HOURS
MAKES: 8 SERVINGS

- 2 packages (10 ounces each) frozen chopped spinach, thawed and well drained
- 2 cups (16 ounces) 4% cottage cheese
- 1 cup cubed process cheese (Velveeta)
- ¾ cup egg substitute
- 2 tablespoons butter, cubed
- ¼ cup all-purpose flour
- ½ teaspoon salt

In a 3-qt. slow cooker, combine all ingredients. Cover and cook on low for 2½ hours or until cheese is melted.

SAUSAGE DRESSING

SLOW COOKER TZIMMES

Slow Cooker Tzimmes

PREP: 20 MIN. • **COOK:** 5 HOURS
MAKES: 12 SERVINGS (⅔ CUP EACH)

- ½ **medium butternut squash, peeled and cubed**
- 2 **medium sweet potatoes, peeled and cubed**
- 6 **medium carrots, sliced**
- 2 **medium tart apples, peeled and sliced**
- 1 **cup chopped sweet onion**
- 1 **cup chopped dried apricots**
- 1 **cup golden raisins**
- ½ **cup orange juice**
- ¼ **cup honey**
- 2 **tablespoons finely chopped crystallized ginger**
- 3 **teaspoons ground cinnamon**
- 3 **teaspoons pumpkin pie spice**
- 2 **teaspoons grated orange peel**
- 1 **teaspoon salt**
  Vanilla yogurt, optional

1. Place the first seven ingredients in a 5- or 6-qt. slow cooker. Combine the orange juice, honey, ginger, cinnamon, pie spice, orange peel and salt; pour over top and mix well.

2. Cover and cook on low for 5-6 hours or until vegetables are tender. Dollop servings with yogurt if desired.

FRANCES MOORE'S
CHEESY SPINACH

Cheesy Spinach

My daughter often serves this easy Florentine specialty at church suppers. Even people who don't usually eat spinach like the flavorful dish once they try it. In fact, there is never any left!

—**FRANCES MOORE** DECATUR, IL

PREP: 10 MIN. • **COOK:** 5 HOURS
MAKES: 6-8 SERVINGS

- 2 packages (10 ounces each) frozen chopped spinach, thawed and well drained
- 2 cups (16 ounces) 4% cottage cheese
- 1½ cups cubed process cheese (Velveeta)
- 3 eggs, lightly beaten
- ¼ cup butter, cubed
- ¼ cup all-purpose flour
- 1 teaspoon salt

In a large bowl, combine all ingredients. Pour into a greased 3-qt. slow cooker. Cover and cook on high for 1 hour. Reduce heat to low; cook 4-5 hours longer or until a knife inserted near the center comes out clean.

Green Beans in Bacon Cheese Sauce

I like to make this side dish for potlucks because it's easy to make, serves a crowd and is always popular.

—**KAREN LEWIS** PLEASANT GROVE, AL

PREP: 10 MIN. • **COOK:** 5 HOURS
MAKES: 10 SERVINGS

- 2 packages (16 ounces each) frozen French-style green beans, thawed
- 1 can (10¾ ounces) condensed cream of mushroom soup, undiluted
- 1 can (10¾ ounces) condensed cheddar cheese soup, undiluted
- ¾ cup chopped onion
- ¾ cup bacon bits
- ½ cup shredded cheddar cheese
- 1 jar (4½ ounces) sliced mushrooms, drained
- 1 jar (4 ounces) diced pimientos, drained
- ½ teaspoon pepper

In a 3- or 4-qt. slow cooker, combine all ingredients. Cover and cook on low for 5-6 hours or until beans are tender.

CREAMY CORN

⑤ INGREDIENTS Creamy Corn

A handful of ingredients and a slow cooker are all you'll need for this rich dish. I first tasted it at a potluck with our camping club. It's so easy to assemble!

—**JUDY MCCARTHY** DERBY, KS

PREP: 5 MIN. • **COOK:** 4 HOURS
MAKES: 6 SERVINGS

- 2 packages (16 ounces each) frozen corn
- 1 package (8 ounces) cream cheese, cubed
- ⅓ cup butter, cubed
- ½ teaspoon garlic powder
- ½ teaspoon salt
- ¼ teaspoon pepper

In a 3-qt. slow cooker, combine all ingredients. Cover and cook on low for 4 hours or until heated through and cheese is melted. Stir well before serving.

Potato Mushrooms

I dress up sliced potatoes with mushrooms, onions, canned soup and cheese to create this versatile side dish. With its comforting flavor, it's a nice accompaniment to most meats.

—**LINDA BERNARD** GOLDEN MEADOW, LA

PREP: 25 MIN. • **COOK:** 6 HOURS
MAKES: 8-10 SERVINGS

- 7 medium potatoes, peeled and thinly sliced
- 1 medium onion, sliced
- 4 garlic cloves, minced
- 2 green onions, chopped
- 1 can (8 ounces) mushroom stems and pieces, drained
- ¼ cup all-purpose flour
- 2 teaspoons salt
- ½ teaspoon pepper
- ¼ cup butter, cubed
- 1 can (10¾ ounces) condensed cream of mushroom soup, undiluted
- 1 cup (4 ounces) shredded Colby-Monterey Jack cheese

In a 3-qt. slow cooker, layer half of the potatoes, onion, garlic, green onions, mushrooms, flour, salt, pepper and butter. Repeat layers. Pour soup over the top. Cover and cook on low for 6-8 hours or until potatoes are tender; sprinkle with cheese during the last 30 minutes of cooking time.

Winter

ENTREES

There's no doubt...winter is truly slow cooker season. From hearty roasts perfect for entertaining to comforting spaghetti sauces ideal for weeknights, these main courses add heartwarming goodness when Old Man Winter calls.

JUDY CLARK'S
SAVORY MUSHROOM
& HERB PORK DINNER

Savory Mushroom & Herb Pork Dinner

Dried thyme, rosemary and marjoram do a wonderful job of seasoning this moist and tender pork roast. In addition, carrots round things out nicely, so you can come home to a delightful meal-in-one sensation. I thicken the cooking juices into a gravy so I can serve the meal alongside mashed potatoes.
—**JUDY CLARK** ADDISON, MI

PREP: 25 MIN. • **COOK:** 5 HOURS • **MAKES:** 8 SERVINGS

- 2 **medium onions, chopped**
- 12 **fresh baby carrots**
- 1 **boneless pork shoulder butt roast (3 to 4 pounds)**
- 1 **can (10¾ ounces) condensed cream of mushroom soup, undiluted**
- ¾ **cup chicken broth**
- 1 **can (4 ounces) mushroom stems and pieces, drained**
- ½ **teaspoon dried thyme**
- ½ **teaspoon Worcestershire sauce**
- ¼ **teaspoon dried rosemary, crushed**
- ¼ **teaspoon dried marjoram**
- ¼ **teaspoon pepper**
- 1 **tablespoon cornstarch**
- 2 **tablespoons cold water**
  French-fried onions, optional

1. Place onions and carrots in a 5-qt. slow cooker. Cut roast in half; add to slow cooker. In a small bowl, combine the soup, broth, mushrooms, thyme, Worcestershire sauce, rosemary, marjoram and pepper; pour over pork. Cover and cook on low for 5-6 hours or until meat is tender.

2. Remove pork to a serving platter; keep warm. Skim fat from cooking juices; transfer to a large saucepan. Bring liquid to a boil. Combine cornstarch and water until smooth; gradually stir into the pan. Bring to a boil; cook and stir for 2 minutes or until thickened.

3. Serve pork with gravy. Sprinkle servings with French-fried onions if desired.

top tip

Dinner Additions

If you have a little time when preparing the Savory Mushroom & Herb Pork Dinner, try browning the French-fried onions in a dry skillet over low heat. This makes them extra crunchy and really brings out their flavor. Top individual plates with the onions right before serving.

I like to round out the meal with mashed potatoes, but warm buttered noodles make an excellent accompaniment as well.
—**JUDY C.** ADDISON, MI

Mexican Pot Roast Filling

My son's friends always requested this recipe when they came over and are still talking about it more than a decade later! The meat absorbs the juices, which give fantastic flavor. It is perfect as a filling for tacos, burritos or enchiladas, and it also freezes well.

—CONNIE DICAVOLI SHAWNEE, KS

PREP: 25 MIN. • **COOK:** 8 HOURS • **MAKES:** 9 SERVINGS

- 1½ teaspoons chili powder
- 1 teaspoon ground cumin
- ½ teaspoon smoked paprika
- ½ teaspoon crushed red pepper flakes
- ¼ teaspoon salt
- 1 boneless beef chuck roast (3 pounds)
- 1 can (4 ounces) chopped green chilies
- ½ cup chopped sweet onion
- 2 garlic cloves, minced
- ¾ cup beef broth
  Taco shells or flour tortillas (8 inches)
  Chopped tomatoes, shredded lettuce and shredded
    Mexican cheese blend

1. In a small bowl, combine the first five ingredients. Cut roast in half; rub spice mixture over meat. Transfer to a 3-qt. slow cooker. Top with chilies, onion and garlic. Pour broth over meat. Cover and cook on low for 8-10 hours or until meat is tender.

2. Remove meat from slow cooker; shred with two forks. Skim fat from cooking juices. Return meat to slow cooker; heat through. Using a slotted spoon, place ½ cup meat mixture on each taco shell. Top with the tomatoes, lettuce and cheese.

MEXICAN POT ROAST FILLING

SLOW-SIMMERING BEEF BOURGUIGNON

Slow-Simmering Beef Bourguignon

Warm up cold days with tender chunks of beef simmered in a rich sauce ladled over steaming noodles.

—ADELE ZUERNER ARDEN, NC

PREP: 30 MIN. • **COOK:** 8 HOURS • **MAKES:** 6 SERVINGS

- 3 pounds beef stew meat
- ¾ teaspoon salt
- ¾ teaspoon pepper
- 3 tablespoons all-purpose flour
- 1½ cups beef broth
- 1½ cups dry red wine or additional beef broth, divided
- ¾ pound medium fresh mushrooms, quartered
- 1 large sweet onion, chopped
- 2 medium carrots, sliced
- 1 thick-sliced bacon strip, chopped
- 2 garlic cloves, minced
- 2 tablespoons Italian tomato paste
  Hot cooked egg noodles

1. Sprinkle beef with salt and pepper. In a large nonstick skillet coated with cooking spray, brown beef in batches. Remove with a slotted spoon to a 4- or 5-qt. slow cooker. Add flour; toss to coat. Add broth and 1 cup wine.

2. In the same skillet, add the mushrooms, onion, carrots and bacon; cook and stir over medium heat until carrots are tender. Add garlic; cook 1 minute longer. Add remaining wine, stirring to loosen browned bits from pan; stir in tomato paste. Transfer to slow cooker.

3. Cover and cook on low for 8-10 hours or until beef is tender. Serve with noodles.

"I love the addition of peanut butter to savory recipes like this. Intensify the flavor by sprinkling with minced fresh cilantro and chopped peanuts for that restaurant-quality look and taste."
—STEPHANIE ANDERSON HORSEHEADS, NY

Pork Satay with Rice Noodles

PREP: 20 MIN. • **COOK:** 4 HOURS
MAKES: 6 SERVINGS

- 1½ pounds boneless pork loin chops, cut into 2-inch pieces
- ¼ teaspoon pepper
- 1 medium onion, halved and sliced
- ⅓ cup creamy peanut butter
- ¼ cup reduced-sodium soy sauce
- ½ teaspoon onion powder
- ½ teaspoon garlic powder
- ½ teaspoon hot pepper sauce
- 1 can (14½ ounces) reduced-sodium chicken broth
- 3 tablespoons cornstarch
- 3 tablespoons water
- 9 ounces uncooked thick rice noodles
- Minced fresh cilantro and chopped peanuts, optional

1. Sprinkle pork with pepper. Place in a 3-qt. slow cooker; top with onion. In a small bowl, mix peanut butter, soy sauce, onion powder, garlic powder and pepper sauce; gradually add broth. Pour over onion. Cook, covered, on low 4-6 hours or until pork is tender.

2. Remove pork from slow cooker and keep warm. Skim fat from cooking juices; transfer cooking juices to a large skillet. Bring to a boil. In a small bowl, mix cornstarch and water until smooth and add to pan. Return to a boil; cook and stir 2 minutes or until thickened. Add pork; heat through.

3. Meanwhile, cook noodles according to package directions; drain. Serve with pork mixture. If desired, sprinkle with cilantro and peanuts.

NOTE *Reduced-fat peanut butter is not recommended for this recipe.*

PORK SATAY WITH RICE NOODLES

Slow-Cooked Meat Loaf

Chopped onion and garlic plus spicy seasonings make this this slow-cooked dinner staple something outstanding!
—**TASTE OF HOME TEST KITCHEN**

PREP: 25 MIN. • **COOK:** 4 HOURS
MAKES: 8 SERVINGS

- 6 tablespoons ketchup, divided
- 2 tablespoons Worcestershire sauce
- 12 saltines, crushed
- 1 medium onion, finely chopped
- 6 garlic cloves, minced
- 1 teaspoon paprika
- ½ teaspoon salt
- ½ teaspoon pepper
- ⅛ teaspoon cayenne pepper
- 2 pounds lean ground beef (90% lean)

1. Cut three 20-in. x 3-in. strips of heavy-duty foil; crisscross so they resemble spokes of a wheel. Place strips on the bottom and up the sides of a 3-qt. slow cooker. Coat strips with cooking spray.

2. In a large bowl, combine 2 tablespoons of the ketchup, the Worcestershire sauce, saltines, onion, garlic, paprika, salt, pepper and cayenne. Crumble beef over mixture and mix well.

3. Shape into a round loaf. Place in the center of the strips. Cover and cook on low for 4-5 hours or until no pink remains and a meat thermometer reads 160°.

4. Using foil strips as handles, remove the meat loaf to a platter. Spread remaining ketchup over top.

top tip Secret Ingredient

Worcestershire sauce is a thin dark-brown sauce used to season meats, gravies, sauces and salad dressing. It is sometimes used as a condiment. It's generally made of soy sauce, vinegar, garlic, onions, tamarind, molasses and various seasonings and is widely available in supermarkets.

CREAMY MUSHROOM, HAM & POTATOES

Creamy Mushroom, Ham & Potatoes

Everyone loves these potatoes and always comes back for more. I like the comforting main dish because it uses only seven ingredients and is finished in the slow cooker.
—**TRACI MEADOWS** MONETT, MO

PREP: 25 MIN. • **COOK:** 4 HOURS
MAKES: 4 SERVINGS

- 1 **can (10¾ ounces) condensed cream of mushroom soup, undiluted**
- ½ **cup 2% milk**
- 1 **tablespoon dried parsley flakes**
- 6 **medium potatoes, peeled and thinly sliced**
- 1 **small onion, chopped**
- 1½ **cups cubed fully cooked ham**
- 6 **slices process American cheese**

In a small bowl, combine the soup, milk and parsley. In a greased 3-qt. slow cooker, layer half of the potatoes, onion, ham, cheese and soup mixture. Repeat layers. Cover and cook on low for 4-5 hours or until the potatoes are tender.

Italian Roast with Alfredo Potatoes

Surprise! This extra-special meal is easy enough for any night of the week. Since the roast is made in the slow cooker, you'll have plenty of time to make the delicious homemade mashed potatoes.
—**TASTE OF HOME TEST KITCHEN**

PREP: 20 MIN. • **COOK:** 7 HOURS
MAKES: 10 SERVINGS

- 1 **boneless beef chuck roast (4 pounds), trimmed**
- 1 **envelope brown gravy mix**
- 1 **envelope Italian salad dressing mix**
- ½ **cup water**
- 1 **medium sweet red pepper, cut into 1-inch pieces**
- 1 **cup chopped green pepper**
- ⅔ **cup chopped onion**
- 8 **medium red potatoes, quartered**
- 2 **tablespoons cornstarch**
- ¼ **cup cold water**
- ¾ **cup refrigerated Alfredo sauce**
- 2 **tablespoons butter**
- ¼ **teaspoon pepper**
- 1 **tablespoon minced chives**

1. Cut roast in half; place in a 5-qt. slow cooker. In a small bowl, combine the gravy mix, dressing mix and water; pour over roast. Top with peppers and onion. Cover and cook on low for 7-8 hours or until meat is tender.
2. Place potatoes in a large saucepan; cover with water. Bring to a boil. Reduce heat; cover and simmer for 15-20 minutes or until tender.
3. Remove beef from slow cooker and keep warm. Skim fat from cooking juices if necessary; pour into a large saucepan. Combine cornstarch and cold water until smooth; stir into cooking juices. Bring to a boil; cook and stir for 2 minutes or until thickened.
4. Drain potatoes; mash with Alfredo sauce, butter and pepper. Sprinkle with chives. Serve with beef and gravy.

ITALIAN ROAST WITH ALFREDO POTATOES

Beef Roast Dinner

Since this healthy dish is slow-cooked, you can use less expensive roasts and have the same mouthwatering results you would get with more costly cuts. Change up the veggies for variety, nutrition or to suit your tastes, or prepare it on the stovetop if you'd like!

—SANDRA DUDLEY BEMIDJI, MN

PREP: 20 MIN. • **COOK:** 8 HOURS • **MAKES:** 10 SERVINGS

- 1 **pound red potatoes (about 4 medium), cubed**
- ¼ **pound small fresh mushrooms**
- 1½ **cups fresh baby carrots**
- 1 **medium green pepper, chopped**
- 1 **medium parsnip, chopped**
- 1 **small red onion, chopped**
- 1 **beef rump roast or bottom round roast (3 pounds)**
- 1 **can (14½ ounces) beef broth**
- ¾ **teaspoon salt**
- ¾ **teaspoon dried oregano**
- ¼ **teaspoon pepper**
- 3 **tablespoons cornstarch**
- ¼ **cup cold water**

1. Place vegetables in a 5-qt. slow cooker. Cut roast in half; place in slow cooker. Combine the broth, salt, oregano and pepper; pour over meat. Cover and cook on low for 8 hours or until meat is tender.

2. Remove meat and vegetables to a serving platter; keep warm. Skim fat from cooking juices; transfer to a small saucepan. Bring liquid to a boil.

3. Combine cornstarch and water until smooth. Gradually stir into the pan. Bring to a boil; cook and stir for 2 minutes or until thickened. Serve with meat and vegetables.

BEEF ROAST DINNER

STOVETOP BEEF ROAST DINNER *In a Dutch oven, brown the roast on all sides in 1-2 tablespoons canola oil. Add the broth, salt, oregano, pepper and onion; bring to a boil. Reduce heat, cover and simmer for 2 hours. Add the potatoes, mushrooms, carrots, green pepper and parsnip; cover and simmer 45-60 minutes longer or until meat is tender. Remove meat and vegetables to a serving platter and keep warm. For gravy, pour pan drippings and loosened browned bits into a measuring cup; skim and discard fat. Transfer to a small saucepan. Combine cornstarch and cold water until smooth; gradually stir into drippings. Bring to a boil; cook and stir for 2 minutes or until thickened. Slice beef; serve with gravy.*

Saucy Mandarin Duck

For something a little different, try this sweet-savory duck dish that is flavored with Asian seasonings and mandarin oranges. It's a nice change of pace. For flair, garnish each serving with toasted sesame seeds.

—TASTE OF HOME TEST KITCHEN

PREP: 30 MIN. + MARINATING • **COOK:** 4¾ HOURS
MAKES: 3 SERVINGS

- 1 **can (14½ ounces) beef broth**
- ⅓ **cup tomato paste**
- 2 **tablespoons brown sugar**
- 2 **tablespoons orange juice concentrate**
- 2 **tablespoons soy sauce**
- 2 **garlic cloves, minced**
- ½ **teaspoon salt**
- ¼ **teaspoon pepper**
- ⅛ **teaspoon ground allspice**
- 1 **domestic duck (4 to 4½ pounds), skinned, deboned and cut into cubes**
- ¼ **pound sliced fresh mushrooms**
- ½ **cup green pepper strips (¼ in. thick)**
- 1 **tablespoon butter**
- 3 **tablespoons cornstarch**
- ¼ **teaspoon ground ginger**
- ¼ **cup 2% milk**
- 1 **can (11 ounces) mandarin oranges, drained**
    Hot cooked rice, optional

1. For marinade, in a small bowl, combine the first nine ingredients. Pour ¾ cup into a large resealable plastic bag; add the duck. Seal bag and turn to coat; refrigerate for 8 hours. Cover and refrigerate remaining marinade.

2. Drain and discard marinade. Transfer duck to a 1½-qt. slow cooker; add reserved marinade. Cover and cook on low for 4-5 hours or until tender. Skim fat.

3. In a small saucepan, saute mushrooms and green pepper in butter. Combine the cornstarch, ginger and milk until smooth. Stir into mushroom mixture; add to slow cooker.

4. Cover and cook on high for 45 minutes or until sauce is thickened. Just before serving, stir in oranges. Serve with rice if desired.

FRENCH ONION PORTOBELLO BRISKET

French Onion Portobello Brisket

I use this recipe when I go to winter potlucks and want something everyone will love. Though I have seen some kids who will scrape away the mushrooms and onion, they still rave about how the meat tastes and gobble it right up!

—**AYSHA SCHURMAN** AMMON, ID

PREP: 20 MIN. • **COOK:** 8 HOURS • **MAKES:** 9 SERVINGS

- 1   fresh beef brisket (4 pounds)
- 1¾ cups sliced baby portobello mushrooms
- 1   small red onion, sliced
- 2   garlic cloves, minced
- 2   tablespoons butter
- 1   can (10½ ounces) condensed French onion soup
- ¼   cup dry white wine or beef broth
- ½   teaspoon coarsely ground pepper
      Fresh sage, optional

1. Cut brisket in half; place in a 5-qt. slow cooker.
2. In a large saucepan, saute the mushrooms, onion and garlic in butter for 3-5 minutes or until onion is crisp-tender. Add the soup, wine and pepper; mix well.
3. Pour mushroom mixture over beef. Cover and cook on low for 8-10 hours or until meat is tender. Garnish with sage if desired.
NOTE *This is a fresh beef brisket, not corned beef.*

Meaty Slow-Cooked Jambalaya

Sure makes life easy having this wonderful, full-of-flavor dish stashed away in the freezer! Another plus, you throw it all in the crock pot. No skillet necessary.

—**DIANE SMITH** PINE MOUNTAIN, GEORGIA

PREP: 25 MIN. • **COOK:** 7 HOURS
MAKES: 12 SERVINGS (3½ QUARTS)

- 1   can (28 ounces) diced tomatoes, undrained
- 1   cup reduced-sodium chicken broth
- 1   large green pepper, chopped
- 1   medium onion, chopped
- 2   celery ribs, sliced
- ½   cup white wine or additional reduced-sodium chicken broth
- 4   garlic cloves, minced
- 2   teaspoons Cajun seasoning
- 2   teaspoons dried parsley flakes
- 1   teaspoon dried basil
- 1   teaspoon dried oregano
- ¾   teaspoon salt
- ½   to 1 teaspoon cayenne pepper
- 2   pounds boneless skinless chicken thighs, cut into 1-inch pieces
- 1   package (12 ounces) fully cooked andouille or other spicy chicken sausage links
- 2   pounds uncooked medium shrimp, peeled and deveined
- 8   cups hot cooked brown rice

1. In a large bowl, combine the first 13 ingredients. Place chicken and sausage in a 6-qt. slow cooker. Pour tomato mixture over top. Cook, covered, on low 7-9 hours or until chicken is tender.
2. Stir in shrimp. Cook, covered, 15-20 minutes longer or until shrimp turn pink. Serve with rice.

ZIPPY SPAGHETTI SAUCE

BEEF WITH RED WINE GRAVY

Beef with Red Wine Gravy

Slow-cooker convenience means you can prep this on a winter morning and come home to a meal that's ready to serve!
—**PRECI D'SILVA** DALLAS, TX

PREP: 10 MIN. • **COOK:** 6¼ HOURS
MAKES: 6 SERVINGS

- **3 pounds beef stew meat, cut into 1-inch cubes**
- **1 pound medium fresh mushrooms, halved**
- **1 medium onion, sliced**
- **1 can (10½ ounces) condensed beef broth, undiluted**
- **1 cup dry red wine**
- **1 envelope brown gravy mix**
- **2 tablespoons tomato paste**
- **¼ teaspoon salt**
- **1 bay leaf**
- **¼ cup cornstarch**
- **¼ cup cold water**
- **Hot cooked egg noodles**

1. Place the beef, mushrooms and onion in a 5-qt. slow cooker. In a small bowl, combine the broth, wine, gravy mix, tomato paste, salt and bay leaf. Pour over top.
2. Cover and cook on low for 6-7 hours or until beef is tender. Discard bay leaf.
3. Combine cornstarch and water until smooth; stir into meat mixture. Cover and cook on high for 15 minutes or until thickened. Serve with noodles.

Cranberry Chicken

I love to collect cookbooks and try new recipes. Here's a favorite that's delicious, easy and especially good when served with rice and a side vegetable.
—**EDITH HOLLIDAY** FLUSHING, MI

PREP: 10 MIN. • **COOK:** 5 HOURS
MAKES: 6 SERVINGS

- **1 broiler/fryer chicken (3 to 4 pounds), cut up**
- **1 can (14 ounces) whole-berry cranberry sauce**
- **1 cup barbecue sauce**
- **1 small onion, finely chopped**
- **1 celery rib, finely chopped**
- **½ teaspoon salt**
- **¼ teaspoon pepper**
- **Hot cooked rice**

Place chicken in a 3-qt. slow cooker. In a small bowl, combine the cranberry sauce, barbecue sauce, onion, celery, salt and pepper; pour over chicken. Cover and cook on low for 5-6 hours or until chicken is tender. Serve with rice.

Sweet and Sour Brisket

Here's one dish that never gets old in our house. We'd eat it every night if we could!
—**JOLIE ALBERTAZZIE** MORENO VALLEY, CA

PREP: 15 MIN. • **COOK:** 8 HOURS
MAKES: 10 SERVINGS

- **1 can (28 ounces) crushed tomatoes**
- **1 medium onion, halved and thinly sliced**
- **½ cup raisins**
- **¼ cup packed brown sugar**
- **2 tablespoons lemon juice**
- **3 garlic cloves, minced**
- **1 fresh beef brisket (3 pounds)**
- **½ teaspoon salt**
- **¼ teaspoon pepper**

1. In a small bowl, combine the tomatoes, onion, raisins, brown sugar, lemon juice and garlic. Pour half into a 4- or 5-qt. slow cooker coated with cooking spray. Sprinkle meat with salt and pepper. Transfer to slow cooker. Top with remaining tomato mixture. Cover and cook on low for 8-10 hours or until meat is tender.
2. Remove brisket to a serving platter and keep warm. Skim fat from cooking juices. Thinly slice meat across the grain. Serve with tomato mixture.
NOTE *This is a fresh beef brisket, not corned beef.*

SWEET AND SOUR BRISKET

EDITH HOLLIDAY'S
CRANBERRY CHICKEN

Slow-Cooked Asian Chicken

It's so nice to find new, tasty ways to serve chicken. I prepare this often for both family and guests. Tender chicken is treated to a slightly sweet sauce and crunchy almonds in this no-fuss dish.
—**RUTH SEITZ** COLUMBUS JUNCTION, IA

PREP: 20 MIN. • **COOK:** 5 HOURS • **MAKES:** 4-6 SERVINGS

- 1 broiler/fryer chicken (3 to 4 pounds), cut up
- 2 tablespoons canola oil
- ⅓ cup soy sauce
- 2 tablespoons brown sugar
- 2 tablespoons water
- 1 garlic clove, minced
- 1 teaspoon ground ginger
- ¼ cup slivered almonds

1. In a large skillet over medium heat, brown the chicken in oil on all sides. Transfer to a 5-qt. slow cooker. Combine the soy sauce, brown sugar, water, garlic and ginger; pour over chicken.

2. Cover and cook on low for 5-6 hours or until chicken juices run clear. Remove chicken to a serving platter and sprinkle with almonds.

PARMESAN PORK ROAST

Parmesan Pork Roast

Fantastic sweet-and-savory flavor comes together with just a few pantry staples in this easy dinner.
—**KAREN WARNER** LOUISVILLE, OH

PREP: 15 MIN. • **COOK:** 5½ HOURS • **MAKES:** 10 SERVINGS

- 1 boneless whole pork loin roast (4 pounds)
- ⅔ cup grated Parmesan cheese
- ½ cup honey
- 3 tablespoons soy sauce
- 2 tablespoons dried basil
- 2 tablespoons minced garlic
- 2 tablespoons olive oil
- ½ teaspoon salt
- 2 tablespoons cornstarch
- ¼ cup cold water

1. Cut roast in half. Transfer to a 3-qt. slow cooker. In a small bowl, combine the cheese, honey, soy sauce, basil, garlic, oil and salt; pour over pork. Cover and cook on low for 5½ to 6 hours or until a thermometer reads 160°.

2. Remove meat to a serving platter; keep warm. Skim fat from cooking juices; transfer to a small saucepan. Bring liquid to a boil. Combine cornstarch and water until smooth. Gradually stir into pan. Bring to a boil; cook and stir for 2 minutes or until thickened. Slice roast; serve with gravy.

SLOW-COOKED ASIAN CHICKEN

ITALIAN CHICKEN CHARDONNAY

Italian Chicken Chardonnay

One day, I needed to have dinner ready when we walked in the door after work and school, so I altered a skillet dish to make this delicious slow cooker meal. It's perfect for a weeknight but nice enough for company, too.

—JUDY ARMSTRONG PRAIRIEVILLE, LA

PREP: 20 MIN. • **COOK:** 5 HOURS • **MAKES:** 6 SERVINGS

- 2 teaspoons paprika
- 1 teaspoon salt
- 1 teaspoon pepper
- ¼ teaspoon cayenne pepper
- 3 pounds bone-in chicken breast halves, skin removed
- ½ pound baby portobello mushrooms, quartered
- 1 medium sweet red pepper, chopped
- 1 medium onion, chopped
- 1 can (14 ounces) water-packed artichoke hearts, rinsed and drained

- 1½ cups chardonnay
- 1 can (6 ounces) tomato paste
- 3 garlic cloves, minced
- 2 tablespoons minced fresh thyme or 2 teaspoons dried thyme
- ¼ cup minced fresh parsley
  Hot cooked pasta
  Shredded Romano cheese

1. Combine the paprika, salt, pepper and cayenne; sprinkle over chicken. Place the chicken, mushrooms, red pepper, onion and artichokes in a 5-qt. slow cooker. In a small bowl, combine the chardonnay, tomato paste, garlic and thyme; pour over vegetables.

2. Cover and cook on low for 5-6 hours or until chicken is tender. Stir in parsley. Serve with pasta; sprinkle with cheese.

SLOW-COOKED LASAGNA

Slow-Cooked Lasagna

My scrumptious version of lasagna is made super-easy in a slow cooker. The finished dish cuts really well! I also like that it makes a smaller batch than most lasagnas so leftovers aren't an issue.

—REBECCA O'BRYAN ALVATON, KY

PREP: 45 MIN. • **COOK:** 4¼ HOURS + STANDING
MAKES: 6 SERVINGS

- 1 **pound ground beef**
- 1 **medium green pepper, chopped**
- 1 **medium onion, chopped**
- 1 **jar (24 ounces) herb and garlic pasta sauce**
- 4 **cups (16 ounces) shredded part-skim mozzarella cheese**
- 1 **carton (15 ounces) ricotta cheese**
- 1 **tablespoon Italian seasoning**
- ½ **teaspoon garlic powder**
- ½ **teaspoon salt**
- ¼ **teaspoon pepper**
- 4 **no-cook lasagna noodles**
- 2 **tablespoons shredded Parmesan cheese**

1. In a large skillet, cook the beef, green pepper and onion over medium heat until meat is no longer pink; drain. Stir in pasta sauce; heat through. In a large bowl, combine the mozzarella and ricotta cheeses, Italian seasoning, garlic powder, salt and pepper.

2. Spread 1 cup meat sauce in an oval 3-qt. slow cooker. Break one lasagna noodle into three pieces. Layer 1⅓ noodles over sauce, breaking noodles to fit as necessary. Top with ⅔ cup meat sauce and 1⅓ cups cheese mixture. Repeat layers twice. Top with remaining sauce.

3. Cover and cook on low for 4-5 hours or until noodles are tender. Sprinkle with Parmesan cheese. Cover and cook 15 minutes longer. Let stand for 10 minutes before cutting.

Stout & Honey Beef Roast

Here's a heartwarming meal that's ideal for cold days and hectic nights. Honey, beer and seasonings make the sauce different and oh, so good!

—TASTE OF HOME TEST KITCHEN

PREP: 15 MIN. • **COOK:** 8 HOURS
MAKES: 4 SERVINGS PLUS LEFTOVERS

- 8 **small red potatoes**
- 4 **medium carrots, cut into 1-inch pieces**
- 2 **medium onions, quartered**
- 1 **boneless beef chuck roast (4 pounds), trimmed**
- 1 **can (14½ ounces) beef broth**
- 1 **cup stout beer or additional beef broth**
- ½ **cup honey**
- 3 **garlic cloves, minced**
- 1 **teaspoon dried marjoram**
- 1 **teaspoon dried thyme**
- ½ **teaspoon salt**
- ½ **teaspoon pepper**
- ¼ **teaspoon ground cinnamon**
- 2 **tablespoons cornstarch**
- ¼ **cup cold water**

1. Place the potatoes, carrots and onions in a 5-qt. slow cooker. Cut roast in half; transfer to slow cooker. In a small bowl, combine the broth, beer, honey, garlic, marjoram, thyme, salt, pepper and cinnamon; pour over top. Cover and cook on low for 8-10 hours or until the meat and vegetables are tender.

2. Remove roast and cut a portion of the meat into cubes, measuring 2 cups; cover and save for another use. Slice the remaining beef and keep warm. Strain cooking juices, reserving vegetables and 1 cup juices; skim fat from reserved juices.

3. Transfer to a small saucepan. Bring to a boil. Combine cornstarch and water until smooth; gradually stir into the pan. Bring to a boil; cook and stir for 2 minutes or until thickened. Serve with beef and vegetables.

STOUT & HONEY BEEF ROAST

Bavarian Pork Loin

I got the recipe for this tender pork roast from an aunt, who made it all the time. It's a delicious taste sensation with sauerkraut, carrots, onions and apples.

—**EDIE DESPAIN** LOGAN, UTAH

PREP: 25 MIN. • **COOK:** 6 HOURS + STANDING
MAKES: 10 SERVINGS

- 1 **boneless pork loin roast (3 to 4 pounds)**
- 1 **can (14 ounces) Bavarian sauerkraut, rinsed and drained**
- 1¾ **cups chopped carrots**
- 1 **large onion, finely chopped**
- ½ **cup unsweetened apple juice**
- 2 **teaspoons dried parsley flakes**
- 3 **large tart apples, peeled and quartered**

1. Cut roast in half; place in a 5-qt. slow cooker. In a small bowl, combine the sauerkraut, carrots, onion, apple juice and parsley; spoon over roast. Cover and cook on low for 4 hours.

2. Add apples to slow cooker. Cover and cook 2-3 hours longer or until meat is tender. Remove roast; let stand for 10 minutes before slicing. Serve with sauerkraut mixture.

STOVETOP BAVARIAN PORK LOIN

Cut roast in half. In a Dutch oven coated with cooking spray, brown roast on all sides. Combine the sauerkraut, carrots, onion, ¾ cup apple juice and parsley; spoon over roast. Bring to a boil. Reduce heat; cover and simmer for 1 hour. Stir in apples. Cover and simmer 20-25 minutes longer or until the apples are tender and a meat thermometer reads 160°. Serve as directed.

top tip · Chef's Secret

To quickly chop an onion, peel and cut in half from the root to the top. Leaving root attached, place flat side down on work surface. Cut vertically through the onion, leaving the root end uncut.

Cut across the onion, discarding root end. The closer the cuts, the finer the onion will be chopped. This method can also be used for shallots.

BAVARIAN PORK LOIN

SLOW-COOKED PORK VERDE

Slow-Cooked Pork Verde

Comforting and hearty, this midweek entree is perfect winter fare. Serve it with French bread and a green salad for a well-rounded supper.

—TASTE OF HOME TEST KITCHEN

PREP: 15 MIN. • **COOK:** 4½ HOURS
MAKES: 8 SERVINGS

- 3 medium carrots, sliced
- 1 boneless pork shoulder butt roast (3 to 4 pounds)
- 1 can (15 ounces) black beans, rinsed and drained
- 1 can (10 ounces) green enchilada sauce
- ¼ cup minced fresh cilantro
- 1 tablespoon cornstarch
- ¼ cup cold water
  Hot cooked rice

1. Place carrots in a 5-qt. slow cooker. Cut roast in half; place in slow cooker. Add the beans, enchilada sauce and cilantro. Cover and cook on low for 4½ to 5 hours or until a thermometer reads 160°. Remove roast to a serving platter; keep warm.
2. Skim fat from cooking juices. Transfer the cooking liquid, carrots and beans to a small saucepan. Bring to a boil. Combine cornstarch and water until smooth. Gradually stir into the pan. Bring to a boil; cook and stir for 2 minutes or until thickened. Serve with meat and rice.

Moist Italian Turkey Breast

This recipe renders some of the juiciest turkey I have ever eaten! High in lean protein, it's a wonderfully smart entree for a special occasion.

—JESSICA KUNZ SPRINGFIELD, IL

PREP: 25 MIN. • **COOK:** 5 HOURS + STANDING
MAKES: 12 SERVINGS

- 1 pound medium carrots, cut into 2-inch pieces
- 2 medium onions, cut into wedges
- 3 celery ribs, cut into 2-inch pieces
- 1 can (14½ ounces) chicken broth
- 1 bone-in turkey breast (6 to 7 pounds), thawed and skin removed
- 2 tablespoons olive oil
- 1½ teaspoons seasoned salt
- 1 teaspoon Italian seasoning
- ½ teaspoon pepper

1. In a 6- or 7-qt. slow cooker, combine the carrots, onions, celery and broth. Place turkey in slow cooker. Brush with oil. Sprinkle with seasoned salt, Italian seasoning and pepper.
2. Cover and cook on low for 5-6 hours or until the meat is tender. Let stand for 15 minutes before slicing. Serve with vegetables.

Sloppy Joe Supper

Here's an easy way to serve up the flavor of sloppy joes in a one-dish dinner. It's great to come home to this simmering away in the slow cooker.

—KARLA WIEDERHOLT CUBA CITY, WI

PREP: 15 MIN. • **COOK:** 4 HOURS
MAKES: 8 SERVINGS

- 1 package (32 ounces) frozen shredded hash brown potatoes, thawed
- 1 can (10¾ ounces) condensed cheddar cheese soup, undiluted
- 1 egg, lightly beaten
- 1 teaspoon salt
- ½ teaspoon pepper
- 2 pounds ground beef
- 2 tablespoons finely chopped onion
- 1 can (15½ ounces) sloppy joe sauce

1. In a large bowl, combine the potatoes, soup, egg, salt and pepper. Spread into a lightly greased 5-qt. slow cooker. In a large skillet, cook beef and onion over medium heat until meat is no longer pink; drain. Stir in sloppy joe sauce. Spoon over potato mixture.
2. Cover and cook on low for 4 to 4½ hours or until a thermometer reads 160°.

SLOPPY JOE SUPPER

Family-Favorite Spaghetti Sauce

My friend Mary shared this wonderful recipe for spaghetti sauce that's become an annual tradition at our campers' potluck.

—HELEN ROWE SPRING LAKE, MI

PREP: 30 MIN. • **COOK:** 6 HOURS
MAKES: 9 SERVINGS (2¼ QUARTS)

- 1   pound bulk Italian sausage
- ½   pound ground beef
- 1   large onion, chopped
- 1   celery rib, chopped
- 3   garlic cloves, minced
- 1   tablespoon olive oil
- 1   can (28 ounces) diced tomatoes
- 1   can (10¾ ounces) condensed tomato soup, undiluted
- 1   can (8 ounces) mushroom stems and pieces, drained
- 1   can (8 ounces) tomato sauce
- 1   can (6 ounces) tomato paste
- 1   tablespoon sugar
- ½   teaspoon pepper
- ½   teaspoon dried basil
- ¼   teaspoon dried oregano
     Hot cooked spaghetti

1. In a large skillet, cook the sausage, beef, onion, celery and garlic in oil over medium heat until meat is no longer pink; drain. In a 4-qt. slow cooker, combine the diced tomatoes, tomato soup, mushrooms, tomato sauce, tomato paste, sugar and seasonings. Stir in sausage mixture.

2. Cover and cook on low for 6-8 hours or until flavors are blended. Serve with spaghetti.

FAMILY-FAVORITE SPAGHETTI SAUCE

NO-FUSS BEEF ROAST

⑤INGREDIENTS No-Fuss Beef Roast

Just a few ingredients are all you'll need for this tangy roast that feeds a bunch. The gravy is tasty on mashed potatoes, too.

—JEANIE BEASLEY TUPELO, MS

PREP: 10 MIN. • **COOK:** 6 HOURS • **MAKES:** 8 SERVINGS

- 1   boneless beef chuck roast (3 to 4 pounds)
- 1   can (14½ ounces) stewed tomatoes, cut up
- 1   can (10¾ ounces) condensed cream of mushroom soup, undiluted
- 1   envelope Lipton beefy onion soup mix
- ¼   cup cornstarch
- ½   cup cold water

1. Cut roast in half. Transfer to a 5-qt. slow cooker. In a small bowl, combine the tomatoes, soup and soup mix; pour over meat. Cover and cook on low for 6-8 hours or until the meat is tender.

2. Remove meat to a serving platter; keep warm. Skim fat from cooking juices; transfer to a large saucepan. Bring liquid to a boil. Combine cornstarch and water until smooth; stir into the pan. Bring to a boil; cook and stir for 2 minutes or until thickened. Serve with roast.

ENTREES

Winter

Spinach & Feta Stuffed Flank Steak

If you're looking for a main dish recipe for the slow cooker that offers an upscale feel, this one is a great choice. Elegant enough for company, the rolled flank steak looks so pretty on a plate.

—STEVEN SCHEND GRAND RAPIDS, MI

PREP: 30 MIN. • **COOK:** 6 HOURS • **MAKES:** 6 SERVINGS

- 1 beef flank steak (1½ pounds)
- 2 cups (8 ounces) crumbled feta cheese
- 3 cups fresh baby spinach
- ½ cup oil-packed sun-dried tomatoes, drained and chopped
- ½ cup finely chopped onion
- 5 tablespoons all-purpose flour, divided
- ½ teaspoon salt
- ½ teaspoon pepper
- 2 tablespoons canola oil
- 1 cup beef broth
- 1 tablespoon Worcestershire sauce
- 2 teaspoons tomato paste
- ⅓ cup dry red wine or additional beef broth
  Hot cooked egg noodles, optional

1. Cut steak horizontally from the long side to within ½ in. of opposite side. Open steak so it lies flat; cover with plastic wrap. Flatten to ½-in. thickness. Remove plastic.

SPINACH & FETA STUFFED FLANK STEAK

2. Sprinkle 1 cup cheese over steak to within 1 in. of edges. Layer with spinach, tomatoes, onion and remaining cheese. Roll up jelly-roll style, starting with a long side; tie with kitchen string. Sprinkle steak with 2 tablespoons flour, salt and pepper.

3. In a large skillet, brown steak in oil; drain. Transfer to an oval 6-qt. slow cooker. Combine the broth, Worcestershire sauce and tomato paste; pour over steak. Cover and cook on low for 6-8 hours or until beef is tender.

4. Remove meat to a serving platter; keep warm. Skim fat from cooking juices; transfer to a small saucepan. Bring liquid to a boil. Combine remaining flour and wine until smooth. Gradually stir into the pan. Bring to a boil; cook and stir for 2 minutes or until thickened. Serve with sliced beef and noodles if desired.

Slow-Cooked Goose

My husband and I own a hunting lodge and host about 16 hunters a week at our camp. The slow cooker makes easy work of fixing this flavorful goose dish, which is a favorite of our guests. The recipe makes lots of savory gravy.

—EDNA YLIOJA LUCKY LAKE, SK

PREP: 20 MIN. + MARINATING • **COOK:** 4 HOURS
MAKES: 4 SERVINGS

- ½ cup soy sauce
- 4 teaspoons canola oil
- 4 teaspoons lemon juice
- 2 teaspoons Worcestershire sauce
- 1 teaspoon garlic powder
- 2 pounds cubed goose breast
- ¾ to 1 cup all-purpose flour
- ¼ cup butter, cubed
- 1 can (10¾ ounces) condensed golden mushroom soup, undiluted
- 1⅓ cups water
- 1 envelope onion soup mix
  Hot cooked mashed potatoes, noodles or rice

1. In a large resealable plastic bag, combine the soy sauce, oil, lemon juice, Worcestershire sauce and garlic powder; add goose. Seal and turn to coat. Refrigerate for 4 hours or overnight.

2. Drain and discard marinade. Place flour in another large resealable plastic bag; add goose in batches and shake to coat. In a large skillet over medium heat, brown goose in butter on all sides.

3. Transfer to a 3-qt. slow cooker. Add the soup, water and soup mix. Cover and cook on high for 4-5 hours or until meat is tender. Serve with potatoes, noodles or rice.

Beef with Red Sauce

Here, a homemade rub spices up tender beef, while tomatoes and gingersnaps add an interesting flavor boost to the sauce. You can substitute graham crackers for the cookies if you'd like.

—LAURIE TIETZE LONGVIEW, TX

PREP: 25 MIN. • **COOK:** 8 HOURS • **MAKES:** 8 SERVINGS

- 2 **tablespoons canola oil**
- 2 **tablespoons baking cocoa**
- 1 **tablespoon chili powder**
- 2 **teaspoons dried oregano**
- 1 **teaspoon salt**
- 1 **teaspoon pepper**
- 1 **teaspoon ground cumin**
- ½ **teaspoon ground cloves**
- ½ **teaspoon ground cinnamon**
- 1 **beef rump roast or bottom round roast (3 pounds), cut into 1½-in. cubes**
- 1 **large onion, chopped**
- 1 **can (28 ounces) whole tomatoes, undrained**
- 3 **tablespoons cider vinegar**
- 1½ **cups crushed gingersnap cookies (about 30 cookies)**
- 9 **garlic cloves, peeled**
- 1 **tablespoon sugar**
  Hot cooked noodles, rice or mashed potatoes

1. In a small bowl, combine the first nine ingredients; set mixture aside.

2. Place beef and onion in a 4-qt. slow cooker; rub beef with spice mixture. Pour tomatoes over the top; sprinkle with vinegar, gingersnaps and garlic. Cover and cook on low for 8-10 hours or until the meat is tender. Stir in sugar. Serve with noodles.

BEEF WITH RED SAUCE

German-Style Beef Roast

My grandmother used to make this, and I adapted it for the slow cooker. You'll love its convenience as much as its flavor.
—**LOIS STANLEY** MYRTLE BEACH, SC

PREP: 10 MIN. • **COOK:** 8 HOURS • **MAKES:** 10 SERVINGS

- 1 **boneless beef chuck roast (4 pounds), trimmed**
- 1 **teaspoon pepper**
- 1 **large onion, thinly sliced**
- 1 **bottle (12 ounces) beer or nonalcoholic beer**
- 1 **cup ketchup**
- ¼ **cup packed brown sugar**
- ¼ **cup all-purpose flour**
- ¼ **cup cold water**

1. Cut roast in half; sprinkle with pepper. Place onion and roast in a 5-qt. slow cooker. In a small bowl, combine the beer, ketchup and brown sugar; pour over top. Cover and cook on low for 8-10 hours or until meat is tender.

2. Remove meat to a serving platter; keep warm. Skim fat from cooking juices; transfer to a small saucepan. Bring liquid to a boil.

3. Combine flour and water until smooth; gradually stir into the pan. Bring to a boil; cook and stir for 2 minutes or until thickened. Serve with roast.

SAVORY PORK CHOPS

GERMAN-STYLE BEEF ROAST

Savory Pork Chops

These chops turn out nice and tender, and fall apart easily after being slow cooked. The light tomato sauce is lovely over rice.
—**LEA ANN SCHALK** GARFIELD, AR

PREP: 20 MIN. • **COOK:** 5 HOURS • **MAKES:** 6 SERVINGS

- 6 **bone-in pork loin chops (8 ounces each)**
- 1 **tablespoon canola oil**
- 1 **large onion, sliced**
- 1 **medium sweet red pepper, cut into rings**
- 1 **can (4 ounces) mushroom stems and pieces, drained**
- 1 **can (28 ounces) diced tomatoes, undrained**
- 1 **tablespoon brown sugar**
- 1 **tablespoon balsamic vinegar**
- 2 **teaspoons Worcestershire sauce**
- ¼ **teaspoon salt**
- ¼ **teaspoon pepper**
  Hot cooked rice

1. In a large skillet, brown chops in oil in batches; drain. Transfer to a 5-qt. slow cooker. Layer with onion, red pepper and mushrooms. Combine the tomatoes, brown sugar, vinegar, Worcestershire sauce, salt and pepper; pour over the vegetables.

2. Cover and cook on low for 5-6 hours or until meat is tender. Serve with rice.

CHICKEN WITH BEANS AND POTATOES

Gingered Short Ribs

Here is a wonderful dish made with meaty short ribs, cabbage, carrots and scallions. It makes a complete meal that is both rich and robust.

—MARIE RIZZIO INTERLOCHEN, MI

PREP: 25 MIN. • **COOK:** 7 HOURS
MAKES: 4 SERVINGS

- 4 pounds bone-in beef short ribs
- 2 medium parsnips, peeled and halved widthwise
- 2 large carrots, halved widthwise
- ½ cup reduced-sodium soy sauce
- ⅓ cup packed brown sugar
- ¼ cup rice vinegar
- 1 tablespoon minced fresh gingerroot
- 2 garlic cloves, minced
- ½ teaspoon crushed red pepper flakes
- 1 small head cabbage, quartered
- 2 tablespoons cornstarch
- 2 tablespoons cold water
- 2 teaspoons sesame oil
- 4 green onions, thinly sliced
  Hot cooked couscous, optional

1. Place the ribs, parsnips and carrots in a 5- or 6-qt. slow cooker. In a small bowl, combine the soy sauce, brown sugar, vinegar, ginger, garlic and pepper flakes; pour over ribs. Top with cabbage. Cover and cook on low for 7-8 hours or until meat is tender.
2. Remove meat and vegetables to a serving platter; keep warm. Skim fat from cooking juices; transfer to a small saucepan. Bring liquid to a boil. Combine cornstarch and water until smooth. Gradually stir into the pan. Bring to a boil; cook and stir for 2 minutes or until thickened.
3. Stir in sesame oil. Serve with meat and vegetables. Sprinkle with green onions. Serve with couscous if desired.

Chicken with Beans and Potatoes

This all-in-one entree is great to make when your afternoon is going to be busy. The veggies and a little onion soup mix give the broth so much flavor.

—TASTE OF HOME TEST KITCHEN

PREP: 20 MIN. • **COOK:** 4 HOURS
MAKES: 10 SERVINGS

- 2 pounds boneless skinless chicken breasts, cut into 1-inch cubes
- ½ teaspoon lemon-pepper seasoning
- 1 tablespoon canola oil
- 1 pound fresh green beans, trimmed
- 1 pound small red potatoes, quartered
- ½ pound medium fresh mushrooms, halved
- ½ cup thinly sliced sweet onion
- 2 cans (14½ ounces each) chicken broth
- 2 tablespoons onion soup mix
- 2 teaspoons Worcestershire sauce
- 1 teaspoon grated lemon peel
- ½ teaspoon salt
- ½ teaspoon pepper
- ¼ teaspoon garlic powder

1. Sprinkle the chicken with the lemon-pepper. In a large skillet, cook chicken in oil over medium heat for 4-5 minutes or until lightly browned.
2. In a 5- or 6-qt. slow cooker, layer the green beans, potatoes, mushrooms and onion. In a small bowl, combine the remaining ingredients; pour over vegetables. Top with chicken.
3. Cover and cook on low for 4-5 hours or until vegetables are tender. Serve with a slotted spoon.

MARIE RIZZIO'S
GINGERED SHORT RIBS

Tuscan-Style Chicken

I found this Italian-style chicken recipe in a magazine and tweaked it to my family's tastes. I have taken it to potlucks and served it at dinner parties, and no one ever guesses that it's made in the slow cooker! I serve the chicken with crusty bread and a spinach salad with lemon vinaigrette.

—MARY WATKINS LITTLE ELM, TX

PREP: 25 MIN. • **COOK:** 6 HOURS • **MAKES:** 4 SERVINGS

- 2 cans (14½ ounces each) Italian stewed tomatoes, undrained
- 10 small red potatoes (about 1 pound), quartered
- 1 medium onion, chopped
- 1 can (6 ounces) tomato paste
- 2 fresh rosemary sprigs
- 4 garlic cloves, minced
- 1 teaspoon olive oil
- ½ teaspoon dried basil
- 1 teaspoon Italian seasoning, divided
- 1 broiler/fryer chicken (3 to 4 pounds), cut up and skin removed
- ½ teaspoon salt
- ½ teaspoon pepper
- 1 jar (5¾ ounces) pimiento-stuffed olives, drained

1. In a 5-qt. slow cooker, combine the first eight ingredients. Stir in ½ teaspoon Italian seasoning. Place chicken on top. Sprinkle with salt, pepper and remaining Italian seasoning. Top with olives.

2. Cover and cook on low for 6-7 hours or until chicken is tender. Discard rosemary sprigs before serving.

Cider-Glazed Ham

Here is a heartwarming and classic way to serve ham. Apple cider and mustard perfectly accent the rich, smoky flavor of the ham.

—JENNIFER FOOS-FURER MARYSVILLE, OH

PREP: 15 MIN. • **COOK:** 4 HOURS • **MAKES:** 8 SERVINGS

- 1 boneless fully cooked ham (3 pounds)
- 1¾ cups apple cider or juice
- ¼ cup packed brown sugar
- ¼ cup Dijon mustard
- ¼ cup honey
- 2 tablespoons cornstarch
- 2 tablespoons cold water

1. Place ham in a 5-qt. slow cooker. In a small bowl, combine the cider, brown sugar, mustard and honey; pour over ham. Cover and cook on low for 4-5 hours or until heated through. Remove ham and keep warm.

2. Pour cooking juices into a small saucepan. Combine cornstarch and water until smooth; stir into cooking juices. Bring to a boil; cook and stir for 2 minutes or until thickened. Serve with the ham.

BAKED CIDER-GLAZED HAM *Place ham on a rack in a shallow roasting pan. Score the surface of the ham, making diamond shapes ½ in. deep. Pour cider over ham. Combine the brown sugar, mustard and honey; spread over ham. Cover and bake at 325° for 45 minutes. Uncover; bake 15-30 minutes longer or until a thermometer reads 140°, basting occasionally. Serve as directed.*

Orange-Glazed Ham *Substitute orange juice for the apple cider.*

TUSCAN-STYLE CHICKEN

top tip — Fast Fixes

Everyone loves a ham sandwich made with the full-flavored leftovers from a ham dinner. But why not get creative with those extras? You can use up leftover ham easily without much fuss.

Dice the ham and add it to your favorite mac-and-cheese recipe or stir it into a can of prepared cream of potato soup or clam chowder. Use the extras to top a baked potato or combine the ham with scrambled eggs in the morning. Top a purchased pizza crust with red sauce, ham, pineapple and cheese for an instant Hawaiian delight or toss cooked ham with pasta and a jarred white sauce for a fast dinner when time is tight.

ROSEMARY MUSHROOM CHICKEN

Rosemary Mushroom Chicken

A delicate hint of rosemary lightly seasons the rich, creamy mushroom gravy in my savory entree. Cooking the chicken and gravy together pares so much time off the dinner rush. Add noodles or rice for a complete and filling supper.

—**GENNY MONCHAMP** REDDING, CA

PREP: 30 MIN. • **COOK:** 7 HOURS •**MAKES:** 6 SERVINGS

- 6 **chicken leg quarters, skin removed**
- 2 **cups sliced fresh mushrooms**
- 2 **cans (10¾ ounces each) condensed cream of mushroom soup, undiluted**
- ½ **cup white wine or chicken broth**
- 1 **teaspoon garlic salt**
- 1 **teaspoon dried rosemary, crushed**
- ½ **teaspoon paprika**
- ⅛ **teaspoon pepper**
  Hot cooked egg noodles

Place chicken in a 5- or 6-qt. slow cooker coated with cooking spray; top with mushrooms. Combine the soup, wine, garlic salt, rosemary, paprika and pepper; pour over top. Cover and cook on low for 7-9 hours or until chicken is tender. Serve with noodles.

CRANBERRY-DIJON PORK ROAST

2 tablespoons all-purpose flour
½ teaspoon salt
½ teaspoon pepper
¼ teaspoon chili powder
2 Cornish game hens
   (20 to 24 ounces each), thawed
1 tablespoon olive oil
1 can (14½ ounces) reduced-sodium
   chicken broth
2 cups cubed peeled eggplant
2 large tomatoes, cut into wedges
   and seeded
2 cups sliced baby portobello
   mushrooms
1 medium onion, sliced
1 medium green pepper, chopped
1 garlic clove, minced
1 bay leaf
2 cups hot cooked couscous

1. In a large resealable plastic bag, combine the flour, salt, pepper and chili powder. Add hens, one at a time, and shake to coat. In a large skillet, brown hens in oil on all sides.
2. Transfer to a 5- or 6-qt. slow cooker. Add broth to the skillet, stirring to loosen browned bits from pan. Bring to a boil. Reduce heat; simmer, uncovered, for 1-2 minutes. Add to the slow cooker.
3. Stir in the eggplant, tomatoes, mushrooms, onion, green pepper, garlic and bay leaf. Cover and cook on low for 3-4 hours or until a thermometer reads 180° and the vegetables are tender. Discard bay leaf. To serve, split hens in half. Serve with couscous and vegetables.

⑤INGREDIENTS Cranberry-Dijon Pork Roast

Five everyday ingredients are all you need for my sweet and tangy pork roast.
—**MARY-ELLEN STEELE** BRISTOL, CT

PREP: 15 MIN.
COOK: 4 HOURS + STANDING
MAKES: 6 SERVINGS

1 boneless pork loin roast
   (2 to 3 pounds)
2 tablespoons butter
1 envelope golden onion soup mix
1 can (14 ounces) whole-berry
   cranberry sauce
2 teaspoons Dijon mustard

1. In a large skillet, brown roast in butter on all sides. Transfer to a 5-qt. slow cooker; sprinkle with soup mix.

Add cranberry sauce to skillet, stirring to loosen browned bits from pan. Pour over roast.
2. Cover and cook on low for 4-5 hours or until meat is tender. Remove the roast to a serving platter; let stand for 10 minutes before slicing. Stir mustard into cooking juices. Serve with roast.

Cornish Game Hens with Couscous

When I invite people to dinner, they often ask if we're going to have this main course. They think I've worked all day in the kitchen, and I don't tell them any different. I suppose my secret's out now!
—**BARBARA LENTO** HOUSTON, PA

PREP: 40 MIN. • **COOK:** 3 HOURS
MAKES: 4 SERVINGS

top tip Slow-Cooking Savvy

When slow cooking a roast heavier than 3 pounds, cut it in half to ensure proper and even cooking. Trim as much fat from the meat before placing it in the slow cooker to avoid greasy gravy. You can add even more flavor to a gravy by first browning the meat in a skillet before setting it in the slow cooker.

Chicken Merlot with Mushrooms

A dear friend who liked cooking as much as I do shared this recipe with me, and I think of her each time I make it. Friends and family love it and request it often.

—**SHELLI MCWILLIAM** SALEM, OR

PREP: 10 MIN. • **COOK:** 5 HOURS
MAKES: 5 SERVINGS

- ¾ **pound sliced fresh mushrooms**
- 1 **large onion, chopped**
- 2 **garlic cloves, minced**
- 3 **pounds boneless skinless chicken thighs**
- 1 **can (6 ounces) tomato paste**
- ¾ **cup chicken broth**
- ¼ **cup merlot or additional chicken broth**
- 2 **tablespoons quick-cooking tapioca**
- 2 **teaspoons sugar**
- 1½ **teaspoons dried basil**
- ½ **teaspoon salt**
- ¼ **teaspoon pepper**
- 2 **tablespoons grated Parmesan cheese**
  Hot cooked pasta, optional

1. Place the mushrooms, onion and garlic in a 5-qt. slow cooker. Top with chicken.

2. In a small bowl, combine the tomato paste, broth, wine, tapioca, sugar, basil, salt and pepper. Pour over chicken. Cover and cook on low for 5-6 hours or until chicken is tender.

3. Sprinkle with cheese. Serve with pasta if desired.

CHICKEN MERLOT MUSHROOM BAKE *In a greased 3-qt. baking dish, combine the mushrooms, onion and garlic. Top with chicken. In a small bowl, combine the tomato paste, broth, wine, tapioca, sugar, basil, salt and pepper; pour over chicken. Cover and bake at 325° for 1¼ to 1½ hours or until the chicken is tender. Proceed as directed.*

CHICKEN MERLOT WITH MUSHROOMS

JANE MCMILLAN'S
TURKEY MEATBALLS AND SAUCE

Turkey Meatballs and Sauce

My sweetie and I have fought the battle of the bulge forever. This is my less-fattening take on meatballs. They're slow-cooker easy, and so flavorful!

—**JANE MCMILLAN** DANIA BEACH, FL

PREP: 40 MIN. • **COOK:** 6 HOURS
MAKES: 8 SERVINGS

- ¼ cup egg substitute
- ½ cup seasoned bread crumbs
- ⅓ cup chopped onion
- ½ teaspoon pepper
- ¼ teaspoon salt-free seasoning blend
- 1½ pounds lean ground turkey

SAUCE

- 1 can (15 ounces) tomato sauce
- 1 can (14½ ounces) diced tomatoes, undrained
- 1 small zucchini, chopped
- 1 medium green pepper, chopped
- 1 medium onion, chopped
- 1 can (6 ounces) tomato paste
- 2 bay leaves
- 2 garlic cloves, minced
- 1 teaspoon dried oregano
- 1 teaspoon dried basil
- 1 teaspoon dried parsley flakes
- ¼ teaspoon crushed red pepper flakes
- ¼ teaspoon pepper
- 1 package (16 ounces) whole wheat spaghetti

1. In a large bowl, combine the egg substitute, bread crumbs, onion, pepper and seasoning blend. Crumble turkey over mixture and mix well. Shape into 1-in. balls; place on a rack coated with cooking spray in a shallow baking pan. Bake at 400° for 15 minutes or until no longer pink.

2. Meanwhile, in a 4- or 5-qt. slow cooker, combine the tomato sauce, tomatoes, zucchini, green pepper, onion, tomato paste, bay leaves, garlic and seasonings. Stir in meatballs. Cover and cook on low for 6 hours. Cook spaghetti according to the package directions; serve with meatballs and sauce.

SPICED CRAN-APPLE BRISKET

Spiced Cran-Apple Brisket

Kids seem to love this recipe the most, although every adult who tastes it becomes an instant fan as well! The apple and cranberry flavors are perfect for the winter season.

—**AYSHA SCHURMAN** AMMON, ID

PREP: 20 MIN. • **COOK:** 8 HOURS
MAKES: 9 SERVINGS

- 1 fresh beef brisket (4 pounds)
- ½ cup apple butter
- ¼ cup ruby port wine
- 2 tablespoons cider vinegar
- 1 teaspoon coarsely ground pepper
- ½ teaspoon salt
- 1 medium tart apple, peeled and cubed
- 1 celery rib, chopped
- 1 small red onion, chopped
- ⅓ cup dried apples, diced
- ⅓ cup dried cranberries
- 2 garlic cloves, minced
- 1 tablespoon cornstarch
- 3 tablespoons cold water

1. Cut brisket in half; place in a 5-quart slow cooker.

2. In a large bowl, combine the apple butter, wine, vinegar, pepper and salt. Stir in the tart apple, celery, onion, dried apples, dried cranberries and garlic. Pour over brisket. Cover and cook on low for 8-10 hours or until meat is tender.

3. Remove meat to a serving platter; keep warm. Skim fat from cooking juices; transfer to a small saucepan. Bring liquid to a boil.

4. Combine cornstarch and water until smooth. Gradually stir into the pan. Bring to a boil; cook and stir for 2 minutes or until thickened. Serve with the meat.

EDITOR'S NOTE *This is a fresh beef brisket, not corned beef. This recipe was tested with commercially prepared apple butter.*

Winter

SOUPS, STEWS & SANDWICHES

This is the ideal season to hunker down and enjoy a bowlful of savory goodness. Come home to a simmering slow cooker of heartwarming soup or stew. Or, enjoy a warm sandwich, piled high with tender beef. This chapter shows you how.

DENISE NYLAND'S EASY ROPA VIEJA STEW

Easy Ropa Vieja Stew

Use your slow cooker for this meaty Cuban classic that offers bold and delicious flavors without a lot of hands-on time.
—**DENISE NYLAND** PANAMA CITY, FL

PREP: 25 MIN. • **COOK:** 6 HOURS • **MAKES:** 8 SERVINGS

- 2 **pounds boneless beef chuck roast, cut in half**
- 2 **tablespoons olive oil**
- 2 **large onions, coarsely chopped**
- 2 **large green peppers, coarsely chopped**
- 4 **jalapeno peppers, seeded and minced**
- 1 **habanero pepper, seeded and minced**
- 3 **cans (14½ ounces each) diced tomatoes, undrained**
- ½ **cup water**
- 6 **garlic cloves, minced**
- 2 **tablespoons minced fresh cilantro**
- 4 **teaspoons beef bouillon granules**
- 2 **teaspoons pepper**
- 1½ **teaspoons ground cumin**
- 1 **teaspoon dried oregano**
- ½ **cup pimiento-stuffed olives, coarsely chopped**
  Hot cooked rice, optional

1. In a large skillet, brown beef in oil on all sides. Transfer meat to a 5-qt. slow cooker. Add onions and peppers. Combine tomatoes, water, garlic, cilantro, beef bouillon, pepper, cumin and oregano; pour over vegetables.
2. Cover and cook on low for 6-8 hours or until meat is tender. Remove beef; cool slightly. Skim fat from cooking juices; stir in olives. Shred beef with two forks and return to slow cooker; heat through. Serve with rice if desired.
NOTE *Wear disposable gloves when cutting hot peppers; the oils can burn skin. Avoid touching your face.*

Wintertime Meatball Soup

If you like, you can vary the vegetables that are added to this soup. For instance, I like to add a bit of chopped jalapeno pepper to my version for some heat, and I serve it with hot corn bread.
—**EUNICE JUSTICE** CODY, WY

PREP: 20 MIN. • **COOK:** 8 HOURS • **MAKES:** 15 SERVINGS (3¾ QUARTS)

- 2 **cans (16 ounces each) chili beans, undrained**
- 2 **cans (14½ ounces each) beef broth**
- 1 **jar (26 ounces) spaghetti sauce**
- ¼ **cup chopped onion**
- 3 **garlic cloves, minced**
- 1 **tablespoon Worcestershire sauce**
- 1 **teaspoon Italian seasoning**
- 1 **package (32 ounces) frozen fully cooked Italian meatballs**
- 1 **package (16 ounces) frozen mixed vegetables**
- 4 **cups chopped cabbage**

In a 6-qt. slow cooker, combine the beans, broth, spaghetti sauce, onion, garlic, Worcestershire sauce and Italian seasoning. Stir in the meatballs, mixed vegetables and cabbage. Cover and cook on low for 8-10 hours or until vegetables are tender.

Barbecued Beef Chili

Served with a hot loaf of bread and a side salad, this slow cooker chili makes a satisfying meal. I was inspired to create the recipe after talking with two friends during a potluck barbecue.

—PHYLLIS SHYAN ELGIN, IL

PREP: 10 MIN. • **COOK:** 6 HOURS • **MAKES:** 12 SERVINGS

- 7 teaspoons chili powder
- 1 tablespoon garlic powder
- 2 teaspoons celery seed
- 1 teaspoon coarsely ground pepper
- ¼ to ½ teaspoon cayenne pepper
- 1 fresh beef brisket (3 to 4 pounds)
- 1 medium green pepper, chopped
- 1 small onion, chopped
- 1 bottle (12 ounces) chili sauce
- 1 cup ketchup
- ½ cup barbecue sauce
- ⅓ cup packed brown sugar
- ¼ cup cider vinegar
- ¼ cup Worcestershire sauce
- 1 teaspoon ground mustard
- 1 can (16 ounces) hot chili beans, undrained
- 1 can (15½ ounces) great northern beans, rinsed and drained

1. Combine the first five ingredients; rub over brisket. Cut into eight pieces; place in a 5-qt. slow cooker. Combine the green pepper, onion, chili sauce, ketchup, barbecue sauce, brown sugar, vinegar, Worcestershire sauce and mustard; pour over meat. Cover and cook on high for 5-6 hours or until meat is tender.

2. Remove meat; cool slightly. Meanwhile, skim fat from cooking juices. Shred meat with two forks; return to slow cooker. Reduce heat to low. Stir in the beans. Cover and cook for 1 hour or until heated through.

NOTE *This is a fresh beef brisket, not corned beef.*

BARBECUED BEEF CHILI

CHILLY NIGHT BEEF STEW

Chilly Night Beef Stew

Hearty and comforting any time of the year, this healthy stew is one of our very favorites.

—JANINE TALBOT SANTAQUIN, UTAH

PREP: 30 MIN. • **COOK:** 8½ HOURS • **MAKES:** 10 SERVINGS

- 6 tablespoons all-purpose flour
- 1½ teaspoons salt, divided
- 1 teaspoon pepper, divided
- 2 pounds beef stew meat
- ¼ cup olive oil
- 4 medium potatoes, peeled and cubed
- 6 medium carrots, sliced
- 2 medium onions, halved and sliced
- 4 celery ribs, sliced
- 2 cans (14½ ounces each) beef broth
- 2 cans (11½ ounces each) V8 juice
- 2 teaspoons Worcestershire sauce
- 6 garlic cloves, minced
- 2 bay leaves
- 1 teaspoon dried thyme
- ½ teaspoon dried basil
- ½ teaspoon paprika
- 6 tablespoons cornstarch
- ½ cup cold water

1. Combine the flour, 1 teaspoon salt and ½ teaspoon pepper in a large resealable plastic bag. Add beef, a few pieces at a time, and shake to coat.

2. Brown beef in oil in batches in a large skillet. Transfer meat and drippings to a 6-qt. slow cooker. Add the potatoes, carrots, onions and celery. Combine the broth, juice, Worcestershire sauce, garlic, bay leaf, thyme, basil, paprika and remaining salt and pepper; pour over top.

3. Cover and cook on low for 8-10 hours or until meat and vegetables are tender. Combine cornstarch and water until smooth; stir into stew. Cover and cook 30 minutes longer or until thickened. Discard bay leaves.

NORTHWOODS STEW

Place beef over vegetables.

2. In a small bowl, combine the soup, wine, tapioca, Italian seasoning, paprika, brown sugar, bouillon and Worcestershire sauce. Pour over the top.

3. Cover and cook on low for 8-10 hours or until meat and vegetables are tender, adding mushrooms during the last hour. Serve with noodles.

Sausage Pumpkin Soup

Here, wintery spices complement pumpkin and sausage for a unique and comforting soup. Maple syrup imparts just a touch of sweetness.

—**LEAH CREMENT** COLLEGE STATION, TX

PREP: 20 MIN. • **COOK:** 3 HOURS 10 MIN.
MAKES: 8 SERVINGS (2 QUARTS)

- 1 **pound bulk pork sausage**
- ⅓ **cup chopped onion**
- 2 **cans (14½ ounces each) chicken broth**
- 1 **can (15 ounces) solid-pack pumpkin**
- ½ **cup maple syrup**
- 1 **teaspoon pumpkin pie spice**
- ½ **teaspoon garlic powder**
- ¼ **teaspoon ground nutmeg**
- 1 **can (12 ounces) evaporated milk**

1. In a large skillet, cook the sausage and onion until sausage is no longer pink; drain.

2. Transfer to a 4-qt. slow cooker. Add the broth, pumpkin, syrup, pie spice, garlic powder and nutmeg. Cover and cook on low for 3-4 hours or until the flavors are blended. Stir in the milk; heat through.

Simple Stand-In

If you rarely use pumpkin pie spice, you may want to make your own instead of buying it. Combine 4 teaspoons ground cinnamon, 2 teaspoons ground ginger, 1 teaspoon ground cloves and ½ teaspoon ground nutmeg. Makes: 7½ teaspoons.

Northwoods Stew

I live in northern Wisconsin, where we appreciate hot and hefty meals during our cold winters. Conveniently prepared in a slow cooker, this beef dish is superb for company.

—**JANICE CHRISTOFFERSON**

EAGLE RIVER, WI

PREP: 30 MIN. • **COOK:** 8 HOURS
MAKES: 11 SERVINGS (2¾ QUARTS)

- 3 **large carrots, cut into 1-inch pieces**
- 3 **celery ribs, cut into 1-inch pieces**
- 1 **large onion, cut into wedges**
- ¼ **cup all-purpose flour**
- ½ **teaspoon salt**
- ¼ **teaspoon pepper**
- 3½ **pounds beef stew meat**

- 1 **can (10¾ ounces) condensed tomato soup, undiluted**
- ½ **cup dry red wine or beef broth**
- 2 **tablespoons quick-cooking tapioca**
- 1 **tablespoon Italian seasoning**
- 1 **tablespoon paprika**
- 1 **tablespoon brown sugar**
- 1 **tablespoon beef bouillon granules**
- 1 **tablespoon Worcestershire sauce**
- ½ **pound sliced baby portobello mushrooms**
  Hot cooked egg noodles

1. Place the carrots, celery and onion in a 5-qt. slow cooker. In a large resealable plastic bag, combine the flour, salt and pepper. Add beef, a few pieces at a time, and shake to coat.

Vegetarian Stew in Bread Bowls

My husband bought a slow cooker after our third baby was born because we didn't have a lot of time to cook. This was our first meal made in it! Make sure all of the vegetables are cut the same size so they cook evenly.

—**MARIA KELLER** ANTIOCH, IL

PREP: 30 MIN. • **COOK:** 8½ HOURS
MAKES: 10 SERVINGS

- 3 cups cubed red potatoes (about 4 medium)
- 2 cups chopped celery (about 4 ribs)
- 2 medium leeks (white portion only), cut into ½-inch pieces
- 1¾ cups coarsely chopped peeled parsnips (about 2 medium)
- 1½ cups chopped carrots (about 3 medium)
- 1 can (28 ounces) Italian crushed tomatoes
- 1 can (14½ ounces) vegetable broth
- 2 teaspoons sugar
- ½ teaspoon salt
- ½ teaspoon dried thyme
- ½ teaspoon dried rosemary, crushed
- 3 tablespoons cornstarch
- 3 tablespoons cold water
- 10 round loaves sourdough bread (8 to 9 ounces each)

1. In a 4- or 5-qt. slow cooker, combine the first 11 ingredients. Cook, covered, on low 8-9 hours or until vegetables are tender.

2. In a small bowl, mix cornstarch and water until smooth. Stir into stew. Cook, covered, on high 30 minutes or until thickened.

3. Cut a thin slice off the top of each bread loaf. Hollow out bottoms of loaves, leaving ½-in.-thick shells (save removed bread for another use). Serve stew in bread bowls.

VEGETARIAN STEW IN BREAD BOWLS

CINDI MITCHELL'S
WHITE CHILI

White Chili

My friend and I created this delicious slow-cooked chicken chili. Jarred Alfredo sauce base makes it stand apart from other white chilis. Reduce the amount of cayenne pepper if you'd like a little less heat in the dish.

—**CINDI MITCHELL** ST MARYS, KS

PREP: 30 MIN. • **COOK:** 3 HOURS
MAKES: 12 SERVINGS (1 CUP EACH)

- 3 cans (15½ ounces each) great northern beans, rinsed and drained
- 3 cups cubed cooked chicken breast
- 1 jar (15 ounces) Alfredo sauce
- 2 cups chicken broth
- 1 to 2 cans (4 ounces each) chopped green chilies
- 1½ cups frozen gold and white corn
- 1 cup (4 ounces) shredded Monterey Jack cheese
- 1 cup (4 ounces) shredded pepper jack cheese
- 1 cup sour cream
- 1 small sweet yellow pepper, chopped
- 1 small onion, chopped
- 3 garlic cloves, minced
- 1 tablespoon ground cumin
- 1½ teaspoons white pepper
- 1 to 1½ teaspoons cayenne pepper
  Salsa verde and chopped fresh cilantro, optional

In a 5- or 6-qt. slow cooker, combine the first 15 ingredients. Cover and cook on low for 3-4 hours or until heated though, stirring once. Serve with salsa verde and cilantro if desired.

Anything Goes Sausage Soup

I call this recipe "anything goes" because you can add or take out a variety of ingredients, and the soup still turns out absolutely perfect. It's impossible to have just one bowl! Canned soups make it easy to throw together.

—**SHEENA WELLARD** NAMPA, ID

PREP: 40 MIN. • **COOK:** 9½ HOURS
MAKES: 15 SERVINGS (ABOUT 4 QUARTS)

- 1 pound bulk pork sausage
- 4 cups water
- 1 can (10¾ ounces) condensed cream of mushroom soup, undiluted
- 1 can (10¾ ounces) condensed cheddar cheese soup, undiluted
- 5 medium red potatoes, cubed
- 4 cups chopped cabbage
- 3 large carrots, thinly sliced
- 4 celery ribs, chopped
- 1 medium zucchini, chopped
- 1 large onion, chopped
- 5 chicken bouillon cubes
- 1 tablespoon dried parsley flakes
- ¾ teaspoon pepper
- 1 can (12 ounces) evaporated milk

1. In a large skillet, cook sausage over medium heat until no longer pink; drain. Transfer to a 6-qt. slow cooker. Stir in the water and soups until blended. Add the vegetables, bouillon, parsley and pepper.

2. Cover and cook on low for 9-10 hours or until the vegetables are tender. Stir in milk; cover and cook 30 minutes longer.

ANYTHING GOES SAUSAGE SOUP

SPICY COWBOY CHILI

Spicy Chicken and Hominy Soup

This slow-cooked soup is also called "posole," a traditional good luck New Year's meal in my native New Mexico. Everyone makes it differently—my soup answers the age-old chili question, "Red or green?" by using both!

—JANET CHRISTINE MCDANIEL
ARLINGTON, TX

PREP: 15 MIN. • **COOK:** 4 HOURS
MAKES: 4 SERVINGS

- 1 **pound boneless skinless chicken breasts, cubed**
- 2 **tablespoons olive oil**
- 1 **medium onion, chopped**
- 3 **garlic cloves, minced**
- 2 **chipotle peppers in adobo sauce**
- 2 **cans (14½ ounces each) chicken broth, divided**
- 1 **can (15 ounces) hominy, rinsed and drained**
- 1 **can (4 ounces) chopped green chilies**
- 1 **teaspoon dried oregano**
- 1 **teaspoon ground cumin**
- ¼ **teaspoon pepper**

1. In a large skillet, brown chicken in oil. With a slotted spoon, transfer chicken to a 3- or 4-qt. slow cooker. In the same skillet, saute onion and garlic in drippings until tender; add to chicken.

2. Place chipotle peppers and ¼ cup broth in a blender or food processor; cover and process until blended. Add to chicken mixture. Stir in hominy, chilies, seasonings and remaining broth. Cover and cook on low for 4-5 hours until chicken is tender.

SPICY CHICKEN AND HOMINY SOUP

Spicy Cowboy Chili

Toasting the peppers for this chili releases their earthy flavors—but do wear gloves when handling dried peppers and seeds.

—RACHEL SPRINKEL HILO, HI

PREP: 45 MIN. • **COOK:** 7 HOURS
MAKES: 14 SERVINGS (3½ QUARTS)

- 1 **whole garlic bulb**
- 2 **to 3 tablespoons olive oil, divided**
- 2 **dried ancho chilies**
- 2 **dried chipotle chilies**
- 1 **bottle (12 ounces) dark beer**
- 3 **pounds beef stew meat, cut into ¾-inch pieces**
- 2 **large onions, chopped**
- 3 **cans (16 ounces each) kidney beans, rinsed and drained**
- 3 **cans (14½ ounces each) diced tomatoes, undrained**
- 2 **cans (8 ounces each) tomato sauce**
- 2 **tablespoons Worcestershire sauce**
- 1 **tablespoon chili powder**
- 1 **teaspoon pepper**
- ½ **teaspoon salt**
  Shredded cheddar cheese, optional

1. Remove papery outer skin from garlic bulb, but do not peel or separate the cloves. Cut off top of garlic bulb, exposing individual cloves. Brush cut cloves with 1 teaspoon oil. Wrap in foil. Bake at 425° for 30-35 minutes or until cloves are soft. Unwrap and cool slightly. Squeeze garlic from skins; mash with a fork.

2. Meanwhile, in a large dry skillet over medium-high heat, toast chilies on both sides until puffy, about 3-6 minutes. (Do not blacken.) Cool. Remove stems and seeds; coarsely chop chilies. Place in a small bowl; cover with beer. Let stand to soften, about 30 minutes.

3. In the same skillet, heat 1 tablespoon oil over medium-high heat. Brown beef in batches, adding additional oil if needed; transfer to a 6-qt. slow cooker. In the skillet, heat 2 teaspoons oil over medium heat. Add onions; cook and stir until tender. Add to beef.

4. Stir in the remaining ingredients, mashed garlic and dried chilies mixture. Cover and cook on low for 7-9 hours or until meat is tender. If desired, serve with cheese.

NOTE *One-half teaspoon ground chipotle pepper may be substituted for the dried chipotle chilies; add ground chipotle with mashed garlic and beer mixture to slow cooker.*

Chicago-Style Beef Sandwiches

I'm originally from the Windy City, so I love Chicago-style beef. I think that these tender sandwiches have an authentic flavor, and they're so simple to prepare using a slow cooker.

—LOIS SZYDLOWSKI TAMPA, FL

PREP: 30 MIN. • **COOK:** 8 HOURS
MAKES: 12 SERVINGS

- 1 **boneless beef chuck roast (4 pounds)**
- 1 **teaspoon salt**
- ¾ **teaspoon pepper**

- 2 **tablespoons olive oil**
- ½ **pound fresh mushrooms**
- 2 **medium carrots, cut into chunks**
- 1 **medium onion, cut into wedges**
- 6 **garlic cloves, halved**
- 2 **teaspoons dried oregano**
- 1 **carton (32 ounces) beef broth**
- 1 **tablespoon beef base**
- 12 **Italian rolls, split**
- 1 **jar (16 ounces) giardiniera, drained**

1. Cut roast in half; sprinkle with salt and pepper. In a large skillet, brown meat in oil on all sides. Transfer to a 5-qt. slow cooker.

2. In a food processor, combine the mushrooms, carrots, onion, garlic and oregano. Cover and process until finely chopped. Transfer to slow cooker. Combine beef broth and base; pour over top. Cover and cook on low for 8-10 hours or until tender.

3. Remove meat and shred with two forks. Skim fat from cooking juices. Return meat to slow cooker; heat through. Using a slotted spoon, serve beef on buns; top with giardiniera.

NOTE *Look for beef base near the broth and bouillon.*

CHICAGO-STYLE BEEF SANDWICHES

Cheesy Cauliflower Soup

If you prefer chunky soup, skip the blender step and stir the cheese and cream right into the slow cooker, then heat on high until the cheese is melted.

—**SHERYL PUNTER** WOODSTOCK, ON

PREP: 25 MIN. • **COOK:** 5½ HOURS
MAKES: 9 SERVINGS (2¼ QUARTS)

- 1 large head cauliflower, broken into florets
- 2 celery ribs
- 2 large carrots
- 1 large green pepper
- 1 small sweet red pepper
- 1 medium red onion
- 4 cups chicken broth
- ½ teaspoon Worcestershire sauce
- ¼ teaspoon salt
- ⅛ teaspoon pepper
- 2 cups (8 ounces) shredded cheddar cheese
- 2 cups half-and-half cream

1. Place cauliflower in a 4-qt. slow cooker. Chop the celery, carrots, peppers and onion; add to slow cooker. Stir in the broth, Worcestershire sauce, salt and pepper. Cover and cook on low for 5-6 hours or until vegetables are tender.

2. In a blender, process soup in batches until smooth. Return all to slow cooker; stir in cheese and cream. Cover and cook on high for 30 minutes or until cheese is melted.

CHEESY CAULIFLOWER SOUP

Beef Stew Provencal

When I was young, my favorite food to order in a restaurant was beef stew. My mother and I decided to create our own and experimented with different ingredients until we came up with this recipe. Everyone liked this slow cooker version so much that now it's a tradition every time the whole family is together!

—**CHELSEY LARSEN** SPARKS, NV

PREP: 25 MIN. • **COOK:** 6 HOURS
MAKES: 6 SERVINGS

- 4 medium carrots, chopped
- 4 celery ribs, chopped
- 1 cup beef broth
- 1 jar (7 ounces) julienned oil-packed sun-dried tomatoes, drained
- 1 can (6 ounces) tomato paste
- 1 small onion, chopped
- ⅓ cup honey
- ¼ cup balsamic vinegar
- 1 garlic clove, minced
- 1 teaspoon dried thyme
- ½ teaspoon onion powder
- ¼ teaspoon white pepper
- 1 boneless beef chuck roast (2½ pounds), cut into 2-inch cubes
- ½ cup all-purpose flour
- ½ teaspoon salt
- ½ teaspoon pepper
- 2 tablespoons olive oil
  Hot cooked mashed potatoes or egg noodles

1. In a 4-qt. slow cooker, combine the first 12 ingredients. In a large bowl, combine the beef, flour, salt and pepper; toss to coat. In a large skillet, brown beef in oil in batches. Transfer to slow cooker.

2. Cover and cook on low for 6-8 hours or until beef is tender. Serve with mashed potatoes.

top tip — Provencal Pointers

Provencal is a region in France and also a savory sauce made of tomatoes, olive oil, garlic and herbs. Mushrooms can be included. It's most often used with beef entrees.

CHELSEY LARSEN'S
BEEF STEW PROVENCAL

HAM AND BLACK BEAN SOUP

Slow Cooker Pulled Pork Sandwiches

These bites are ideal for potlucks because they can be made ahead, which I especially appreciate during the busy holiday season. The sweet-and-spicy sauce is always a hit.

—**MARTHA ANNE CARPENTER** MESA, AZ

PREP: 20 MIN. • **COOK:** 8½ HOURS • **MAKES:** 10 SERVINGS

- 1 boneless pork loin roast (4 pounds)
- 1 can (14½ ounces) beef broth
- ⅓ cup plus ½ cup Worcestershire sauce, divided
- ⅓ cup plus ¼ cup Louisiana-style hot sauce, divided
- 1 cup ketchup
- 1 cup molasses
- ½ cup prepared mustard
- 10 kaiser rolls, split

1. Cut roast in half; place in a 5-qt. slow cooker. In a small bowl, combine the broth, ⅓ cup Worcestershire sauce and ⅓ cup hot sauce; pour over roast. Cover and cook on low for 8-10 hours or until tender.

2. Remove pork; shred with two forks. Drain and discard cooking liquid. Return shredded pork to the slow cooker. For sauce, combine the ketchup, molasses, mustard and the remaining Worcestershire sauce and hot sauce. Pour over pork. Cover and cook on high for 30 minutes or until heated through. Serve on rolls.

Ham and Black Bean Soup

I originally created this slightly spicy soup for my husband, who enjoys black beans. But I ended up loving it, too! Even more compliments came from our neighbors who stopped by and stayed for supper.

—**LAURA MEURER** GREEN BAY, WI

PREP: 25 MIN. • **COOK:** 4 HOURS
MAKES: 8 SERVINGS (ABOUT 2 QUARTS)

- 3 cans (15 ounces each) black beans, rinsed and drained
- 2 cans (14½ ounces each) beef broth
- 1 can (14½ ounces) diced tomatoes, undrained
- 1½ cups cubed fully cooked ham
- 1 can (4 ounces) chopped green chilies
- ¼ cup red wine vinegar
- 1 large onion, chopped
- 3 garlic cloves, minced
- 1 teaspoon dried oregano
- 1 teaspoon dried thyme
- 1 teaspoon pepper

In a 3-qt. slow cooker, combine all ingredients. Cover and cook on high for 4-5 hours or until onion is tender.

SLOW COOKER PULLED PORK SANDWICHES

CREAM OF POTATO & CHEDDAR SOUP

Cream of Potato & Cheddar Soup

Here's a soup of complete and total comfort—with simple ingredients. Yukon Gold potatoes make it taste incredible, and my daughter always shares them from her garden. With sharp cheddar and croutons, it's heavenly!

—CINDI BAUER MARSHFIELD, WI

PREP: 25 MIN. • **COOK:** 7½ HOURS
MAKES: 11 SERVINGS (2¾ QUARTS)

- 8 medium Yukon Gold potatoes, peeled and cubed
- 1 large red onion, chopped
- 1 celery rib, chopped
- 2 cans (14½ ounces each) reduced-sodium chicken broth
- 1 can (10¾ ounces) condensed cream of celery soup, undiluted
- 1 teaspoon garlic powder
- ½ teaspoon white pepper
- 1½ cups (6 ounces) shredded sharp cheddar cheese
- 1 cup half-and-half cream
  Optional toppings: salad croutons, crumbled cooked bacon and additional shredded sharp cheddar cheese

1. Combine the first seven ingredients in a 4- or 5-qt. slow cooker. Cover and cook on low for 7-9 hours or until potatoes are tender.

2. Stir in cheese and cream. Cover and cook 30 minutes longer or until cheese is melted. Garnish servings with toppings of your choice.

CRYSTAL KELSO'S
BROCCOLI POTATO SOUP

Broccoli Potato Soup

For a comforting soup with a nice, creamy texture, try my recipe. It features broccoli, chunks of potato and red pepper flakes that add just the right hint of heat. Fresh herbs season this truly delicious meal-in-one specialty.

—CRYSTAL KELSO SANDY, OR

PREP: 25 MIN. • **COOK:** 4½ HOURS
MAKES: 8 CUPS (2 QUARTS)

- 1 pound small red potatoes, cubed
- 1 large onion, chopped
- 1 large carrot, coarsely chopped
- 7 garlic cloves, minced
- 3 cups water
- 1 can (14½ ounces) condensed cream of broccoli soup, undiluted
- 1 teaspoon each minced fresh thyme, basil and parsley
- 1 teaspoon garlic powder
- ½ teaspoon salt
- ½ teaspoon crushed red pepper flakes
- ¼ teaspoon pepper
- 2 cups frozen chopped broccoli, thawed and drained
- 1 cup (4 ounces) shredded Havarti cheese

1. Place the potatoes, onion, carrot and garlic in a 4- or 5-qt. slow cooker. Add the water, soup and seasonings. Cover and cook on low for 4-5 hours or until heated through.
2. Stir in broccoli and cheese. Cover and cook for 30 minutes or until broccoli is tender.

What's Havarti?

Havarti is a creamy semi-firm cheese that melts quickly, making it a perfect choice for slow-cooked dishes. Buttery Havarti is a Danish cheese that is named after the farm where it was developed at the turn of the 20th century. It offers a distinctive flavor, somewhat similar to Gouda, and is peppered throughout with tiny holes.

Slow & Easy Minestrone

Hot soup on a cold day is something I just can't get enough of. It's a snap to put together, and I don't have to wash pots and pans after a relaxing meal.

—SALLY GOEB NEW EGYPT, NJ

PREP: 25 MIN. • **COOK:** 7 HOURS
MAKES: 6 SERVINGS (2¼ QUARTS)

- 1 can (28 ounces) diced tomatoes, undrained
- 3 celery ribs, cut into ½-inch slices
- 2 medium carrots, cut into ½-inch slices
- 2 small zucchini, halved and cut into ¾-inch slices
- 2 cups vegetable broth
- 1 cup shredded cabbage
- ¼ pound sliced fresh mushrooms
- 1 small onion, chopped
- 2 garlic cloves, minced
- 1 teaspoon dried basil
- 1 teaspoon salt
- ⅓ cup quick-cooking barley
- 1 can (15 ounces) white kidney or cannellini beans, rinsed and drained

1. In a 4- or 5-qt. slow cooker, combine the first 11 ingredients. Cover and cook on low for 7-9 hours.
2. Cook barley according to package directions; stir into soup. Add beans; heat through.

SLOW & EASY MINESTRONE

HUNGARIAN GOULASH

Hungarian Goulash

Talk about heirloom recipes! My grandmother made this for my mother when she was a child, and then Mom made it for us to enjoy. Paprika and caraway add wonderful flavor, and sour cream gives it a creamy richness. It's simply scrumptious!

—**MARCIA DOYLE** POMPANO, FL

PREP: 20 MIN. • **COOK:** 7 HOURS • **MAKES:** 12 SERVINGS

- 3   medium onions, chopped
- 2   medium carrots, chopped
- 2   medium green peppers, chopped
- 3   pounds beef stew meat, cut into 1-inch cubes
- ½   teaspoon plus ¼ teaspoon salt, divided
- ½   teaspoon plus ¼ teaspoon pepper, divided
- 2   tablespoons olive oil
- 1½ cups reduced-sodium beef broth
- ¼   cup all-purpose flour
- 3   tablespoons paprika
- 2   tablespoons tomato paste
- 1   teaspoon caraway seeds
- 1   garlic clove, minced
     Dash sugar
- 12 cups uncooked whole wheat egg noodles
- 1   cup (8 ounces) reduced-fat sour cream

1. Place the onions, carrots and green peppers in a 5-qt. slow cooker. Sprinkle meat with ½ teaspoon salt and ½ teaspoon pepper. In a large skillet, brown meat in oil in batches. Transfer to slow cooker.

2. Add broth to skillet, stirring to loosen browned bits from pan. Combine the flour, paprika, tomato paste, caraway seeds, garlic, sugar and remaining salt and pepper; stir into skillet. Bring to a boil; cook and stir for 2 minutes or until thickened. Pour over meat. Cover and cook on low for 7-9 hours or until meat is tender.

3. Meanwhile, cook noodles according to package directions. Stir sour cream into slow cooker. Drain noodles; serve with goulash.

Lentil & Chicken Sausage Stew

This hearty and healthy stew will warm your family right down to their toes! It's packed with veggies and plenty of comforting goodness. Serve with rolls to soak up every last morsel.

—**JAN VALDEZ** CHICAGO, IL

PREP: 15 MIN. • **COOK:** 8 HOURS • **MAKES:** 6 SERVINGS

- 1   carton (32 ounces) reduced-sodium chicken broth
- 1   can (28 ounces) diced tomatoes, undrained
- 3   fully cooked spicy chicken sausage links (3 ounces each), cut into ½-inch slices
- 1   cup dried lentils, rinsed
- 1   medium onion, chopped
- 1   medium carrot, chopped
- 1   celery rib, chopped
- 2   garlic cloves, minced
- ½   teaspoon dried thyme

In a 4- or 5-qt. slow cooker, combine all ingredients. Cover and cook on low for 8-10 hours or until lentils are tender.

LENTIL & CHICKEN SAUSAGE STEW

SLOW COOKER SPLIT PEA SOUP

Slow Cooker Split Pea Soup

When I have leftover ham in the fridge, I always like to make this soup. Just throw the ingredients in the slow cooker, turn it on and dinner is done! You can also drain a small can of corn and toss that in, or experiment with your favorite herbs.

—**PAMELA CHAMBERS** WEST COLUMBIA, SC

PREP: 15 MIN. • **COOK:** 8 HOURS • **MAKES:** 8 SERVINGS

- 1 package (16 ounces) dried green split peas, rinsed
- 2 cups cubed fully cooked ham
- 1 large onion, chopped
- 1 cup julienned or chopped carrots
- 3 garlic cloves, minced
- ½ teaspoon dried rosemary, crushed
- ½ teaspoon dried thyme
- 1 carton (32 ounces) reduced-sodium chicken broth
- 2 cups water

In a 4- or 5-qt. slow cooker, combine all ingredients. Cover and cook on low for 8-10 hours or until peas are tender.

top tip ## Simple Additions

When it comes to split pea soup, there's a lot of room to get creative! Stir in some cooked and crumbled bacon, sliced mushrooms, shredded cheese or even a little red wine.

Machete Shredded Beef Sandwiches

Beef sirloin tip roast makes the base for these tangy sandwiches. A hit of brown sugar gives the hearty handheld specialties an extra touch of flavor that everyone adores.

—**TASTE OF HOME FOOD STYLING TEAM** GREENDALE, WI

PREP: 10 MIN. • **COOK:** 8 HOURS • **MAKES:** 12 SERVINGS

- 1 beef sirloin tip roast (2½ pounds)
- ½ teaspoon salt
- ¼ teaspoon pepper
- 1 tablespoon canola oil
- 1 cup each ketchup and water
- ½ cup chopped onion
- ⅓ cup packed brown sugar
- 3 tablespoons Worcestershire sauce
- 2 tablespoons lemon juice
- 2 tablespoons cider vinegar
- 2 tablespoons Dijon mustard
- 2 teaspoons celery seed
- 2 teaspoons chili powder
- 12 kaiser rolls, split

1. Sprinkle roast with salt and pepper. In a nonstick skillet, brown roast in oil on all sides over medium-high heat; drain.
2. Transfer roast to a 5-qt. slow cooker. Combine the ketchup, water, onion, brown sugar, Worcestershire sauce, lemon juice, vinegar, mustard, celery seed and chili powder; pour over roast.
3. Cover and cook on low for 8-10 hours or until meat is tender. Remove meat; shred with two forks and return to slow cooker. Spoon ½ cup meat mixture onto each roll.

MACHETE SHREDDED BEEF SANDWICHES

Winter

DESSERTS

From Gingerbread Pudding Cake perfect for cozy nights at home to Chocolate Peanut Drops ideal for holiday cookie trays, the comforting deserts here are sure to bring smiles and warm souls on even the chilliest winter night.

LATONA DWYER'S
SLOW-COOKER
CHOCOLATE LAVA CAKE

Slow-Cooker Chocolate Lava Cake

Everyone who tries this dessert falls in love with it! Using a slow cooker makes cleanup a breeze.

—**LATONA DWYER** PALM BEACH GARDENS, FL

PREP: 15 MIN. • **COOK:** 3 HOURS • **MAKES:** 12 SERVINGS

- 1 package devil's food cake mix (regular size)
- 1⅔ cups water
- 3 eggs
- ⅓ cup canola oil
- 2 cups cold 2% milk
- 1 package (3.9 ounces) instant chocolate pudding mix
- 2 cups (12 ounces) semisweet chocolate chips

1. In a large bowl, combine the cake mix, water, eggs and oil; beat on low speed for 30 seconds. Beat on medium for 2 minutes. Transfer to a greased 4-qt. slow cooker.
2. In another bowl, whisk milk and pudding mix for 2 minutes. Let stand for 2 minutes or until soft-set. Spoon over cake batter; sprinkle with chocolate chips. Cover and cook on high for 3-4 hours or until a toothpick inserted in cake portion comes out with moist crumbs. Serve warm.

Apple Comfort

Years ago, we were without electricity for nine days during an ice storm, but I was able run the slow cooker from our generator. The situation called for a dessert that would raise our spirits, and this has been a favorite ever since!

—**AWYNNE THURSTENSON** SILOAM SPRINGS, AR

PREP: 30 MIN. • **COOK:** 4 HOURS • **MAKES:** 8 SERVINGS

- 8 medium tart apples, peeled and sliced
- 1 cup sugar
- ¼ cup all-purpose flour
- 2 teaspoons ground cinnamon
- 2 eggs
- 1 cup heavy whipping cream
- 1 teaspoon vanilla extract
- 1 cup graham cracker crumbs
- ½ cup chopped pecans
- ¼ cup butter, melted
  Vanilla ice cream, optional

1. In a large bowl, combine the apples, sugar, flour and cinnamon. Spoon into a greased 3-qt. slow cooker. Whisk the eggs, cream and vanilla; pour over apple mixture. Combine the cracker crumbs, pecans and butter; sprinkle over top.
2. Cover and cook on low for 4-5 hours or until apples are tender. Serve warm with ice cream if desired.

Slow-Cooked Bread Pudding

My warm, hearty dessert is perfect on any cold, blustery winter evening. The slow cooker fills the kitchen with such an amazing aroma, my stomach growls just thinking about it!
—**MAIAH MILLER** CARLSBAD, CA

PREP: 15 MIN. • **COOK:** 3 HOURS • **MAKES:** 8 SERVINGS

- 4 whole wheat bagels, split and cut into ¾-inch pieces
- 1 large tart apple, peeled and chopped
- ½ cup dried cranberries
- ¼ cup golden raisins
- 2 cups fat-free milk
- 1 cup egg substitute
- ½ cup sugar
- 2 tablespoons butter, melted
- 1 teaspoon ground cinnamon
- 1 teaspoon vanilla extract

1. In a 3-qt. slow cooker coated with cooking spray, combine the bagels, apple, cranberries and raisins. In a large bowl, whisk the milk, egg substitute, sugar, butter, cinnamon and vanilla. Pour over bagel mixture and stir to combine; gently press bagels down into milk mixture.
2. Cover and cook on low for 3-4 hours or until a knife inserted near the center comes out clean.

SLOW-COOKED BREAD PUDDING

HOT CARAMEL APPLES

Hot Caramel Apples

Whoever thinks of making dessert in a slow cooker? This old-time favorite goes together quickly, and it's such a treat to come home to the comforting delight of cinnamon baked apples.
—**PAT SPARKS** ST. CHARLES, MO

PREP: 15 MIN. • **COOK:** 4 HOURS • **MAKES:** 4 SERVINGS

- 4 large tart apples, cored
- ½ cup apple juice
- ½ cup packed brown sugar
- 12 Red Hots
- ¼ cup butter
- 8 caramels
- ¼ teaspoon ground cinnamon
  Whipped cream, optional

1. Peel about ¾ in. off the top of each apple; place in a 3-qt. slow cooker. Pour juice over apples. Fill the center of each apple with 2 tablespoons of sugar, three Red Hots, 1 tablespoon butter and two caramels. Sprinkle with cinnamon.
2. Cover and cook on low for 4-6 hours or until apples are tender. Serve immediately with whipped cream if desired.

DIANE HALFERTY'S
CARAMEL PEAR PUDDING

Caramel Pear Pudding

Here's a lovely winter dessert that uses pears, which are seasonally available. It's easy to fix and a comforting treat after any meal. I enjoy snacking on it in front of the fireplace.

—**DIANE HALFERTY** CORPUS CHRISTI, TX

PREP: 20 MIN. • **COOK:** 3 HOURS
MAKES: 10 SERVINGS

- 1 cup all-purpose flour
- ½ cup sugar
- 1½ teaspoons baking powder
- ½ teaspoon ground cinnamon
- ¼ teaspoon salt
- ⅛ teaspoon ground cloves
- ½ cup 2% milk
- 4 medium pears, peeled and cubed
- ½ cup chopped pecans
- ¾ cup packed brown sugar
- ¼ cup butter, softened
- ½ cup boiling water
  Vanilla ice cream, optional

1. In a large bowl, combine flour, sugar, baking powder, cinnamon, salt and cloves. Stir in milk until smooth. Add pears and pecans. Spread evenly into a 3-qt. slow cooker coated with cooking spray.
2. In a small bowl, combine brown sugar and butter; stir in boiling water. Pour over batter (do not stir). Cover and cook on low for 3-4 hours or until pears are tender. Serve warm with ice cream if desired.

Warm Rocky Road Cake

I didn't think a cake made in a slow cooker could be so beautiful and delicious. When it's warm, it reminds me of those ooey-gooey lava cakes.

—**SCARLETT ELROD** NEWNAN, GA

PREP: 20 MIN. • **COOK:** 3 HOURS
MAKES: 16 SERVINGS

- 1 package German chocolate cake mix (regular size)
- 1 package (3.9 ounces) instant chocolate pudding mix
- 1 cup (8 ounces) sour cream
- ⅓ cup butter, melted
- 3 eggs
- 1 teaspoon vanilla extract
- 3¼ cups 2% milk, divided
- 1 package (3.4 ounces) cook-and-serve chocolate pudding mix
- 1½ cups miniature marshmallows
- 1 cup (6 ounces) semisweet chocolate chips
- ½ cup chopped pecans, toasted
  Vanilla ice cream, optional

1. In a large bowl, combine the first six ingredients; add 1¼ cups milk. Beat on low speed 30 seconds. Beat on medium 2 minutes. Transfer to a greased 4- or 5-qt. slow cooker. Sprinkle cook-and-serve pudding mix over batter.
2. In a small saucepan, heat remaining milk until bubbles form around sides of pan; gradually pour over the dry pudding mix.
3. Cook, covered, on high 3-4 hours or until a toothpick inserted in cake portion comes out with moist crumbs.
4. Turn off slow cooker. Sprinkle marshmallows, chocolate chips and pecans over cake; let stand, covered, 5 minutes or until marshmallows begin to melt. Serve warm. If desired, top with ice cream.
NOTE *To toast nuts, spread in a 15x10x1-in. baking pan. Bake at 350° for 5-10 minutes or until lightly browned, stirring occasionally. Or, spread in a dry nonstick skillet and heat over low heat until lightly browned, stirring occasionally.*

Slow Cooker Baked Apples

Coming home to this irresistible dessert on a dreary day is just wonderful. Best of all, it's slow-cooker easy!

—**EVANGELINE BRADFORD** ERLANGER, KY

PREP: 25 MIN. • **COOK:** 4 HOURS
MAKES: 6 SERVINGS

- 6 medium tart apples
- ½ cup raisins
- ⅓ cup packed brown sugar
- 1 tablespoon grated orange peel
- 1 cup water
- 3 tablespoons thawed orange juice concentrate
- 2 tablespoons butter

1. Core apples and peel top third of each if desired. Combine the raisins, brown sugar and orange peel; spoon into apples. Place apples in a 5-qt. slow cooker.
2. Pour water around apples. Drizzle them with orange juice concentrate. Dot with butter. Cover and cook on low for 4-5 hours until apples are tender.

SLOW COOKER BAKED APPLES

GINGERBREAD PUDDING CAKE

Gingerbread Pudding Cake

A handful of spices and a half cup of molasses give this delightful dessert a yummy old-fashioned flavor. It's pretty, too, with a dollop of whipped cream and a mint sprig on top.

—**BARBARA COOK** YUMA, AZ

PREP: 20 MIN. • **COOK:** 2 HOURS + STANDING
MAKES: 6-8 SERVINGS

- ¼ cup butter, softened
- ¼ cup sugar
- 1 egg white
- 1 teaspoon vanilla extract
- ½ cup molasses
- 1 cup water
- 1¼ cups all-purpose flour
- ¾ teaspoon baking soda
- ½ teaspoon ground cinnamon
- ½ teaspoon ground ginger
- ¼ teaspoon salt
- ¼ teaspoon ground allspice
- ⅛ teaspoon ground nutmeg
- ½ cup chopped pecans

TOPPING

- 6 tablespoons brown sugar
- ¾ cup hot water
- ⅔ cup butter, melted

1. In a large bowl, cream butter and sugar until light and fluffy. Beat in egg white and vanilla. Combine molasses and water. Combine the flour, baking soda, cinnamon, ginger, salt, allspice and nutmeg; gradually add to creamed mixture alternately with molasses mixture, beating well after each addition. Fold in pecans.

2. Pour into a greased 3-qt. slow cooker. Sprinkle with brown sugar. Combine hot water and butter; pour over batter (do not stir).

3. Cover and cook on high for 2 to 2½ hours or until a toothpick inserted near center of cake comes out clean. Turn off heat. Let stand for 15 minutes. Serve warm.

Butterscotch-Pecan Bread Pudding

Bread pudding fans just might hoard this yummy butterscotch version. Toppings like whipped cream and a butterscotch drizzle make this dessert absolutely irresistible!

—**LISA VARNER** EL PASO, TX

PREP: 15 MIN. • **COOK:** 3 HOURS • **MAKES:** 8 SERVINGS

- 8 slices white bread, cubed
- ½ cup chopped pecans
- ½ cup butterscotch chips
- 4 eggs
- 2 cups half-and-half cream
- ½ cup packed brown sugar
- ½ cup butter, melted
- 1 teaspoon vanilla extract
  Whipped cream and butterscotch ice cream topping

1. Place the bread, pecans and butterscotch chips in a greased 4-qt. slow cooker. In a large bowl, whisk the eggs, cream, brown sugar, butter and vanilla. Pour over top.

2. Cover and cook on low for 3-4 hours or until a knife inserted in the center comes out clean. Serve warm with whipped cream and butterscotch topping.

BUTTERSCOTCH-PECAN BREAD PUDDING

Slow Cooker Apple Pudding Cake

A comforting dessert like this is a superb treat on a chilly night. Since the pudding is made in a slow cooker, it does not require any attention from you, so it's great when entertaining. It separates into three layers—apples, cake and sauce—making it look like a lot of work on your part!

—**ELLEN SCHROEDER** REEDSBURG, WI

PREP: 15 MIN. • **COOK:** 2 HOURS • **MAKES:** 10 SERVINGS

- 2 cups all-purpose flour
- ⅔ cup plus ¼ cup sugar, divided
- 3 teaspoons baking powder
- 1 teaspoon salt
- ½ cup cold butter
- 1 cup 2% milk
- 2 medium tart apples, peeled and chopped
- 1½ cups orange juice
- ½ cup honey
- 2 tablespoons butter, melted
- 1 teaspoon ground cinnamon
- 1⅓ cups sour cream
- ¼ cup confectioners' sugar

1. In a small bowl, combine the flour, ⅔ cup sugar, baking powder and salt. Cut in butter until mixture resembles coarse crumbs. Stir in milk just until moistened. Spread into the bottom of a greased 4- or 5-qt. slow cooker; sprinkle apples over batter.

2. In a small bowl, combine the orange juice, honey, melted butter, cinnamon and remaining sugar; pour over apples.

Cover and cook on high for 2-3 hours or until the apples are tender.

3. In a small bowl, combine sour cream and confectioners' sugar. Serve with warm pudding cake.

Burgundy Pears

These spiced pears elevate slow cooking to a new level of elegance, yet they're incredibly easy to make. Your friends won't believe this fancy-looking dessert came from a slow cooker.

—**ELIZABETH HANES** PERALTA, NM

PREP: 10 MIN. • **COOK:** 3 HOURS • **MAKES:** 6 SERVINGS

- 6 medium ripe pears
- ⅓ cup sugar
- ⅓ cup Burgundy wine or grape juice
- 3 tablespoons orange marmalade
- 1 tablespoon lemon juice
- ¼ teaspoon ground cinnamon
- ¼ teaspoon ground nutmeg
  Dash salt
  Whipped cream cheese

1. Peel pears, leaving stems intact. Core from the bottom. Stand pears upright in a 5-qt. slow cooker. In a small bowl, combine the sugar, wine or grape juice, marmalade, lemon juice, cinnamon, nutmeg and salt. Carefully pour over the pears.

2. Cover and cook on low for 3-4 hours or until tender. To serve, drizzle pears with sauce and garnish with whipped cream cheese.

(5) INGREDIENTS
Chocolate Peanut Drops

This is a recipe I received from a friend, who got it from her sister, and between the three of us we've handed it out everywhere! The chocolaty candies couldn't be easier to make in the slow cooker, and depending on the size of your spoon, you can get at least several dozen candies from this one recipe. They make wonderful holiday gifts.

—**ANITA BELL** HERMITAGE, TN

PREP: 20 MIN. • **COOK:** 1½ HOURS + STANDING
MAKES: ABOUT 11 DOZEN

- 4 **ounces German sweet chocolate, chopped**
- 1 **package (12 ounces) semisweet chocolate chips**
- 4 **packages (10 to 12 ounces each) white baking chips**
- 2 **jars (16 ounces each) lightly salted dry roasted peanuts**

1. In a 6-qt. slow cooker, layer ingredients in order listed (do not stir). Cover and cook on low for 1½ hours. Stir to combine. (If chocolate is not melted, cover and cook 15 minutes longer; stir. Repeat in 15-minute increments until chocolate is melted.)

2. Drop mixture by rounded tablespoonfuls onto waxed paper. Let stand until set. Store in an airtight container at room temperature.

Spiced Sweet Potato Pudding

One of my favorite winter desserts, this treat's rich flavors are suited to the chillier months. I like to serve it over a slice of pound cake.

—**AYSHA SCHURMAN** AMMON, ID

PREP: 15 MIN. • **COOK:** 3 HOURS
MAKES: 7 SERVINGS

- 2 **cans (15¾ ounces each) sweet potatoes, drained and mashed**
- 3 **eggs**
- 1 **can (12 ounces) evaporated milk**
- ⅔ **cup biscuit/baking mix**
- ½ **cup packed brown sugar**
- ½ **cup apple butter**
- 2 **tablespoons butter, softened**
- 2 **teaspoons vanilla extract**
- ⅓ **cup finely chopped pecans**
  Pound cake, optional

In a large bowl, beat the first eight ingredients until well-blended. Pour into a greased 3-qt. slow cooker. Sprinkle with pecans. Cover and cook on low for 3-4 hours or until a thermometer reads 160°. Serve with pound cake if desired.

NOTE *This recipe was tested with commercially prepared apple butter.*

Apple-Nut Bread Pudding

Traditional bread pudding gives way to cool-weather influences in this comforting treat. I top warm servings with ice cream.

—**LORI FOX** MENOMONEE FALLS, WI

PREP: 10 MIN. • **COOK:** 3 HOURS
MAKES: 6-8 SERVINGS

- 8 **slices cinnamon-raisin bread, cubed**
- 2 **medium tart apples, peeled and sliced**
- 1 **cup chopped pecans, toasted**
- 1 **cup sugar**
- 1 **teaspoon ground cinnamon**
- ½ **teaspoon ground nutmeg**
- 3 **eggs, lightly beaten**
- 2 **cups half-and-half cream**
- ¼ **cup apple juice**
- ¼ **cup butter, melted**
  Vanilla ice cream

Place bread cubes, apples and pecans in a greased 3-qt. slow cooker. In a bowl, combine the sugar, cinnamon and nutmeg. Add the eggs, cream, apple juice and butter; mix well. Pour over bread mixture. Cover and cook on low for 3-4 hours or until a knife inserted in the center comes out clean. Serve with ice cream.

CHOCOLATE PEANUT DROPS

LORI FOX'S
APPLE-NUT BREAD PUDDING

GRETA IGL'S
AUTUMN TOSSED SALAD
page 347

Bonus

Ready when you are and loaded with meal-in-one convenience, slow-cooked dinners can't be beat. Add flair to menus with this section of bonus recipes. Simply toss a salad or bake a loaf of quick bread to round out a slow-cooked supper, and you'll have a dinner to remember.

Bonus

SALADS

No matter what the season is, salads add a pop of color to the dinner table...and extra veggies to the menu! This special section offers green, vegetable, pasta, potato and bean salads that are ideal for all of your slow-cooked main courses.

MARY MARLOWE LEVERETTE'S
FALL HARVEST SALAD

"For a change, you can swap roasted butternut squash or pumpkin for sweet potatoes in this tasty salad. Any combination of dried fruit and nuts will work as ingredients, so pick your favorites."
—**MARY MARLOWE LEVERETTE** COLUMBIA, SC

Fall Harvest Salad

PREP: 30 MIN. • **BAKE:** 25 MIN. • **MAKES:** 6 SERVINGS

- 2 large sweet potatoes, peeled and cubed
- 2 tablespoons olive oil
- ¼ teaspoon salt
- ¼ teaspoon pepper
- 2 cups cubed cooked turkey breast
- 2 medium apples, cubed
- 1 cup chopped walnuts, toasted
- 4 green onions, thinly sliced
- ½ cup raisins
- ½ cup minced fresh parsley

DRESSING

- ¼ cup olive oil
- 2 tablespoons rice vinegar
- 2 tablespoons orange juice
- 2 tablespoons maple syrup
- 1 tablespoon lemon juice
- 2 teaspoons minced fresh gingerroot
- ¼ teaspoon salt
- ¼ teaspoon ground cinnamon
- ⅛ teaspoon ground nutmeg
- ⅛ teaspoon pepper

1. Place sweet potatoes in an ungreased 15-in. x 10-in. x 1-in. baking pan; drizzle with oil and sprinkle with salt and pepper. Toss to coat.
2. Bake at 400° for 25-30 minutes or until tender, stirring occasionally. Cool to room temperature.
3. In a large bowl, combine the turkey, apples, walnuts, onions, raisins, parsley and sweet potatoes.
4. In a small bowl, whisk the dressing ingredients. Pour over turkey mixture; toss to coat. Serve immediately.

top tip

Wise Choice

Rice vinegar is made with fermented rice and has a milder flavor than white vinegar. There are both Japanese (colorless) and Chinese (white, red or black) rice vinegars. For this salad choose a colorless or white rice vinegar.

Cilantro Couscous Salad

Since this serves 12, I regularly make it for potlucks, and it is always appreciated. My 11-year-old daughter liked it so much, we served it at her birthday tea party.

—CINDY GIFFORD CEDAR CITY, UT

START TO FINISH: 25 MIN. • **MAKES:** 12 SERVINGS (⅔ CUP EACH)

- 1 package (10 ounces) couscous
- 1 medium cucumber, finely chopped
- 2 medium tomatoes, seeded and finely chopped
- ⅔ cup minced fresh cilantro
- ⅓ cup olive oil
- ¼ cup lemon juice
- 3 garlic cloves, minced
- 1 package (8 ounces) feta cheese, crumbled

1. Prepare couscous according to package directions; let cool to room temperature.

2. In a large serving bowl, combine cucumber, tomatoes, cilantro and couscous. In a small bowl, whisk the oil, lemon juice and garlic. Drizzle over salad; toss to coat. Add cheese and toss gently to combine. Chill until serving.

CILANTRO COUSCOUS SALAD

AUTUMN TOSSED SALAD

Autumn Tossed Salad

For a company-special dish, whip up this simple homemade dressing the night before and toss with salad just before serving.

—GRETA IGL MENOMONEE FALLS, WI

START TO FINISH: 10 MIN. • **MAKES:** 6 SERVINGS

- 1 package (6 ounces) fresh baby spinach
- 1 medium pear, sliced
- 1 celery rib, chopped
- ¼ cup dried cranberries
- ¼ cup chopped pecans, toasted

VINAIGRETTE

- ¼ cup canola oil
- 2 tablespoons sugar
- 2 tablespoons cider vinegar
- 1 tablespoon minced fresh parsley or 1 teaspoon dried parsley flakes
- ¼ teaspoon salt
  Dash hot pepper sauce

In a large bowl, combine the first five ingredients. In a small bowl, whisk the vinaigrette ingredients. Pour over salad; toss to coat.

ALL-SPICED-UP RASPBERRY AND MUSHROOM SALAD

Creamy Red Potato Salad

We love red potatoes for their color and shape in this perfect combo with radishes, green onions and a touch of vinegar.
—**BETSY KING** DULUTH, MN

PREP: 30 MIN. • **COOK:** 20 MIN.+ CHILLING
MAKES: 12 SERVINGS

- 2½ pounds small red potatoes, cut into ¼-inch slices

VINAIGRETTE
- ⅔ cup canola oil
- ⅓ cup red wine vinegar
- 2 tablespoons Dijon mustard
- ¾ teaspoon salt
- ½ teaspoon dill weed
- ¼ teaspoon garlic salt
- ¼ teaspoon pepper

SALAD
- ⅔ cup mayonnaise
- ⅔ cup sour cream
- 2 cups sliced radishes
- ⅔ cup thinly sliced green onions
- ½ cup minced fresh parsley
- 4 hard-cooked eggs, coarsely chopped

1. Place potatoes in a Dutch oven; cover with water. Bring to a boil. Reduce heat; cover and cook potatoes for 15-18 minutes or until tender. Drain.

2. Transfer potatoes to a large bowl. In a small bowl, whisk the vinaigrette ingredients. Pour over warm potatoes; gently toss to coat. Cool slightly. Cover and refrigerate until chilled.

3. In a small bowl, combine the mayonnaise and sour cream; stir in the radishes, onions and parsley. Add to potatoes; mix gently. Top with the eggs. Chill until serving.

CREAMY RED POTATO SALAD

All-Spiced-Up Raspberry and Mushroom Salad

Here's a refreshing salad for summer or anytime. You'll love the easy homemade raspberry vinaigrette with allspice.
—**ROXANNE CHAN** ALBANY, CA

START TO FINISH: 30 MIN.
MAKES: 4 SERVINGS

- 2 tablespoons raspberry vinegar
- 2 tablespoons olive oil, divided
- 1 tablespoon red jalapeno pepper jelly
- ¼ teaspoon ground allspice
- 1 pound small fresh mushrooms, halved
- 4 cups spring mix salad greens
- 1 cup fresh raspberries
- 2 tablespoons chopped red onion
- 2 tablespoons minced fresh mint
- 2 tablespoons sliced almonds, toasted
- ¼ cup crumbled goat cheese

1. In a small bowl, whisk the vinegar, 1 tablespoon oil, pepper jelly and allspice until blended. In a large skillet, heat remaining oil over medium-high heat. Add mushrooms; cook and stir until tender; cool slightly.

2. In a large bowl, combine salad greens, raspberries, onion, mint and almonds. Just before serving, add mushrooms and vinaigrette; toss to combine. Top with cheese.

NOTE *To toast nuts, spread in a 15x10x1-in. baking pan. Bake at 350° for 5-10 minutes or until lightly browned, stirring occasionally. Or, spread in a dry nonstick skillet and heat over low heat until lightly browned, stirring occasionally.*

SUMMER SALADS WITH MANDARIN ORANGES

Summer Salads with Mandarin Oranges

Fresh and pretty, my arranged salad is a terrific way to get fruit and veggies into your day. Sweet oranges and a tangy dressing make a delightful match.
—FRANCIS GARLAND ANNISTON, AL

START TO FINISH: 25 MIN.
MAKES: 6 SERVINGS

- **3** tablespoons red wine vinegar
- **1** tablespoon lemon juice
- **1** garlic clove, minced
- **¾** teaspoon minced chives
- **¾** teaspoon minced fresh parsley
- **⅛** teaspoon salt
- **⅛** teaspoon coarsely ground pepper
- **½** cup olive oil
- **4** cups torn Boston lettuce
- **2** plum tomatoes, chopped
- **1** medium ripe avocado, peeled and cubed
- **½** small cucumber, halved and sliced
- **1** can (11 ounces) mandarin oranges, drained
- **¼** cup sliced ripe olives

1. In a small bowl, whisk the first seven ingredients. Gradually whisk in oil. Set aside.
2. Divide lettuce among six serving plates. Top with tomatoes, avocado, cucumber, oranges and olives. Drizzle with dressing.

Black-Eyed Pea Pasta Salad

Having Southern cuisine tonight? Here's a salad that'll go great with it. A creamy Italian dressing enhances the chopped vegetables, cheese and pasta.
—JOAN HUGGINS WAYNESBORO, MS

PREP: 30 MIN. + CHILLING
MAKES: 8 SERVINGS

- **1** jar (7½ ounces) marinated quartered artichoke hearts
- **1** cup uncooked tricolor spiral pasta
- **1** can (15½ ounces) black-eyed peas, rinsed and drained
- **4** slices provolone cheese, cut into thin strips
- **½** cup chopped green pepper
- **½** cup chopped sweet red pepper
- **½** cup thinly sliced red onion
- **½** cup sliced pepperoni, cut into thin strips
- **½** cup mayonnaise
- **¼** cup prepared Italian salad dressing

1. Drain artichokes, reserving ¼ cup liquid; chop and set aside. Cook pasta according to package directions.
2. Meanwhile, in a large bowl combine the artichokes, peas, cheese, peppers, onion and pepperoni. Drain pasta; add to artichoke mixture.
3. In a small bowl, combine the mayonnaise, salad dressing and reserved artichoke liquid. Pour over pasta mixture; toss to coat. Cover and refrigerate for at least 1 hour.

BLACK-EYED PEA PASTA SALAD

Mediterranean Romaine Salad

My mother taught me how to make a salad of artichoke hearts, roasted red peppers, red onion and olives. It's a traditional Genovese accompaniment to a family dinner, or it can be used as a light supper when you add chicken or shrimp.

—TRISHA KRUSE EAGLE, ID

START TO FINISH: 30 MIN. • **MAKES:** 6 SERVINGS

- 2½ cups cubed French bread
- 1 tablespoon olive oil
- 1 garlic clove, minced
- 1 jar (7½ ounces) marinated quartered artichoke hearts, drained
- 1 cup roasted sweet red peppers, thinly sliced
- 1 medium cucumber, peeled and thinly sliced
- 1 celery rib, sliced
- 1 can (2¼ ounces) sliced ripe olives, drained
- ⅓ cup thinly sliced red onion
- ½ cup balsamic vinaigrette
- 1 bunch romaine, torn
- ¼ teaspoon coarsely ground pepper
  Shaved Parmesan cheese, optional

1. Place cubed bread on an ungreased 15-in. x 10-in. x 1-in. baking pan. Combine oil and garlic; drizzle over bread and toss to coat. Bake at 400° for 6-8 minutes or until golden brown, stirring once. Set aside.

2. In a large bowl, combine the artichokes, red peppers, cucumber, celery, olives and onion; add vinaigrette and toss to coat. Just before serving, place romaine in another bowl. Add artichoke mixture and croutons; toss to coat. Sprinkle with pepper; top with cheese if desired.

TOSSED SALAD WITH CILANTRO VINAIGRETTE

Tossed Salad with Cilantro Vinaigrette

This is not a salad you'll see everywhere...with its unique mix of veggies that are tossed with romaine. But everybody asks for seconds after they've tried it!

—LARI MONTESINO ELKHART, IN

START TO FINISH: 25 MIN. • **MAKES:** 16 SERVINGS (¾ CUP EACH)

- ⅓ cup olive oil
- ¼ cup minced fresh cilantro
- ¼ cup lime juice
- ⅛ teaspoon salt
- 8 cups torn romaine
- 1 medium zucchini, chopped
- 1 medium cucumber, chopped
- 1 medium sweet yellow pepper, chopped
- 5 to 10 radishes, sliced

1. In a small bowl, whisk the oil, cilantro, lime juice and salt.

2. In a large bowl, combine the romaine, zucchini, cucumber, yellow pepper and radishes. Drizzle with dressing; toss to coat. Serve immediately.

top tip Smart Shopping

Fresh bunch radishes should be free of dirt and have dark green tops with no yellowing. They can be stored in the refrigerator for 1 to 2 weeks. Radishes packaged in bags are more economical and can be stored in the refrigerator for 3 to 4 weeks.

MEDITERRANEAN ROMAINE SALAD

My Underground Vegetable Salad

PREP: 20 MIN. • **BAKE:** 40 MIN. • **MAKES:** 8 SERVINGS

- 1 pound medium fresh mushrooms, halved
- 8 small carrots, peeled and halved lengthwise
- 2 cups cubed peeled celery root (about ½ pound)
- 2 cups cubed peeled rutabaga (about 1 medium)
- 2 cups cubed peeled sweet potatoes (about 1 medium)
- 2 tablespoons olive oil
- ¼ teaspoon salt
- 2 cups cherry tomatoes, halved
- 8 cups torn curly endive

VINAIGRETTE
- 3 tablespoons apple cider or juice
- 2 tablespoons lemon juice
- 2 tablespoons cider vinegar
- 1 teaspoon stone-ground mustard
- 1 teaspoon grated lemon peel
- ½ teaspoon fennel seed, crushed
- ¼ teaspoon salt
- ¼ teaspoon pepper
- ½ cup olive oil

1. Preheat oven to 400°. In a large bowl, combine the first five ingredients. Add oil and salt; toss to coat. Transfer to a greased shallow roasting pan. Roast 30-35 minutes or until vegetables are tender, stirring occasionally. Add tomatoes; bake 10 minutes longer.

2. Place endive in a large bowl. In a small bowl, whisk the first eight vinaigrette ingredients. Gradually whisk in oil until blended. Pour over endive; toss to coat. Divide endive among eight plates; top with roasted vegetables.

Citrus & Roasted Beets Salad

Glistening oranges, tangerines and grapefruit star in this colorful, tangy salad that I created at Showcase of Citrus, where I help to manage the market. Just add chicken to this refreshing mix of bright flavors—and you have a complete meal!

—PETER ELDRIDGE CLERMONT, FL

PREP: 20 MIN. • **BAKE:** 1 HOUR + COOLING • **MAKES:** 6 SERVINGS

- 3 medium fresh beets (about 1 pound)
- 8 cups fresh arugula or baby spinach
- 1 can (14 ounces) hearts of palm, drained and sliced
- 1 medium grapefruit, peeled and sectioned
- 1 medium orange, peeled and sectioned
- 1 tangerine, peeled and sectioned
- 1 cup crumbled goat cheese

DRESSING
- 3 tablespoons balsamic vinegar
- 4 teaspoons grated orange peel
- 2 teaspoons grated tangerine peel
- 1 tablespoon orange juice
- 2 teaspoons Dijon mustard
- 2 teaspoons honey
- ¼ cup olive oil

1. Scrub beets and trim tops to 1 in. Wrap in foil; place on a baking sheet. Bake at 400° for 1 hour or until tender. Remove foil; allow beets to cool.

2. Peel beets and cut into ½-in. cubes. On six salad plates, arrange arugula, beets, hearts of palm, grapefruit, orange and tangerine; sprinkle with cheese. Whisk vinegar, orange and tangerine peels, orange juice, mustard and honey; gradually whisk in oil. Drizzle over the salads. Serve immediately.

MY UNDERGROUND VEGETABLE SALAD

Bonus SALADS

BARBARA BURKS'
GARDEN BOW TIE SALAD

Garden Bow Tie Salad

Originally a vegetable dish, this mix only got better when I added pasta. It's great for family gatherings and church potlucks. Try adding sliced mushrooms and diced tomatoes before serving.

—**BARBARA BURKS** HUNTSVILLE, AL

PREP: 30 MIN. + CHILLING • **COOK:** 10 MIN.
MAKES: 24 SERVINGS (¾ CUP EACH)

- 1 medium cucumber
- 1 medium yellow summer squash
- 1 medium zucchini
- 1 medium sweet red pepper
- 1 medium green pepper
- 4 cups fresh broccoli florets
- 3 cups fresh cauliflowerets
- 1 small red onion, finely chopped
- 2 packages Italian salad dressing mix
- 4½ cups uncooked bow tie pasta
- ¼ cup olive oil
- ¼ cup red wine vinegar
- ¾ teaspoon salt
- ½ teaspoon pepper

1. Wash the first five ingredients but do not dry; chop and transfer to a large bowl. Add remaining vegetables. Sprinkle with dry dressing mix; toss to coat. Refrigerate, covered, 4-6 hours or overnight.
2. Cook pasta according to package directions. Drain; rinse with cold water. Add to the vegetable mixture. In a small bowl, whisk the remaining ingredients. Add to salad; toss to coat.

top tip Good Greens

Baby spinach is spinach that was picked after 15 to 35 days of growing. It is more tender and has a more delicate flavor than the larger, more mature leaf spinach. Check the "use-by" or "enjoy-by" date on bagged baby spinach before purchasing.

It can be eaten raw or cooked, used in place of lettuce on sandwiches or in salads. One of the quickest ways to cook baby spinach is to saute it with a little olive oil and minced garlic.

"This is a favorite summertime salad. Fresh parsley, tarragon and chives give the homemade dressing special flavor. Precut matchstick carrots make it a snap to fix!"
ELISABETH LARSEN PLEASANT GROVE, UT

White Bean and Spinach Salads

START TO FINISH: 20 MIN.
MAKES: 4 SERVINGS

- ¼ cup olive oil
- 2 tablespoons white wine vinegar
- 2 teaspoons minced fresh parsley
- 2 teaspoons minced fresh tarragon
- 2 teaspoons lemon juice
- 1 teaspoon minced chives
- 1 teaspoon Dijon mustard
- ½ teaspoon sugar
- ½ teaspoon salt
- ⅛ teaspoon pepper
- 1 can (15 ounces) cannellini or white kidney beans, rinsed and drained
- ½ cup julienned carrot
- ¼ cup roasted sweet red peppers, chopped
- 2 tablespoons chopped red onion
- 4 cups fresh baby spinach

1. In a small bowl, whisk the first 10 ingredients. In another bowl, combine the beans, carrot, red peppers and onion. Add dressing and toss to coat.
2. Divide spinach among four serving plates. Top with bean mixture.

WHITE BEAN AND SPINACH SALADS

Bonus

BREADS

A bite of freshly baked bread with melting butter is one of life's little pleasures. Spread this joy around with one of the breads feature here. Have no worries; there's a bread to complement every schedule, slow-cooked entree and season!

CHRISTINA PITTMAN'S
BEST DINNER ROLLS

Best Dinner Rolls

If you can't decide which enticing topping to use, just make them all! Then each person can choose his or her favorite.
—**CHRISTINA PITTMAN** PARKVILLE, MO

PREP: 35 MIN. + RISING • **BAKE:** 15 MIN. • **MAKES:** 2 DOZEN

- 4½ to 5 cups all-purpose flour
- ¼ cup sugar
- 1 package (¼ ounce) active dry yeast
- 1¼ teaspoons salt
- 1 cup whole milk
- ½ cup water
- 2 tablespoons butter
- 2 eggs
- 1 egg, lightly beaten

FOR EVERYTHING DINNER ROLLS
- 1 teaspoon poppy seeds
- 1 teaspoon kosher salt
- 1 teaspoon dried minced garlic
- 1 teaspoon sesame seeds
- 1 teaspoon dried minced onion

FOR PARM-GARLIC DINNER ROLLS
- 2 tablespoons grated Parmesan cheese
- ½ teaspoon dried minced garlic

FOR ALMOND HERB DINNER ROLLS
- 2 tablespoons chopped sliced almonds
- ½ teaspoon kosher salt
- ½ teaspoon dried basil
- ½ teaspoon dried oregano

1. In a large bowl, combine 2 cups flour, the sugar, yeast and salt. In a small saucepan, heat milk, water and butter to 120°-130°. Add to dry ingredients; beat on medium speed 3 minutes. Add 2 eggs; beat on high speed for 2 minutes. Stir in enough remaining flour to form a soft dough (dough will be sticky).

2. Turn onto a floured surface; knead until smooth and elastic, about 6-8 minutes. Place in a greased bowl, turning once to grease the top. Cover with plastic wrap and let rise in a warm place until doubled, about 1 hour.

3. Punch dough down. Turn onto a lightly floured surface; divide into 24 portions. Shape into balls. Divide between two greased 13-in. x 9-in. baking pans. Cover with a clean, lightweight towel and let rise until doubled, about 30 min.

4. Preheat oven to 375°. Brush with lightly beaten egg. Sprinkle with toppings for rolls of your choice. Bake for 10-15 minutes or until golden brown. Remove from the pans to wire racks.

CLOVERLEAF ROLLS *Make dough as directed; divide into 24 portions. Divide each into three equal pieces; shape into balls. Place three balls in each greased muffin cup. Let rise, top and bake as directed.*

TWISTS *Make dough as directed; divide into 24 portions. Shape into balls; roll each into a 10-in. rope. Fold in half and twist two or three times, holding both ends. Pinch rope ends to seal. Let rise, top and bake as directed.*

Corn Bread with a Kick

To me, nothing says Southern cooking like crisp corn bread made in a traditional cast-iron skillet. I use a very old skillet that once belonged to my great-aunt.

—**GEORDYTH SULLIVAN** CUTLER BAY, FL

PREP: 20 MIN. • **BAKE:** 20 MIN. • **MAKES:** 8 SERVINGS

- ⅔ cup all-purpose flour
- ⅔ cup cornmeal
- 1 tablespoon sugar
- ½ teaspoon baking powder
- ½ teaspoon salt
- ¼ teaspoon baking soda
- 1 egg
- 1 cup buttermilk
- 3 tablespoons butter
- 3 chipotle peppers in adobo sauce, drained and chopped
- 6 bacon strips, cooked and crumbled

1. In a large bowl, combine the first six ingredients. In another bowl, whisk egg and buttermilk.
2. Place butter in an 8-in. ovenproof skillet; heat skillet in a 425° oven for 3-5 minutes or until butter is melted. Meanwhile, stir egg mixture into dry ingredients just until moistened. Fold in peppers and bacon.
3. Carefully swirl the butter in the skillet to coat the sides and bottom of pan; add batter. Bake at 425° for 18-22 minutes or until a toothpick inserted near the center comes out clean. Cut into wedges; serve warm.

PEPPERY CHEESE BREAD

Peppery Cheese Bread

This is my daughter, Kendra's, favorite savory quick bread. Your first bite of the warm, moist bread will have you reaching for a second slice—it's just heavenly! This bread never lasts long in our house.

—**SHARON BOREN** SALEM, OR

PREP: 15 MIN. • **BAKE:** 45 MIN. + COOLING
MAKES: 1 LOAF (16 SLICES)

- 2½ cups all-purpose flour
- 1 tablespoon sugar
- 1½ teaspoons coarsely ground pepper
- 1 teaspoon baking powder
- ¾ teaspoon salt
- ½ teaspoon baking soda
- 2 eggs
- 1 cup (8 ounces) reduced-fat plain yogurt
- ½ cup canola oil
- ¼ cup 2% milk
- 1 tablespoon spicy brown mustard
- 1 cup (4 ounces) shredded cheddar cheese
- 2 green onions, thinly sliced

1. In a large bowl, combine first six ingredients. In a small bowl, whisk eggs, yogurt, oil, milk and mustard. Stir into dry ingredients just until moistened. Fold in cheese and onions.
2. Transfer to a greased 9-in. x 5-in. loaf pan. Bake at 350° for 45-55 minutes or until a toothpick inserted near the center comes out clean. Cool for 10 minutes before removing from pan to a wire rack

CORN BREAD WITH A KICK

KRISTINA VANNI'S
TRIPLE-TASTY CLOVERLEAF ROLLS

Triple-Tasty Cloverleaf Rolls

Three types of dough—white, wheat and cornmeal—dress up my everyday cloverleaf rolls. Pass a basket for an eye-catching addition to your table!

—**KRISTINA VANNI** NORTH HOLLYWOOD, CA

PREP: 40 MIN. + RISING • **BAKE:** 15 MIN.
MAKES: 2 DOZEN

- 1 package (¼ ounce) active dry yeast
- 1½ cups warm water (110° to 115°)
- ½ cup sugar
- ¼ cup canola oil
- 2 eggs, lightly beaten
- 1½ teaspoons salt
- 4 cups all-purpose flour
- 1 cup whole wheat flour
- 1 cup yellow cornmeal
- ¼ cup butter, melted

1. In a large bowl, dissolve yeast in warm water. Add sugar, oil, eggs, salt and 3 cups all-purpose flour. Beat on medium speed for 3 minutes. Divide dough into three portions; place in separate bowls. Add the remaining all-purpose flour to one bowl, whole wheat flour to another bowl and the cornmeal to the last bowl.

2. Turn each portion onto a floured surface; knead until smooth and elastic, about 6-8 minutes. Place each portion in a greased bowl, turning once to grease the top. Cover and let rise in a warm place until doubled, about 1 hour.

3. Divide each portion of dough into 24 pieces. Shape each into a ball. Place one of each of the balls in greased muffin cups; brush with butter. Cover and let rise until doubled, about 30 minutes.

4. Preheat oven to 375°. Bake for 15-18 minutes or until golden brown. Remove from pans to wire racks.

Hazelnut Wheat Bread

In an effort to match the flavors of one of our favorite store-bought breads, I developed this recipe, adapting it to a recipe in my bread machine manual. It makes such a hearty, great-tasting loaf!

—**RUTH FANGER** MONROE, OR

PREP: 20 MIN. • **BAKE:** 3 HOURS
MAKES: 1 LOAF (1½ POUNDS, 12 SLICES)

- 1 cup water (70° to 80°)
- 1 tablespoon honey
- 1 tablespoon butter, softened
- 3 tablespoons toasted wheat germ
- 2 tablespoons mashed potato flakes
- 1 tablespoon nonfat dry milk powder
- 1 tablespoon ground flaxseed
- 1 tablespoon sesame seeds
- 1 tablespoon poppy seeds
- 1 teaspoon salt
- 1¼ cups whole wheat flour
- 1 cup bread flour
- ¼ cup chopped hazelnuts
- 1½ teaspoons active dry yeast

1. In bread machine pan, place all the ingredients in the order suggested by the manufacturer. Choose crust color and loaf size if available.

2. Check dough after 5 minutes of mixing; add 1 to 2 tablespoons of water or flour if needed. Bake according to bread machine directions.

Sunflower Cranberry Bread

I embellished this recipe from my sister-in-law with dried cranberries and sunflower seeds. It's a wonderful bread to share.

—**JULIET KONIECZNY** AMSTERDAM, NY

PREP: 15 MIN. • **BAKE:** 3 HOURS
MAKES: 1 LOAF (2 POUNDS, 16 SLICES)

- 1 cup warm 2% milk (70° to 80°)
- 2 eggs, lightly beaten
- 2 tablespoons butter, softened
- ½ teaspoon salt
- ⅓ cup sugar
- ⅓ cup dried cranberries
- ¼ cup sunflower kernels
- 3⅓ cups bread flour
- 2¼ teaspoons active dry yeast

1. In bread machine pan, place all the ingredients in the order suggested by the manufacturer. Select basic bread setting. Choose crust color and loaf size if available.

2. Check dough after 5 minutes of mixing; add 1 to 2 tablespoons of water or flour if needed.

3. Bake according to bread machine directions.

NOTE *We recommend you do not use a bread machine's time-delay feature for this recipe.*

SUNFLOWER CRANBERRY BREAD

BUTTERHORNS

⑤ INGREDIENTS Savory Biscuit-Breadsticks

START TO FINISH: 20 MIN.
MAKES: 10 BREADSTICKS

- ½ **cup grated Parmesan cheese**
- 2 **teaspoons dried minced garlic**
- ¼ **teaspoon crushed red pepper flakes**
- 1 **tube (12 ounces) refrigerated buttermilk biscuits**
- 2 **tablespoons olive oil**

1. In a shallow bowl, mix cheese, garlic and pepper flakes. Roll each biscuit into a 6-in. rope. Brush lightly with oil; roll in cheese mixture.
2. Place on a greased baking sheet. Bake at 400° for 8-10 minutes or until golden brown.

Butterhorns

These mouthwatering, buttery rolls never last long so I always double the recipe. You can shape them any way you like, but to me, a crescent shape is so pretty.
—**KELLY KIRBY** WESTVILLE, NS

PREP: 35 MIN. + RISING • **BAKE:** 10 MIN.
MAKES: 2 DOZEN

- 1 **tablespoon active dry yeast**
- 1 **teaspoon plus ⅓ cup sugar**
- ½ **cup warm water (110° to 115°)**
- ½ **cup butter, softened**
- ½ **cup warm 2% milk (110° to 115°)**
- 1 **egg**
- ¾ **teaspoon salt**
- 4 **cups all-purpose flour**

1. In a large bowl, dissolve yeast and 1 teaspoon sugar in warm water. Add butter, milk, egg, salt, remaining sugar and 2 cups flour. Beat until smooth. Stir in enough remaining flour to form a soft dough.
2. Turn dough onto a floured surface; knead until smooth and elastic, about 6-8 minutes. Place in a greased bowl, turning once to grease top. Cover and let rise in a warm place until doubled, about 1 hour.
3. Punch dough down. Turn onto a lightly floured surface; divide in half. Roll each portion into a 12-in. circle; cut each circle into 12 wedges. Roll up wedges from the wide end and place point side down 2 in. apart on greased baking sheets. Curve ends to form crescents. Cover and let rise in a warm place until doubled, about 30 minutes.
4. Preheat oven to 350°. Bake the rolls 10-12 minutes or until golden brown. Remove from pans to wire racks.

SAVORY BISCUIT-BREADSTICKS

Five-Topping Bread

I love to make bread from scratch and this has become one of our tried and true favorites to serve with any meal, casual or formal.

—**TRACI WYNNE** DENVER, PA

PREP: 45 MIN. + RISING • **BAKE:** 25 MIN.
MAKES: 1 LOAF (25 SLICES)

- 1 package (¼ ounce) active dry yeast
- ¾ cup warm water (110° to 115°)
- 1 cup warm 2% milk (110° to 115°)
- ¼ cup butter, softened
- 2 tablespoons sugar
- 1 egg yolk
- 1½ teaspoons salt
- 4 to 4½ cups all-purpose flour
- 1 egg white
- 2 teaspoons water
- 1 teaspoon coarse sea salt or kosher salt
- 1 teaspoon dried minced onion
- 1 teaspoon each sesame, caraway and poppy seeds

1. In a large bowl, dissolve yeast in warm water. Add the milk, butter, sugar, egg yolk, salt and 2 cups flour. Beat on medium speed for 3 minutes. Stir in enough remaining flour to form a firm dough.

2. Turn onto a floured surface; knead until smooth and elastic, about 6-8 minutes. Place in a greased bowl, turning once to grease the top. Cover and let rise until doubled, about 1 hour.

3. Punch dough down. Turn onto a lightly floured surface; divide dough into thirds. Shape each into a 20-in. rope. Place ropes on a large greased baking sheet and braid; pinch ends to seal and tuck under. Cover and let rise until doubled, about 45 minutes.

4. Preheat oven to 375°. Combine egg white and water; brush over dough. Combine sea salt, onion and seeds; sprinkle over the bread. Bake 22-28 minutes or until bread is golden brown. Remove from the pan to a wire rack to cool.

⑤ INGREDIENTS

Wonderful White Bread

Here's a wonderful bread with a light texture. It's great for sandwiches or toast.

—**KAREN KALOYDIS** FLUSHING, MI

PREP: 10 MIN. • **BAKE:** 3 HOURS
MAKES: 1 LOAF (1½ POUNDS, 16 SLICES)

- 1 cup plus 1 tablespoon water (70° to 80°)
- 1 egg
- 4½ teaspoons canola oil
- ¼ cup sugar
- 1½ teaspoons salt
- 3¼ cups bread flour
- 1 package (¼ ounce) active dry yeast

1. In a bread machine pan, place all the ingredients in the order suggested by the manufacturer. Select basic bread setting. Choose crust color and loaf size if available.

2. Check dough after 5 minutes of mixing; add 1 to 2 tablespoons of water or flour if needed. Bake according to bread machine directions.

Irish Soda Bread

My husband's family is Irish. Wanting to impress my future mother-in-law, I baked a bread and took it along with me when I met her the first time. Needless to say, it worked!

—PADMINI ROY-DIXON COLUMBUS, OH

PREP: 20 MIN. • **BAKE:** 50 MIN. + COOLING
MAKES: 1 LOAF (16 SLICES)

- ¾ cup raisins
- 1 cup boiling water
- 2 cups all-purpose flour
- 1 cup whole wheat flour
- ⅓ cup sugar
- 3 teaspoons baking powder
- 1 teaspoon baking soda
- 1 teaspoon salt
- 1 egg
- 2 cups buttermilk
- ¼ cup butter, melted

1. Place raisins in a small bowl. Cover with boiling water; let stand for 5 minutes. Drain and pat dry.

2. In a large bowl, combine the flours, sugar, baking powder, baking soda and salt. In a small bowl, whisk the egg, buttermilk and butter. Stir into dry ingredients just until moistened. Fold in raisins.

3. Transfer to a 9-in. x 5-in. loaf pan coated with cooking spray. Bake at 350° for 50-60 minutes or until a toothpick inserted near the center comes out clean. Cool for 10 minutes before removing from pan to a wire rack.

IRISH SODA BREAD

HONEY & OAT YEAST BREAD

Honey & Oat Yeast Bread

This recipe meets the three most important requirements I have for a recipe: easy, healthy, and kid approved! A woman my husband knows shared the directions for this moist, multi-grain bread with us.

—LISA BEDORD POWER, MT

PREP: 30 MIN. + RISING • **BAKE:** 25 MIN. + COOLING
MAKES: 1 LOAF (12 WEDGES)

- ½ cup water
- 6½ teaspoons butter, divided
- ½ cup old-fashioned oats
- ½ cup unsweetened applesauce
- ¼ cup honey
- 1 teaspoon salt
- 2 teaspoons active dry yeast
- 2 tablespoons warm water (110° to 115°)
- 1 egg
- 1½ cups whole wheat flour
- 1¼ to 1¾ cups all-purpose flour

1. In a small saucepan, bring water and 4½ teaspoons butter just to a boil. In a small bowl, pour boiling liquid over oats. Add the applesauce, honey and salt. Let stand until mixture cools to 110°-115°, stirring occasionally.

2. In a large bowl, dissolve yeast in warm water. Add the oatmeal mixture, egg, whole wheat flour and 1 cup all-purpose flour. Beat until smooth. Stir in enough remaining all-purpose flour to form a soft dough (dough will be sticky).

3. Turn onto a floured surface; knead until smooth and elastic, about 6-8 minutes. Place in a greased bowl, turning once to grease the top. Cover and let rise in a warm place until doubled, about 1 hour.

4. Punch dough down. Shape into an 8-in. round loaf on a greased baking sheet. Cover and let rise in a warm place until doubled, about 30 minutes.

5. Melt remaining butter; brush over loaf. Bake at 375° for 25-30 minutes or until golden brown. Cool on wire rack.

Caraway Cheese Biscuits

PREP: 10 MIN. • **BAKE:** 15 MIN. • **MAKES:** 10 BISCUITS

- 2 **cups all-purpose flour**
- 3 **teaspoons baking powder**
- ¾ **teaspoon salt**
- 6 **tablespoons cold butter, cubed**
- 1 **cup (4 ounces) finely shredded cheddar cheese, divided**
- 1½ **teaspoons caraway seeds**
- ¾ **cup 2% milk**

1. Preheat oven to 425°. In a large bowl, whisk flour, baking powder and salt. Cut in butter until mixture resembles coarse crumbs. Stir in ¾ cup cheese and caraway seeds. Add milk; stir just until moistened.

2. Drop by ¼ cupfuls onto ungreased baking sheets. Sprinkle with remaining cheese. Bake 12-15 minutes or until golden brown. Serve warm.

CARAWAY CHEESE BISCUITS

GARLIC ASIAGO BREAD

Garlic Asiago Bread

My friends and family rave about this loaf. It has chunks of cheese and fabulous garlic flavor. We have bread sales at our school, and this is always one of the top sellers!

—**CHARLOTTE THOMAS** POLLOCK PINES, CA

PREP: 30 MIN. + RISING • **BAKE:** 20 MIN. + COOLING
MAKES: 2 LOAVES (10 WEDGES EACH)

- 1 **package (¼ ounce) active dry yeast**
- 1¼ **cups warm water (110° to 115°)**
- 2 **tablespoons plus 2 teaspoons olive oil**
- 7 **garlic cloves, minced**
- 1 **tablespoon sugar**
- 2 **teaspoons salt**
- 1½ **teaspoons white vinegar**
- 3 **to 3¼ cups bread flour**
- 1 **cup cubed Asiago cheese**

EGG WASH
- 1 **egg**
- 1 **tablespoon water**

1. In a large bowl, dissolve yeast in warm water. Add the oil, garlic, sugar, salt, vinegar and 2 cups flour. Beat until smooth. Stir in enough remaining flour to form a firm dough. Stir in cheese.

2. Turn onto a floured surface; knead until smooth and elastic, about 6-8 minutes. Place in a greased bowl, turning once to grease the top. Cover and let rise in a warm place until doubled, about 1 hour.

3. Punch dough down; divide in half. Shape into 5-in.-round loaves. Place on lightly greased baking sheets. Cover and let rise in a warm place until doubled, about 30 minutes.

4. For egg wash, in a small bowl, combine egg and water. Brush over loaves. Bake at 375° for 20-25 minutes or until golden brown. Cool on wire racks.

General Recipe Index

This handy index lists recipes by food category and major ingredient so you can easily find recipes that suit your needs.

BUFFET MEATBALLS, P. 185

BANANAS FOSTER, P. 96

BEST DINNER ROLLS, P. 354

CHEESY SPINACH, P. 293

Index · GENERAL RECIPE

CRANBERRY CHICKEN, P. 300

MINTY HOT FUDGE SUNDAE CAKE, P. 173

COBBLERS & CRISPS

Black and Blue Cobbler, 180
Blueberry Cobbler, 179
Butterscotch Apple Crisp, 88
Granola Apple Crisp, 94
Slow-Cooker Berry Cobbler, 172

COCONUT

Butternut Coconut Curry, 113
Coconut-Pecan Sweet Potatoes, 200
Mango & Coconut Chicken Soup, 161
Pecan-Coconut Sweet Potatoes, 28

CORN

Corn and Broccoli in Cheese Sauce, 119
Corn Spoon Bread, 197
Creamed Corn, 121
Creamy Corn, 293
Fiesta Corn and Beans, 121
Jalapeno Creamed Corn, 116
Shoepeg Corn Side Dish, 22

CORNISH HENS

Cornish Game Hens with Couscous, 316

CORNMEAL

Corn Bread-Topped Chicken Chili, 236
Corn Bread with a Kick, 355
Triple-Tasty Cloverleaf Rolls, 357

CRANBERRIES

Cranberry Apple Topping, 201
Cranberry BBQ Pulled Pork, 242
Cranberry Chicken, 300
Cranberry-Dijon Pork Roast, 316
Cranberry-Ginger Pork Ribs, 226
Cranberry Hot Wings, 275
Cranberry Pork Roast, 221

DESSERTS

*(also see Bread Pudding, Candies,
Cobblers & Crisps)*

HOT CHILI DIP, P. 102

TANGY LAMB TAGINE, P. 44

ZIPPY SPAGHETTI SAUCE, P. 61

ZESTY ITALIAN SOUP, P. 171

BLACK BEAN POTATO AU GRATIN, P. 31

TURKEY WITH CRANBERRY SAUCE, P. 230

SLOW COOKER RATATOUILLE, P. 114

Alphabetical Index

This handy index lists every recipe in alphabetical order, so you can easily find your favorite dishes.

CHILI CONEY DOGS, P. 125

ENCHILADA PIE, P. 124

GREEN BEANS AND NEW POTATOES, P. 122

LIME CHICKEN TACOS, P. 133

SATAY-STYLE PORK STEW, P. 81

STUFFING FROM THE SLOW COOKER, P. 205

TURKEY SLOPPY JOES, P. 74

Cook Time Index

On a schedule? Let this index help! Stop here to find slow cooker recipes that fit into your time frame.

SUNNY AMBROSIA PUNCH, P. 101

Index

COOK TIME

PORTOBELLO BEEF BURGUNDY, P. 234

Substitutions & Equivalents

EQUIVALENT MEASURES

3 teaspoons	=	1 tablespoon	16 tablespoons	=	1 cup
4 tablespoons	=	¼ cup	2 cups	=	1 pint
5⅓ tablespoons	=	⅓ cup	4 cups	=	1 quart
8 tablespoons	=	½ cup	4 quarts	=	1 gallon

FOOD EQUIVALENTS

GRAINS

Macaroni	1 cup (3½ ounces) uncooked	=	2½ cups cooked
Noodles, Medium	3 cups (4 ounces) uncooked	=	4 cups cooked
Popcorn	⅓ to ½ cup unpopped	=	8 cups popped
Rice, Long Grain	1 cup uncooked	=	3 cups cooked
Rice, Quick-Cooking	1 cup uncooked	=	2 cups cooked
Spaghetti	8 ounces uncooked	=	4 cups cooked

CRUMBS

Bread	1 slice	=	¾ cup soft crumbs, ¼ cup fine dry crumbs
Graham Crackers	7 squares	=	½ cup finely crushed
Buttery Round Crackers	12 crackers	=	½ cup finely crushed
Saltine Crackers	14 crackers	=	½ cup finely crushed

FRUITS

Bananas	1 medium	=	⅓ cup mashed
Lemons	1 medium	=	3 tablespoons juice, 2 teaspoons grated peel
Limes	1 medium	=	2 tablespoons juice, 1½ teaspoons grated peel
Oranges	1 medium	=	¼ to ⅓ cup juice, 4 teaspoons grated peel

VEGETABLES

Cabbage	1 head	=	5 cups shredded	Green Pepper	1 large	=	1 cup chopped
Carrots	1 pound	=	3 cups shredded	Mushrooms	½ pound	=	3 cups sliced
Celery	1 rib	=	½ cup chopped	Onions	1 medium	=	½ cup chopped
Corn	1 ear fresh	=	⅔ cup kernels	Potatoes	3 medium	=	2 cups cubed

NUTS

Almonds	1 pound	=	3 cups chopped	Pecan Halves	1 pound	=	4½ cups chopped
Ground Nuts	3¾ ounces	=	1 cup	Walnuts	1 pound	=	3¾ cups chopped

EASY SUBSTITUTIONS

When you need...		Use...
Baking Powder	1 teaspoon	½ teaspoon cream of tartar + ¼ teaspoon baking soda
Buttermilk	1 cup	1 tablespoon lemon juice or vinegar + enough milk to measure 1 cup (let stand 5 minutes before using)
Cornstarch	1 tablespoon	2 tablespoons all-purpose flour
Honey	1 cup	1¼ cups sugar + ¼ cup water
Half-and-Half Cream	1 cup	1 tablespoon melted butter + enough whole milk to measure 1 cup
Onion	1 small, chopped (⅓ cup)	1 teaspoon onion powder or 1 tablespoon dried minced onion
Tomato Juice	1 cup	½ cup tomato sauce + ½ cup water
Tomato Sauce	2 cups	¾ cup tomato paste + 1 cup water
Unsweetened Chocolate	1 square (1 ounce)	3 tablespoons baking cocoa + 1 tablespoon shortening or oil
Whole Milk	1 cup	½ cup evaporated milk + ½ cup water